CAREER
DEVELOPMENT
CONCEPTS AND PROCEDURES

CAREER
DEVELOPMENT
CONCEPTS AND PROCEDURES

David J. Srebalus
West Virginia University

Robert P. Marinelli
West Virginia University

Jeffrey K. Messing
West Virginia University

Brooks/Cole Publishing Company
Monterey, California

Brooks/Cole Publishing Company
A Division of Wadsworth, Inc.

Printed in the United States of America

10 9 8 7 6 5 4 3 2 1

Library of Congress Cataloging in Publication Data

Srebalus, David J.
　　Career development.

　　Bibliography: p.
　　Includes index.
　　1. Vocational guidance.　I. Marinelli,
Robert P.　II. Messing, Jeffrey K.
III. Title.

HF5381.S7365　　　650.1′4　　　81-17957
ISBN 0-8185-0471-4　　　　　AACR2

Subject Editor: *Claire Verduin*
Manuscript Editor: *Meredy Amyx*
Production Editor: *Patricia E. Cain*
Interior Design: *Angela Lee*
Cover Design: *Jamie Sue Brooks*
Typesetting: *Boyer & Brass, Inc., San Diego, California*

To Our Parents

PREFACE

Much like its clients, career counseling is maturing. At one time largely a practice for facilitating adolescent occupational decision making, career counseling and related interventions are now being directed to an increasingly broad range of people coping with many different career-related concerns.

Prior to the last several years, career counseling and guidance were hardly regarded as wide-ranging treatments. When we ourselves were introduced to the area of vocational guidance as graduate students, what we studied was for the most part the use of occupational information. Frankly, after that rather dull first meeting, none of us really thought he would ever become so committed to the area as to write a textbook for it. Our attitudes changed both with our own maturity and with that of career counseling and systematic career planning.

Only in the last five or so years have two of us become heavily involved in the career area. Prior to that time one or another of us devoted significant effort to rehabilitation counseling, program management, long-term therapy with psychiatric outpatients, consultation strategies, group counseling, counseling theory and metatheory, and several other allied areas. At one time all these varied interests and experiences on our part may have had no place within the traditional specialty of vocational guidance. That is not so today. Contemporary career practitioners can come from many disciplines to promote lifelong career development on the part of people in all age groups.

The expansion of career counseling and systematic career planning has made many narrow but previously popular ideas and practices obsolete. If we did not believe in that change, we would not have admitted so readily our relatively recent enthusiasm for this area. Nor would we be so proud of a broad background beyond the scope of traditional career guidance. As we grew, and the career area likewise enlarged itself, we began to feel at home as counseling-oriented persons in a traditionally guidance-oriented field. But we were able also to rediscover and appreciate more fully the potent aspects of many traditional career interventions.

In writing this book, we have constructed a survey text designed for an initial course in career counseling. However, because much of the text is devoted to career topics not found in older texts, the experienced counselor may find at least part of it useful as update information.

We have included many familiar topics and issues along with some rather new ones. The mix of content represents not only our personal view but the outcome of our publisher's extensive market analysis. The latter has been very helpful in moderating our excesses while generating confidence in the utility and appeal of what ultimately was to be included in the text.

Readers familiar with promoting career development will recognize the established elements of career counseling and guidance treated in this text. The history of the field is presented, along with familiar theoretical concepts. The assessment of career interests, the use of occupational information, and comprehensive career-guidance programming are other familiar areas. All these topics are given considerable space in the text because of their contemporary significance.

In treating those topics often found in other texts, we direct attention more clearly to their connection with the counseling process. As one of our early reviewers said, "The field does not need one more vocational-guidance text." What an analysis of the market indicated was a need for a career-counseling text.

Contemporary trends indicate that promoting career development, while it retains valuable traditions and proven practices, does not rely on only one kind of intervention. Nor does it ignore populations most often targeted for vocational guidance. Thus, we do not overlook adolescents and their initial career decisions or the handicapped and their placement. We do, however, treat more fully than do most comparable texts the normal adult career-adjustment issues, mental-health problems, and problems in job seeking and placement. We believe that, by emphasizing both career decision making and the process of adaptation to work, we provide material of interest to a wide range of practitioners. Certainly school and rehabilitation counselors should find the text useful. Also, mental-health counselors, social workers, and private-practice psychologists will have an opportunity to examine the tie between career and mental health to facilitate greater overall client adaptation. Our government estimates that average workers spend 80,000 hours of their lives being employed—an amount that far exceeds the time they spend with spouses and family. Thus, career counseling has to be a potent mental-health intervention of importance at least equal to that of family-therapy and group procedures.

Career consultation receives extensive coverage in the text. In the future, counselors will need to consider greater involvement in the consultation process in order to expedite the change/adaptive process, extend services to new populations, involve the reservoir of community talent in career-related services, and provide training and receptivity to the career-development process. An overriding consideration is time. Counselors functioning as consultants are in essence extending their influence to many more persons than they could assist directly, by training helpers to promote the achievement of career-development goals. More and more experts in careers are viewing consultation as equal in potential to any newer trend. The effectiveness of consultation as a tool for change has been established in business and industry. The material we include is intended to broaden the reader's skill and interaction potential.

With assistance from our editor, her assistant, and eight reviewers, we have attempted to construct a readable text that uses examples freely and provides practical suggestions throughout. At the same time, we have made an effort to balance conceptual issues and practical applications. Finally, to give the text lasting value, we sought to make it a well of resource information. This plan included allotting considerable space to important references such as the *Dictionary of Occupational Titles.* We treated the third as well as the fourth edition; the former remains a basis for important work-sample systems both in rehabilitation assessment and in general employment counseling and placement.

We thank our series editor, Claire Verduin, for her support and direction; Patricia E. Cain, our production editor; Meredy Amyx, our manuscript editor; Ann Drake, Madelo Lambert, and Jane Haines for manuscript preparation. We also thank those who reviewed the manuscript during various stages of its development: Stephen S. Feit, Frank M. Fletcher, Abraham Gelfond, Joan Hartzke McIlroy, Robert C. Reardon, Richard J. Riordan, Howard E. A. Tinsley, and Jane L. Winer. Finally we thank our students for helping us evaluate text content; and our wives and families for both proofreading/editing and tolerance.

David J. Srebalus
Robert P. Marinelli
Jeffrey K. Messing

CONTENTS

1
Career Counseling in Perspective   1

2
Career-Development Theory   15

3
Counseling for Career Decisions   41

4

Career Assessment   68

5

Overview of Career Information   96

6

Career Exploration: Resources and Strategies   107

7

Career Understanding: Resources and Strategies   120

8
Career Action: Resources and Strategies   152

9
Counseling for Career Adjustment   189

10
Career Consultation   224

11

Comprehensive Career Guidance   249

CAREER
DEVELOPMENT
CONCEPTS AND PROCEDURES

CHAPTER ONE

CAREER COUNSELING IN PERSPECTIVE

The goal of this chapter is orientation to the practice of career counseling and guidance and its evolution from concern over the vocational decisions that most persons must make in our culture. The issue of career choice is broader in scope than most people recognize. Many persons do not reflect on the complexity of a career decision, particularly after the decision is made. This complexity is, in part, due to the fact that our careers are related to our individual makeup: who we are—physically, intellectually, and emotionally—will significantly affect the careers we choose. Career counselors consider this complex interaction while serving persons who are making career decisions.

The complexity of the career-decision process and the considerable differences in clientele served often result in career counselors' assuming multiple roles. Generally the role of career counselor is combined with other helper roles. Elementary and secondary school counselors, in addition to contributing to clients' increased career awareness and improved decision making, are concerned with facilitating clients' overall development. Rehabilitation and mental health counselors share a common concern regarding the coping and adjustment of clients with disabilities as well as the impact of disabilities on their clients' careers. College counselors, employment counselors, and practically all other types of counselors generally wear these different hats. To illustrate the multiple roles played by career counselors and the various competencies used in their practice, we will look at two counselors-in-training.

Marion and Jack are students in a counselor-preparation program. Each has had course work in counseling theories, counseling techniques, tests and measurement, human growth and development, research methods, and issues in the counseling profession. They are about to begin a course entitled "Career Counseling and Life-Span Planning." In addition to students of counseling, others in this course include several industrial-relations majors and several social-work students.

Jack is reasonably sure that he will specialize in promoting career development among high school students. He has been a business educator for the past four years, with additional experience in industry as a sales representative. On the other hand, Marion is a recent graduate in psychology from a small liberal-arts college. She is certain that she wishes to enter a service-oriented occupation, probably as some type of counselor. Her own career plans are not specific.

In deciding to specialize in helping people prepare for and adjust to their

1

lifelong roles as workers, what significant factors will each of these individuals consider? What are career counselors like as people? What does their job involve? How are they alike and different from other specialists in counseling? How do they compare with psychologists or social workers? We imagine that these and other questions would cross the minds of persons like Jack and Marion as they begin a more detailed inquiry into the role of the career counselor.

For Jack and Marion to make career counseling part of their own careers requires them to recognize that what career counselors do is useful, needed by others, and also personally challenging. Marion, maybe more than Jack, can speak personally about the importance of assisting an individual with initial career decisions and the process of job entry. Like many people whose careers are undecided, she is anxious regarding her future as a worker. Recently engaged, she is concerned about the compatibility of her own career with that of her future husband's and with the demands of a family life, one that may eventually include children.

Jack has already had two full-time jobs and an employment history of six years. Most recently a teacher, Jack spent a considerable amount of time with students and advisees on career matters. Being single and having wide interests, including some rather unconventional ones (sewing, for example), Jack has become interested in alternate lifestyles. Specialized training in career counseling and the promotion of career development fit well with both Marion's and Jack's varied interests and ambitions.

Jack and Marion do have common questions regarding continued work as a career counselor. Both are confident about their human relations and communications skills. What role will these skills play in career counseling? More specifically, they wonder about the respect career counselors enjoy among social service professionals and the energy and momentum in the career-counseling profession itself. Will the work of career counseling retain its relevance for both counselor and client alike in the future?

CAREER COUNSELING VIEWED HISTORICALLY

A definitive response to the questions posed by Jack and Marion is seldom possible. Career counseling has developed considerable variability in its practice over 70 years of progressive effort. A look at that history may give a perspective on career counseling as a profession. In an overview, counselors-in-training, like Marion and Jack, may discover at least partial answers to some of their important questions.

Early career counselors

Marion and Jack would find that prior to the 20th century, career counselors, in the sense that we know them now, did not exist. Foundations of career counseling were, however, being laid. Literature designed to advise youth in choosing educational and vocational goals existed as far back as the 15th century—more than 400 years ago (Zytowski, 1972). These publications, which frequently outlined information about a large number of occupations, were widely used, a fact evidenced by their appearance in numerous languages and many editions. Zytowski (1972) speculates that while most of those early texts were designed primarily to inform learned persons of the breadth and variety of occupations, they may have been used by parents and perhaps by priests who, in the roles of counselors, assisted young people with career decisions.

In the 1880s and 1890s a number of individuals began to make significant contributions to assisting youth in their choice of jobs and careers. Williamson (1964) cites Charles Eliot, William Harper, and Daniel Giliam as examples of individuals who, during that period, helped to outline informal diagnostic procedures for use in vocational guidance. Galton (1883), Cattell (1890), and Binet and Henri (1895), pioneers of the mental-testing movement, began to lay the base which would evolve into our current formal assessment procedures. Munsterberg (1889, 1913), a founder of industrial and applied psychology, began to identify through tests the abilities required of workers in various occupations. Not all contributors during this period provided the building blocks on which career counseling and guidance would later be built. Some like Richards (1881) recommended the use of phrenology as a tool for occupational decision making. Perhaps Jack and Marion, had they been early advisors of youth, could have used some of the rudimentary methods and tools suggested by these pioneers.

At the same time (approximately 1895), an individual by the name of Frank Parsons began to advise underprivileged youth in Boston. Due to his work in developing and describing methods for vocational guidance, his impact became such that today he is considered the father of vocational guidance. Miller (1971) presents a concise biography of this extremely talented engineer, teacher, lawyer, politician, social worker, and college dean, whose influence on the field came with the publication, several months after his death, of *Choosing a Vocation* (1909). In this book, Parsons presented a three-step approach to vocational guidance. He said:

> In the wise choice of vocation there are three broad factors: (1) a clear understanding of yourself, your aptitudes, abilities, interests, ambitions, resources, limitations, and their causes; (2) a knowledge of the requirements and conditions of success, advantages and disadvantages, compensation, opportunities, and prospects in different lines of work; (3) true reasoning on the relations of these two groups of facts [1909, p. 5].

As simple and obvious as it sounds, this approach represents some of the most basic elements of career counseling as it is practiced today. It is often described as "matching people to jobs." If Jack and Marion had been colleagues of Parsons at Breadwinner's College and the Vocational Bureau of Boston, they would have spent much of their time interviewing adolescents and assisting them in self-appraisal relevant to career decisions. They would also have worked hard to learn of employment opportunities in the Boston area. Developing good relations with employers and other social service agencies would have been as important for them then as it is today.

After Parsons death the Boston Vocational Bureau's new director was Meyer Bloomfield, another influential pioneer in vocational guidance. Other important contributors to vocational guidance prior to World War I include Frank P. Goodwin in the Cincinnati School System, Eli W. Weaver in New York, and Jesse B. Davis in Grand Rapids, Michigan (Miller, 1971). A short time later the development of the first paper-pencil tests of intelligence by Yerkes (1921) led to the extensive study of the intelligence levels of workers in different occupations.

If Jack and Marion had been vocational guidance specialists at that time, they might have been charter members of the National Vocational Guidance Association (NVGA), formed in 1913. This organization was to become the principal professional association for vocational or, as they were later to be called, career counselors. Impetus for its formation developed as a result of the First National Conference on Vocational Guidance, held in 1910 in Boston. In 1912 the second conference was held in New York, leading to the formation of NVGA.

With the growing professionalism of vocational guidance, counselors were increasingly able to discuss principles and techniques with colleagues. Still, their efforts in this new field were based largely on common sense and trial-and-error learning. Marion or Jack would have had little recognition as a vocational counselor, more than likely having some other job title and other duties to perform. They would not have fit our present-day concept of counselors, since their highly cognitive and directive approach would have more closely resembled what we know as academic advising.

Career counseling after 1930

As a result of the Great Depression and the expansion of the federal government during the New Deal, other changes occurred in the practice of vocational counseling. The changes were stimulated by congressional passage of the Wagner-Peysner Act of 1933, which organized the United States Employment Service as part of the Department of Labor. Through this agency an enormous pool of data was beginning to be generated concerning the working conditions, worker requirements, and employment opportunities in various occupations. Much of this information was incorporated into a *Dictionary of Occupational Titles* (1939). The use of information had always been an important part of vocational guidance. Although information resources were improving, counselors, then and now, have been handicapped by many information voids and many questions regarding the validity and reliability of available data.

In the 1930s and 1940s Marion and Jack would have experienced a dramatic increase in the precision of their counseling or advising efforts, not only because of better available information but also because of improved guidance methods, including client-assessment strategies. Williamson (1965) describes the progress that had been made by then in the assessment of individual performance differences by psychologists working for business and industry. Much of this self-awareness information would be applied to the first step of Parsons' approach to vocational guidance. Leadership in the effort to transform vocational guidance into a precise data-based treatment emanated from the Minnesota Stabilization Research Institute under the leadership of Donald G. Paterson. The vocational counseling approach emerging in Minnesota would later be called trait-factor counseling. It will be described in detail in Chapter 3.

After this period, Marion and Jack would likely have approached their work as career counselors in a much different manner. Helping people with career problems would for the most part continue to emphasize decision making. In this process counselors could now rely on their background in tests and measurement to assist in client self-assessment. Knowledge of the work world would be based on a library of occupational information containing both references for clients and technical manuals for counselor use. It is clear that vocational counseling was becoming much more sophisticated. In addition, social and economic conditions after World War II made new demands on the work force and necessitated greater emphasis on vocational planning and occupational placement. Consequently, increased numbers of counselors began to achieve greater recognition for their efforts (Miller, 1971).

The professionalization of vocational counseling would have been quite noticeable to Jack and Marion in the 1940s. The National Vocational Guidance Association had evolved into the American Personnel and Guidance Association (APGA). Professional journals such as the *National Vocational Guidance Bulletin* had been published regularly since 1921 (Siegel, 1972). Texts describing the counseling process were available (for example, Williamson, 1939; Williamson & Darley, 1937). In some universities, among them the University of Minnesota, it was now possible for a student to plan a graduate-degree program emphasizing the assessment techniques used in vocational guidance and counseling.

Recent developments

If Jack and Marion had been counselors in the early 1950s, a major rethinking of the career counselor's role would have affected them. The former emphasis on the cognitive processing of information shifted to more of an awareness of the psychological variables affecting career choice, particularly those variables that relate to the process of human development. At that time important contributions from several individuals (for instance, Eli Ginzberg, Ann Roe, and Donald Super) allowed for the integration of career decision making with normal growth and development. Super's work (1951) well represents the expansion of vocational guidance into genuine life-span planning. To support his position, Super later argued:

> Work and occupation play an important part in determining the social status, values, attitudes, and style of living of an individual. Important though some of these are as determinants of occupation, they in turn are in part determined by occupation. Occupation is not merely a means of earning a livelihood, but also a way of life, a social role [Super, 1957, p. 35].

Prior to the contributions of developmental theorists like Super and Ginzberg, vocational decisions were frequently treated as a one-time event. A person's lifelong involvement with work, his or her career, would increasingly become a more significant focus of attention. Now career counselors have begun to view an important life event such as a vocational decision in the context of the person's developmental history.

Jack and Marion could no longer be experts only in techniques of standardized assessment and the use of occupational information; they would need a clearer concept of human development. This would be valuable in understanding the context in which, for example, an employment crisis could occur. Recognizing that career issues are lifelong, Marion and Jack might now serve clients of many different age ranges. They would now have to examine their career interventions to see if each were developmentally appropriate for the client.

During the 1950s the professionalization of career specialists gained added momentum. Super (1955) notes the progressive integration of vocational guidance into the much broader specialty of counseling psychology. Through his efforts and those of individuals such as C. Gilbert Wrenn, Leona Tyler, Francis P. Robinson, and Edward S. Bordin, many vocational counselors came to view their practice as concerned with the overall adjustment of their clients. These vocational counselors began to represent a large segment of counselor-education faculties. In the 1960s and 1970s these faculties trained thousands of elementary- and secondary-school counselors. In addition to these practitioners, in more recent years rehabilitation and mental-health counselors have been trained and influenced by similarly oriented counselor educators, firmly grounded in counseling psychology and its close attention to vocational development. Of late, more and more doctoral graduates from these same training programs have entered private practice as licensed psychologists. Through the professions of counseling and guidance, rehabilitation counseling, and counseling psychology, thousands of practitioners today, in a multitude of treatment settings, share the traditions of the 1950s in their respect for developmental issues and general social/emotional adjustment. Because of this diversity of practice, individuals from different backgrounds, like Marion and Jack, can find themselves a place as career-development specialists working in a variety of settings with a broad spectrum of clients.

One of the most significant events of the 1950s occurred on October 4, 1957. On that day the U.S.S.R. launched Sputnik I into orbit. With it began the Space Age. In a sense, counselors, particularly secondary-school counselors, responded to a governmental mandate to ensure the entry of talented young people into scientific and technical careers so that this country could catch up with the Soviets. In 1958 Congress passed the National Defense Educational Act (NDEA), which sponsored a massive effort to train and support school counselors, especially in career-planning activities. NDEA was not the first legislation of importance in the development of the career-counseling profession; prior to it, for example, were the Vocational Education Act of 1917 and the Vocational Rehabilitation Act of 1920. This type of legislation and subsequent amendments has resulted in considerable expansion of counseling methods and opportunities for the training and employment of counselors. Many other pieces of legislation important to career development were also passed in the 1960s and 1970s, including the Manpower Development and Training Act of 1962, the Economic Opportunity Act of 1964, the Elementary and Secondary Education Act of 1965, the Higher Education Act of 1965, and the Mental Health – Mental Retardation Act of 1966. Just this sampling of legislation indicates the significant role of the federal government in career counseling and guidance.

For Jack, because of his teaching background and interest in working with adolescents, this governmental effort to support and train school counselors would have greatly simplified his entry into the career-counseling profession. If he had been a student in one of the many NDEA institutes, Jack probably would have received training not only in the competency areas already discussed but also in counseling procedures applicable to a wide variety of personal and emotional difficulties. As the NDEA training institutes for school counselors developed in the 1960s, many trainees were influenced by the writings of Carl Rogers (1942, 1951). At that time the same was true of the students in rehabilitation counseling and other social-service training programs. Rogers' client-centered therapy, as we shall see in Chapter 3, influenced career counselors' interview behavior, allowing it greater flexibility to deal with career concerns as they interact with the emotional and social adjustment of the client.

Both Marion and Jack might have recognized that career counseling was continuing its evolution from what might at first have been advice and information dissemination to a form of psychological treatment relying on interpersonal and communication skills. Its roots, however, go beyond the discipline of psychology into areas of economics, sociology, and other fields, making it truly multidisciplinary in its conception and practice. With client-centered contributions and those from other forms of therapy, a true form of counseling for a career was emerging.

If Jack and Marion had been employed as career counselors in the 1960s, their continuing professional development would have reaffirmed the multidisciplinary nature of their practice. It would have been a multi-intervention practice, acknowledging that client goals could be achieved through a variety of means. Coordinating the functions of therapist and interventionalist into an integrated professional role was an important objective during that time. Another was the need to formulate career-oriented programs, which in turn would structure and coordinate the multiple interventions.

The need for large-scale career-development programs continued to be recognized. Bailey and Stadt (1973, p. 268) credit then U.S. Commissioner of Education James Allen with being, in 1970, the first influential person to use the term *career education.* Allen's successor, Sidney P. Marland, provided concrete leadership in the formation of legislation and funding guidelines for this curriculum innovation, which would provide career-related input in public schools.

In the 1970s, the era of systematic programming for career development began, bringing with it added management responsibilities for career counselors. With extensive funding from the Career Education Incentive Act (Public Law 95-207) and the Education Amendments of both 1976 and 1978 (Public Laws 94-982 and 95-561), many school districts were able to develop programs demonstrating comprehensive career guidance and career education. But it was not the intent of the national leadership to restrict career guidance to public schools. Other legislation made it possible to assist persons of many different ages within the community who were not attending public school. As the 1980s began, greater emphasis was placed on comprehensive programs for adults. The ideal became a unified community program "without walls," incorporating many different service agencies and professionals (Hoyt, Evans, Mackin, & Mangum, 1974).

As promoters of career development recognized the need for life-span career-planning programs, it also became evident that practitioners were unprepared for such extensive programs. Through federal and state funding and the sponsorship of professional organizations, a concerted effort has been made to upgrade in-service training of practicing career-development specialists, in addition to improving entry-level graduate-school preparation.

As the 1980s continue, the spread of life-span career-planning programs is uncertain. However, it is expected that closer attention will be paid to the career-adjustment problems affecting thousands of workers and their families. With the prevailing negative attitudes of individuals toward their jobs (Sheppard & Herrick, 1972; U.S. Department of Health, Education and Welfare, 1973), it is unlikely that this vast problem can be solved completely by life-span career-planning programs. Complete service with respect to career problems would seem to demand a follow-up to initial aid in making career decisions. In a comprehensive career-guidance program, career planning would be extended to later stages of life rather than restricted to early years. This very personalized form of treatment for the unique aspects of career planning and adjustment would examine alternatives to the assumption that career changes constitute the only pathways toward ultimate career development. More appropriate means of adapting to the current work environment would also be considered. This enriched form of career counseling may be called counseling for career adjustment or counseling for career satisfaction.

EMPLOYMENT FOR CAREER COUNSELORS

Career counselors now occupy many diverse professional roles, opening opportunities for employment in many different settings. Counseling-program graduates like Jack and Marion, if they enlarge on their backgrounds and training ultimately could pass through a wide variety of employment experiences in their careers. Some of their positions could be similar or parallel to previous ones, using similar skills and differing only in setting and clientele, as when switching jobs from one secondary school to another. However, clients of widely different developmental ages will require markedly different assistance as a consequence of their developmental readiness and unique personal circumstances. Individual practitioners in different work settings will require significantly different educational preparation and work experiences. Marion, for example, could become an elementary-school counselor or a rehabilitation counselor. Her work would differ greatly in the two settings even though either job would involve direct service to clients and consultation with others who have impact on her clients.

On the other hand, beginning career counselors, like workers in other occupations, have before them a career ladder: a series of changes in job or position, through promotion and transfer, while remaining in the same field. As one moves up, salary and status increase. Jack, for example, might graduate from his degree program and accept a position as a secondary-school counselor. With experience and further education, he might secure a position either as guidance director in that school district or as career-education coordinator.

Marion might begin as a counselor in a correctional setting, applying her background to a prerelease program involving career planning. Later, following completion of a doctorate, Marion might join the staff of a university counseling center, later to become its director or even dean of students. A move into counselor education or private practice might be a possibility.

In the 1980s many employment opportunities exist for those trained in career counseling and guidance. Other than the obvious positions in school, correctional, and rehabilitation centers, more career-related service components are developing in mental-health and community agencies. Many of these programs serve the career needs of special populations. Changes in cultural conditions both offer new occupations and stimulate effort to find additional employment opportunities. Edwards and Bloland (1980) describe a relatively recent interest in providing leisure counseling and consultation services. Christiani and Christiani (1979) note that counselors in the 1980s cannot expect significant growth or vacancies in education and other settings in which many of the career services of the present and past have been provided. They attempt to demonstrate how counselor competencies, including those related to promoting career development, can fit well in business and industry. Graduates of counselor education programs have not for the most part sought employment in the commercial area, even though counselors have much to offer in this setting. Employee training and personnel development have many facets, allowing room for a variety of counseling and consultation strategies (Griffith, 1980).

CAREER-DEVELOPMENT COMPETENCIES

Jack and Marion will eventually have more specific career decisions to make. In what settings and with what kinds of clients will they work? Will their practice focus primarily on career concerns or will those concerns be secondary to personal and social problems that clients present? Jack's and Marion's choices will depend in part on their unique combinations of personal characteristics. In a broad sense, their individual needs, interests, competencies, values, and opportunities considered together will affect their choices (Super, 1953). Considerations such as preferred climate and topography, desire to live near friends and loved ones, salary, tolerance for stressful working conditions, and many others may be significant choice variables for Jack. Personal values and a long-time interest in serving youthful offenders may be tested for Marion when the opportunity for a much higher-paying job in a private-for-profit rehabilitation agency becomes available.

Areas of competence in career counseling will also affect Marion's and Jack's choices of practice. Different positions will require different combinations of competencies.

While counseling practice is often general in its focus, it is possible for Jack or Marion to specialize, emphasizing a number of specific skills. Specialized positions are typical in two types of work settings: those that offer a narrow scope of services and those that combine the efforts of many specialists. For example, a counselor in an employment agency may require considerably more competence in job placement than in other areas. In contrast, a secondary-school counselor in a small rural school may need to be competent in a great variety of areas. Facilities that provide a comprehensive service may employ counselors with diverse specialties. In a comprehensive rehabilitation center, for instance, vocational evaluators, job-placement specialists, and work-adjustment counselors may work in concert with rehabilitation counselors and more than a dozen other human-service professionals to help clients achieve personal goals.

Since this book is about career-counseling competencies, the chapters that follow will discuss particular competencies in detail. The brief overview here will serve as an introduction. When reviewing these ability areas, consider those that interest you most at this time, and also think of counseling positions that may emphasize certain sets of competencies over others.

The mastery of career-development theory

Career counseling must have a conceptual basis for its interventions. Knowledge of career development from theory, and the research stimulated by theory, permits the counselor to base practice on a sound rationale. Chapter 2 discusses theoretical approaches to career counseling.

Counseling for career decision making

While career-guidance programs with structured interventions can be helpful to a majority of clients, idiosyncratic needs and high levels of anxiety often require serving clients with personal career counseling. In personal, one-to-one career counseling, the practitioner can develop systematic, precise assistance in decision making (Turner, 1979). Contributions from many theoretical orientations (Crites, 1974) not only accommodate counselors with different personalities but also enable clients with diverse backgrounds and cognitive styles to benefit from different counseling approaches (Johnson, 1978). Various approaches to counseling for career decisions are described in Chapter 3.

Career assessment

For decades career counseling and guidance have utilized standardized instruments to measure the expression of career interests. Recently they have taken advantage of inventories intended to assess career maturity. Competence in the use of both kinds of instruments can differentiate practitioners trained in career counseling from other psychological-treatment specialists (Crites, 1976a). Because extensive use of aptitude and personality assessment as part of career counseling has declined in recent years, this text will not treat such devices to any significant extent. Chapter 4 thus restricts its discussion of assessment to interest inventories and measures of career development.

The use of occupational information

The use of occupational information is traditional in the promotion of career development, especially in the process of making career decisions. Our discussion of occupational information in Chapters 5, 6, 7, and 8 has been based largely on the procedures used in the counseling process. This discussion, like Carkhuff's (1969), is organized in phases common to the helping or counseling process (see also Egan, 1975) and attempts to promote greater recognition of occupational information as a key counselor competency.

Job placement

Most perspectives on promoting development include concrete action taking by clients. To complete the process of career exploration, self-exploration, and career decision making, the client, aided by the counselor, ideally seeks actual placement in an occupation or in a preparation program for an occupation. In Chapter 8 we explore the important components of job seeking, summarizing empirical data on employment search and emphasizing teachable skills.

Consultation practice

In most career-practice settings, counselors actually function as counselor/ consultants. Probably as often as they counsel they work for the welfare of their clients through third parties; that is, they serve as consultants. Consultation has a special set of competencies. Because counselors-in-training often do not systematically study consultation strategies prior to a course of study in career development, we have included a general overview in Chapter 9 of consultation in the context of promoting career development.

Counseling for career adjustment

Recent authors have taken issue with the view of working as a means of implementing self-concept (Super, 1951) or of expressing one's personality (Bordin, Nachmann, & Segal, 1963). Instead they depict work as secondary to other avenues of fulfillment (Green, 1968; Lasson, 1972; Terkel, 1975; Warnath, 1975). An even more pessimistic point of view is shared by those authors who see work as contributing to psychological and physical maladjustment in workers (Cooper & Marshall, 1976; Cunnick & Smith, 1977; Kasl, 1978; Wool, 1975). Career counselors will often find themselves involved with clients who are suffering pain from work. Chapter 10 discusses such work-related problems and suggests interventions.

Planning and managing career-guidance programs

The last decade has emphasized the promotion of career guidance as a multi-disciplinary, multi-intervention practice. Comprehensive career-guidance programs involve many different professionals, among them the counselor, working in various roles. Chapter 11 describes career-guidance programming, stressing counselor role and function, and extensively treats career education as it illustrates current effort in comprehensive career programming.

THE INTERRELATIONSHIP OF COUNSELOR COMPETENCIES

The foregoing discussion highlights the repertoire of competencies counselors bring to the process of career exploration, the making of career decisions, and adjustment to work. While the range of skills may appear awesome at first, it is not long before the interrelationship among them becomes evident. Thus, in learning one skill the counselor is already preparing for the mastery of still others. For example, it would be difficult not to learn something about counseling for career decisions while studying the diagnosis of career maturity, part of career-assessment competency.

Up to this point we have shown the development of the career-counseling profession and counselor competency through the eyes of Jack and Marion, two counselors-in-training. Not all readers of this text will be beginning counselors. Just as Jack and Marion would be expected to carry on the traditions of the profession and contribute to it in the future, other readers, especially practicing counselors, have had to work to remain current with career-counseling practice. The assumptions and recommended interventions may have changed since they were in training. For them, this text may provide a useful update on developments in their field. Other practicing career counselors may be reading this text for such reasons as the considerable space it devotes to adult clients. Still others may have examined this book in the hope that it will give more attention to counseling-related practices than do the more information- and guidance-oriented texts.

No text can be truly comprehensive, nor can it remain up-to-date. Thus career counselors must rely on more than books. Career journals are important reading. Some useful ones include *The Counseling Psychologist, Personnel and Guidance Journal, The Vocational Guidance Quarterly, Journal of Counseling Psychology, Journal of Vocational Behavior,* and *Journal of Occupational Psychology.* In addition to reading, the career practitioner can build skills through membership in professional organizations and through attending workshops and conferences.

In concluding this introductory chapter, we suggest that the reader review the index to gain additional understanding of what is contained in this text. Subheadings of chapters listed in the Table of Contents also preview material.

SUMMARY

Important material covered in this chapter included historical factors that influenced the development of career counseling and planning: social attitudes and social changes, persons instrumental in promoting career development, and pertinent governmental action and legislation.

Much of this survey was to serve as a backdrop for current theory and practice in career counseling. The relationship was drawn among those elements, historical factors, and current employment opportunities for career counselors. A rationale was provided for the topics to be given more detailed coverage in later chapters.

RECOMMENDED READINGS

Christiani, T. S., & Christiani, M.F. The application of counseling skills in the business and industrial setting. *Personnel and Guidance Journal,* 1979, *58*(3), 166–169.

An example of recent journal articles exploring career options for counselors in settings and roles not traditional to the profession. In this selection the emphasis is on the use of a counseling background in the area of training and personnel development.

Parkinson, T., Bradley, R., & Lawson, G. Career counseling revisited. *Vocational Guidance Quarterly,* 1979, *28,* 121–128.

An inquiry into the relevance of contemporary counseling practices in the context of Frank Parsons' broad philosophy of self-improvement and the value of work. Current practices in career counseling are put into this philosophic perspective.

Williamson, E.G. An historical perspective of the vocational guidance movement. *Personnel and Guidance Journal,* 1964, *42,* 854–859.

An article treating material similar to that included in the author's 1965 book entitled *Vocational Counseling: Some Historical, Philosophical, and Theoretical Perspectives.* The latter is a major work by this pioneer of the counseling profession, summarizing more than 50 years of effort to add precision to the process of career decision making and employee selection.

LEARNING ACTIVITIES

1. List several important developments that have affected the career-counseling profession for each decade in the 20th century up to the current decade.
2. Describe both recent and traditional employment opportunities for practitioners with special training in career counseling.
3. Briefly interview three individuals, each of a different generation, and compare their attitudes regarding job entry and career planning. Learn how these individuals made decisions regarding jobs and what resources they used in the process.
4. Write a brief description of the general competencies required of a career counselor.
5. Review several recent issues of the *Personnel and Guidance Journal* and *The Vocational Guidance Quarterly* to identify recent trends in promoting career development.

CHAPTER TWO

CAREER-DEVELOPMENT THEORY

IMPORTANCE OF THEORY

Counselors who devote their efforts to career work are faced with a difficult task. Complicated at every stage in development, a client's career experience can be difficult to understand and to integrate with other life experience. The committed counselor is beset with questions. How do elementary school counselors, for example, gain confidence that their efforts contribute to important career decisions in adolescence? How can a secondary school counselor feel comfortable that services offered in junior and senior high school will foster later adjustment and career satisfaction? Similar questions are the concern of parents, teachers, college counselors, counselors of adults, and numerous others interested in facilitating an individual's career.

Most career counselors seek to understand how childhood experience influences later work patterns, how career decisions are made and what factors determine job dissatisfaction. Understanding these and other issues enables the counselor to develop thoughtful action steps that emanate from sound and explicable reasoning. Thoughtful action is to a considerable extent a function of one's grasp of theory. Theory also provides constructs and dynamics by which one's efforts may be communicable and comprehensible to others. The ability to develop and express the rationale behind the practice enhances professional esteem and credibility. Practice unsupported by theory is questionable on ethical grounds. Career-development theory can assist counselors to practice their professions wisely and ethically and can help to answer some of the difficult questions that arise.

A theory of career development can be defined as a conceptual system that identifies, describes, and interrelates important factors affecting lifelong human involvement with work. It is a group of ideas or concepts that allow us to make both generalizations and discriminations regarding career development. Beyond simply providing concepts (symbolized by representative words or signs), a theory coordinates or associates one concept with another to make statements about the dynamics of career development. It generates predictions or testable hypotheses of career development, and, even more than that, it organizes and interrelates hypotheses. Theory resembles a manuscript containing words (concepts), sentences (hypotheses or theorems), and paragraphs (interrelated hypotheses). Each of these elements is an essential component of a workable theory. When a theory is tested by experience (through many different forms of

15

research), the resulting evidence is integrated back into the theory itself; thus a *theoretical system* gradually evolves.

The theory-building process is as complicated as it sounds. It takes a long time to develop and refine a theoretical system. In fact, most existing systems are the result of generations of human effort and not attributable to a single person. One individual may initiate the theory, but many others over time invest effort to test, refine, and fully develop it.

A system under construction

Theoretical work in the area of career development is yet only in the preliminary stages. At least rudimentary career-development theories do exist. Certainly "theorizing" has occurred, and theoretical concepts have been developed and appropriated for application. Many conjectural or predictive statements have been made. Some individuals have applied their efforts to specific issues in career development, making intensive but limited contributions. Others have summarized or synthesized a number of ideas into more general theoretical statements. The extensive endeavors of theory testing, expansion, and refinement have been initiated and are currently under way, but fully comprehensive theoretical systems have not been completed. Existing theoretical constructs and hypotheses can, however, provide practitioners with concepts that will be valuable in their career-related work. Hence this chapter will explore recurring career issues in the perspective of current theory.

We will treat career-development theory in a manner somewhat different from those of other texts. Rather than successively summarizing the theoretical contributions of different individuals, we will examine general career-development problems and issues and integrate the contributions of several important individuals with these topics. John Holland's work will be the principal exception to this.

We have selected questions in career development that we believe to be of most interest to counseling practitioners and of central importance in their work. Essential to the role of counselors in promoting career development is acquisition of expertise in career theory, both to guide their own practice of counseling and to explain the sequence of career development to others. This educational component of the counselor's role is not often discussed but is nonetheless important, especially to the counselor serving as a consultant in career education and other extended programs.

Related disciplines

Career-development theory has already been defined essentially in terms of conceptual systems that explain the lifelong process of change in people who work. Developmental theories in psychology are for the most part descriptive in nature, portraying changes that occur naturally as a result of growth or maturation. They are often concerned with organismic changes; for example, changes in skill or competence levels attributable to individuals' internal structures. Mental and emotional as well as physical structures are often postulated.

Career-development theories contain elements of such psychological theories, but often include sociological elements as well. They can therefore be described as theories of a social-psychological nature, being concerned with the interaction of an individual with various social forces and social units. Cultural mores and expectations are examples of social forces that have a bearing on career-development theory. Economic issues also are important among the phenomena that permeate career development. Hence, a major challenge to the career-development theorist and practitioner is the understanding and integration of multidisciplinary thought.

DEVELOPMENTAL THEORIES

Developmental stages

Human development, as a more or less orderly process of change, is usually viewed as a passage through a series of stages over a period of time. A developmental theory can attempt to describe growth and maturation from birth to death, then, by positing a series of developmental steps or stages. Usually such theories are epigenetic in nature; that is, early stages provide the foundation for later stages and are thus incorporated into them. A weak foundation results in continued inferior development. Thus, if early development is hindered, the prognosis is poor for the entire course of development.

The discipline of psychology provides numerous developmental theories that have application for career development—for instance, those of Erikson (1963) and Havighurst (1953). These contributions have been effectively synthesized in a number of sources, a recent one being Herr and Cramer (1979). This resource is well worth study, for it integrates the broad stages of psychological development with stages posited for career development.

More specific to our topic are several proposals regarding the stages through which people pass in making career decisions and in adjusting to work. Probably the earliest of these was put forward by Ginzberg, Ginsburg, Axelrad, and Herma (1951), later to be critically analyzed and expanded by Super (1953, 1957). Over the past several decades Donald E. Super has consistently provided important contributions to career-development theory and research, through both his individual effort and those of his many colleagues and students. Hence, we will discuss Super's developmental stages in greatest depth. A brief examination of Ginzberg's views will be preparatory to this primary discussion.

Ginzberg's three periods.   Ginzberg articulated his views of occupational choice in 1952 and updated his work 20 years later (Ginzberg, 1952, 1972c). The stages he proposed present three steps in the process of career decision making:

1. The Fantasy Period (0 to 11 years). Children imagine themselves in occupations, basing them on early family and peer identifications. Their interpretations are ideal, stylized, and fictional, as are the games the child plays.
2. The Tentative Period (11 to 17 years). Adolescents consider mostly subjective or personal factors such as interests, capacities, and values, in that order of priority. This stage ends with a substage termed *transition,* in which interests, capacities, and values become integrated.
3. The Realistic Period (17 to young adulthood). A person seeks to become acquainted with available alternatives. It is a period marked by exploration followed by crystallization represented by a choice, which is subsequently further delimited. The crystallization stage usually occurs between 19 and 21.

Ginzberg cautioned against rigid adherence to his estimated age ranges, noting that much variation occurs; for example, working-class members tend to make occupational choices earlier than white-collar or middle-class members.

Super's five stages.   Super (1957, p. 71) attributed his view of vocational or career development to the influence of Charlotte Buehler and her concept of life stages. These stages seemed to Super to be more useful in formulating research than the more basic life-stage concepts such as infancy, childhood, adolescence, and so forth. Thus, Super used Buehler's five psychological life stages as the basic structure for his theory.

1. The Growth Stage (0 to 14 years)
2. The Exploratory Stage (15 to 25 years)
3. The Establishment Stage (26 to 45 years)
4. The Maintenance Stage (46 to 65 years)
5. Decline (65 to death)

Super was careful to note that these stages were indeed life stages, applicable to more than involvement with work. As he elaborated his Growth Stage, he incorporated much of the Fantasy and early Tentative Periods of Ginzberg. The Exploratory Stage, essentially comprising adolescence, included the balance of the Tentative Period along with what was to be a Trial Substage in which job entry occurs and an initial career selection is made. It remains a trial phase because it is experimental, involving one or more early choices that may precede permanent decisions.

The beginning of Super's Establishment Stage is a substage of continuing trial and gradual adjustment. Very often several changes take place before a relatively permanent occupation is chosen. Between the ages of 30 and 45 a period of occupational stabilization generally occurs. The period from age 45 until retirement is usually a stage that involves simply continuing work, maintaining one's family, and sustaining those endeavors initiated earlier. At about age 65, Decline may begin. For the working person, lowered energy and the effects of aging can require a reduction in work load; for some, this phase even requires a change to a less demanding job. At home, this Decline may interfere with one's ability to care for oneself.

It might be appropriate to mention here that Super (1953) criticized Ginzberg for distinguishing between career choice and career adjustment, as we do in this text. Super believed that career choices are continuous throughout life; that they represent an adjustment mechanism and cannot be separated from it. In contrast to Super, Crites (1976b) noted that, despite its importance, the issue of young-adult career adjustment has been greatly undertreated.

Implications for counseling.   The broad developmental stages described above provide counselors with a framework to which to attach other more specific concepts helpful in understanding client concerns and in formulating counseling goals. Knowledge of this material also prepares a counselor for at least a rudimentary assessment of a client's career maturity or immaturity. For example, the perspective of Ginzberg may help the counselor to understand a college student's repeated change of majors and lack of success in each if the student is basing curriculum decisions on needs for peer identification and parental approval rather than on considerations of personal interest and aptitude. Parental approval and peer identification are fantasy-based concerns, whereas personal interests and aptitude are typical of the early adolescent and the Tentative Period. We might understand that the 20-year-old college student is approaching career decisions in the manner of a 10-year-old. This client needs to mature, and the counselor can facilitate this process by increasing the client's self-awareness, specifically with regard to interests, capacities, and values. Then follows the generation of alternatives, exploration of the alternatives, and finally the making of a decision, taking into account the job market and other environmental factors. Theory related to developmental stages provides a basis for this plan.

A developmental theoretical perspective might also enable a marriage counselor to assist a 28-year-old couple who need to renegotiate their relationship after 7 years of marriage. Perhaps as just-married college students they shared a primary interest in career exploration and dreams of the future. Seven years later, well into Super's Establishment Stage, the major issues have become coordinating work, family, and community roles. The couple's understanding that they are currently in a different life stage may help them to clarify and justify the effort required to work on their relationship. Knowing, too, that satisfaction during this stage often depends in part on broader participation in the community may stimulate a necessary review of the marital contract. Interpretations in counseling based on developmental stage changes are generally easily understood by clients and viewed as a sensible way of approaching adjustment problems.

Early childhood experiences

The name of Ann Roe (1956) is most often associated with the study of effects of parent-child relations on later career decisions. Roe predicted that parental warmth would affect the choice of occupation; children who receive less affection, for example, will likely choose more impersonal work. However, there exists a lack of empirical evidence to support her early point of view. She subsequently modified her position (Roe & Siegelman, 1964) to a general and much less definitive prediction of a later person-orientation as a function of early social experience. She hesitated to predict more specific career choices based on early child-parent relations, because those hypotheses had not been borne out in theory-testing research.

Erikson's association of age ranges with particular developmental stages (1963) has influenced career theorists. Tiedeman (1961) based many of his proposals on Erikson's work. In recent years Munley (1977) has attempted to demonstrate the applicability of Erikson's formulations to career development. Those formulations have been used more as a basis for viewing career decisions as developmental in nature than as a specific predictor of career-related behavior. Little has been done to establish more direct links. The general contributions of Erikson regarding early childhood and later psychopathology do not contain specific implications for career development and related counseling.

EXPLORATORY STAGE

Self-concept

The influence of self-concept or self-identity is probably as popular an idea as any in current use in explaining career decision making, decision problems, and career adjustment. Most often associated with Super's theoretical statements (1953, 1957), an individual's self-concept is believed to express itself in career decisions and overall career pattern.

If self-concept is viewed as analogous to self-insight and self-understanding, it is also essentially the same as Erikson's concept of identity: all represent a stable and integrated view of self. Thus, it is possible to combine self-concept and identity-formation theory to reveal an influential factor in the process of career development.

It is important here to distinguish between self-concept and self-esteem. Self-esteem is similar to self-regard or self-acceptance. It is a function of the degree of correspondence between what we perceive ourselves to be (real self) and what we would like to be (ideal self); an evaluation or a pricing of our identity or

Self - concept - identity
self - esteem - how we (see)our identity (self -(concept)
value

Career-Development Theory 21

self-concept. We would expect both self-concept and self-esteem to be important in career development, but not necessarily in the same way.

Other vocational theorists besides Super support the influence of self-concept or identity formation in career development. Client-centered therapy, as we shall see in Chapter 3, has played an important part in alerting counselors to effects of occupational roles (real or perceived) on the self-concept and on self-esteem (Patterson, 1964). Identity formation is very important in psychoanalytically oriented approaches (Bordin, 1968).

Adolescent identity formation.   According to Erikson (1968), the shaping of personal identity begins very early in life, achieving its first workable, more or less stable form in adolescence. In infancy the mutual recognition between mother and child generates a sense of relatively undifferentiated identity. The will to be oneself in early childhood and the experiences of school and an enlarged social sphere provide a balance between conformity and the exercise of one's own volition. According to Erikson, to develop a sense of self requires the enculturation of the person. Social and personal identity are inseparable. It is extremely important that children have the opportunity to attach themselves to teachers or other adults beyond their parents, to imitate peers, and to test roles through play.

In adolescence several crises arise that affect identity formation. Teenagers desperately need to identify with role models but often find few they can admire. Erikson (1968) describes a heightened desire to offer service to others, but frequent hesitation arising from fear of ridicule. Often adolescents cannot acquire satisfaction through making choices because their independently desired choices are often dictated by others in advance. Some of the most important choices during this time are career related.

One of the last crises faced by many adolescents is what is described as a safe return to the traditional. Students in high school and college experiment with a variety of behaviors and attitudes in which they do not believe strongly, appearing more radical in their beliefs than they really are. Resolution of these disparities gradually crystallizes a stronger sense of identity. Erikson defines the final crisis of adolescence (1968, pp. 135–136) as the achievement of a sense of personal identity only to have it threatened by the inception of adulthood and its task of establishing intimacy. The question arises: "Will I lose my identity, so hard fought and attained, when I fuse myself in love with another?"

Research has supported the importance of self-perceptions in career development. Workers in similar occupations reflect similar developmental histories and self-concepts (Galinsky & Fast, 1966; Nachman, 1960). Often for workers to experience satisfaction with their jobs, the type of satisfaction must be consistent with their self-images (Korman, 1976). Sense of identity and the need for enculturation are related to satisfactory job placement (Hershenson, 1967). Finally, as the next chapter will elaborate, many clients presenting serious

career-choice difficulty are most accurately diagnosed as having identity problems (Bordin & Kopplin, 1973).

Implications for counseling.   The influence of self-concept formation on
career development provides a strong justification for counseling as an appropriate intervention for career-related concerns. This is so because counseling
bases its objectives and practices so firmly on the process of self-exploration and
self-clarification. Although the specific goals of counseling do vary, this process is
always an inherent part of counseling and is in itself an intermediate objective.
An increase in self-understanding almost always results from effective counseling. Thus, career counseling is not a form of treatment radically different from
social-personal counseling; knowledge, skills, and experience relevant to general
counseling apply directly to work with career concerns.

Career maturity

Career or vocational maturity has been treated extensively by both Donald
Super and John Crites (Super, 1974) and less comprehensively by numerous
others. Such a broad concept as career maturity is difficult to define succinctly.
Probably the best way to understand the definitions of Crites and Super is to
study the instruments both have developed to measure it. Crites's diagnostic
device to evaluate this phenomenon is his Career Maturity Inventory; for Super
it is his Career Development Inventory. Both are examined in Chapter 4 of
this text.

To describe career maturity we attempt to represent the accomplished growth
of a person in terms of career much as a biologist attempts to describe attainment
of maturation in a cell or organism. Because we never view career development
as completed, however, we measure maturity by comparing career factors
across age. For instance, to the question "Who is a career-mature sixth grader?"
an appropriate response might be a description of a person who acts as a ninth
grader in some important aspects of career behavior. Because career maturity is
defined according to age, there is a direct or monotonic relationship between age
or grade level and career maturity.

Factors in mature choice.   With respect to the concept of career maturity,
only the age range of adolescence has received comprehensive study (Super &
Hall, 1978). To date such factors as self-knowledge and knowledge of
occupations—that is, mostly cognitive variables (Westbrook, 1974)—have been
emphasized as indexes of career maturity.

In addition to retaining the information they have, the relatively more
career-mature adolescents are usually active in increasing their information.
Their subjective view of their career goals is better defined and they can articu-
late it more clearly to others. If asked to specify the career alternatives they are

considering, they usually express more realistic options, and, if asked repeatedly over time, they will state increasingly consistent alternatives and will likely evidence an increasingly coherent interest pattern.

The ideas of realism and consistency of choice warrant further discussion. Consistency is a matter simply of repetition of similar choices. Important to consider is consistency not only across time but also across level, occupational field, and job family (see Crites, 1969). Occupational level can be defined in several ways but most often is related to the complexity of the work and the training required (for example, unskilled versus skilled labor). The concept of job family divides occupations into groups according to both worker characteristics and the product or service produced by the worker. Realism of choice (Crites, 1969) is typically understood as the compatibility of a choice with the individual's abilities, interests, personality, and social class. The first three factors are usually assessed in research by people trained in career counseling and theory who review stated choices within the context of a person's personnel or academic record, including scores on standardized tests. Social class is a factor in that it can act as a barrier to following an occupational preference even though the choice may be realistic in terms of the other factors.

An important measure of career maturity is certainty of career choice: the client's level of confidence (from very sure to very unsure) that he or she will act on an expressed choice by applying for a position or training program associated with the choice. Another key factor in career maturity is differentiation or crystallization of interests and values. The more distinct a person's interest profile becomes, the more mature that person is considered to be. Specificity in actual planning for career decisions often accompanies such a profile and demonstrates that the individual is not using avoidance to deal with the anxiety common to making important choices. In general the combination of these factors reflects a person's assumption of the responsibility for making career decisions. Responsibility of this sort is indicative of career maturity.

Implications for counseling.   The work of Super, Crites, and others in identifying career-maturity variables is extremely useful in the diagnosis of career-decision problems. As we shall see in Chapter 3, diagnostic activity is common to most career-counseling approaches. Chapter 4 will discuss standardized instruments that assess career maturity.

ESTABLISHMENT STAGE AND BEYOND

Career patterns

Common patterns.   Another significant contribution by Donald Super and his colleagues has been the careful study and delimitation of career patterns: the various job sequences common to workers. Super based his study of career patterns (Super, Crites, Humme, Moser, Overstreet, & Warnath, 1957; Super & Overstreet, 1960) on the earlier work of Form and Miller (1949). In the beginning Super (1957) divided such career patterns into male and female types. Such sex-role differences being less appropriate now, we will omit them in describing some of Super's more common patterns:

1. Vocationally stable.   An individual has a series of positions in which the same type of work is performed, but not necessarily in the same industry or for the same employer. For example, an accountant may change jobs or employers but perform the same work throughout a career. This is a pattern common to professional careers.

2. Industry stable.   A person is employed in the same industry or by the same employer but does different work over the duration of a career. He or she may have one entry job, be promoted to another, be retrained on the job for still another, and so on. This pattern has been romanticized in the "from broom-pusher to company president" story.

3. Conventional.   A worker's career follows Super's developmental stages: it begins with an initial job, goes through a trial period, and finally evolves into a stable position. It is a pattern common to management.

4. Unstable.   A worker does not become established in a lifelong occupation. For many with this pattern one potential career is sacrificed for another. The changes may derive from dissatisfaction, illness, economic conditions, or other sources. This pattern is common to semiskilled and clerical workers.

5. Multiple-trial.   The worker makes frequent job changes, from one type of work to another, and as a result never really establishes a career. This is the least stable pattern, most typical of unskilled and semiskilled workers.

6. Double-track.   A worker follows two careers at one time. This pattern is most often exhibited by women who sustain careers both inside and outside the home.

7. Interrupted.   One career is temporarily interrupted for another, then reestablished. This pattern is characteristic of women who suspend a career in order to have and care for children. It also applies to individuals who for certain periods in their lives set aside one career to perform missionary work or another form of service, then return to the earlier type of work.

Variations.   The above career patterns represent only select sequences of work. If we expand our perspective to include more than chronological work histories, we can examine other interesting viewpoints. Under the label "career pattern" Hansen (1978) described the union of careers among couples. A *shared* career is one in which one spouse is actively involved in the other's work, but more or less as an unrecognized partner. The wife of a United States president often shares her husband's career, for example. A *joint* career is an arrangement in which spouses act as co-equals; for instance, married professors teaching, writing, and doing research jointly in the same field. The products of joint careers are attributed to each partner in the belief that the union produces more than either could achieve alone, while recognizing the unique contribution of each.

Implications for counseling. Familiarity with career patterns can help the counselor of adults to verify important factors in a client's overall life adjustment. Without favoring one pattern over another, counselors can employ an understanding of the various patterns to explore client values related to such issues as stability and change. Has the client, for example, endured boredom or dissatisfaction for the sake of security and stability? For what recompense has another client undergone the anxiety associated with frequent change? In general, are the client's personality and ability to handle stress suitable to the career pattern being followed? Examination of such questions can point the way to solutions.

Knowledge of career patterns can also help counselors working with adolescents on career planning. For example, since a professional career frequently leads to a stable pattern, will clients who pursue one profession continue to derive satisfaction from their careers as they themselves change? Will other clients likely to find themselves in less stable patterns be able to withstand the stress of job changes? Do they even recognize the possibility of career instability into middle age?

It seems natural for counselors, whose professional careers generally follow a stable pattern, to see a stable career as desirable and also to support other culturally endorsed patterns, such as the one termed *conventional*. However, the experienced counselor knows that such patterns are not without their disappointments and dissatisfactions. The overall value of a job sequence is ultimately subjective.

Such broad concepts as career patterns obviously cannot tell the complete story of job sequence and stability in an occupation. Dalton, Thompson, and Price (1977) describe how some important interpersonal roles change in the course of even a professional career. In such careers an individual typically goes through four stages: (1) apprentice, (2) colleague, (3) mentor, and (4) sponsor. Each role involves different tasks, relationships, and psychological adjustments. Some individuals may not adjust well to one or more of those roles. Thus, it repeatedly seems evident that every career pattern and role demands personal adaptation, which sometimes prompts an appropriate quest for counseling.

Job and career satisfaction

No career-related issue has received more research attention than job satisfaction. Hundreds of published articles have reported on large numbers of worker groups across a great range of different work settings. In these studies, job satisfaction has been operationally defined in many different ways, with widely varied outcomes and conclusions. Here we will endeavor to distill this research literature by examining it within the context of the underlying theoretical constructs.

Need-satisfaction theory.   Need-satisfaction theory, best known by Maslow's (1954) theory of motivation, provides the basis for much of the literature on job and career satisfaction. From this perspective, as lower-order needs (those related to simple survival) are met, workers will evaluate their jobs and careers according to how higher-order needs (those increasingly related to self-actualization) are satisfied. After an extensive review of the pertinent literature, Zytowski (1970, p. 73) reports a similar conclusion, identifying need satisfaction as the basis for job satisfaction.

A major need-satisfaction theory in the area of careers has been that of Frederick Herzberg (1966). In his theory the following two groups of factors are important:

1. Motivators (satisfiers).   Factors related to the intrinsic nature of a job. These include achievement, potential for advancement, recognition, responsibility, and the nature of the work itself.
2. Hygiene factors (dissatisfiers).   Extrinsic factors, including type of supervision, company policy, administrative style, interpersonal relations, working conditions, and salary or wages.

Herzberg's theory proposes some interesting views. It asserts that hygiene factors alone do not govern job satisfaction. Even if negative conditions (dissatisfiers) were removed (for instance, low salary or noisy surroundings), job satisfaction would not be guaranteed; workers would still not voice positive attitudes toward work. To Herzberg the opposite of satisfaction is not dissatisfaction but absence of satisfaction. In order for true work satisfaction to result, attention must be given to the motivator category.

Motivation is not necessarily simple, however, because cultural background and individual experience along with personal value system dictate what a worker seeks in a job and ultimately in a career. For example, a person with college-educated parents in professional careers might place greater value on self-expression and self-actualization in work than someone from an impoverished family. The latter might attach more importance to hourly wage and job security. Accordingly, we would expect more satisfaction from professional careers than from unskilled ones. Unskilled and semiskilled workers may not always be dissatisfied with their work, but they will be more likely to seek gratification in life from a source other than work.

To analyze job and career satisfaction, the student could take Herzberg's list of factors and construct a questionnaire to administer to workers. This has been done hundreds of times. But for our purposes, career satisfaction most likely can be summarized by the answer of a worker to the following question: "If you had to do it all over again, would you do it in the same way?" If the answer were yes, we would conclude that the worker is and has been satisfied with jobs and career.

According to Hoppock (1976), need satisfaction is the principal motive behind career decisions: people choose jobs to meet needs. Hoppock also confirms the relationship between need satisfaction and job satisfaction.

Implications for counseling. Understanding factors related to job satisfaction has application beyond work; it provides a framework for broader life-style planning. It can enable clients and counselors to explore not only work satisfaction but also the value of leisure, family, and community involvement. Need satisfaction comes from many different sources. The use of need satisfaction theories to explain job and career satisfaction provides strong ties to general counseling theories that are humanistic in approach.

Adult career development

For the most part career-development theory has been concerned with adolescent development and decision making. Even after the concept of life-span development was introduced by Super in the 1950s, it was another 20 years before much interest or effort was directed toward his post-Exploratory Stage. Crites (1976b) has begun to conceptualize work adjustment during Super's Establishment Stage (26 – 45 years). Since career development is epigenetic in nature, Crites believes that success in earlier stages will contribute to later career adjustment.

Career adjustment. Crites (1969) has proposed the coping mechanisms of compliance, control, compromise, and integration as important in work adjustment. These are personal characteristics that increase people's likelihood of adapting to work settings. Although these mechanisms can be extremely important, they do not guarantee satisfaction, because the organizational climate on the job can be a determining factor. Drawing from Hall and Schneider (1973, p. 12), Crites (1976b) discusses four important features of the organizational climate: (1) leadership or supervisory style, (2) interpersonal relations, (3) intrinsic meaning in work, and (4) extrinsic reward characteristics.

Crites forewarns the reader that the term *career adjustment,* to warrant its literal meaning, implies coping with a situation in which everything does not go well; the worker faces barriers or "thwarting conditions" that require personal adjustment. Without the need to adapt despite negative conditions, there would be no meaning to the concept of adjustment. Some such conditions, borrowed by Crites (1976b, p. 116) from Forer (1957), include criticism, challenge, orders, and failure. Using characteristic coping mechanisms, the worker attempts to circumvent such barriers to career satisfaction.

Consider the following example: Brenda, a recent college graduate, takes a job as a social worker with the welfare department. This particular department has what could be described as a paternalistic set of employee management policies, among them strict monitoring of work time. Many of the case workers have become irate over receiving frequent memoranda of a rather punitive nature. As a result of this approach to supervision, in addition to the fact that welfare work is difficult and often frustrating, turnover of case workers is high. Brenda is careful to be civil with her supervisor, refraining from angry outbursts over memos and recurring punitive attitudes. She tells herself "I cannot change the people running the department. Anyway, the memos are only pieces of paper; the threats are never enacted." Despite numerous frustrations the work is sometimes satisfying, but because of low salary and poor morale, and with friends continually resigning, Brenda believes that in a year or two she also will change jobs. It would be accurate to say that Brenda has adjusted to her work better than some of her colleagues because she exercises greater self-control, is able to compromise, and can tolerate annoying but minor grievances. She plans to change jobs because her present one is lacking in effective supervision, has little extrinsic reward value, and has uneven intrinsic meaning, with vague criticism directed toward her and other workers.

Implications for counseling. One of the most valuable features of Establishment-Stage theory is its framework for understanding occupational stress and sources of job dissatisfaction. The concepts are compatible with those typically used by counselors to understand general social adaptation.

Adulthood and the mid-life transition

In recent years Daniel Levinson and associates (Levinson, 1977; Levinson, Darrow, Klein, Levinson, & McKee, 1978) have made a significant contribution to our understanding of adult development. Adulthood is divided into different time periods, some stable and some marked by change. Stable periods are times (6–7 years) when a person has decided on a lifestyle or life structure based on regularities within work, intimate relationships, and his or her view of self. Unstable periods, called transitions, are periods (4–5 years) of reevaluation when an attempt is made to change life to meet unsatisfied needs and desires. This period of reevaluation leads to a new stable period. During the late teens and early 20s people are faced with the task of finally leaving their families and establishing their identity on their own; in the late 20s they establish interpersonal relationships, career, and leisure activities of a more or less stable nature.

Settling down. An important transition period comes at about the age of 30. Entering their 30s, people often conclude that much of what they once used to organize their lives no longer provides for the satisfaction of important interests and needs. The decisions of the 20s are now brought into question, with some resultant turmoil. Usually, however, the person regains equilibrium, retains or recaptures order and balance, and continues to pursue predominant goals and dreams. For some this Settling-Down Stage is marked by significant achievement, which, if it occurs, is likely to arise within the context of a career.

Mid-life crisis. By the late 30s or early 40s there occurs what Levinson (1977) calls the Mid-Life Transition. In a very real and often disillusioning way men and women recognize that they have reached the midpoint in their lives. Compounding the realization of advancing age may be adjustment to such circumstances as the permanent departure of children from the home, major illness or deterioration of health, and the need to care for an elderly parent. It may become clear that goals established in early adulthood will never be achieved. A startling but recurring phenomenon is that persons at this point begin to consider themselves failures. This universal dysphoria develops especially in the area of career ambitions; no matter how competent and successful a person has been by external standards, a discrepancy invariably exists between dreams and actual accomplishments. The superior achiever suffers just as much as anyone else, having had proportionately higher ambitions. Generally, too, the tokens of past achievement provide diminished gratification in middle-age years. Resolving these feelings is one of the most significant of all of life's challenges.

At this mid-life crisis it is natural for self-examination to raise questions about past career decisions and to provoke consideration of new, perhaps even radically different career choices. In some cases such mid-career decisions do occur, but most do not eventuate in drastic change in job or occupation. For the majority the culmination of this reappraisal process is a decision to remain in the current employment situation but to alter work perceptions and performance expectations and to change nonwork involvements to satisfy other needs.

Rappoport (1976) describes how middle-aged couples can undergo a form of sex-role reversal. The husband often may reduce work involvement and become more concerned with affiliative and nurturant activities, whereas the wife may invest herself more in activities outside the home, approach others more assertively, and generally evidence more independence. In this phase both must deal more directly with the inevitability of death. The confrontation of these middle-age crises and changes offers a fertile opportunity for furthering of self-actualization. A new balance and role-free lifestyle can result for both men and women.

Implications for counseling. In a stimulating discussion of counseling strategies with adults, Moreland (1979) argues that cycles of stability interspersed with crisis are natural to human development. These cycles will at times leave the adult depressed, apathetic, angry, or anxious. Such feelings accompany normal development; it is important to understand that they are not always symptomatic of psychopathology. To treat a developmental crisis reaction as pathology is likely to be a tactical error.

Another potential pitfall for career counselors is to view dissatisfaction and questioning of a career as mandating an actual change. Until only recently career counseling has stressed decision making. This emphasis has seemed inadvertently to narrow the function of career counseling with middle-aged adults to a matter, by and large, of assisting mid-career changers or persons with career reentry concerns. In fact, very few mid-life clients become career changers, especially in terms of the precise definition of career changes as shifting to a job in which past training and employment experience have no applicability to the new position.

Moreland (1979) alerts counselors to a number of normal developmental changes that may arise in treatment. The mid-20s male often must cope with the recognition that status can no longer be achieved solely by physical strength or sexual prowess. Rather, the attainment of objectives must eventually be based more on intellectual and interpersonal skills, which are less subject to deterioration with advancing age. It may be difficult for some men to become more sensitive, reflective, and responsive and to begin to substitute cooperation for competition. Moreland (1979, p. 301) notes that females in their mid-20s frequently experience conflicting role expectations. Many clients will be college educated and have promising career futures but suffer conflict between external pressure to marry and start a family and equally strong personal desires. The age-30 crisis amplifies these issues for both sexes.

Counseling with clients in the Mid-Life Transition may be primarily concerned not with mid-career change but with feelings of failure and reappraisal of sex-role stereotypes adopted over life. Moreland (1979, p. 302) identifies the need of many men at this point to work toward establishing greater intimacy, especially with other men. Goldberg (1976) notes that most men in actuality have very few close friends; many "buddies" or associates, but few truly intimate friends. Intimacy may indeed become increasingly important for the middle-age male because, traditionally dependent on females for emotional support, he may be married to a woman now striving to become more independent. The mid-life female is also in a period of reappraisal, often contemplating whether it is too late to explore new sources of gratification.

A recommended counseling strategy for adults in transition from one stage to another is simply to teach them about their own development and the normalcy of those feelings that typify developmental crises. This strategy not only is supportive but also motivates the client to tackle the challenge of transition, in the belief that equilibrium and a sense of well-being will follow. Because of the influence of mutual sex roles in this developmental view, regular consultation with spouse separately or jointly may be indicated.

Work and old age

Old age can be defined as the final period of life, a time when the process of aging has effected significant changes in human functioning. This period of life has often been misunderstood and devalued; only recently has attention been given to it in our society. Many difficulties arise in describing this stage of life, because there are such vast differences in the aging rate among people. We know that, as people complete growth and continue to age, certain biological changes occur. Most obvious are the reduced efficiency of the senses, the presence of gray hair, and poorer skin and muscle tone. Many also believe that there is a reduced ability to learn, remember, and make decisions, and accordingly older persons are often viewed as less effective and less capable of making a useful social contribution.

Transitions. Besides obvious biological facts, old age gains its definition from social influences; the period itself becomes established culturally. In the United States there is a legal definition of old age: when one becomes 70 years old, one is a senior citizen, even if biologically less aged than someone in mid-life. What is important for career counselors in this legal definition is that retirement from one's past work role frequently occurs and a new work life or career must begin. Important also is the fact that believing one is old has no real age limits; it is not unusual for even college students to consider themselves old (Maynard, 1973).

Gerontology, the study of the aging process, has steadily increased our understanding of this period, often dispelling old myths and cultural misconceptions. As Jarvik (1975) describes, aging's most pronounced effect on mental functioning is a gradual slowing down. People in advanced age can perform the same mental functions as the young, only it takes them longer. Often the speed differential is insignificant in the context of everyday activity. It appears to be true that mental inactivity can hasten deterioration, just as a sedentary life can lead to muscular decline. Real changes with age often involve major functional losses through disease or injury. A critical loss can occur, hastening the process of mortality (Jarvik, 1975, p. 579).

Understanding the aged is indeed a complex task. Havighurst (1963) describes the differences among older persons as greater than the differences among adolescents. The true diversity of people becomes apparent with advancing age, as years of experience alter people's attitudes and lifestyles. This is not to say that the elderly do not have common concerns and problems: reduced income and physical strength promote concern over finances, security (for example, police protection), adequate housing, finding a useful role, and remaining independent.

On the other hand, Sarason, Sarason, and Cowden (1975) caution against premature closure regarding the elderly, especially with respect to their attitudes toward work and working. In our culture the proportion of elderly to youth is increasing, bringing with it a new type of senior citizen. This person is much better educated, more self-assertive, and better prepared for life as a 60- and 70-year-old. Thus, our theories of old age may require considerable revision in the coming years.

Implications for counseling. Some counseling services are aimed at obvious needs of people past 50 years old. Planning for retirement is one of the most important. This transition point is becoming more and more a time for new work and a new lifestyle, rather than simply the termination of a career. So many options are available to retirees in so many different circumstances that the counselor must be flexible and aware of any personal stereotypes regarding the aged. It is important to show genuine respect for the client's dignity, even though at times youthful counselors will feel patronized by the elderly client. Our personal contacts with counselors working with senior citizens confirm informally that these clients are often extremely interesting persons, eager to share their wealth of knowledge and to serve others. Career counseling with them seems best approached in an open-ended fashion; the counselor may at times learn more from the client than the reverse.

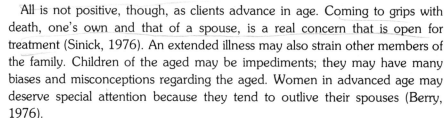

All is not positive, though, as clients advance in age. Coming to grips with death, one's own and that of a spouse, is a real concern that is open for treatment (Sinick, 1976). An extended illness may also strain other members of the family. Children of the aged may be impediments; they may have many biases and misconceptions regarding the aged. Women in advanced age may deserve special attention because they tend to outlive their spouses (Berry, 1976).

The feedback we have received from counselors active with this age group indicates that senior citizens work well together. They are enthusiastic helpers of one another, and they are tolerant of one another's idiosyncrasies. It is worthwhile to structure group treatments for them and explore peer-related interventions.

PERSONALITY THEORY

We have selected John Holland's theory to represent the influence of stable personality characteristics on career development. It far overshadows any other theoretical system, having prompted hundreds of articles and investigations in recent years. First published in 1959, Holland's theory is accompanied by standardized assessment instruments to measure his constructs, including the Vocational Preference Inventory (VPI) and the Self-Directed Search (SDS). It is unusual today to read a career-related journal without encountering at least one article dealing with Holland's theory. No chapter on career development theory in the 1980s would be complete without this theory.

Holland's typology

Holland's theory, essentially a trait-factor theory (a category elaborated in Chapter 3), classifies people according to six different types, each having a different kind of work and interpersonal environment. This theory is clearly applicable to the issues of career choice and adjustment: if a person chooses a career with a work setting in which the other workers are generally compatible with the person's own personality, choice satisfaction and job satisfaction will result.

Early in the development of the theory, Holland (1966) proposed that every person could be described as belonging to one of the following personality types, in which interests or preferences are the essential determinants.

1. Realistic (R). A person with an interest in manual labor, preferring to spend time with things or machinery rather than with people. Concrete tasks are favored over abstract ones. Realistic personality types appropriately choose careers as farmers and machinists.

2. Investigative (I). A person best represented by the role of a scientist; one who is thoughtful and precise. Investigative people can deal well with abstractions, but tend not to be sociable or interested in leadership activities.

3. Artistic (A). Creative, nonconforming, and expressive individuals, best represented by artists such as painters and musicians. They usually do not perform routine or repetitive tasks well.

4. Social (S). Individuals preferring person-oriented activities, generally of a service nature. Teachers and counselors are good examples of this type, since they tend to be outgoing and interested in understanding people. However, they may tend to be less than well organized in their affairs, untidy, and low in mechanical ability.

5. Enterprising (E). A sociable person who has the potential to use social skills to manipulate others, especially for economic gain. Careers as salespersons and attorneys are examples of those chosen by persons of this personality type. They differ most from the Investigative and may not perform well on analytical tasks.

6. Conventional (C). People of this type like to manipulate information rather than people or things. They prefer routine to ambiguous activities. Accountants and bookkeepers are examples of the Conventional type.

From these broad descriptions we might postulate that Investigative types might be more academically oriented than other types, Enterprising persons more achievement-oriented, and so forth.

Interrelationships of types. Besides giving a more detailed description of these six types, Holland (1973) also stated that individuals are rarely of one pure type. Although one type may predominate in an individual, he or she will show characteristics of other types, too. The mix of the three most dominant types in a person has been the major element in Holland's contemporary theory. Holland believes that career-interest inventories can serve as measures of personality. Through his standardized devices (such as the SDS) for measuring personality types, we can now classify people by a Holland Three-Letter Code. For example, the code SAE indicates a combination of Social, Artistic, and Enterprising types, with Social being the most significant.

In addition to classifying people, the three-letter code can be used to classify work environments. In fact, Holland (1973) provides a two-way conversion table between his code and the one in the *Dictionary of Occupational Titles*. This correlation greatly simplifies the trait-factor task of matching jobs and people. When the codes for occupation and person are the same or very nearly so, the person has achieved *congruence* in career choice.

One of the most significant features of Holland's theory is the relationship among types demonstrated by a hexagonal model (see Figure 2-1). The relationship of each personality type to another can be determined by the linear distance between points on the perimeter of the hexagon.

A comparison of the length of the solid line (a side of the hexagon) between Social and Artistic to the lengths of the broken lines yields an index of similarity between Social and Artistic, Social and Investigative, and Social and Realistic. Social is most like Artistic and least like Realistic. One can make similar comparisons for any of the types.

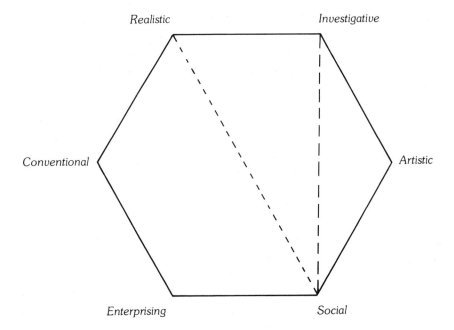

FIGURE 2-1. Holland's model of the relationships among personality types.

The three-letter code of a client can to some degree represent career maturity or immaturity through use of the concepts of *consistency* and *differentiation*. A consistent profile is one evidenced by a three-letter code whose letters are adjacent to one another on the hexagon. This pattern indicates more harmonious than conflicting characteristics in the personality. For example, an SAE code is more consistent than an SRI code. Consistent codes indicate greater career maturity, and together these concepts are related to increased ease of career decision and higher probability of career satisfaction.

The concept of differentiation is a function of the configuration of a client's scores across all six of Holland's types. A differentiated code is one in which sizable differences exist among categories on a person's interest profile; that is, the range of scores includes some very high and some very low interests. An undifferentiated profile, conversely, is one in which no distinct interests are expressed; no high and low points appear on the graphed profile (generally referred to as a "flat" profile). A differentiated profile reflects greater career maturity.

As mentioned earlier, a close match between an individual's three-letter code and the code of a selected work environment signifies congruence of occupational choice. Congruent matches of workers and work environments, in Holland's view, will lead to greater career satisfaction and fewer problems of adjustment.

Implications for counseling. Holland's theory provides counselors with many concepts important to both career decision making and career-adjustment counseling. In the former the typology provides a coding method useful in exploratory activities. The three-letter code can be used to categorize occupational information, to help interpret adult work histories, and to promote self-understanding (Helms, 1973). Because career satisfaction (as defined by the concept of congruence) and maturity (as defined through consistency and differentiation) enter so much into career counseling, it is valuable to have them interrelated in one theoretical system.

The use of Holland's typology need not be restricted to career issues alone. Bruch (1978), for example, has proposed a system using the typology to predict male satisfaction or dissatisfaction with the counseling process itself. In this connection, there may be a rude awakening for some counselors, who discover for the first time that the majority of clients represent only a few personality types (Social and Artistic?). Most people (Realistic and Conventional?) do not by nature perceive a verbal/abstract form of treatment such as counseling as an appropriate forum for their concerns. Even the general issue of client readiness for treatment may be studied using Holland's concepts. In the specific area of career decisions, the inconsistent/undifferentiated client seems more ready for broad life experience than for intensive personal counseling.

Finally, knowledge of Holland types may enable counseling centers to assign both style of treatment and specific counselor according to client code. Counselor evaluation and self-evaluation can be facilitated through the contributions of John Holland.

OTHER CAREER ISSUES

To conclude this section we will discuss some career-development concepts that appear important but that are either unexplored or ambiguous with respect to their impact.

Career saliency

This concept refers to the importance a person attaches to an occupation and how that occupation contributes to overall life satisfaction. Persons with high career saliency expect to receive much from their jobs. Those with low career saliency find work a necessary requirement and expect satisfaction to come from other sources (Zytowski, 1970).

High and low career saliency both have advantages and disadvantages. The high-career-salient person might conform better to cultural values and thus achieve greater financial rewards and greater social recognition. However, if one spends too much time on the job, family life and avocational pursuits may suffer. To date little evidence exists to suggest the clear advantage of high or low career saliency. We speculate that overall life satisfaction is related to career saliency in a curvilinear fashion, with moderate saliency associated with overall satisfaction.

We also assume that some clients may be highly involved in their jobs to compensate for lack of involvement elsewhere through inability or fear. For example, a person with a fear of intimacy might work long hours to justify avoidance of intimate contact. Conversely, low-career-salient clients may be avoiding work as a consequence of some neurotic trait. The importance of a client's job may be symptomatic of general personal traits in need of attention during counseling. In any case, when high or low saliency is reflective of non-adaptive behavior and results in reduced gratification, its more detailed exploration seems to be worthwhile.

Differing views of career importance can also affect a marriage. It is not uncommon for one spouse to find fault with the other's valuing of work, the effort put into it, and the degree of advancement achieved. This may be of double importance in a marriage in which both partners work full time outside the home.

Aptitudes and abilities

Throughout most of the history of vocational counseling it has been assumed that both specific and general aptitudes are related to occupational behavior. Counselors have thus spent a great deal of time with clients in assessing various kinds of aptitudes. It is important however, to mention Zytowski's conclusion 1970, p. 35) on reviewing the literature on special abilities and occupational performance: "We are unable to show that the possession of any given psychological factor, ability or motivation, will result in the superior performance of any given occupation." He went on to say that workers in the same occupations do share some common abilities but differ on others. This inconsistency prevents precise prediction of occupational performance or satisfaction based on aptitudes.

For some long-time members of the career guidance and counseling professions, this reality has been difficult to accept. Historically there has been a deep desire to apply scientific rigor to career work. One example has been the prediction of occupational performance from factors that include general and specific aptitudes.

For years such prediction was attempted through the use of the General Aptitude Test Battery (GATB) and resulting aptitude profiles. While many questioned the validity of this method for individual clients, it was deemed defensible from a management position in that, over a large number of cases, predictive validity was sometimes evident. In recent years, however, the use of aptitude profiles to make occupational placement decisions has become increasingly unpopular. Legal verdicts and general sentiment have altered the use of aptitude assessment from prediction of occupational performance to guidance of client career exploration. The shift is represented in the materials developed by the Appalachian Educational Laboratory and marketed through McKnight Publishing Company of Bloomington, Illinois. The materials are called the Career Information System (CIS). In this system self-assessment of aptitudes is one of several data systems used to guide career exploration. We must note that the use of aptitude assessment in career exploration has never been as popular or as easily defended as the use of career interests.

Learning theory

In much of the theory discussed so far, little attention has been paid to the learning concepts of academic psychology—concepts such as those of operant learning and social-learning theory. One could argue that career development can be effectively summarized in terms of a person's conditioning history, exposure to occupational role models, and so forth. In the next chapter we will discuss learning concepts when we describe a behavioral approach to career counseling.

PRACTICAL APPLICATIONS OF THEORY

Career theory enters into counseling as a cognitive aid in diagnosing problems, setting goals, and charting progress. It does not tell a counselor exactly what to say or what to do in a particular interview. Because of its nature, some counselors and counselor trainees have questioned the practicality of career development theory; they believe it should be more of a concrete aid in counseling. It is easier for most of us to see the practical application of a specific technique than the practicality of broad theoretical concepts. Both are useful, although not in the same ways.

A simplified grouping of the essential competencies for counselors in the context of the counseling relationship might be (1) therapeutic personal traits, (2) mastery of interview technique, and (3) a workable understanding of human behavior. The first two competencies alone can allow a counselor to perform well in a given interview, as is continually proved in counselor education; first-semester students, after a counseling laboratory, can conduct an interview as well as do noted authorities in the profession. A single interview, however, seldom constitutes effective counseling.

What beginning counselors often cannot do well and must take more time to learn is to link a series of counseling interviews together in a sensible way. Frequent concerns among practicum students are maintaining continuity among several interviews, establishing achievable goals, and gaining assurance that

TABLE 2-1. Relationship of career-development theory to practical issues

Approximate age	Theoretical stage	Normal developmental concerns
	Growth	Parental nurture
0	Fantasy	Family turmoil
11	Interest	School adjustment
		Social adjustment
13	Capacity	Accurate self-appraisal
	Exploratory	
15	Tentative	Initial career decisions
		Choice anxiety
		Lack of information
		Lack of role models
18	Transition	Leaving the family
		Diffuse identity
		Intimacy fears
22	Trial	Frustrated job search
	Establishment	
26	Trial	Job dissatisfaction
31	Stabilization	Settling down
		Questioning of earlier decisions
		Renegotiation of marriage
		Career reentry
		Divorce
		Frustrated ambitions
		Mid-life transition
46	Maintenance	Feelings of failure
		Role reversals in marriage
		Recognition of intimacy needs
		Major Illness
		Retirement Planning
65	Decline	Adjustment to Retirement
		Terminal Illness
		Death of Spouse

progress is being made toward the goals. Neither therapeutic personality nor interview technique can settle these issues for the trainee. Although they are common problems, they seem more apparent among trainees and practicing counselors with below-average grasp of theory. When counseling is concerned with career development, a grasp of theory is a practical tool in dealing with these crucial counseling issues.

The impact of career-development theory has been significant in the organization of comprehensive career-guidance and career-education programs. Table 2-1 summarizes some of its contributions toward understanding potential concerns or developmental issues clients might bring to counseling.

SUMMARY

This chapter provided a definition of career development theory along with a discussion of factors treated in various career theories. Each important factor or issue was followed by a discussion of its implications for counseling practice. Through this discussion emerged the current view that people of different developmental histories often have different career problems and concerns. Those differences require flexibility in a counselor's approach to the problem. Thus, one's grasp of career-development theory provides important and practical direction for the interventions employed to help clients.

RECOMMENDED READINGS

Holland, J. L. *Making vocational choices: A theory of careers.* Englewood Cliffs, N.J.: Prentice-Hall, 1973.

A brief, primary source for one of the most popular career theories. The book contains many practical tools for the career counselor.

Moreland, J. R. Some implications of life-span development for counseling psychology. *Personnel and Guidance Journal,* 1979, *57,* 299–304.

This article, based primarily on Levinson's view of adult development, associates different counseling strategies with important developmental changes or crises of postadolescence. The emphasis is on normal age-related problems sometimes mistaken by counselors as signs of serious emotional difficulties.

Munley, P. H. Erikson's theory of psychosocial development and career development. *Journal of Vocational Behavior,* 1977, *10,* 261–269.

A succinct review of Erikson's developmental concepts and how they explain career-related behavior.

Osipow, S. H. *Theories of career development* (2nd ed.). Englewood Cliffs, N.J.: Prentice-Hall, 1973

A useful reference on career theory and the research it has stimulated.

Super, D. E., & Hall, D. T. Career development: Exploration and planning. In *The Annual Review of Psychology,* Vol. 29, Palo Alto, Calif.: Annual Reviews, Inc., 1978.

A recent review of the research trends in the area. Look for such reviews to follow in this series. Reviews are also available in the related areas of developmental psychology, personnel management, and counseling.

LEARNING ACTIVITIES

1. Write a brief essay defining and describing factors associated with career maturity.
2. List significant career-adjustment problems of adult workers.
3. Explain why career-development theory up to the 1980s was one primarily concerned with adolescent career decisions.
4. Write a brief summary of John Holland's theory.
5. Explain how a person's self-concept affects career development.
6. Write a defense of the practicality of career-development theory.
7. Interview several retired persons to learn about important adjustments they needed to make at retirement.
8. Write a plan for a one- or two-day workshop that describes important transitions encountered in typical career patterns. Include several application or participant-involvement exercises.
9. Discuss how work is portrayed on television and in the cinema. Name a movie character who by most standards has failed in an occupation. Use your understanding of career-development theory to explain the failure.

CHAPTER THREE

COUNSELING FOR CAREER DECISIONS

An important monograph by Crites (1974) reviews dominant theories of vocational counseling and concludes that the unifying theme among various career-counseling approaches is the goal of facilitating effective career decisions. While various theoretical systems approach this objective in different ways, those viewed as career oriented do not deviate from this primary goal, whatever other outcomes they may serve.

Crites's conclusion is not seriously disputed among the leadership in career counseling; his paper has been reprinted several times in other important career-related publications (Peters & Hansen, 1977; Whiteley & Resnikoff, 1978). Support for his position comes from additional sources. For example, Herr and Cramer (1979, p. 274) argue that a presumably free society, with an almost unlimited array of career options, needs to provide assistance in the complex task of career decision making. They also posit decision making as one of the two primary purposes for career counseling; the other is development.

The consistent emphasis on a single outcome implies that career counseling is a specialized form of treatment, requiring special training of its practitioners, and that clients seek counseling expressly for decision-making assistance. It also suggests that career counseling should involve some rather specialized techniques if in fact it is more than multipurpose counseling applied to career decisions. In his monograph (1974), Crites does attempt to identify specialized process/technique issues in career counseling.

While one can hardly discount assistance in career decision making as a worthwhile service, apparently counseling as a vehicle for this service can be and has been criticized. Holland (1976) sees the use of the counseling relationship for career exploration and decision making as an expensive treatment. Like others he appears to advocate a "funnel" approach to career development: clients first receive the less expensive treatments, such as group guidance, with personal counseling reserved for only the more difficult client problems. Holland (1976) would administer his Self-Directed Search (SDS), a 1½-hour instrument described by Weinrach (1979) as a comprehensive career-guidance experience, to many clients; only a few would receive extended counseling.

Holland is directly critical of counseling as an everyday vehicle for making career decisions, and other experts in the area seem at least partly to agree. For example, Herr and Cramer devote at most a dozen of more than 400 pages in

41

their text on career guidance (1979) specifically to counseling. Does this scant treatment mean that the process of counseling is viewed as essentially unimportant in promoting career development and decision making? Some would say so. Others might argue that texts devoted to career issues need not duplicate the student's or practicing counselor's background in general-purpose counseling but should concentrate on career issues. Presumably the readers then synthesize into their counseling activity the specialized material in the career text.

A glance at the table of contents of this text shows that the authors take a different position. We believe that the process of counseling toward career decision making has been neglected in favor of career guidance or programmed-learning activities distinct from counseling. One reason for this neglect is a misconception common to many members of this counseling profession, expressed in the cliché: "There are real counselors, and there are those who cannot do 'real' counseling and are called career-guidance specialists." Such a misconception may be perpetrated by insufficient attention to counseling strategies in career texts.

We believe that more counselors and counselors-in-training are interested in career problems than ever before. Counselors are committed to doing what they believe they do best, and their expertise resides in the counseling relationship. This chapter is given primarily to an overview, critique, and synthesis of approaches to career counseling. Finally, we will examine the components of a career-counseling theory, with the purpose of assisting the reader in the formulation of a personal approach to career counseling.

APPROACHES TO CAREER COUNSELING

An approach to career counseling has been defined by Crites (1969) as "a relatively well-articulated model and method of assisting individuals in making decisions about their lifelong roles in the world-of-work and in solving problems which arise in the course of the choice process." This definition is for the most part clear; its only ambiguity is the meaning of "*relatively* well-articulated."

When Crites (1974) attempted an overview of the major approaches to career counseling, he apparently found five that were relatively well articulated. Crites began with an historical investigation into vocational psychology, concluding that vocational guidance rather than counseling predominated until the 1930s and 1940s, when trait-and-factor counseling began to take form. In the late 1940s, client-centered counseling was applied to career decision making; a decade later followed contributions from a psychoanalytic framework. At about the same time, Donald Super (1957) proposed a developmental framework with implications for counseling. Finally, Crites (1974) noted the application in the late 1950s of behavioral principles to career information seeking and decision making. Thus, he concluded that historically there are five approaches. Later, Crites (1976a) articulated his own synthetic approach to career counseling.

Of the approaches named, only trait-and-factor counseling was developed specifically for career problems. It remains the best-developed approach and is the standard to which other approaches are compared. We will therefore treat this approach at length, along with the behavioral approach to career counseling, which also seems to be well articulated. The remaining approaches, those less well articulated in terms of career work, will receive less attention.

Client-centered approach

The most significant statement of client-centered career counseling does not come from Carl Rogers, nor is there any systematic statement of it as an approach to career issues in the 1940s and 1950s. During that period client-centered counseling seems to have emphasized social-emotional adjustment, of which career decision making and career adjustment were part. No special constructs or procedures were offered for career counseling.

According to Crites (1974), Patterson (1964) articulates the best statement of client-centered theory as applied to career counseling. It emphasizes outcomes and counselor characteristics consistent with the approach. The goals of counseling are self-congruence and implementation of the self-concept. Counselor-offered congruence, empathy, and unconditional positive regard remain the principal therapeutic elements in the counseling dyad (Rogers, 1957).

Patterson (1964) stresses that career counseling, especially when the use of tests and occupational information is considered, must remain a relationship built on client self-direction. If the client requests occupational information or the administration of standardized tests, then the use of both would be consistent with client-centered counseling.

In summarizing this approach, Crites (1974) views its most important contribution to career counseling as heightened counselor sensitivity to the client's role in decision making and recognition of how an occupational role can affect a person's self-concept. In reality, there is little in client-centered counseling specific to career decision making and coping with work-related problems.

Psychoanalytic approach

Early psychoanalytic contributions to career counseling come for the most part from Edward S. Bordin and his associates at the University of Michigan (Bordin, 1968; Bordin & Kopplin, 1973; Bordin, Nachmann, & Segal, 1963). Bordin (1968), in particular, emphasized the interplay between a client's general personality and vocational decisions, an approach Crites (1974) labels "psychodynamic." The label may be appropriate, since Bordin's view of career counseling goes beyond psychoanalytic concepts to a synthesis of psychoanalytic and other developmental theories. For example, he cites Roe, Rogers, and Super as important contributors to vocational counseling (Bordin, 1968). At the core of his approach is the assumption that internal (intrapsychic) factors explain the difficulties clients have in making career decisions.

As one would expect, Bordin and others incorporate in their writing about career counseling only a handful of the many concepts in psychoanalytic theory. They call their approach a developmental one with developmental goals. They view life in cycles that include a series of transition points; people move from one stage to another, climbing from one plateau (stable period) to the next. A vocational decision usually marks a point of transition. When personal hangups (intrapsychic blocks) or developmental deficiencies interfere with these decisions, the pain of increased anxiety will motivate the client to seek counseling.

While it will begin with the career-decision problem, the psychodynamic approach will evolve quickly into personal counseling. In fact, Bordin (1968, p. 729) describes vocational counseling as a form of "self-confrontation"; career indecision is really a symptom of something else. Bordin, like so many others, views a career choice as an expression of one's self-concept or self-identity. Of all the things, then, that make career decision making difficult, an incomplete or faulty sense of identity is the most common.

Bordin and Kopplin (1973) have developed a diagnostic system that attempts to categorize career-decision problems. A simplified version of the categories follows. This synopsis omits elaboration as well as subcategories, which warrant separate investigation.

1. Synthetic difficulties. Situations in which insufficient cognitive review has occurred for the client to see career options clearly.
2. Identity problems. Cases in which self-perception is associated with the choice problem.
3. Gratification conflict. Instances in which approach/avoidance and approach/approach conflicts occur.
4. Change orientation. Cases in which self-dissatisfaction and the desire to change personally become portrayed as a career choice.
5. Overt pathology. Circumstances in which personal functioning is insufficient to allow career choices or even to do work.
6. Unclassified problems.

In an attempt to use the above system, Bordin and Kopplin (1973) classified 82 college-student cases. Of these cases, 59% were diagnosed as related to identity problems, a result they explained by reminding the reader that identity formation is one of the most significant developmental tasks for late adolescence and early adulthood. Their heavy reliance on the work of psychoanalytic and developmental theorist Erik Erikson is evident. Erikson's ideas on ego identity (1946, 1956, 1963, 1968) are cited frequently in the literature on psychodynamic career counseling.

The counseling process for this approach has been described by Bordin (1968) as one in which the counselor attempts to optimize the client's self-confrontation at that transition point in life marked by the career decision. It is to be hoped that the client expresses minimal (only therapeutic) anxiety during this process. Three stages in this process can be observed: thorough *exploration* of the problem, *contract setting* (making the decision), and *working through* the developmental problems making the decision difficult.

Counseling usually begins with a superficial and cognitive review of the career-decision problem. We would probably find it difficult to discriminate this beginning from that of trait-factor counseling, to be described later. As the process continues, though, the counselor skillfully integrates personal counseling with the career-decision problem. For example, one would expect the psychodynamic career counselor to promote investigation of dependency needs and methods of handling and expressing aggression. Both will have eventual relevance to a career choice, since work can provide gratification of both. Examination of client fears and wishes would be appropriate and relevant.

Eventually the critical decision point would be reached: in some way counselor and client negotiate whether or not counseling will go beyond the career decision and strive for personality change. We assume that in most cases of synthetic difficulties (cognitive review of career options) this would not be necessary. However, as discussed earlier, most career-choice problems in adolescents are identity related and thus require personal counseling.

If a contract is made to do psychodynamic personal counseling, *working for change* follows a path similar to face-to-face psychoanalytically oriented therapy. The techniques used in this last stage are primarily interpretations aimed at insight or increased self-understanding. Tests, especially interest inventories, would be used and interpreted. The view of the counselor remains keyed to developmental issues such as parental/identity figures, and so forth. Ego strength is evaluated and enhanced through therapeutic interpretations. After counseling, the less-conflicted client with increased psychic energy and a stronger ego should have less difficulty making the career decision.

Evidence exists that identity problems are related to career-choice issues (Galinsky & Fast, 1966; Hershenson, 1967). However, the appeal of psychodynamic career counseling probably depends on one's overall attraction to psychoanalytic theory, ego psychology, and the modern treatments associated with them. Important to note is Bordin's broad experience as a clinician and practicing therapist, in contrast to the rooting of many other approaches in the thought of educators or researchers. Clinically trained, practicing therapists, the majority of whom subscribe to some form of analytically based therapy (Garfield & Kurtz, 1976), may be interested in using this career-counseling approach in treatment settings such as mental health centers, private practice, and others not traditionally involved directly with career problems.

Developmental approach

In his review of career counseling, John Crites (1974, p. 17) calls the developmental approach "the most comprehensive and coherent system of assisting clients with career problems which has yet been formulated." While not as old as trait-factor counseling, the developmental approach begins with the early writing of Donald Super. Refer to Chapter 1 for the principles on which the counseling approach is based.

In terms of counseling process and objectives, the developmental approach is a composite of both client-centered and trait-factor techniques (Crites, 1974). The goals of counseling are essentially the general objectives of promoting career development. Paralleling the developmental stages of Super, the goals become more specific as they are defined by the next developmental step appropriate for the client. At each developmental stage, though, there may be several competencies that may be worked on consistent with career-development theory. More of a developmental approach will be manifested later in our discussion of Crites's comprehensive approach to career counseling.

Trait-factor approach

Dating as far back as the 1930s, trait-factor counseling is the traditional approach to career decision making and the standard by which all other forms of career counseling are measured. Although dominant in the history of vocational psychology, it has been much criticized for numerous reasons. Still, it seems that counselors of many different orientations, when faced with psychologically well-adjusted clients wanting to make educational or vocational decisions, turn almost instinctively to an approach similar to what we will describe as trait-factor. Because of its widespread use, this approach will receive a more detailed description than others.

The trait-factor approach to counseling is based on trait theory, which essentially states that people can be understood in terms of the traits they possess. Traits are stable characteristics, believed to be finite in number, that enable people to respond consistently to similar situations. Examples of commonly understood traits are intelligence, ambition, aptitude, and self-esteem. While traits are internal to the person and unobservable in that sense, they can be measured by observing behavior that reveals them. Standardized assessment, especially self-report devices, has been the means by which we learn about traits. In a counseling context, then, if one can learn about clients' traits that are relevant to work, one can help clients select employment best suited to them. It soon becomes clear why trait-factor counseling has been described as "matching people to jobs" and criticized as "the square-peg, square-hole theory."

Historical background. Much of the development of this approach emanated from the University of Minnesota. In the 1920s Donald G. Paterson began an effort to bring scientific rigor to the vocational-guidance approach of Frank Parsons. Parsons, called the father of vocational guidance, proposed that self-knowledge and knowledge of the world of work, with "true reasoning on the relations of these two groups of facts" (Parsons, 1909, p. 5), would provide assistance in career planning. This was discussed briefly in Chapter 1.

As a student and later colleague of Paterson, E. G. Williamson would further develop trait-factor counseling and then become its best representative. In Williamson's major publications (1939, 1950, 1965), one finds a detailed description of its methods and objectives. It is important to note that Williamson's approach, later expanded to include other counseling problems, began with career decision making specifically in mind. This is quite the reverse of most other approaches. Trait-factor counseling is also the only counseling approach with its origins in education, designed to assist high school and college students in planning for the future.

Counseling goals. Future planning and the making of related decisions best represent the goals of trait-factor counseling. While often discussed in connection with client self-actualization or personal growth, the element of decision making as an objective remains strong. An objective, intermediate to the decision, is increased self-understanding.

In particular, educational and career decisions provide direction for the counseling. Williamson (1950) often mentions an individual's social responsibility; the decisions made, if effective, not only are personally satisfying but also make a social contribution.

Counselor characteristics. As we shall see, trait-factor counseling is direct and straightforward in its procedure; it was at one time what came to be called directive counseling. Consistent with this terminology, the counselor is direct, freely giving opinions and suggestions without exerting control or limiting the client's right to make the ultimate decision.

The counselor is viewed as a wise person, a teacher, experienced in living, mature enough to have a workable set of values; knowledgeable about careers and how people make decisions, effective in assessing human traits and behaviors. Since standardized tests are important counseling tools, the counselor is skilled in their use, especially in their interpretation. One might further expect that the counselor would enjoy disseminating information, making predictions, and so forth. E. G. Williamson himself was Dean of Students for many, many years at the University of Minnesota. Maybe a stereotype of a kindly dean with psychological training represents many trait-factor counselors.

The counseling process. As we shall see, trait-factor counseling is intended for normal adolescents and adults with adequate intellectual capability. We would expect many counselors of this orientation to refer severely disabled clients to other therapists.

Trait-factor counseling is a direct, rational activity: To feel good, you must think clearly. It is information-based: Knowledge about oneself and the world of work makes effective career decisions more probable. Testing is usually one important part of the process.

Williamson (1950) describes the counseling process as having six flexible steps: (1) analysis, (2) synthesis, (3) diagnosis, (4) prognosis, (5) counseling, and (6) follow-up. To complete these steps it is clear that the counselor does more than interview the client; much important work is done between sessions.

Usually in the first interview the client presents the career-decision problem and, together with the counselor, explores personal information related to it. The counselor may explain the process of choosing a vocation, thus structuring the counseling activity. Early in the process most clients complete a battery of tests, assigned by the counselor and taken between interviews. Earlier in its history, the assigned test battery was to be comprehensive, including interest, aptitude, and personality testing. Since a prognosis was to be made, there was an effort to estimate probability of success in various occupations using multiple regression procedures. In recent years, the practice of prediction has declined, and with it "saturation testing." Career-interest assessment remains, though, an important part of the counseling process.

Using interview data, test results, and school records, the counselor attempts to profile the client's assets, liabilities, and possible maladjustments. In counseling, these conclusions are presented to clients in an educational atmosphere. The counselor may also help the client to learn new skills, change attitudes, and plan to change environments or select new ones. Planning a program of action, especially for career exploration, is very important.

The techniques used are intended to promote rapport and deal directly with the issues at hand. The counselor advises, explains, persuades, serves as a model, and makes referrals to appropriate sources as needed. To some this may sound more like advising than counseling; if so, it would be a very personalized form of advising, with great care taken to generate as complete a picture as possible of all factors related to the decision. This is not often done in normal academic advising.

Evaluation. As with most dominant approaches in a field whose members differ widely in ideology, critiques of trait-factor counseling have often been emotional and severe. Anyone who has been a counselor since the 1960s has no doubt heard references to this type of counseling as "three interviews and a cloud of dust." In the first interview the career decisions are explored and tests assigned; in the second, the tests and general measurement concepts (use of percentiles, for example) are explained; the third interview discusses potential career choices along with sources of career information.

Although three sessions may be sufficient for some clients, most seem to need more time to assimilate all the information required, to learn more career information-seeking behaviors, and to receive a heavier dose of support to help control some of the anxiety associated with important career decisions. We have seen appeals to career counselors to refrain from putting clients into an information overload, to be sure to develop an interview style that achieves active client participation, and to recognize that readiness for decision making is more complex, involving more than content-knowledge recall. Of course, E. G. Williamson recognized these complexities, and said so in his numerous publications over his professional career of almost 50 years.

It seems that trait-factor counseling has also responded to other criticisms as it has matured. Overtesting is less common today. Very early criticisms that this approach viewed career choice as a one-time event have diminished considerably as proponents have acknowledged the necessity of viewing career choice as a developmental process. Still, for some the practice of trait-factor counseling seems to be an oversimplified and therefore invalid attempt at people/job matching.

Behavioral approach

With all that has been published applying behavioral principles to career counseling and career development, it is difficult in a text of this size and nature to represent fully all it has to offer. Thus, to introduce behavioral career counseling we will treat primarily the points of view of John D. Krumboltz, Carl E. Thoresen, and their students from Stanford University (Krumboltz, 1976; Krumboltz & Thoresen, 1969). As one would expect, behavioral career counseling had as a goal the development of a scientifically precise approach to career decision making, both in theory and in practice. Utilizing learning concepts from academic psychology, career decision making was to be understood as a product of instrumental learning, teachable both inside and outside the counseling relationship through structured activities.

Career-related behavior (such as career information seeking and job-interview behavior) was understood as resulting from the reinforcing or nonreinforcing consequences of an individual's past behavior. Most of the behavior required in career choice and development is rather complex in nature, including more than one type of behavior, but if carefully studied it can be broken down into its component parts. The client can then learn the complex behavior in simple steps.

The approach we will describe, however, is not merely operant conditioning applied to career problems; cognitive factors do intervene in the learning process. Such mediating cognitions, though, can be studied and modified, according to this approach, with precision similar to that observed in conditioning experiments (Meichenbaum, 1977). Important to note is the preference for putting the technology of behavior modification and cognitive restructuring in the hands of the client. The behavioral approach may be simply understood as the counselor teaching clients self-control skills (Mahoney & Thoresen, 1974; Thoresen & Mahoney, 1974).

In an attempt to develop a more comprehensive theory of career selection, Krumboltz, Mitchell, and Jones (1978) labeled many of the cognitive variables, along with some performance abilities and emotional predispositions, as *task-approach skills*. They include work habits, mental sets, perceptional and thought processes, performance standards and values, problem orienting, and emotional responses.

Counseling goals. True to form, the behavioral approach constantly re-quires counseling goals to be specific and observable (Krumboltz & Baker, 1973). This emphasis, typifying the precision sought in practice, also simplifies the evaluation of results. For example, if a client says something vague, such as, "I want to find a job I'll like," the counselor and client work to translate that goal into observable behavior, such as setting up a certain number of interviews with local employers for the coming week.

In counseling, a number of specific intermediate goals may relate to increasing skill levels in areas important to career decision making. These include value clarifying, goal setting, predicting future events, alternative generating, informa-tion seeking, estimating, reinterpreting past events, eliminating and selecting alternatives, planning, and generalizing (Krumboltz & Baker, 1973). The client's circumstances will dictate which of these areas are emphasized. In all cases the client decides the goals for counseling. To form the treatment contract, the counselor must then agree to the goals. If a counselor's value system or compe-tence in a specific area will not allow agreement with the client's chosen goals, then a referral is in order.

Counseling process. Krumboltz and Baker (1973, p. 240) outline the counseling process as follows:

1. Defining the problem and the client's goals
2. Agreeing mutually to achieve counseling goals
3. Generating alternative problem solutions
4. Collecting information about the alternatives
5. Examining the consequences of the alternatives
6. Resolving goals, alternatives, and consequences
7. Making the decision or tentatively selecting an alternative contingent on new developments and new opportunities
8. Generalizing the decision-making process to new problems

The sequence listed is flexible and should not be viewed as a recipe. Much of this process is consistent with behavioral models for decision making (Gelatt, 1962).

We have already discussed goal setting. The process of alternative generating is a form of brainstorming in which as many options are listed as can come to mind. Initially no alternatives should be eliminated due to apparent unfeasibility.

Most clients benefit from learning more about the decision-making process and gaining information on careers. The behavioral career counselor will use reinforcement techniques and both live and recorded models in helping the client learn information and develop skills useful in career decisions. Simulation techniques, represented by the *Job Experience Kit* (1970), were developed by Krumboltz; the kit is marketed through Science Research Associates. Such direct experience in an occupationally related activity is highly recommended in the behavioral approach.

One thing that may change during counseling is the client's career interests. Behavioral counselors view interests not as inborn traits but as learned characteristics.

Finally, the process undertaken by a client in career decision making cultivates skills applicable to other life choices. It is therefore recommended that attention be given to generalizing this skill to other issues, further increasing the benefit of career counseling.

Evaluation. In a critique of Krumboltz's view of career decision making, Holland (1976) reminded us that approaches based on precision and comprehensiveness are not always the most practical for actual use with clients. This objection may apply to behavioral career counseling. The use of performance objectives and live and recorded models may be too costly for individual counseling. Highly structured interactions and practice experiences as described are not always economical or useful in counseling situations. Furthermore, the behavioral explanation of career-decision problems may provide no more precision than any other system. For example, reinforcement histories relevant to decision making ability depend, like histories used in other approaches, on client report after the fact.

Although such criticisms can be made, one certainly cannot conclude that this system is any less practical than others. While at times abstract, the concepts used in this approach are relatively easy to understand. Due to their popularity in counselor education, the concepts and practices of behavioral counseling are taught by many skilled educators.

An important advantage of the behavioral approach comes from the easy translation of its methodology back and forth between counseling and structured guidance experiences in both small groups and classrooms. Learning this system may well help the counselor to develop a comprehensive career-development program. Thus, consistency and uniformity of practice are possible.

Synthesis: Crites's comprehensive approach

After having reviewed what he considered to be the major approaches to career counseling, Crites (1974, 1976a) published another major article in which he presented a synthesis of career counseling, relying not only on other counseling approaches but also on some of his own earlier efforts. He felt that no one counseling approach was comprehensive enough to provide an adequate guide for practice. However, each system he reviewed did make significant contributions to the practice of career counseling. Thus, a synthesis of leading approaches may provide the best basis for both theory and practice.

In attempting his synthesis, Crites (1976a) arranged a taxonomy of career-counseling approaches, comparing and contrasting them according to theory and method. Theoretical contributions were further divided into issues of diagnosis, counseling process, and proposed outcomes. He felt that career-counseling methods could be understood best when subdivided into interview techniques, method of test interpretation, and the use of occupational information. In each of these areas, Crites presented a synthesis of his own and other counseling approaches. He drew on and enriched much of what trait-factor and developmental career counseling had to offer.

Diagnosis. Crites believes that a practical diagnosis answers the *what* and *why* of the client's problem in making a career decision. In generating the diagnosis, both test and interview information is useful. He recommends the use of the Career Maturity Inventory (see Chapter 4) for its precision in assessing career-choice attitudes and competencies. It provides important information regarding the client's decision-making readiness and style. Crites calls this diagnosis a *decisional* one, which is different from the *dynamic* diagnosis mentioned in our discussion of the psychodynamic approach (see p. 44). Finally, Crites sees as useful a *differential* diagnosis, common in trait-factor counseling. This is diagnosis of the realism of an expressed choice from a determination of differences between that choice and the client's aptitudes and interests.

Process. In surveying the career-counseling process generally, Crites identifies the three commonly recognized stages of problem solving. First the counselor/client team gathers background information regarding the problem; second, the team clarifies and states the problem; finally, it discusses and executes solutions. The middle stage is the longest.

Crites also presents recommendations regarding the quality of the relationship between counselor and client. He thinks the career-counseling relationship at best is a modified combination of the paternalism of trait-factor counseling and the laissez-faire orientation of early client-centered counseling. The counselor shares experiences and knowledge with the client but accepts the client's perception of events as valid. While career-decision counseling may be more cognitive and straightforward than personal-social counseling, it can be an extremely therapeutic and growthful experience. Thus we would assume that the process includes the use of many different techniques.

Outcomes. Crites repeatedly emphasizes that the diagnosis in counseling determines the outcomes. For counseling to be purposeful from beginning to end, diagnosis and outcome must be related. Thus development of the maturity necessary for career decisions often becomes an outcome. Strongly emphasized in the discussion of outcome is the connection between career-related outcomes and overall adjustment. Client movement toward personal growth and fuller functioning is an imperative consideration during counseling. Increased self-esteem, stability, and other indexes of enhanced adjustment would therefore be anticipated or at least desired outcomes.

Interviewing. To achieve desired outcomes, Crites recommends a broad repertoire of interviewing techniques. In the beginning of counseling, when problem background is being explored, reflective counselor responses seem in order. Crites sees the middle stage of counseling as the period in which the counselor becomes more interpretive, relating present to past behavior. As actual problem resolution begins in the final stage of counseling, the technical aspects of trait-factor and behavioral counseling seem appropriate. Thus Crites's view of interview techniques appears consistent with contemporary views of interviewing strategy, probably most thoroughly described and organized by Cormier and Cormier (1979).

Test interpretation. Crites acknowledges that test interpretation has a long tradition in career counseling, especially for predicting career satisfaction. However, he documents the declining interest in tests and their use, suggesting that a new approach to interpretation might retain the usefulness of tests as an important source of feedback but eliminate the confusion and error common in their past use. He calls this approach "interpreting the tests without the tests."

In the past, the trait-factor approach called for the administration of a comprehensive test battery, later to be interpreted at a single session. As one might imagine, the large amount of test information was difficult for clients to understand and remember accurately. Thus much confusion and error resulted.

Crites recommends using Career Maturity Inventory (CMI) results and interview data to make a decisional diagnosis; interview data to make a dynamic diagnosis; and aptitude and interest assessment to make the differential diagnosis mentioned earlier. The counselor makes use of standardized tests but never formally interprets them to the client. Rather, while interviewing the client, the counselor can introduce test results into the dialogue at appropriate times. For example, if a client is seriously considering the occupation of bank teller, results of an interest inventory such as the Career Assessment Inventory may be discussed to reveal similar or dissimilar client interests compared to bank tellers. The interpretation of test results are woven into the ongoing effort to make career decisions.

Use of occupational information. Crites identifies the use of occupational information as the most underdeveloped method in career counseling. He claims that its value in making career decisions has been minimal mainly because occupational information is poorly integrated with other aspects of career counseling, even the use of self-information by the client.

It does not necessarily follow that Crites favors counselors' disseminating occupational information during interviews; this practice puts the counselor too much in the role of expert rather than collaborator. Crites sees the reinforcement of information seeking by the client between sessions as the counselor's best alternative. In this respect, Crites may be advocating behavioral strategies as a useful career-counseling method for supplying occupational information.

Evaluation. Both Holland (1976) and Roe (1976) have written critiques of Crites's approach. The former notes that Crites may have overemphasized diagnosis, especially since that activity has moderate support at best from both research and practice. Crites's description of the counseling relationship and the parallels between career and personal development is also criticized by reviewers, especially Holland, who asserts that individual counseling is an uneconomical treatment compared to other career decision-making programs (such as Self-Directed Search). Noted, of course, in the reviews is the heavy reliance upon the Career Maturity Inventory and its associated decisional diagnosis.

Such criticisms are to be anticipated since at present structured guidance activities seem to predominate in the field. The approach of Crites is a promising contribution to those more or less full-time counseling practitioners who leave structured guidance activities to colleagues more interested in such forms of service.

One might suspect that many counselors may never become enthusiastic about using the Career Maturity Inventory as broadly as recommended in this approach. However, Crites has an advantage over many other theorists in that his theoretical system describes in detail the components of career decision making. Thus, decisional diagnoses merit investigation by researchers and experimentation by practitioners. The coherence of his views warrants testing.

STATE-OF-THE-ART IN CAREER COUNSELING

In concluding an overview of dominant approaches for facilitating career decisions through counseling, one must evaluate what each contribution offers and what general conclusions can be drawn from the sum total of these contributions. Clear-cut conclusions are not evident, since multiple points of view (as we find in the field of career counseling) seem to raise more questions than they answer. By way of conclusion, then, we will direct attention toward questions commonly raised about counseling for career decisions.

Is there a dominant approach to career counseling?

If there is a dominant approach, it has to be a trait-factor approach matured through developmental contributions. This approach is not viewed as a general counseling approach that would be applicable, for example, to personal/social problems. Thus, few counselors in general practice call themselves by its name. We imagine that most practitioners would label their orientation otherwise but nevertheless adopt strategies that are essentially trait-factor in origin when confronted directly with a career-decision problem.

If the three-interview format of traditional trait-factor counseling does not work, the counselor might revert back to his or her stated theoretical approach to explain why little movement resulted from the trait-factor approach at the outset. It seems that in the majority of instances trait-factor counseling is the chosen technique when the problem presented is clearly a career-decision dilemma.

What we have called "a trait-factor approach matured through developmental contributions" essentially summarizes Crites's (1976a) comprehensive approach. The rigid reliance on tests as predictors of career satisfaction is certainly not popular and thus represents a part of the trait-factor approach that is largely unacceptable to most active counselors.

From the consumer's point of view, however, if clients were asked to describe what they thought career counseling would be like, their conceptions would most resemble trait-factor counseling. This approach, then, in addition to being popular among counselors, has evidently been popularized with the public and remains consistent with client expectations. To approach career-choice problems otherwise may result in some client resistance.

Is career counseling really different from personal counseling?

As this chapter has so far discussed, the approaches of psychodynamic, client-centered therapy, and Crites's comprehensive theory all minimize differences between career and personal problems and emphasize the similarities. The trait-factor and developmental approaches note differences in treating career-decision problems and more general client personal-social problems.

One can observe clearly on many high school and college campuses that career counseling represents a special service provided at offices or centers where personal counseling of any duration rarely occurs. In fact, many institutions may designate an entirely different place for one to receive personal counseling. It is evident that many educational institutions view career and personal counseling as distinctly different enterprises.

From our review it seems difficult to make this distinction consistently. At times a counselor can deal very little with issues beyond a career decision; the focus is on such things as career-decision involvement, extent and accuracy of occupational information, and so on. In Bordin and Kopplin's (1973) diagnostic system, such instances present "synthetic difficulties": problems in which accumulated knowledge needs to be sorted for cognitive clarity. Direct, cognitively oriented career counseling seems appropriate for these clients, who are mainly adaptive and not manifesting psychopathology. Since millions of people fall into this category, one could easily be employed working only with them, leaving the more psychologically disabled and career confused to others. In fact, the specialized career counselor may not be competent to do personal counseling. In the same vein, however, the clinical counselor who lacks background in straightforward career counseling may not be as able to help the more disabled client with career-decision problems.

Is special training required for career-decision counseling?

We have just speculated that specific training in career counseling may increase the overall competence of clinical counselors. This hypothesis assumes that many counselors, even those who are generally well trained, possess training deficiencies that specialized career counselors do not have. These deficiencies pertain chiefly to diagnostic training specific to career decisions. Full-time career counselors are more likely to be certified in the use of the General Aptitude Test Battery (GATB) and to have much more experience with interest inventories and the more recent measures of career maturity such as the Career Maturity Inventory. Also, they are most familiar with career development theory and theories of job satisfaction. This kind of specialized background certainly can be expected to increase one's competence to perform counseling for career decision making. We would recommend this background as a useful adjunct to mental health counselors, social workers, and clinical psychologists, as well as counseling psychologists and guidance counselors.

If a clinical psychologist, for instance, recognizes the importance of a career decision in a therapy case and does not have the appropriate background, the psychologist might be wise to request a consultation with a school counselor or someone else more specifically trained in the area of career decisions. Generally, the counseling psychologist with doctoral training and a specialized background in career counseling is the most capable consultant and referral source.

In addition to aptitude and interest assessment, special training in occupational information or, more appropriately, the process of career exploration seems necessary to achieve efficiency in counseling for career decisions. Knowledge of the *Dictionary of Occupational Titles* and *Occupational Outlook Handbook* (to be discussed in Chapter 7) enriches the counseling process. Crites (1974, 1976a) is probably correct in the view that the use of occupational information is a specialized technique in career counseling. Such specialized techniques require special training.

Rarely does a counseling practitioner do individual or group counseling exclusively, spending all his professional time in an interviewing room or office with clients. The variety of a counselor's job normally includes consultation work. Consultation for career development and decision making requires an extensive background. Thus the usual combination of counseling with consultation in the specific area of career decision making demands specialized training.

Is career guidance more effective than counseling in promoting career decisions?

The tone of this question may suggest that structured learning activities, commonly termed *guidance,* are in competition with the less structured and more individualized process of counseling. In truth, guidance activities and counseling are complementary; both are of unique and essential value to a complete program. Sometimes errors in judgment occur in selecting and timing the use of each.

In the early stages of career decision making, usually a phase of general career exploration, structured experiences seem most appropriate and cost effective. The subsequent phase of sorting and collating a vast array of personal and occupational information also seems most efficiently managed in a guidance-technique format. Also, for a person who has made appropriate career decisions and seeks simple confirmation of them, a programmed guidance experience is the method of choice.

For many young people, these guidance services, usually available on a general basis in school settings, will supply all that is needed to facilitate an appropriate career decision. For other young people the decision-making process is more complex and difficult; occupational and general assessment information acquired through guidance programs are not sufficient to their needs, and individualized assistance through counseling is indicated. Some young people who approach adulthood and the termination of public education recognize with seriousness and considerable anxiety the importance of the impending career decision. This anxiety frequently is of such magnitude as to diminish the benefit they gain from even the best of structured guidance activities. The counseling relationship can provide the potential to channel this age-appropriate anxiety therapeutically into individualized and supportive exploration of relevant internal and external factors, to promote appropriate decision making, and hence to increase emotional equilibrium.

Counseling may also be the process most beneficial to persons already at the terminal phase of a career choice when, following ample information seeking and exploration, they have narrowed the selection to a few equally attractive though uniquely different options. At this point, subjective data generated through counseling, evaluated and integrated with occupational data, may help resolve this traditional approach/approach conflict. Counseling may also be indicated for an individual with very limited realistic career opportunities, confusion or conflict regarding career choices versus other life factors of high value (such as geographical ties, family concerns, or financial considerations), or lack of any cohesive career-interest pattern even partially identified through some programmed device.

As an individual matures into adulthood, counseling seems increasingly to be the preferred form of career-decision assistance. A primary reason for this situation is the paucity of well-developed structured guidance programs for adults. Also, adults tend to present particularly complex career-decision problems, in that they generally have some work experience and are likely to be exploring career options due to dissatisfaction with their current employment situation. Thus they need to both gain an understanding of their current dissatisfaction and consider alternatives consistent with their enhanced self-understanding. At some future time, organized, structured guidance activities may be available to assist adults in this common dilemma. At present, however, counseling, with its flexibility and individual emphasis, must be seen as the treatment of choice.

ONE COUNSELOR'S APPROACH:
AN ILLUSTRATION

The following dialogue shows how one counselor has developed and applied a career counseling theory.

Interviewer: Tom, at present you are working in a career center in a community college. Can you briefly describe how you begin career counseling with one of your students?

Counselor: If I have to put a label on what I do, I think I would call myself more of a trait-factor career counselor than anything else. But because at the college we have students differing widely in age and many other factors, I have to be flexible in my thinking and technique. To answer your question, though, trying to diagnose or understand my client's career choice problem is what I see as my first task. How I diagnose it determines the rest of what I do.

Interviewer: What kind of diagnostic system do you use?

Counselor: I usually begin by using the differential diagnosis Williamson talked about in the 1930s. I simply ask the following questions.

1. Has my client made a career choice?
2. If a choice has been made, how certain is it?
3. Was the choice made a realistic one? By that I mean, did it show a discrepancy between client interests and aptitudes? There are times when I really don't need to do much counseling; that is when I have a

client who has made a realistic career choice that he or she is certain about. We really need only to devise a plan to implement that choice.

Interviewer: But, Tom, what happens if your client in a sense fails the first question—really has not made a career choice?

Counselor: Clients frequently fall into this category for various reasons. Some simply have not devoted time and effort toward making a decision. In these cases my efforts are directed toward encouraging their involvement—helping them to see career decision making as their responsibility. For others no choice was made because that process is too anxiety provoking. With this diagnosis my task becomes one of working to identify what contributes to the anxiety. In such instances I'm pretty reflective or nondirective in my interview technique. In some other instances I have become involved with clients who are generally indecisive, who reflect almost a lifetime of difficulty in making decisions. It's taken me at times quite a few sessions to decide this. These clients are tough to deal with because we're talking about a personal trait not easily changed. When you come across a client like this, I think the career indecision is only an example of generalized difficulty. Many other personal problems usually surface to broaden the goals of counseling.

Interviewer: Let's talk a little about your second question, whether or not the client who has made a career decision is really certain about it.

Counselor: This is important both as an initial counseling problem and as a later one for those beginning counseling without a decision. Frequently to learn how certain my clients are, I ask them to rate their choice on a scale from 1 to 10 with 10 being "very certain." For those clients still pretty tentative (7 or less) I structure my efforts around Parsons' equation that "certain choices are based upon more and more accurate self- and occupational information." Sometimes to increase certainty the client really needs greater self-clarification; sometimes more knowledge of the work world is required. For self-concept and values clarification I rely primarily on feeling-oriented responses and other nondirective techniques. For increasing knowledge of occupations I become a teacher; I assign homework or a study plan close to the interests expressed by the client. Let me add, though, that certain career choices do not come easily; most have to work at it. This takes time. Sometimes all it takes is time—that is, to be with the client and listen until sufficient reflection produces certainty. In a last breath I might note that a number of my recent clients really were certain about their career plans, but these plans were shaken by some crisis. In one case it was failing a required course that could have been easily passed. When this happens, I usually interpret the uncertainty as a by-product of the crisis situation.

Interviewer: O.K. What do you do with clients who express unrealistic choices?

Counselor: In most of these cases my style is pretty direct; I tell them in a straight way that I personally think their choice is unrealistic, and give them my reasons for saying so. I don't do this too soon, I hope. I try to weigh all the evidence I have for making such a strong stand. But when I give my opinion, I give it. I figure that they can accept or reject it; that direct communication is less manipulative than subtle implications.

Interviewer: How do you follow up your opinion?

Counselor: To take issue with their choice, as I described, I believe obligates me to help in supplying more realistic alternatives. I think one would hold back until at least a few more realistic options begin to emerge. I think my knowledge of occupational clusters and hierarchies helps here. If it's a matter of a choice being discrepant with ability, I help find an alternative consistent with expressed interests and values but more in line with at least measured aptitude or past actual performance. I might add that many of my clients, maybe because of low self-esteem, aspire to careers requiring less ability than they have. It is not always a matter of deciding on something one will fail at; many times it's a choice that will not provide enough opportunity for self-actualization.

Interviewer: So unrealistic career choices pretty much relate to accurately determining aptitudes and interests by the client or you?

Counselor: Not always. I've had clients in my time who evaluate themselves pretty accurately and even agree with me that a career decision lacks realism. But sometimes they want to pursue it anyway. To understand this is at times difficult. Often I try to grasp the situation by trying to identify a personal need that must be gratified, even at the expense of a foolish career decision. This overriding need must be attended to in counseling. See! Even a trait-factor type like me gets into counseling of a very personal and emotional nature.

Interviewer: I'm sure we have not exhausted all the issues that come up early in career counseling. And I'm sure those who listen to us will recognize that your approach to diagnosis is an ongoing one. Also, that your approach is not always a stereotypic trait-factor one. But for a few minutes, let's talk about counseling interviews that follow the first or second session; what happens to them?

Counselor: For the majority of my clients I do use standardized interest inventories and sometimes other tests. I often actually summarize my understanding of the client in an informal handwritten profile I construct during one of the sessions. I keep a carbon of it for myself. I assign homework, mostly in terms of occupational exploratory activity. At times I even use written contracts for such tasks. For me, I use the time available for counseling as a means of getting the client to the point where a realistic set of career options is expressed. After that I usually suggest some of our center's ongoing programs oriented toward implementing such decisions. For example, we offer résumé-writing workshops, seminars on job-hunting techniques, and so forth. However, if a client reaches a decision with one of the more realistic options and enters one of those programs I mentioned earlier, I try to have a follow-up session to review the combined outcome of the earlier counseling along with the structured program.

Interviewer: So your counseling and structured group work go hand-in-hand.

Counselor: Yes! But since we are now concerned with counseling, let me make a few more comments regarding it. I do not think one can beat this service when clients have heightened levels of choice anxiety; when self- and occupational information require more of a synthesis; when a client has narrowed choices to a few alternatives, but ones almost equally attractive. When choice anxiety is high I rely on listening and attending skills—my ability to be supportive and build client confidence in self. However, I also interpret client "self-talk" that heightens anxiety. When information synthesis is needed I sometimes find myself guiding fantasies, helping the client to project him- or herself into a career or life role. In a real way I try to recall all my counseling training and see it applied to career issues.

Interviewer: Real quickly before we end, how do you evaluate your efforts?

Counselor: Mostly by client self-report. When one says 'no choice' was replaced by at least a tentative one, I've achieved something. When tentative choices are verbalized as more certain, I feel joy for that client. When a client says that an unrealistic choice is abandoned, I think something has been achieved. In the end, though, I hope these verbalizations are acted on in a behavioral way so I can be more certain and ultimately more realistic about the value of counseling.

DEVELOPING A PERSONAL THEORY

For most counselors-in-training, the study of counseling theory is intended to serve as a basis for the development of their own personal approaches to counseling. While some may hope to find an existing theoretical approach to adopt in its entirety, most counselors recognize early that their own view or theory of counseling will be unique to them, usually some mixture of concepts from several of the published approaches. As discussed earlier, practitioners must of necessity often look to several of the popular theories in order to develop a comprehensive theory; most approaches studied leave many important questions unanswered. Many times, however, what we have described is not really borrowing ideas from theories of others; there occurs a recognized agreement between what one person believes and what has been published by another.

To aid in the formation of a conceptual system or theory to explain career counseling, we will identify and discuss the primary components of a comprehensive career-counseling theory. In the sections following the general one on foundation, the components are represented by important questions pertinent to the practitioner. A complete personal theory will attempt to deal with each question or issue. Like all other good theories, it will strive for a degree of internal consistency, in that the response to one issue will not contradict another.

Components of a career-counseling theory

Foundation. Ultimately one's view of counseling is connected to one's definition of helping. What constitutes helpfulness is in turn connected to a view of human nature. Building a theory could easily result in the consideration of many abstract, metaphysical issues. For most practitioners, however, it is usually sufficient to begin with a study of personality. By this we mean an investigation into the characteristics that enable people to cope with everyday challenges. From a personality theory comes a view of how behavior changes or is changed to meet life's challenges. A theory of behavior change results.

Changes in behavior are consequences of many different forces. Counseling, just one of many means for changing human behavior, draws on only a few of these forces. Thus, counseling theory is essentially a specialized theory of behavior change encapsulated in an individual's theoretical view of personality. A theory of career counseling is a specialized part of one's counseling theory, directed toward goals related to career development (see Figure 3-1). Because of these interrelationships, it is no wonder that counseling-theory courses usually introduce a counseling theory by reviewing its parent personality theory.

Likewise, some background in general counseling theory is valuable in approaching the study of career counseling. Because not every student will have this background, we will cover some general counseling theory to ensure broader relevance of the material.

Client prerequisites. Counseling theories seldom purport to serve all human beings. When well developed, an approach will describe the cognitive, emotional, and behavioral characteristics necessary for a client to benefit from the treatment. Minimal age, ability to verbalize, and so on, are discussed.

In developing one's own approach to career counseling, one might begin by reflecting on the population to be served. Who are they? What typical problems do they have? What special career-development needs do they reflect? What resources are available to them that could be utilized in counseling? Are there any client factors that might make it impossible for counseling to be successful? Do the prerequisites listed generalize to other populations of clients?

Client concerns and counseling goals. Following the identification of the population one intends to serve comes the important issue of outcome. Counseling outcomes usually take the form of changes that will occur in the client. For the changes to be valid, they are to be viewed as necessary in order to satisfy an important set of client needs. One can see how counseling goals are

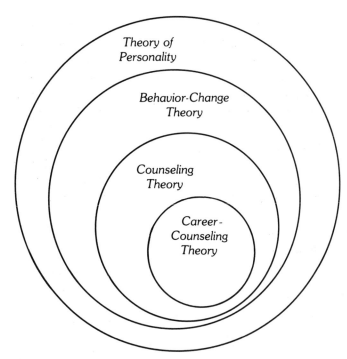

FIGURE 3-1. The interrelationship of career-counseling theory with other theoretical approaches.

anchored in an understanding of client behavior. What goals, then, can be achieved in career counseling? How do they relate to client needs? Are specific career-counseling goals similar or dissimilar to other counseling goals? Do some of these goals imply other goals or changes? If so, is a certain sequence of change to be expected? Can some goals be classified as final goals and others as intermediate objectives? When the outcomes are considered together, are there negative consequences connected to positive ones? What risks will the client undergo in achieving some goals? Who decides on the goals of counseling? Will it be difficult for clients to commit themselves to some goals? How are changes to be made concerning goals?

Counselor characteristics. With the client population and goals identified, consideration of counseling strategy or technique is warranted. The first element to consider would be the person of the counselor: those personal qualities likely to affect interactions with clients. It might be appropriate to begin by considering fundamental attitudes and behaviors associated with the effective career counselor. Does adherence to a specific belief system predict effective career counseling? Is a specific form of preparation necessary? Are there differences between career counselors and other special types of therapists?

Counselor/client relationship. Taken together, the prerequisite characteristics of both counselor and client determine, at least in part, their interactions
during counseling. One factor that has been strongly validated in relation to
outcome has been the quality of the counselor/client relationship (Bergin, 1966).
This relationship is understood to exist when the counselor offers high levels of
empathy and the client freely explores deep feelings and beliefs. The presence of
the relationship is viewed by the majority of therapists as the *sine qua non* of
psychotherapy. In a functional theory of career counseling, will there be a difference between its counselor/client relationship and that of psychotherapy and
intense personal counseling? If so, how will it be different? How will it be similar?

Diagnostic procedures. As mentioned earlier in this chapter, the diagnoses of career maturity and psychopathology have played an important role in
vocational counseling. How are concerns or problems to be identified? Will the
counseling interview serve as a diagnostic tool? Will standardized tests be used?
If so, what types of instruments? How will the diagnosis occur? How is it com-
municated to the client? What precautions are taken to ensure the accuracy and
objectivity of the diagnosis? How does the client contribute to the diagnosis?

Counseling technique and strategy. By technique we mean in general
the various methods used by the counselor to enable the client to explore,
define, and attain treatment goals. In career counseling, as in most other forms,
much of what is considered technique is verbal statements by the counselor. Are
there special interview techniques for career counseling? Does the counselor
avoid or seldom use some techniques associated with psychotherapy? What
techniques are utilized in common by career counseling and other specialized
treatments? How can one demonstrate the relationship among diagnosis, counseling goals, and technique? Do certain counseling techniques or strategies have
adverse side effects? Are there special techniques employed between sessions,
outside the interview? Is there a sequence of procedures to be followed? Is client
readiness a factor in the use of certain techniques? Are types of clients matched
with special techniques or group of techniques?

The change process. In a well-developed counseling theory, the order of
events or changes would be described. What are the special features to note
early, in the middle, and toward the end of career counseling? Must certain
events precede others? Are certain changes necessary for others to follow? How
is progress or movement defined or described? How is a setback noted? Are
there critical periods in the process? When is attrition most likely? Can the
counseling process be described by a number of steps or stages? How do gains
in counseling generalize to real life? How do changes in attitude affect observable behavior? How does one behavior change affect other behavior? How is

the sequence of change in career counseling similar to or different from sequences in other forms of counseling?

Evaluation of counseling outcome. In order to verify one's theory, one must often make difficult decisions regarding the nature of evidence. As in a courtroom, counselors and the counseling profession in general argue about what constitutes admissible evidence. Some take a very narrow view of valid evidence, often in the form of observable changes in behavior. Others accept more subjective evidence, such as client self-reports of change and expressed satisfaction with counseling. What criteria best represent the attainment of counseling goals? Do different types of goals require different forms of evidence? How are criteria for goal attainment established? In the absence of adequate criteria, what compromises in evaluation can be considered? How are the criteria for evaluating career counseling similar to or different from those of other forms of treatment?

A practical theory of career counseling

After entertaining so many questions that a theory could conceivably answer, one should see clearly how complicated and exhausting the development of a comprehensive approach can be. Furthermore, perseverance cannot guarantee the practicality of the product. We can see how a theory, intended to aid our understanding, could become so complex that it introduces more confusion than understanding. Counselors, like most others who need to utilize theory, must achieve a balance between conceptual systems that overexplain and those that oversimplify the phenomena to be understood.

No doubt readers without much background in counseling theory will feel overwhelmed by the series of questions just posed to represent elements in a career-counseling theory. It would require years of counseling experience and years of reflection on that experience to complete a theoretical view. For the counselor-in-training, simplified explanatory systems seem appropriate. A more sophisticated theoretical view can come later in one's career. To become more proficient in the understanding of career counseling, one might consider the following:

1. Read as much as possible regarding general counseling theory and theory specific to career counseling. Do not restrict reading to secondary sources only; read some of the original authors.

2. Anchor a reading of theory in actual counseling practice. Before taking practicum, gain vicarious experience through the study of written cases. Seek out experienced counselors; ask them to describe their counseling in cases that exemplify aspects of theory. Organize a seminar that includes practicing coun-

selors and counselor educators; give it a theme such as "Interesting clients I have had." Case studies help demonstrate the use of theory better than role playing, since what happens over a series of interviews is difficult to role play but can be understood with the help of theory.

3. When beginning to see real clients, keep careful notes. Record data as objectively as possible, but leave sections or even a special diary for forecasting what will happen to a client. This practice will test one's theory. Follow up predictions to verify them with evidence. While counseling, reread some texts on counseling theory.

4. Observe and study other people besides clients being treated. Do not treat these people; see what happens to them, what events help or hinder the attainment of their goals. Were observed results consistent with one's theory? Likewise, apply one's theory to one's own career development.

5. Seek out supervisors and colleagues interested in the discussion of theory and case studies. Allow them to play the "devil's advocate" as you discuss your own counseling cases. Try not to be defensive. Remember that a discussion of theory includes more than technique.

6. Write down thoughts at different periods in one's professional career. Save them and compare versions. Risk sharing thoughts with other counselors. Consider submitting for publication an article that reflects one's counseling theory.

7. When confused and frustrated by the hardships associated with being a helper, do not cover up or defend the confusion by paying lip service to anti-intellectualism. Recycle through some of the steps suggested earlier. Do not let others with deficiencies in their understanding of counseling persuade you to compromise your own.

SUMMARY

This chapter surveyed counseling theories that have addressed specific issues in career decision making. The approaches receiving greatest attention were trait-factor and behavioral counseling. In addition, the role of counseling in conjunction with more structured career-guidance or planning activities was discussed. The chapter also provided an outline for the formation of a personal counseling theory by posing important questions requiring answers from career-counseling practitioners.

RECOMMENDED READINGS

Bordin, E. S., & Kopplin, D. A. Motivational conflict and vocational development. *Journal of Counseling Psychology,* 1973, *20,* 154–161.
    An interesting piece of research that also provides a useful diagnostic system briefly described in this chapter.

Crites, J. O. Career counseling: A review of major approaches. *The Counseling Psychologist,* 1974, *4,* 3–23.

A well-accepted summary of career-counseling approaches. In the same journal (1976, Volume 6, No. 3) is the author's own synthetic approach to career counseling.

Whiteley, J. M., & Resnikoff, A. *Career counseling.* Monterey, Calif.: Brooks/ Cole, 1978.

A compilation of articles appearing in *The Counseling Psychologist,* including the ones above by John Crites. A useful addition to any career counselor's permanent library.

LEARNING ACTIVITIES

1. Compare and contrast three approaches to career counseling with regard to the use of diagnosis, testing, and occupational information.
2. Explain the apparent popularity of trait-factor career counseling.
3. Write a critique of the counseling position presented in the section of this chapter entitled "One Counselor's Approach: An Illustration."
4. Describe how counseling and structured group work complement one another.
5. List client career problems that seem to be effectively treated by the counseling relationship.
6. Use the outline provided near the end of the chapter to write your own career-counseling theory.
7. Visit a career-planning center and discuss with its staff useful theoretical concepts for the career-counseling process.

CHAPTER FOUR

CAREER ASSESSMENT

In directing its attention toward assessment, the present chapter emphasizes a competency that is very important to the counselor's specific role in the career-development process. The measurement of vocational interests has been a traditional and often unique responsibility of the vocational counselor or counseling psychologist. In the last decade the assessment of career development, sometimes called *career maturity,* has been added to the measurement of interests.

In this chapter we do not intend to review general psychometric theory. Nor do we intend to provide such technical evaluations of instruments as are easily found in journal reviews and *The Mental Measurement Yearbook* (Buros, irregular years). Rather, we intend to focus on what is specific to the measurement of career interests and career development in applied practice. We will assume that we need not review the basics of test-construction theory and thus will attend primarily to the application of testing in career-related counseling and consultation situations. We also assume that important technical information on specific instruments will be gained from further reading.

In organizing this chapter, we have given primary attention to the assessment of career interests, followed by the measurement of career development. Under topics that are closely related to both activities, they will be discussed together.

WEIGHING VOCATIONAL TESTING

Vocational-interest and career-development tests are usually expensive if used properly. While they may be worth the price, a counselor should consider dollar outlay and time investment before becoming heavily involved in the use of standardized vocational-interest and career-development assessment. Although standardized assessment is a traditional service of counselors, their purpose and cost may not be compatible at all times with a person's job description.

Cost

In selecting a standardized assessment device, one might consider the following factors:

1. the initial purchase price of answer forms and test booklets;
2. the possible cost of scoring completed forms;
3. the purchase price and scoring costs of other tests in an assessment battery;

4. the time it takes to administer the tests;
5. the effort required to have the instruments scored;
6. the time it takes to interpret test results;
7. the time it takes to record and store the results;
8. the time it takes to write reports related to the assessment;
9. the cost of storage facilities for completed tests and those awaiting use;
10. the cost of specimen sets, reference books, journal subscriptions, professional meetings, and other money/time expenditures necessary for practitioners to keep current with career-assessment procedures;
11. the time it takes to explain the purposes of this form of testing to clients and their families;
12. the time-and-materials.cost to train other professionals affected by the assessment program;
13. the cost of physical facilities that provide the space and privacy for the administration and interpretation of the instruments;
14. the added time and money required for repeating the assessment over time in order to gain more reliable measures of the expression of career interests or development.

Certainly an accountant would include other direct and indirect costs in arriving at the true cost of career-assessment procedures. In many cases the counseling practitioner will be concerned more with time expenditure than with dollar outlay, since the latter is usually the concern of some administrator. In any case, career assessment is expensive. Probably the real way to compute the cost for any one practitioner is to keep careful records of all activities, including those of colleagues, related to the assessment effort.

Not to be neglected in considering costs are the potential risks associated with testing. While interest assessment has not been as controversial as some other areas of measurement, there still are legal issues attached to the process, such as the client's right to privacy. In addition, tests have a tradition of being misrepresented and misinterpreted. Resulting work-related stress for the practitioner is itself a cost item in the use of formalized assessment.

Uses

The most common uses of both standardized and nonstandardized assessment in career-related issues are:

1. to predict job satisfaction or success (see commentary below);
2. to predict satisfaction or success in an educational program related to a future career (see commentary below);
3. to verify a career-related decision;
4. to stimulate career-exploratory behavior;

5. to identify individuals in need of special services;
6. to evaluate services and programs;
7. to encourage self-exploration;
8. to aid in the formation of a self-image;
9. to personalize and increase participation of students in career education;
10. to assist clients in convincing third parties (parents, spouses, advisers, and others) of the appropriateness of a career decision;
11. to help clients understand their own vocational/educational dissatisfaction.

One might speculate that other reasons exist for the use of standardized assessment in career counseling. For example, using computer-scored instruments with an attractive printout suggests that the counseling process has at least a few scientific elements to it. The precision with which such tests organize and categorize client self-report information simplifies the investigation of such material. The impact seems to promote client confidence in the counseling process and optimism with regard to its outcome. These factors are important and may be reason enough for the investment in career-interest assessment.

The use of testing to predict success or client satisfaction in a job or educational program is probably the least-valid reason for the use of such instruments. The Strong Vocational Interest Blank (SVIB), the most widely researched of all interest inventories, is not viewed by its authors as having sufficient predictive validity for such purposes. The manual of the most recent modification of the SVIB—the Strong-Campbell Interest Inventory (SCII)—does not recommend its use as a predictor (Campbell, 1977). The same limitation would hold true for all other interest inventories. In fact, critical reviews of interest inventories note the lack of predictive validity attached to the instruments (see reviews in the editions of *The Mental Measurements Yearbook*).

Most of the other purposes noted, with the exception of program evaluation, are closely related to common counseling goals. Thus, the use of interest inventories seems defensible as progress in counseling seems to warrant their use. Finally, the selection of any instrument must consider the career maturity of the client. Differential developmental levels call for different criteria to be used in making a test selection.

SELECTING AN INSTRUMENT

Standardized or nonstandardized?

As in most other specialized areas of assessment, the career-counseling practitioner initially has the choice of selecting standardized instruments, usually well normed and well packaged by commercial test producers. For group-testing purposes, these tests are obviously more reliable than nonstandardized instruments, but they are expensive to produce and use. Nonstandardized instruments can in most cases be viewed as "homemade" devices, intended to stimulate and promote investigation. Since an accurate description of the test taker is not the primary purpose, reliability and validity concerns in testing are not as important as they have been traditionally. Not all so-called "homemade" interest inventories are in fact such; commercial publishing houses market these items too. Sometimes a practitioner can purchase a printed master unit (ditto carbon) with a one-page inventory ready for reproduction in quantity.

For most people, vocational interests do not become stable until early adulthood. Thus, some may argue that the expense of standardized instruments for clients under the age of 18 may not be warranted. However, few would argue in favor of inaccurate client portrayal through instruments of unknown validity. This caution must be considered in using brief homemade inventories to report client career interests. Granted, with younger clients the cost of interest assessment may be too high a price to pay to measure an unstable factor. Sensitive to this, we have not devoted much space to instruments intended for youthful clients. We will describe only the Ohio Vocational Interest Survey (OVIS) and the Vocational Interest, Experience and Skill Assessment (VIESA) when we discuss the early measurement of interests.

In the area of interest assessment there are many instruments. We have made the decision to review only selected inventories that both are quality instruments in themselves and represent measurement approaches of interest to the practitioner. Several instruments other than the ones described in the text are listed in Table 4-1.

Inventories for adults

As clients gain in age, they become more likely candidates for standardized interest inventories. Selection of an instrument can create a challenge because adult clients represent a diverse population. Since one interest inventory seldom contains scales for occupations from semiskilled to professional,[1] counselors must first decide on an instrument with the client's educational preparation and occupational level in mind. The college-bound senior in high school, for example, will need something different from the graduate interested in immediate placement. In the past a counselor may have used the Strong Vocational Interest Blank for the former, the Minnesota Vocational Interest Inventory for the latter. More recently, interest assessment has been simplified somewhat through a new generation of instruments represented by the Strong-Campbell Interest Inventory and the Career Assessment Inventory. We will describe these two instruments as representative and worthwhile inventories for mature counseling clients.

[1]Both the California Occupational Preference Survey (COPS) and the Kuder Occupational Interest Survey, Form DD, claim to measure both professional and nonprofessional occupations.

TABLE 4-1. Vocational-interest inventory selection

Clientele	Purpose/situation	Instrument	Alternate instruments
Adult/college	Professional preparation	SCII	Kuder, Form DD; SDS
Adult/college	Mid-career change; job dissatisfaction	SCII	SDS
Adult/noncollege	Vocational placement; job dissatisfaction	CAI	OVIS; WOWI*
High school graduate	Career-entry/vocational decision	CAI	OVIS
High school dropout	Vocational counseling placement	OVIS	CAI
High school student	Vocational-Education placement	OVIS	Kuder, Form E
High school or junior high school student	Vocational exploration	Nonstandardized/ self-report	VIESA; COPS**; OVIS
Middle school student	Career awareness	Nonstandardized/ self-report	What Could I Be?

*World of Work Inventory
**California Occupational Preference Survey

Strong-Campbell Interest Inventory (SCII) and Career Assessment Inventory (CAI). Popular use of Edward K. Strong's inventory began in 1927 with the first Strong Vocational Interest Blank. With the assistance of many other test developers, Strong revised and validated the instrument. In 1974 a major revision of the Strong Vocational Interest Blank occurred (SVIB Form T325); another major revision was made in 1981. For most purposes the SVIB has now been replaced by the Strong-Campbell Interest Inventory (SCII) (see Figure 4-1). The major work on these revisions was done by Dr. David Campbell, then professor of psychology at the University of Minnesota and director of the Center for Interest Measurement Research. Charles B. Johansson, an associate of Campbell who assisted in the research and development of the SCII, completed work in 1976 on the initial form of the Career Assessment Inventory (CAI) (see Figure 4-2). The SCII is viewed as most applicable to college-bound and college-educated adults, whereas the CAI is used with individuals seeking immediate career entry or seeking training in business or technical school. While both instruments are descendants of the SVIB, the CAI is intended to fill the need satisfied earlier by the Minnesota Vocational Interest Inventory. The SCII and the CAI represent a major innovation in interest inventories in that they incorporate a theoretical framework to aid in organizing and interpreting results. The framework used is that of John Holland, first proposed by him in 1959. Holland's system, closely tied to psychometric research, was discussed in Chapter 2, "Career-Development Theory." A second major revision in both the above instruments is the incorporation of both male and female occupational scales into one form. Earlier versions of the SVIB had separate male and female forms. As reflected in the manuals of both instruments, empirical reality cannot eliminate sex differences; males and females in the same occupations demonstrate different interest patterns and thus respond differently to interest inventories. Such responses are not measures of sexual identity, as most counselors recognize. For example, education and general cultural enrichment can contribute to higher scores on female scales, regardless of a respondent's actual gender or gender identity.

Counselors who are expected to make repeated use of either the SCII or the CAI or both should study the manuals carefully. Here are some interesting aspects to note in investigating these instruments:

1. Both inventories include three different sets of scales (see sample profiles in Figures 4-1 and 4-2).
   a. General Occupational Themes. Each of the inventories has six scales, corresponding to the six Holland types or themes. These scales were included to aid in the interpretation of career interests. Items used to form the scales were those that correlated strongly with appropriate scales from Holland's (1965) own Vocational Preference Inventory (VPI).
   b. Basic Interest Area Scales. The SCII has 23, and the CAI 22, scales developed from the intercorrelation of inventory items (internally consistent items) that are supposed to assess pure interest areas. By this we mean general interests with significance in our society and used in everyday language. These scales are more specific than the previous theme scales (for example, the Investigative Theme is divided into basic interests in science and numbers). Like the theme scales, they are viewed by the authors as useful in interpreting the occupational scales.
   c. Occupational Scales. The SCII contains 162 occupational scales; the original CAI for commercial use contained 42 occupational scales, with others to be added. These scales are the most reliable and most important portions of both instruments. Empirically developed, the scales compare an individual's response to the entire inventory with responses from a group of people used as the criterion (norm group) for each occupation presented.
2. Both instruments reflect 30-day test-retest reliabilities in the high .80s and low .90s.
3. On the average both instruments can be completed in 30 minutes. (This is a moderate time period when compared to those of other instruments.)
4. Both instruments use standard t scores ($\overline{X} = 50$, $\sigma = 10$).
5. Both instruments contain occupational scales free of item overlap; that is, one scale score does not affect another.

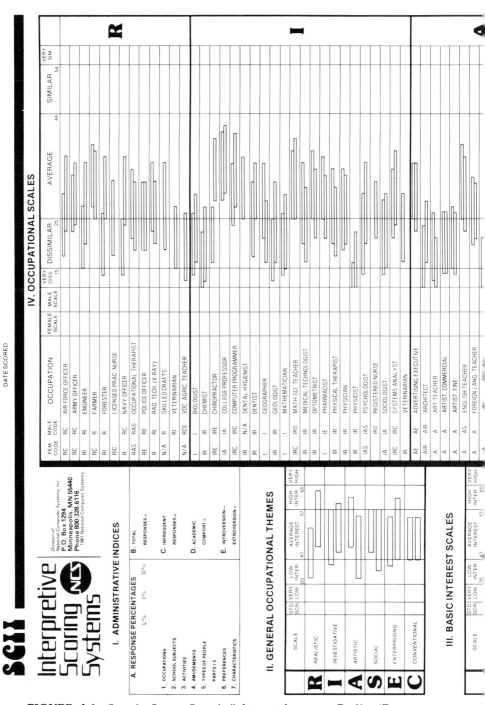

FIGURE 4-1. Sample Strong-Campbell Interest Inventory Profile. (From Strong-Campbell Interest Inventory, Form T325 of the STRONG VOCA-TIONAL INTEREST BLANK by Edward K. Strong, Jr., and David P. Campbell

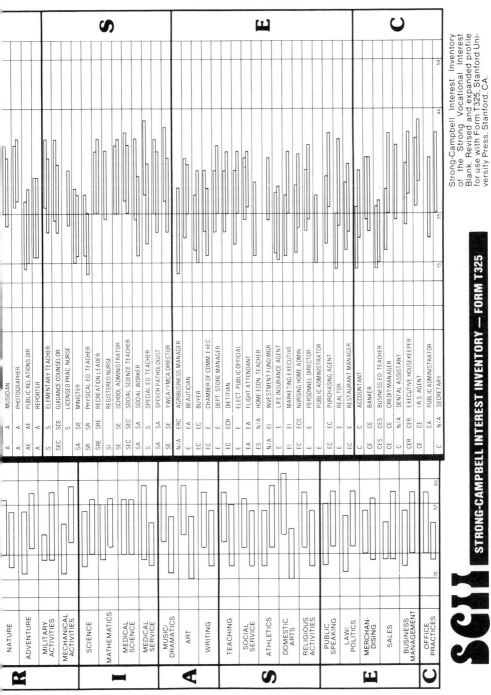

STRONG-CAMPBELL INTEREST INVENTORY — FORM T325

SCII

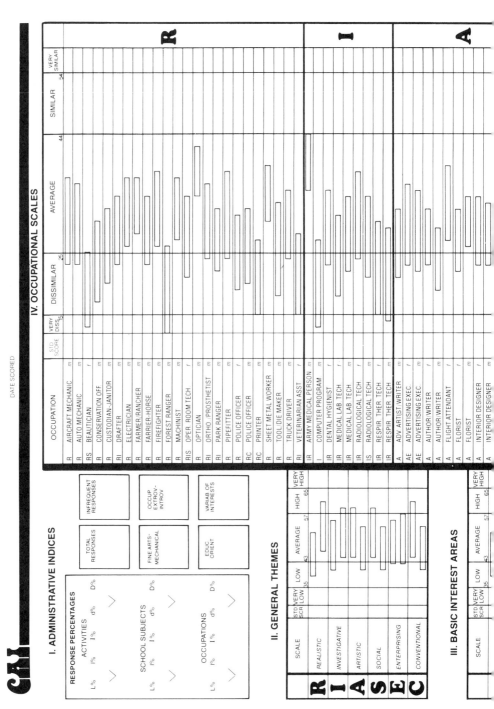

FIGURE 4-2. Sample Career Assessment Inventory Profile. (©1980 Dr. Charles B. Johansson, National Computer Systems, P.O. Box 1294, Minneapolis, Minnesota, 55440, 612/830-7600. All rights reserved.)

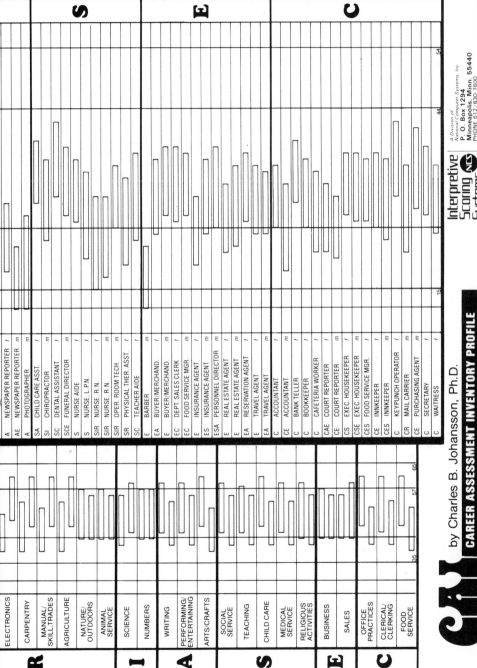

by Charles B. Johansson, Ph.D.

CAREER ASSESSMENT INVENTORY PROFILE

Interpretive Scoring Systems

A Division of
National Computer Systems, Inc.
P. O. Box 1294
Minneapolis, Minn. 55440
PHONE 612/830-7600
© 1980 National Computer Systems

8802-54321

6. The weighting of items in different scales is copyrighted material, prohibiting counselor scoring and score-weighting inspection.
7. The SCII and CAI correlate with one another, on the average, at .85.
8. Occupational scales are scored according to both likes and dislikes.
9. The scales related to Holland's Realistic theme are the most reliable on both instruments.
10. Both instruments can be computer-scored promptly through a test service; for a larger fee, both can be accompanied by a computer-prepared interpretive report.

While the above comments reflect general and mostly well-known characteristics of these instruments, the SCII and CAI have, like many other instruments, subtle characteristics not as well known. Here are some characteristics identified in the manuals and in journal articles.

1. Many times social-service-oriented individuals receive deflated scores on Social Scales on the inventories because of negative responses toward religious items. Such items are weighted in generating scores on these scales.

2. Males and females tend to respond differently to items (one-third of the items show a difference).

3. Norm groups for different sexes sometimes differ markedly. For example, male nurses came mostly from the military; male "pharmacists" worked in drugstores, females in research. Check the manual for a description of the norming groups.

4. Contradictions among basic-interest and occupational scales can and do occur. For example, farmers often show high scores on the occupational scale for farming but low scores on agriculture as a basic interest. Such contradictions occur in part because basic-interest scales are scored using "like" responses to transparent or face-valid items, whereas occupational scales are based on "like" and "dislike" responses to a variety of items, many not so transparent.

Recommendations for use.   In order to avoid misrepresenting the results of the SCII and the CAI, the counselor is wise periodically to review the assumptions on which the instruments are based. To simplify this effort, we have provided the following notes:

1. Do not simply tell your client, "This inventory will help us understand what you are most and least interested in." This statement gives the impression that the inventory supplies an internal ordering of interests; it fails to say, "This inventory compares your responses to those of individuals employed in various occupations." Do not forget that these inventories provide normative data.

2. A large number of neutral responses from one client does not invalidate the

profile. What you should expect, though, is a "flat" (undifferentiated) profile of little use for most of the purposes for which interest assessment is performed.

3. Remember that these instruments do not predict either success in an occupation or job satisfaction. The high scores are usually the most reliable. You might say, as Strong recommends, "Before disregarding an occupation whose members have interests similar to yours, you should consider your decision carefully."

4. Remember that male and female occupational scales exist on the instruments. Your client may need to be alerted to both since job placement may put him or her in a work setting dominated by the opposite sex. Make sure you select a scoring service that prints both male and female scores on the profile.

5. A great deal of data can be generated from these instruments if the counselor is well versed in the vocational theory of John Holland. Review, if needed, such concepts as the "differentiated" and the "consistent" profile. Holland's *Making Vocational Choices: A Theory of Careers* (1973) contains a table that transforms Holland's three-letter codes into related *Dictionary of Occupational Titles* (DOT) codes and adds a useful exploratory dimension to these interest inventories. Practiced counselors can almost instinctively identify an inconsistent profile (elevated scores on themes opposite to one another on the hexagon; see Figure 2-1) and give it careful attention during counseling, checking appropriateness of development and possible self-identity problems.

6. The most common profile to expect, especially with young clients, is a "flat" or undifferentiated profile. This usually suggests the desirability of exploration or enrichment experiences. After further life experience, the client should undergo follow-up testing. It seems reasonable for counselors on limited budgets to test few clients more often than to test many only once. You may communicate early to a client that the plan is to administer the inventory periodically even if counseling sessions are not planned on a regular basis for the entire period in which assessment will occur.

7. As you may recall from Chapter 2, John Holland has proposed the use of interest inventories as measures of personality. Thus, from an SCII or CAI profile one could project how a client might adapt to situations other than work. Without evidence to support such projections, this use of interest-inventory results is suspect.

8. In Chapter 3, we mentioned the recommendation of John Crites to interpret the tests without the tests—that is, to introduce assessment results when they fit naturally into interview dialogue, avoiding a formal test interpretation. A formal test interpretation will be described later in this chapter. Crites's recommendation may merit investigation. Careful scrutiny of a profile does appear at times to create an information overload for the client. While elaborate interpretations may impress the client, their ultimate benefit may be less than a more modest effort would provide.

Self-Directed Search (SDS).   Another instrument of possible utility with more mature clients may be John Holland's Self-Directed Search. This instrument is described by the author as a self-administered, self-scored, and self-interpreted vocational counseling tool. In 40 to 60 minutes a person uses the test booklet and an occupational classification booklet called *The Occupations Finder* and generates a three-letter code consistent with Holland's theory of vocational choice (*see* Chapter 2). This code represents a personality type. Upon completing the SDS, the client also identifies a series of occupations consistent with that personality. In addition, the identified occupations are coded according to educational level required and to DOT listing. In completing the SDS, the client lists previous jobs, states preferred activities and occupations, assesses personal competencies, and so forth. The final three-letter summary code, the outcome of the inventory, is a listing of the three highest numerical scores for each of the six Holland types.

While many clients will have little difficulty in completing and utilizing the instrument, the instrument is subject to error; many individuals make computational errors in generating the three-letter summary code, thus misrepresenting the results (Gelso, Collins, Williams, & Sedlacek, 1973). The newer versions of the SDS have improved instructions, reducing scoring errors. Also, the flat profile creates problems because the differences among the three scores used to generate the letter code may be very small. For example, a person could have an IAS (Investigative/Artistic/Social) three-letter code with only three points separating the three scores. *The Occupations Finder* would list these occupations as worthwhile for the client to investigate: economist, mathematician/statistician, marketing research worker. If the slight differences in scores were reversed to achieve an SAI three-letter code, the person would be encouraged to investigate the following careers: minister/priest/rabbi, librarian, special-education teacher, speech and hearing clinician, and so forth. One can see why the inventory recommends investigating all "top" codes separately. With all but the very mature, monitoring of the instrument is warranted. Finally, the terminology (and some say Holland's theory in general) of the SDS seems to have a sex bias. Research (Boyd, 1976) indicates that the terminology does not seem to affect the results. The SDS enables a counselor in two hours to provide a minimally supervised vocational guidance experience (Weinrach, 1975, p. 128). For poor readers, Form E of the SDS may merit consideration.

Inventories for adolescents

We have said that for the most part we do not believe that the purposes of career guidance with teenagers and younger students warrant the cost of using most commercially prepared interest inventories, especially those requiring machine scoring. Again, the most common reason for interest assessment with younger students is to encourage exploration of careers, for which purpose noncommercial materials are effective. But, as mentioned earlier in the chapter, placement for vocational education and the counseling of "dropouts" seem to be limited instances in which counselors may need to use every resource available, including standardized interest assessment. Two representative inventories for use in such cases are the Ohio Vocational Interest Survey (OVIS) and the Vocational Interest, Experience and Skill Assessment (VIESA).

Ohio Vocational Interest Survey (OVIS). The OVIS is an instrument that evolved from the Vocational Planning Questionnaire, a survey developed by the Ohio Division of Guidance and Testing in 1953 to assist in planning vocational education in that state. It was revised in 1966 to incorporate a cubistic theory of interests like that in the DOT. A theory of this nature essentially plots interests in three dimensions. Thus, as a cube is considered by its height, width, and breadth, so the general nature of career interest is divided three ways—by the interest dimensions of people, data, and things. The inventory was normed in 1969 on 50,000 students across the country. The plan was to have an interest inventory for students in grades eight through 12 who planned to select a vocation on completion of high school.

The OVIS provides a profile of interest across 24 scales that contain the more than 21,000 jobs in the DOT. The close relationship with the DOT is one of the major strengths of the instrument. Thus, the counselor, familiar with worker trait groups (to be discussed in Chapter 7), can effectively apply that knowledge in the use of the OVIS. In the same regard the General Aptitude Test Battery (GATB) has been linked with the OVIS to take fuller advantage of all three devices. The AEL Career Information System (CIS), useful material for applying these relationships, has been developed and marketed by Career Decision-Making Program, Appalachia Educational Laboratory, Inc., Charleston, West Virginia 25325. McKnight Publishing Company markets revised versions of this material.

The following describe some additional important characteristics of the OVIS:

1. The instrument was developed to generate internal consistency for each scale and to reduce item overlap as much as possible.
2. While the reliability of scales varies, a two-week test-retest indicates a median coefficient of about .80.
3. The OVIS usually requires one to one and one-half hours to administer.
4. The instrument contains a questionnaire that seeks self-expressed occupational plans and curricular interests.
5. A school district can include up to eight additional questions relevant to local issues.
6. The inventory appears to follow guidelines for sex fairness.

7. In addition to comparing a student's responses to the norm group (expressed in percentiles and stanines), the OVIS computer printout also rank-orders the respondent's own interests from high to low.

8. By virtue of the local questionnaire items and expression of students' own educational/vocational plans, the OVIS is claimed to be a useful instrument for schools in the planning of career-guidance programs.

9. Like most other interest inventories, the OVIS cannot predict career satisfaction or success.

Vocational Interest, Experience and Skill Assessment (VIESA). The Vocational Interest, Experience and Skill Assessment is a rather recent instrument (1976) developed by the American College Testing Program and marketed by Houghton Mifflin Company. In reality the VIESA is a complete kit with the goal of helping students, grades eight to 12, to expand self-awareness and develop career awareness toward the identification of personally relevant career options. It contains a self-scored inventory that assesses interests and a workbook that provides a self-estimate of general skill and expression of job choice.

The VIESA, like other American College Testing (ACT) Program career systems (for example, the Career Planning Program for high school students, published in 1976), takes advantage of ACT's Occupational Classification System (ACT-OCS). Occupations in this system are classified at a very general level within what are called job clusters. These clusters are similar in nature to Roe's (1956) and Super's (1957) occupational groups. Job clusters are divided again into job families. In the ACT-OCS there are six job clusters and 25 job families. Each job cluster has three to seven job families within it. Using this system and the results of the interest inventory, a client can reduce career alternatives to a manageable number for exploration purposes.

Once the inventory is completed and scored, and the results plotted, job families are described within the area of a student's interests/skills/choices. The student then lists job titles to be explored following completion of the VIESA. Thus, in addition to the self-assessment described earlier, the student learns a way to organize occupations that is simple yet comprehensive. The publisher claims that the VIESA "bridges the gap between test scores (data) and their implications (information)."

The manual for the instrument estimates 40- to 45-minute completion time for the self-assessment/job-identification parts. There is significant cost for the materials, if used extensively. While the format is attractive and the instructions clear, the VIESA is not easy to complete due to the need to follow many directions and read numerous charts and tables. We believe that an intelligent and literate group of students would benefit most from it, although its use could be extended to others by reading instructions aloud and carefully supervising completion. The instrument would seem to have a place in small-group guidance with students keenly motivated for career exploration.

Test batteries for career counseling

In both Chapter 2 and Chapter 3 we have noted the changes that have occurred in career counseling, including the modifications of trait-factor counseling and its use of tests. Those changes have reduced interest in the clinical interpretation of tests in career counseling. Use of large test batteries has likewise decreased.

Because state-wide and college-entry test programs provide standardized assessment of aptitudes and general achievement, school counselors already have on file partial descriptions of their clients. They can use college-entry tests such as those of ACT in career counseling to provide an indication of academic aptitude and an opening for discussion of abilities. Various personality inventories may be used as part of a battery and may be helpful in promoting self-exploration. Some instruments used in vocational counseling, especially in higher education, include the California Personality Inventory (CPI), Omnibus Personality Inventory, Minnesota Counseling Inventory, and Edwards Personal Preference Schedule (EPPS). The Institute for Personality and Ability Testing (IPAT), 1602 Coronado Drive, Champaign, Illinois 61820, has developed a special service called "Personal Career Development Profiles," in which the 16 Personality Factor Questionnaire is interpreted with "career development considerations," according to IPAT's advertisement of the service.

Remember that personality inventories have little if any predictive validity in a one-to-one counseling and/or decision-making context. With the integration of Holland's theory into several interest inventories, sufficient stimulation may exist for a client's self-exploration without incurring the expense of a multi-instrument test battery.

General Aptitude Test Battery (GATB). Because of the important role the General Aptitude Test Battery (GATB) plays in the U.S. Employment Service, counselors must pay special attention to this instrument. There is an enormous amount of data related to the GATB, since much of the U.S. Department of Labor's job-analysis effort uses its subscales to describe aptitudes and levels of aptitudes judged important for a job. We will not provide a detailed description of the GATB; it is a focal point of many references on testing, and certified training in its use is part of a quality counselor-education program. A counselor who has not been trained and certified in the GATB may contact the state Employment Service for information on training. Counselors working directly with adult-placement concerns recognize full well the extent to which this aptitude test is used. The GATB also receives attention from school counselors, since it often is administered to applicants for vocational education. In recent years, however, the use of minimal GATB scores as a "cutoff score" for employment has declined. With the decline in the use of cutoff scores has come the reliance in counseling on client self-estimates of ability, especially for the planning of career exploration. At present a definitive position on aptitude self-estimates does not seem to exist; research on the topic is recommended.

For the counselor of the college-bound, some use of the Differential Aptitude Test (DAT) may be warranted, since the manual includes useful profiles of students in various professional schools and colleges in a large university. The profiles give some idea of the general aptitudes dominant in various groups of professionals. While it is doubtful that the counselor of skilled and semiskilled workers could avoid contact with the GATB, the counselor of professional, white-collar workers could conceivably be effective without long-term contact with the DAT.

Interest-Inventory Publishers

Publisher/test-scoring service	*Instrument(s)*
Consulting Psychologists Press 577 College Avenue Palo Alto, California 94306	The Self-Directed Search (SDS) Strong-Campbell Interest Inventory (with scoring service) (SCII)
Chronicle Guidance Publications, Inc. Moravia, New York 13118	The Harrington/O'Shea System for Career Decision-Making
EDITS Publishers P.O. Box 7234 San Diego, California 92107	The California Occupational Preference System (COPS)
Harcourt Brace Jovanovich, Inc. 757 Third Avenue New York, New York 10017	Ohio Vocational Interest Survey (OVIS)
Houghton Mifflin Company One Beacon Street Boston, Massachusetts 02107	Vocational Interest, Experience and Skill Assessment (VIESA)
National Computer Systems (NCS) 4401 West 76th Street Minneapolis, Minnesota 55435	Strong-Campbell Interest Inventory (with scoring service) (SCII) Career Assessment Inventory (CAI) World of Work Inventory (WOWI)
Roche Testing Service Hoffman-LaHoche, Inc. Nutley, New Jersey 07110	Strong-Campbell Interest Inventory (with scoring service) (SCII)
Science Research Associates, Inc. (SRA) 259 East Erie Street Chicago, Illinois 60611	Kuder Occupational Interest Survey, Form DD Kuder General Interest Survey, Form E What Could I Be?

Armed Services Vocational Aptitude Battery (ASVAB).   It has been estimated (Cronbach, 1979) that each year the Armed Services Vocational Aptitude Battery (ASVAB) is administered to more than one million individuals in schools and military recruitment centers. The extent of its use may make the ASVAB a more important test than even the GATB.

In recent years the ASVAB has become a somewhat controversial instrument (Conrad, Gulick, & Kincaid, 1977) because of its connection to some of the alleged abuses of military recruitment. On the other hand, because the ASVAB has been made available to schools at no cost for students interested in either military or civilian careers, it has in part filled an assessment need during times of tight budgets.

At one time the various armed forces used different classification batteries as part of their respective recruitment and training efforts. The ASVAB was later devised to streamline testing efforts for both the military institutions and the public schools.

The ASVAB has twelve subtests, which cover a range of content similar to that of the GATB and the DAT. The subtests are:

Word Knowledge (WK)
General Information (GI)
General Science (GS)
Arithmetic Reasoning (AR)
Mathematics Knowledge (MK)
Attention to Detail (AD)
Space Perception (SP)
Mechanical Comprehension (MC)
Automotive Information (AI)
Shop Information (SI)
Electronic Information (EI)

Cronbach (1979) has questioned some of these subtests on the 1977 version of the ASVAB with respect to gender fairness, reliability, and validity, especially predictive validity in career placement. Since the ASVAB is well funded and able to be revised each year, more recent versions may or may not have the problems of earlier ones.

Because this test is often part of a school's career-guidance effort, Cronbach (1979) recommends the development of a policy that requires, at a minimum, counselor inspection and interpretation of results along with the use of other information to verify and be verified by ASVAB results. Ciborowski (1978, 1980) makes similar recommendations for information balance and counselor involvement when the ASVAB is used in schools.

INTERPRETING INTEREST INVENTORIES TO CLIENTS

The interpretation of interest inventories does not ordinarily present the counselor with any special issues not found in other testing situations. Thus, much of this section is a review of relatively standard interpretation procedures, at least up to the concluding phases of the interpretation, when the purposes for testing are realized more fully through the planning of follow-up activities. We assume that the expense of using interest inventories warrants an individual or small-group interpretation. If not, results are woven into counseling when appropriate.

Fundamental to the effective use and interpretation of any instrument is the relationship between the counselor and client. This relationship has been well explained and seems well understood by most counselors. Within the essential context of the positive relationship, the interpretation session is a way to gain use of the information contained in the inventory itself and the information generated by its review. We recommend the following procedures for the interpretation of test results.

1. *Prepare a set of materials that simplify your job of explaining and interpreting the inventory.* If you have ever had a person try to sell you a set of encyclopedias or a life insurance policy, you may have had a demonstration of something that would be helpful in interpreting tests. Remember the large printed cards (mini-posters) used by the salesperson? You might easily incorporate a summary of our suggestions into a packet of reusable materials. This may include colorful mini-posters, worksheets, and so forth.

2. *Use your interpretation packet and a copy of the actual inventory to help the client recall the inventory to be interpreted.* Say the test name and indicate the date on which it was taken. Often counselors will show the client the completed answer sheet and point out two or three responses, saying something like this: "Marlene, on item 16, for example, you were asked if you like to 'conduct business by telephone' and you said you did not like to do that." At this time a counselor might see if the client can recall any special circumstances or events prior to taking the test that might have affected its results. Usually clients do not recall much that is relevant. But since the inquiry takes little time, it may be worthwhile; the occasional recollection that invalidates results (an event contributing to testing error) is important enough to remain alert for it.

3. *Review with the client both the general purposes for the use of such inventories and the specific reasons why the decision was made to have the client take the inventory.* This is rather self-explanatory. At this early point in the interpretation, such a recall of purpose can be followed by something like: "Marlene, we are taking the time to remember the reasons why we're using the inventory because after we see its results we will want to discuss some plans to make good use of the information we acquired. The plans we make will have a lot to do with the purposes or goals we had in the first place."

4. *Give a simple explanation of such testing concepts as validity and reliability. If need be, explain any standard scores used in the inventory.* Most people who are able to complete standardized instruments already understand percentiles, the most commonly used standard score; other standard scores can be converted into percentiles. To explain reliability, the counselor might say: "Marlene, before we go over all the results, let's look here. This part of the profile indicates a percentile score of 57. As you may already know, this means that, compared to other students taking the inventory, about half of them expressed less interest in the area than you; some, though, differed from you by just a very little bit. Inventories like this one are affected by so many things that if you took the

instrument several different times even in the same week, we would not expect the exact same results. For example, most of the time the score we're looking at now [57] may vary, say from 47 to 67 [counselor uses standard error for this instrument]. Because scores really reflect a range—by that I mean a score somewhere between 47 and 67—let's be careful not to see scores as exact numbers. Let's always talk more generally than that and think of scores as meaning high, low, or medium interests when compared to other people's.''

For validity, the interpreter might say: "Marlene, let me tell you what will go through my mind when I look at the results. I will remind myself that Marlene Janovic is not completely represented by this sheet of paper [points to profile]. You and your interests just can't be figured out so easily. Some of this I will, and you will, believe is true about you, but maybe not all of it. That's the way people and tests are; tests are not perfect mirrors of you. But let's see what the results have to say, and let's talk about what can be learned from them."

5. *If time permits, attempt to have the client provide self-estimates of profile scores prior to discussing inventory results.* To do this you will need a blank profile or worksheet facsimile in order to record self-estimates. It may be necessary to simplify or abbreviate complex and lengthy profiles and to explain subscales. A self-estimate for the Strong-Campbell Interest Inventory might involve 20 occupational scales keyed to a one-letter rather than a three-letter Holland code; for example, use an accountant scale (coded C) but not a beautician scale (coded CRE). (Refer to the discussion of Holland in Chapter 2 and the SCII Profile). Clients, however, are reticent at times to risk such self-estimates and require some prodding. Your ability to generate self-estimates therapeutically will determine usage of this tactic. Gaining self-estimates may be too time-consuming for general use. Also, self-estimates have not been shown to improve client recall of inventory results.

6. *Preview test results by emphasizing areas of high interest, followed by very low-interest patterns. Deemphasize midband (average) interest scores.* In reviewing test results, continually describe results in general terms, as bands of scores, using expressions such as "very similar" and the like. Leave time for questions, and be alert to nonverbal cues indicating surprise or confusion. Since it is assumed that you know the client and have reviewed the results prior to the interpretation, you may be able to anticipate controversial or unexpected results. Spend time at first on high-interest areas, then low. Since average interest patterns provide less useful information, describe them in a neutral way; for example, "These scores provide little help in making future plans." Make sure the whole profile receives consideration and the client does not focus on only one or two scores.

7. *If you begin to run short on time, plan to reschedule rather than rush through the results.* It is common to the experience of counselors to hear clients say, "I took this test and it said I should be . . . ." Careful interpretation, clearly understood by the client, takes time. If your client will continue in counseling, plan to reintroduce results in future sessions when appropriate.

8. *When the discussion of separate scales is completed, ask the client to summarize the results of the inventory.* A summary or general conclusion needs to be drawn from the data provided by the inventory. If the client begins providing it, the counselor has a check with regard to the client's understanding of the data. If the client's summary should indicate invalid conclusions, the counselor can deal with them immediately. For those reasons we recommend that the client's summary precede the counselor's whenever possible.

9. *Be sure to check and discuss any discrepancies between client-estimated scores and obtained scores.* You will have done this, no doubt, during the examination of the obtained profile. When summarizing the profile, one can also incorporate a discussion of any discrepancies and a plan of action to resolve them.

10. *Conclude the interview or reschedule in order to make an action plan based on the results of the inventory.* Action on the part of the client is one of the main objectives of using the instrument. If the results of the inventory are uncomplicated, providing no unexpected scores, then planning exploratory and other activities provides no major difficulty. However, the confused client just beginning to structure career exploration may require an incubation period to assimilate the data supplied by the inventory. Thus, the planning of activities after the interpretation may benefit from a delay. Sometimes it is difficult to decide whether action-taking behavior is in the interest more of the counselor seeking concrete results or of the client approaching important career decisions. As follow-up plans are made, counselors often find it beneficial to write such plans down instead of just discussing them. Printed summary sheets, listing future plans or activities, may simplify doing this. A written record certainly is helpful when a follow-up is made: it refreshes the memory concerning past efforts.

11. *Plan to follow up the interpretation/planning session periodically.* Since the demise of the "square peg/square hole" theory of vocational decision making, the emphasis has shifted to regarding career decisions as a process. Thus the follow-up of interest inventories can be viewed as a series of contacts over time. These contacts need not be full counseling sessions, which would probably be possible for only a few clients. Rather, vocational counselors seem to become masters of the brief note, the passing comment in the hallway, the telephone call, and so forth. Such contacts supplement formal, more lengthy sessions. Follow-up occurs repeatedly, then, in little ways. Each, however, is a professional transaction and not a social visit.

ASSESSING CAREER DEVELOPMENT

The assessment of career development, while primarily within the domain of school counseling, is an effort appropriate for other practitioners working with school-age adolescents and young adults. It is especially applicable for individuals working in corrections, special programs, and other situations in which corrective strategies can be implemented when assessment of development indicates a need.

With the expansion of career-education programs, counselors have had both to identify the needs of students and to assess outcomes of programs developed to meet those needs. Even in schools and facilities without comprehensive programs oriented toward occupational awareness and career planning, one may find the methods of assessing career development useful. Because most of the instruments deal primarily with a person's cognitive knowledge of careers, the form of assessment is related more to overall program evaluation than to individual/small-group assessment. In other words, there is not at present a clinical instrument standardized for use in identifying and diagnosing career-immature individuals.

Instruments

The assessment of career development or maturity can be viewed as being in its infancy. Super's view of career development dates back only to 1953, and Crites's developmental model was described only in 1961. Both views of career development, as seen in Chapter 2, are of historical significance, cast not very long ago. Since that beginning, much work has been done. Westbrook (1974) cites the ETS Guidance Inquiry, published in 1958, as probably the first significant measure of career development. Since then numerous instruments have been devised. Some fairly well-known instruments are the Readiness for Vocational Planning (Gribbons & Lohnes, 1968), the Cognitive Vocational Maturity Test (Westbrook, 1970), and Super's Career Development Inventory (Super, Bohn, Forest, Jordaan, Lindeman, & Thompson, 1971). The three instruments to be examined in this chapter are the Assessment of Career Development, developed by the American College Testing Program (ACT) and marketed by Houghton Mifflin Company; the Planning Career Goals, developed by the American Institutes for Research and marketed by CTB/McGraw-Hill; and the Career Maturity Inventory by John O. Crites, marketed by McGraw-Hill. These instruments can be used in research and program evaluation. Another instrument, the Career Development Inventory (Form III), is nearing completion of standardization and publication (Super & Thompson, 1979). It will no doubt join the above instruments as one of the important means to assess career maturity.

Assessment of Career Development (ACD).   The Assessment of Career Development (ACD) is an instrument developed both for the purpose of assessing student career needs and for assessing outcomes of career-guidance programs. Westbrook's work on the Cognitive Vocational Maturity Test (CVMT) and ACT's own work on the ACT Guidance Profile were merged in the development of the ACD. From 1971 to 1974 the test developers for ACT conducted research on various forms of the test, finally norming the ACD on a stratified sample of 8th, 9th, and 11th graders totaling 28,298. It is one of the most sophisticated measures of vocational maturity to date, with great care given to its construction. It has 11 scales, requires 125 minutes to administer, and must be scored by the publisher's (Houghton Mifflin) computerized scoring service.

The ACD has six parts or units: job knowledge, preferred job characteristics (job values), career plans, career-planning activities, career-planning knowledge, and exploratory job experiences. These units gather data on what a student knows about occupations, preferences in terms of job families, theoretical knowledge of how career planning occurs, actions taken related to exploring and seeking employment, and reactions to the school career-guidance program. In addition, a set of 19 local items can be included to gather other data of specific interest to career-guidance program managers and evaluators. For the career-program manager, the test-scoring service provides an alphabetized student list for each group for which a summary report is requested, simplifying the reporting of group data.

The manual for the ACD lists a reading grade level of 7.2 for the instrument. At the cost of sacrificing national norms and time limits, the ACD could be read to poor readers. This option may make its use possible with persons from different cultural and linguistic backgrounds. Westbrook's analysis (1974) of the ACD indicates that it measures more than cognitive knowledge of occupations. About one-third of the items ask the test takers to indicate what kinds of worker activities they have engaged in (psychomotor domain). Another 10% of the questions deal with career-planning activities. A few other questions are related to attitudes and values, providing some measurement in the affective domain.

The ACD user's guide is in effect a bibliography of career-development materials. The intent of the guide is to increase student career development. The materials cited are organized for programs for grades seven through 12. Some counselors may find this guide useful, provided that the publisher updates the reference periodically.

Planning Career Goals (PCG).   In a review of this instrument, Robert E. Wurtz (1977) describes it as "probably the most comprehensive testing battery developed in the last 30 years." It is in effect a combination aptitude, interest, and career-development test. It is expensive and takes over six hours to complete. The instrument emerged from Project TALENT, being normed in 1960 on about 38,000 of the project's 400,000 participants.

In addition to the instrument itself (four test booklets and an answer booklet), the computer-scored narrative profile for the test can be compared to 151 job profiles found in the *Career Handbook,* a supplemental scoring and materials service. This comparison adds considerably to the dollar cost of utilizing the instrument.

Obviously, to adopt the PCG would constitute a major decision for a career-development program, warranting careful review of the instrument itself, its *Technical Bulletin,* and its *Counselor's Handbook.* Because of its size alone it may be appropriate only for 11th and 12th grade students.

Career Maturity Inventory (CMI). The Career Maturity Inventory (CMI), formerly called the Vocational Development Inventory (VDI), is probably the most economical instrument to use of the three described in this chapter, with regard to both dollar outlay and time investment. The purpose of the instrument, as described in the manual, is "to measure the maturity of attitudes and competencies that are critical in realistic career decision-making." As mentioned in Chapter 2, John Crites is the author of this inventory.

The CMI is actually a set of two instruments, one for attitudes and one for competencies. One can be administered without the other.

The Attitude Scale (CMI-AS) is designed to elicit subjective reactions (feelings) toward the process of selecting a career. It contains 50 true/false items designed to test the following dimensions: consistency of career choice over time, realism of career choices in relation to personal capabilities and employment opportunities, career-choice attitudes, and career-choice competencies. While these five areas are measured, the Attitude Scale yields only one total score. The instrument can be administered in 30 minutes and can be hand-scored easily. It has a 6th-grade reading level and a sufficient range of scores to make it appropriate for many varied populations. The author claims, for example, that sufficient "ceiling" exists in the device to serve in assessing career-undecided college juniors and seniors. However, the instrument is standardized for grades 8, 9, 10, and 11.

The Attitude Scale of the CMI has been used extensively by Crites and others in research. More than 200 studies have used this part of the CMI (CMI-AS). The CMI-AS used in past research has been called the "Screening Form." There is also a "Counseling Form," a longer, more involved instrument. It yields a single score much like that of the "Screening Form."

At present it seems that the CMI-AS has been principally a research instrument. For the practitioner it may have some use in screening individuals for counseling. In program development and evaluation it may also be useful. One attraction of the CMI-AS is its ease in administration, low cost, and brief administration time.

The Competence Test of the CMI (CMI-CT) is described by the author as measuring the more cognitive variables involved in choosing an occupation. The five parts or sections of this instrument are: Self-Appraisal (Knowing Yourself), Occupational Information (Knowing about Jobs), Goal Selection (Choosing a Job), Planning (Looking Ahead), and Problem-Solving (What Should be Done). The instrument itself requires roughly two hours to administer, is normed for grades 8 through eleven, and has a 6th-grade reading level.

Care was taken to make the test interesting and involving. Each item is a brief case study of a person involved in some aspect of career development. The little case description is followed by a five-choice set of answers.

The potential uses of the CMI-CT, according to the author (Crites, 1973), include: studying career development, assessing curricular and guidance needs, evaluating career education, and testing in career counseling. Of these four applications, the first three have been identified as reasons for other career-development inventories. The last use, as a counseling tool, is not so clearly emphasized in other instrument manuals. However, in the administration manual Crites states that as yet the CMI-CT has not actually been used in career counseling. He speculates, though, that it may serve as a standardized measure of occupational information, a measure of self-appraisal, goal selection, planning, and problem solving. One gets the impression that the CMI-CT may serve as both a diagnostic and an evaluative instrument. To date no significant body of evidence supports this speculation. Chapter 3 described how Crites recommends its uses in counseling.

STATE-OF-THE-ART IN ASSESSING CAREER DEVELOPMENT

With the rapid expansion of career-education programs in the 1970s, there has arisen an increasing need for instruments to evaluate the results of such programs. Three of the most sophisticated of these devices have been described in this chapter. Very often, when an instrument is developed that gains the respect of the individuals who use it, one finds that, as in education, users begin "teaching the test." Thus one way to evaluate the state-of-the-art in the assessment of career development would be to ask: If programs were developed specifically and pointedly to improve scores on the test, would clients/students be better off? We might ask further: If counselors study and utilize available measures of career development, will they be better prepared to provide service to their clients? Will they have a better understanding of career maturity? Will they develop greater diagnostic competence? We believe at this point that an affirmative response can be given to these questions.

One may ask why these questions need to be raised; in testing we should be able to determine the value of an instrument merely by measuring its validity and reliability. The questions just raised are in a sense an informal way of establishing some validity to measures of career development. The formal effort of validating these instruments can conceivably take decades of research by behavioral scientists. In the meantime, practitioners will need some guide to determine the value of using the instruments.

As is probably obvious from reading this chapter, we have taken a rather conservative view of standardized assessment. This is not difficult to justify; it is common knowledge that more clients have been abused through overtesting and overinterpretation of instruments than the reverse. Interest assessment is the most common form of personality testing, and thus the most frequently misused.

We have tried to deal not so much with test-construction issues as with issues in the utilization of interest assessment by the practitioner. In doing this we have treated issues that are not as specific and objective as those commonly found in a typical journal review of an instrument: its validity and reliability and the clarity of its manual. Thus at times we probably were less conservative than we could have been. Being a helping practitioner is sometimes risky because of the ambiguity associated with the work and its outcome.

THE ETHICS OF CAREER ASSESSMENT

With the last statement we have opened the door for the final topic for discussion in this chapter: ethics. A more appropriate sectional title may have been "The Prudent Use of Assessment in Career Counseling and Program Development." We assume that most readers of this text are familiar with the ethical codes of both The American Personnel and Guidance Association and the American Psychological Association. In conjunction with the latter, though, some readers may not be familiar with APA's *Standards for Educational and Psychological Tests and Manuals* (1966) and *Ethical Principles in the Conduct of Research with Human Participants* (1973). Both of these documents also apply to the topics discussed in the chapter, the first being more relevant to the test developer, the second to the behavioral scientist. Practitioners at times do assume the roles of both and are then bound by the principles contained in these documents.

While much of our professional ethics applies generally to career assessment, there is little actually specific to it. As a form of testing it is covered by those sections of the codes related to testing (APGA, 1974, Section C; APA, Principle 8) but by little else. For example, the sections on testing do not reflect a belief that there are any special competencies required for the administration and interpretation of interest or career-development inventories beyond those of most other tests.

If anything is recognized as unique about career-interest assessment, it seems to be the fact that clients are frequently given copies of their actual test profiles to keep. The ethical codes state that this practice involves risks through neglecting to advise the client that such profiles change over time and may very well become nonrepresentative. Rarely does one find a counselor who writes on a profile, "Disregard in six months unless verified by a later profile." But how does one arrive at an estimate of obsolescence for an interest inventory?

Another source of potential difficulty specifically in the area of career assessment may be the increasing use of self-administered, self-scored instruments. Earlier in the chapter we discussed this trend and the frequency of subjects' scoring errors. Too little supervision of such instruments may not reflect good judgment.

Related to the issue just discussed is the use of narrative profiles, which are also becoming quite popular. These lengthy, computer-prepared descriptions of the results of the inventory would seem at first glance to free the counselor of the chore of interpretation. Professional ethics indicate that such narrative profiles are professional-to-professional communication. The counselor responsible for administering the inventory is also responsible for the contents of the narrative profile. Ethics would dictate that one read the narrative; most of them should at least be screened to be sure of their contents.

It can be a sobering experience in the realm of interest assessment to read the reviews of most interest inventories in various issues of the *Mental Measurements Yearbook* (Buros, irregular years) and examine the questionable or unreported validity of most instruments. Again, counselors in counseling use interest inventories more often than any other kind of standardized device. The area of career-development assessment is still very new; it must be further developed and evaluated. As career-development assessment progresses, so also must the counselor's competence in its use progress in order for our profession to be certain that the best interests of clients are being served.

As a footnote, it is reasonable to expect that individuals trained as career counselors may at some time change jobs, possibly moving into personnel management or some similar position. In such cases new issues arise concerning the use of tests and inventories, especially with regard to employee selection. Those who follow such a career pathway will be wise to rethink the use of tests, the ethics attached, and the legal pitfalls involved.

SUMMARY

The treatment of career assessment was restricted for the most part to interest inventories and measures of career development. A few representative inventories were described that portray both different assessment strategies and different age-group applications.

Important ethical and cost issues related to career assessment were discussed. The overall view presented of testing in career counseling was a cautious one; it emphasized test selection only in the context of one's counseling goals. Also considered were various aspects of interpreting interest inventories.

RECOMMENDED READINGS

Campbell, D. P. Stability of interests within an occupation over thirty years. *Journal of Applied Psychology,* 1966, *50,* 51–56.

A classic that reviews the follow-up research on the Strong Vocational Interest Blank. It demonstrates both the reliability of such instruments and the precautions needed in their use, especially in the counseling relationship.

Buros, O. K. (Ed.). *The mental measurements yearbook.* Highland Park, N.J.: Gryphon Press, irregular years.

A standard reference work in several volumes that reviews most standardized tests and inventories, including interest inventories. Use this work to assess the many different inventories used in career counseling.

Super, D. E. (Ed.). *Measuring vocational maturity for counseling and evaluation.* A monograph of the National Vocational Guidance Association. Washington, D.C.: American Personnel and Guidance Association, 1974.

An important source for early efforts by numerous individuals to measure the concept of career maturity. This work can be viewed also as a primary source on career-development theory.

Westbrook, B. W. Content analysis of six career development tests. *Measurement and Evaluation in Guidance,* 1974, 7, 172 – 180.

The title is descriptive of this article. Using cognitive, affective, and psychomotor domains, it compares various measures of career maturity. A brief historical survey of assessment in this area is provided.

LEARNING ACTIVITIES

1. Discuss the ethics and costs attached to career-assessment practices.
2. Refer to the recent issues of professional journals listed at the end of Chapter 1. List the ones that regularly include research on career assessment and reviews of recently published inventories.
3. If you are a student in counseling, your instructor may provide sample interest-inventory profiles and opportunities to role-play the interpretation of those profiles.
4. Investigate sources in your area where you can gain access to files of manuals and specimen sets of currently used interest inventories and measures of career development.
5. If planning to attend a professional conference oriented in part toward career counseling, visit the exhibit area to secure information on career inventories and related materials.
6. Devise a checklist to be used in reminding counselors of important points to remember and procedures to follow in the interpretation of interest inventories.

CHAPTER FIVE

OVERVIEW OF CAREER INFORMATION

The use of career information in career counseling has been described as "the most inarticulate" and "most neglected aspect of career counseling" (Crites, 1976a, pp. 8−9). There are multiple reasons for describing career information in this manner.

This chapter surveys these problems, discusses the scope of career information, and presents a general model for its use in career development. It also serves as an introduction to the next three chapters, which discuss the use of career information resources and strategies in more detail.

Authors generally agree on what is meant by *career information* (Hoppock, 1976; Isaacson, 1977). However, the various types of career information and the proper times for their use are unclear (Barak, Carney, & Archibald, 1975). In addition, there has been little effort to integrate the use of career information with appropriate decision-making models (Barry & Wolf, 1962; Crites, 1976a; Osipow, 1973).

Whereas all major theoretical approaches assign some value to career information, there are considerable differences regarding the importance of its use (Crites, 1978). The trait-factor theorists, following the Parsonian Equation (Parsons, 1909) that *knowledge of self + knowledge of work + counseling = ability to choose,* assign career information a central role (Barak, Carney & Archibald, 1975; Calia, 1966; Crites, 1974, 1976a, 1978). Client-centered counselors, on the other hand, generally consider career information to be of secondary importance (Crites, 1976a, 1978; Patterson, 1964).

Evaluations of the use and effects of career information have been few (Barry & Wolf, 1962; Osipow, 1973; Remenyi & Fraser, 1977). A recent five-year review by Holcomb and Anderson (1977) found career information to be the least-researched area in vocational guidance.

Because of this state of confusion and neglect, the career counselor has been provided with little external guidance regarding the kind of career information to disseminate and the manner of disseminating it. Supplying career information to clients—on the surface a straightforward process—when viewed in depth turns into a quagmire.

Although the use of career information is a confusing and controversial subject, one irrefutable fact remains: virtually all counseling practitioners, theoreticians, and researchers agree that career information is a necessary component of career counseling.

SCOPE OF CAREER INFORMATION

In order to understand and use career information appropriately in career counseling, it is important that practitioners use common terminology and understand the concepts related to the terms used. Without this common language and understanding, confusion may result in the counselor's application of career information, thus hindering client career development. This section defines the most commonly used terms that apply to career information. In addition, it reveals the conceptual breadth of careers and career information.

The term *career information* is easily and often confused with the term *occupational information*. This confusion stems from a lack of understanding regarding the difference between a career and an occupation. Emphasizing the developmental nature of careers, Super and Bohn (1970) define a *career* as "the sequence of occupations, jobs, and positions engaged in or occupied throughout the lifetime of a person" (p. 113). Super further notes that this concept may be expanded by including prevocational and postretirement years. In a study of careers the emphasis is on the dynamic, developmental change occurring throughout the person's working life, particularly on those developmental tasks in which a person must achieve success in order for work to be a means of expressing self and relating to society.

Super and Bohn's definition of *career* presupposes the definitions of *occupation, job,* and *position.* In modern usage these definitions, as well as those of *career* and *work,* have very different meanings depending on who is using them and how and why they are being used. Fortunately, the career literature provides us with commonly accepted definitions.

An *occupation* is generally understood to be a group of similar jobs in various establishments (Shartle, 1959). In studying occupations the focus has been "essentially a static *differential* psychology" (Super, 1957, p. 4). This attention to the differences among occupations emphasizes knowledge regarding the various components and requirements of different occupations. *Occupational information* typically includes various facts about occupations, including employment prospects, nature of the work, work environment, qualifications, earnings, preparation for entry, and so forth. In general, the purpose of this information is to facilitate clients' selecting occupations that are compatible with their interests, abilities, and personalities.

A *job* is generally defined as "a group of similar positions in a single plant, business establishment, educational institution, or other organization" (Shartle, 1959, p. 23). A *position* is "a collection of tasks constituting the total work assignment of a single worker. There are as many positions as there are workers in the country" (U.S. Department of Labor, 1972, p. 3).

When a carpenter in the Home Construction Company retires, there is an opening for this worker's *position*. A description of the position and its special requirements would probably be included in the position announcement used in hiring a worker to fill the vacancy. For example, specialized skill in building stairs may be a unique requirement of this position. According to the 1978–1979 *Occupational Outlook Handbook* (U.S. Department of Labor, 1978), there were 1,010,000 carpenters employed in the United States during 1976. Each of those carpenters filled a single position, so in 1976 there were 1,010,000 positions of carpenter in the United States.

The Home Construction Company employs 73 carpenters carrying out a variety of tasks in residential construction; these 73 *positions* make up the *job* of carpenter in this company. The Dock Construction Company builds docks for boats; the 14 *positions* of carpenter in the Dock Construction Company make up the *job* of carpenter in this company. Although the jobs of carpenter in the Home Construction Company and the Dock Construction Company are similar in many ways, their requirements would differ as the work environments, qualifications, preparation for entry, nature of the work, employment prospects, and so on, differed. The general and broad information provided in occupational descriptions could not be adequate to describe the job of carpenter as it is practiced at either the Home or the Dock Construction Company.

The jobs of carpenter for the Home Construction Company, the Dock Construction Company, and all other establishments employing carpenters throughout North America would make up the *occupation* of carpenter. Although the information describing the occupation of carpenter would be broad enough to represent all the jobs and positions of carpenter, it would not be so general as to disallow discrimination between carpenters and other construction workers, such as bricklayers or plasterers.

The *career* of carpenter would consist of the patterns or paths followed by carpenters as they move through their lives, particularly their work lives. Information included in a description of this *career pattern* would emphasize the entry, intermediate, and regular occupations involved in the career, the rate and direction of movement through these occupations, and the effect of parental socioeconomic and occupational levels on entry and movement (Super, 1954).

In the case of the career of a carpenter, typical considerations (based on Super, 1953, 1954, 1957) might include:

1. What are the socioeconomic class, race, and occupational levels of the parents of carpenters and how do they affect the exposure of their children to occupational and educational opportunities?
2. What effects do the psychological characteristics of carpenters such as intelligence, interests, values, and needs have on their entering and progressing through their careers?

3. What are the typical education and training received by carpenters in preparing for and progressing through their careers?
4. What effect do economic and cultural changes such as technological change, business cycles, war, and natural disasters have on the career pattern of carpenters?
5. What are the different occupations through which carpenters move as they progress through their careers, with a particular focus on the entry, intermediate, and terminal occupations?
6. How are admission to occupations, behavior on the job, and behavior away from the job regulated?
7. How do carpenters prepare for retirement and what are the primary activities in which carpenters engage following retirement?

Unfortunately, information required to respond to the above questions is generally very difficult to collect. Much of this information, such as the retirement patterns of carpenters, simply does not exist in published form. Other information, which may be available through publications that describe occupations, must be pieced together in a time-consuming, frustrating, and often incomplete manner. Because the primary focus in counseling has been on occupational information and its collection and dissemination, information about career patterns is largely unavailable in published form (Crites, 1976a). In general, counselors base their information on the knowledge they have developed from the few available resources on the sociology and psychology of careers (Caplow, 1954; Miller & Form, 1951; Super, 1957; Terkel, 1974) and from observing and reflecting on their own careers and those of family, friends, and clients. The term *career pattern* or *career-pattern information* will be used to describe this information.

Career information will be used in a broad context to mean all information related to the world of work that can be useful in the process of career development. This includes career-pattern information and occupational information, as well as educational and psychosocial information that relates to working. Our use is similar to Isaacson's (1977) use of the term.

Occupational information includes information such as the employment prospects, nature of work, qualifications, earnings, work environment, preparation for entry, and related information about occupations. In addition, it includes information about jobs and positions that would be most useful after the client has made an occupational choice and is seeking entry into a position.

Educational information describes the educational and training opportunities that relate to occupations and careers. This material typically describes in-school and out-of-school work-experience programs, particularly information such as the nature of the education or training experience, its availability, costs, facilities, and related information.

Psychosocial information describes the psychological and social environment in which workers are embedded and the interaction between the workers and this environment. It includes information about the status of workers in different occupations, psychological and social adjustment to working, and related information. Career-pattern information, educational information, and psychosocial information, for our purposes, are all components of the broad rubric *career information*.

PROBLEMS WITH CAREER INFORMATION

The average individual, and particularly the younger person, is exposed to little direct information about occupations and careers. Through the information acquired indirectly from parents, relatives, friends, and mass media, people frequently develop inaccurate stereotypes of various occupations. Stereotyping is most likely to happen in occupations with which people are most familiar (Crowther & More, 1972; Remenyi & Fraser, 1977). Incomplete and inadequate information is frequently the only material that young people use in the process of comparing self to jobs. The widespread and documented dissatisfaction with work (Cooper & Marshall, 1976; Srivastava, 1977) may be due in part to inadequate information, inappropriately disseminated, that is used as a basis for decision making.

Another major problem with career information can be its lack of organization. There are more than 22,000 occupations defined in the *Dictionary of Occupational Titles* (U.S. Department of Labor, 1977). The fact that for most of these 22,000 occupations there is a variety of sources of information—either written or oral—means that the volume of data is huge. If this mass of data is not organized in some way, it cannot be translated into knowledge and assimilated by the individual. Without assimilation it serves little useful purpose in career development. Adams (1973) emphasizes the importance of organizing career information so that "it represents work as it occurs both in the community and society" (p. 141). He also stresses the importance of relating career information to the developmental needs of the receiver.

The valence of information on a positive/negative dimension appears to have a significant effect on how occupations are viewed. Given highly positive information, people tend to construe an occupation with cognitive simplicity; that is, they view it using fewer cognitive dimensions (Bodden & James, 1976). Some amount of negative information appears to overcome these simplifying effects, allowing occupations to be viewed more realistically (Haase, Reed, Winer & Bodden, 1979). Potentially this more-accurate view would lead to better decision making. Considering that the majority of occupational information provided through written materials is generally neutral or positive, these findings strongly suggest a need for including information about the deficits of occupations so that the user may acquire a balanced picture.

Information disseminated must also be appropriate in content and timing to meet the needs of the individual, particularly the needs of the person who is involved in making a career decision. Such questions as these may be at issue:

What courses should I sign up for next semester?
Should I take a job at Sam's Auto Body or the Broadway Deli?
What should my major be in college?
What else can I do besides put up with this crummy job that I have now?
Should I retire now?

Obviously, adequate and accurate career information is a vital component in making the decisions implied by these questions. Certain kinds of required career information may be adequately provided at the time of decision making, but frequently it is information assimilated at an earlier stage in life and held in memory that is used at the time of decision making.

Consider an example. Suppose that Janice Jones drops in to see you, her high school counselor, regarding her plans to enter Clarksville State College after graduation, which is four months away. Janice is enrolled in the college prep program and, thus far, has a solid "C" average. Her grades are strikingly stable—a few "B's" and "D's," but primarily "C's." Although she has a "C" average, her admittance to Clarksville State is all but guaranteed, since all state residents with at least a "C" average are assured admittance.

Early in the session Janice expresses her ambivalence about going to college—particularly her uncertainty regarding a major. Her parents would like her to be an elementary school teacher, largely because that's what Mom did and because they consider it a "profession appropriate for a young lady." Mom and Dad, but especially Mom, have emphasized the benefits of going to college and becoming a school teacher: (1) people will respect you, since you are making a positive contribution to society and since you will be "educated"; (2) you will have the opportunity to meet the "right type of young man," and this matters because Charleton High has given you little exposure to "decent people." (Incidentally, Mom and Dad met in college.)

In some ways Janice agrees with her parents' point of view. However, she expresses concern about her lack of interest and abilities in academic areas. "Boy, did I work hard to even get a 'C' average!" What has her most concerned is her nervousness in front of groups. She tells you, "It doesn't matter who it is—younger kids, older kids, or adults—if I have to say or do anything in groups larger than two or three people, I freak out!" She describes her "lousy performance" in her third-grade piano recital, even though she played her piece perfectly during practice sessions.

As you listen, Janice lets you know, hesitantly at first, that there is something that she would really like to do—become a hairdresser. She proceeds to describe vividly her early recollections of visits to the beauty shop with her mother and her fascination with the "hum and whirl" of the machines and the pleasant chatter of the women. With rising energy and enthusiasm, she tells you how much she loved to play beauty shop as a kid and how she now enjoys cutting and styling her younger sister's and girlfriends' hair. "But why talk about it? It's impossible. Mom and Dad will never agree," she concludes. "Boy, am I in a mess! How can I ever decide what to do?"

There are obviously many issues that have to be considered in helping Janice make the decision of what to do following graduation. Some of the obvious factors are:

1. Janice's apparent limited ability and interest in college and in being a school teacher;
2. Janice's response to parental pressure to go on to college; and
3. Janice's anxiety in performing in front of groups.

Although these factors are personal characteristics of Janice, they are significant in Janice's struggle with her career decision. Their implications for career planning must be considered, particularly as they relate to Janice's fund of career information.

Rather than focusing on these factors or attempting to solve her career problem at this time, let us look at the sources and inadequacies of the career information that are critical in this career-decision dilemma:

1. Janice's parents appear to have a limited and stereotypic view of college and teaching that they are transmitting to her. The information does not appear to consider significant dimensions such as the current job market for teachers, the day-to-day duties that school teachers carry out, and many other factors. Probably most significant, they are not considering this career information in relation to Janice.

2. The information that Janice has about the occupations of teacher and hairdresser also appears to be restricted. She is probably not aware of or is not considering many factors, such as pay, nature of the duties, and so forth. At this point she has not considered the long-term career implications of either occupation, particularly as they may relate to her future plans for marriage and/or children.

Considering the decision facing her, the information that she has acquired about jobs while growing up should be modified by career information provided to her now, since the time for her decision is now. Accurate and appropriately disseminated career information integrated with counseling that focuses on the other critical elements in this situation is necessary. Regardless of its accuracy and adequacy of dissemination, career information at this point may not overcome the destructive stereotypes of the past.

To be effective, career counselors must have some understanding of how career information is acquired, particularly since they work on a daily basis with individuals who have been negatively impacted by inadequate information. Many career counselors are also in a position to play critical roles in the manner in which young people acquire information about careers. As influencers of children and adults, counselors must understand career information from the perspective of how it is acquired and used in the process of career development.

CAREER INFORMATION IN CONTEXT

A useful context for understanding the role of career information in counseling is the three-stage helping model of Carkhuff (1969). This developmental model (Egan, 1975) proposes that helping moves through the three stages of *exploration, understanding,* and *action.* During the *exploration* stage the focus is on helping clients determine where they are with respect to particular life situations. Clients are frequently confused and often their primary concerns relate to problems or situations affecting them. The *understanding* stage focuses on where clients would like to be in the future with regard to those situations or problems. Helping clients select realistic goals and reduce confusion are preferred outcomes of this stage. In the *action* stage systematic programs involving concrete steps provide the means for assisting clients to move from where they are to where they wish to be with their lives. These programs are intended to provide the means for resolving the negative life situations.

This developmental model is particularly applicable to career counseling: clients must *explore* where they are in relation to work, *understand* where they wish to be in relation to work, and *act* on their understanding to develop means of entering and moving through their careers (Friel & Carkhuff, 1974). Within each of these stages there are certain processes in which the individual is involved:

1. In the *exploration* stage, individuals must become more aware of the broad spectrum of work. They also begin to conceptualize the relationships among occupations. As part of this conceptualization process, distortions about occupations become reduced.

2. In the *understanding* stage they differentiate among occupations according to occupational characteristics. Comparing self to occupations is part of this process. Increased knowledge of the components of self and improved ability to differentiate among occupations permits persons to begin decision making about those occupations that meet their needs and whose requirements can be met.

3. In the *action* stage the active preparation for entry into the occupational world begins. Individuals eventually enter into the occupational world in a more or less permanent manner during this period. Later in this stage, involvement in maintaining and enriching their career occurs.

In all these stages there is an active need for career information. In the school system this need is beginning to be met through career-education programs. In addition to career information acquired through the educational system, contacts with people (parents, friends, neighbors, relatives, employers, and others) add to the repertoire of information and contribute to the movement in this process.

Dependent in part on the unique characteristics of the individual involved and the quality of the information provided, movement through these stages may be somewhat organized and predictable or disorganized and unpredictable. The movement is never so systematic as to presuppose the clear-cut termination of any stage or any period within a stage at a certain time and the immediate beginning of the next. Rather than discrete steps, these stages should be considered a continuous process. Blended together by slow movement from one to another and overlapping one another to an extent, they are difficult, if not impossible, to distinguish clearly.

Although it may appear that an earlier stage or operation within a stage has been completed, unique situations may force a delayed or impaired entry to the career process (LoCascio, 1964). Problems with career entry may be due to disadvantagement, a disabling condition, and/or institutionalization that prevented an earlier exploration of the world of work and thus impeded the acquisition of some vocationally relevant information or behavior. For example, a 45-year-old long-term-institutionalized person recently discharged from a state school for the mentally handicapped may have an awareness of occupations equivalent to that of a 10-year-old. There may also be unique characteristics of the individual that impair or delay the career-choice process, such as indecisiveness (Tyler, 1969) or limited risk-taking propensity (Slakter & Cramer, 1969; Ziller, 1957).

Mid-career change due to job dissatisfaction, a handicap, forced occupational change, or other reason may require recycling through earlier stages of the process. Homemakers whose youngest children are entering elementary school frequently engage in a process of exploring and understanding themselves in relation to work prior to entering a "second" career.

SUMMARY

In this chapter, we have discussed the role of career information in career counseling. Despite its generally recognized importance to career counseling, there is little direction as to how or why career information should be integrated within the career counseling process. Other problems that relate to career information were discussed: presentation of stereotypical information about jobs, lack of organization of information, and inappropriate content and timing of information. Important terms related to career information were presented and the differences among careers, occupations, jobs, and positions clarified. The developmental helping model of Carkhuff, which emphasizes the movement of counseling through the stages of exploring, understanding, and action, was presented as a useful context for understanding the role of career information in counseling.

RECOMMENDED READINGS

Friel, T., & Carkhuff, R. R. *The art of developing a career.* Amherst, Mass.: Human Resource Development Press, 1974.

This workbook, based on the Carkhuff three-stage helping model, guides the user through a series of exercises designed to facilitate career development.

Hoppock, R. *Occupational information* (4th ed.). New York: McGraw-Hill, 1976.

This textbook, first published in 1957, provides information about the various kinds of career information, discusses career-development theories, and describes a variety of ways in which occupational information may be presented to groups. The latter area, discussed in Chapters 12 to 24, is a definite strength of the book.

Isaacson, L. E. *Career information in counseling and teaching* (3rd ed.). Boston: Allyn & Bacon, 1977.

This textbook, in addition to the standard review of career-development theories and career-information resources, provides thorough coverage of the psychological, physical, social, and economic factors affecting workers and their careers.

Norris, W., Hatch, R. N., Engelkes, J. R., & Winborn, B. B. *The career information service* (4th ed.). Chicago: Rand McNally, 1979.

This text provides a comprehensive coverage of the major career-information resources.

Terkel. S. *Working.* New York: Avon Books, 1975.

Terkel interviewed workers from more than 100 occupations and provides highly personal accounts of their jobs and lives. Definitely worth reading.

LEARNING ACTIVITIES

1. Discriminate among the terms *career, occupation, job,* and *position.*
2. What are the major differences between career information and occupational information? What are the different kinds of career information?
3. Interview at least two middle-aged adults, focusing on their career patterns. Compare the differences and similarities in their career patterns. Select at least two workers from Terkel's *Working* and carry out the same analysis.
4. Reflect on your own career pattern. What is your career goal? Where are you now with respect to the goal? What are your future plans related to your career?
5. Reflect on your personal attitudes about sex stereotyping in occupations. Do you believe that certain jobs are "man's work" or "woman's work"? What appears to be the basis for your decision?

6. Has inappropriate, inaccurate, or poorly timed career information ever been provided you? How did it affect you?
7. Interview a person who is or has been involved with a mid-career change. What are the nature of the change and the reasons for it? How has it affected the person?

CHAPTER SIX

CAREER EXPLORATION: RESOURCES AND STRATEGIES

THE EXPLORATION STAGE

In the exploration stage, individuals begin to become more aware of the world of work around them. They also begin the process of awareness of self with respect to personal strengths and deficits, interests, and goals.

In the case of a preschool or elementary-school child, increased awareness of work may mean an improved understanding of workers—police officers, dairy workers, fire fighters, and others—acquired through field trips or through class visits by persons representing different occupations. Toys and picture books provide further exposure to a wide variety of occupations. The child's vague notion of occupational roles is usually expanded by discussion, observation, and identification with the work roles of mother, father, teacher, or other significant persons (Goldhammer & Taylor, 1972). As time brings increased exposure to more people and to the mass media, the child develops a broadened view of the work world. The danger in accumulating information in this vicarious, haphazard fashion rather than systematically is the risk of acquiring a distorted, fairylandish view.

Children also begin to acquire simple manual and mental skills by performing chores, school work, or other tasks. In this early stage, children begin at a superficial, fantasy level to compare themselves to people in occupations (Ginzberg et al., 1951). Children in these formative years, frequently enthusiastic and unbridled by occupational stereotypes, are vulnerable to misperceptions and distortions (Herr & Cramer, 1972). Unfortunately, occupational distortions appear to pervade our culture. For example, research suggests that sex-stereotyped ideas about work are reinforced by television (Kaniuga, Scott, & Gade, 1974) and elementary readers (Stefflre, 1969).

As individuals develop a deepening awareness of the work world, they begin to conceptualize occupations in a manner that allows them to compare themselves with the requirements and other characteristics of occupations. This comparison process occurs as a result of an increased awareness of one's abilities, interests, and values and an increased awareness of occupations in terms of what they require and what they offer (Gribbons & Lohnes, 1968). Improved cognitive capacity, ability to be abstract and to use symbols (Piaget, 1970), increased academic ability, especially in reading, and increased contact with the work environment contribute to children's acquiring more specific information about a wider variety of occupations. Early subtle pressures from the environment, particularly the school and family, to begin thinking about whether or not to move toward occupations requiring considerable preparation exert more influence at this time.

The person in the exploration stage proceeds from acquiring broad information about occupations to filling in the details about groups of occupations. Career information provided during this period must include more specific data such as the general training requirements and rate of compensation for certain classes of occupations, as well as broad-based information such as the relationships between occupations and the general structure of the work world. For example, persons involved in this conceptualization period would probably be able to recognize that certain categories of occupations, such as school teaching, require a college education, whereas other categories, such as construction work, generally require a high school education in addition to on-the-job training.

RESOURCES AND STRATEGIES
FOR EXPLORATION

There is a great wealth of resources available for the counselor involved in helping persons to improve their awareness and conceptualization of work. Frequently they are difficult to locate and organize. The primary purpose of this section is to present a variety of useful resources and strategies that relate to career awareness and conceptualization and briefly to describe them.

The resources discussed in this section are methods developed through career education, as well as methods developed through other sources and reported on in career-education, information, and counseling texts and other sources of career literature. While the resources discussed are generally most relevant to our exploration stage, they include activities that are potentially useful in the career understanding and action stages. They are included in this section either because they are more pertinent to the exploration stage than to the others or because their application begins in this stage.

Career education

The advent of career education in the early 1970s (Marland, 1971, 1972a, 1972b) provided a significant impetus for the development of career-information resources. Career education requires the integration of career information into the school curriculum. Adams (1973, pp. 142–143) accentuates the centrality of career information in career education through the following concepts.

1. Career information is essential to the conduct of career education.
2. Career information includes information about occupations, educational development, career preparation, and the labor market.
3. Curriculum subject matter or content knowledge is career information when related to preparation for or performance of occupational tasks.
4. Career development is facilitated by having information about educational and occupational requirements.
5. Career development is facilitated by having information about community, state, and national labor-market conditions.
6. Career development is facilitated by having information about economic conditions.
7. The meaning of educational and occupational experience is enriched through career information.
8. Career information is essential to the development of occupational and career competency.
9. Career information is essential to clarification of values, formulating goals, and making career choices.

Although the goal of career education is to refocus American education so "that every young person completing our school program at grade 12 be ready to enter higher education or to enter useful employment" (Marland, 1972a, p. 188), the early years of school are seen as important in developing an awareness of work. The stimulation offered by career education has contributed to the development of a variety of resources that can assist the counselor interested in understanding or developing methods and programs to facilitate clients' exploration of work.

A number of career-education textbooks, both general (Bailey & Stadt, 1973; Goldhammer, 1974; Goldhammer & Taylor, 1972; Hoyt, Evans, Mackin, & Mangum, 1974; Magisos, 1973; Marland, 1974; McClure & Buan, 1973; Tiedeman, Schreiber, & Wessell, 1976) and specific to our career-exploration stage (Gysbers, Miller, & Moore, 1973; Hoyt, Pinson, Laramore, & Mangum, 1973) have been published. The general career-education textbooks, for the most part, provide basic information, such as the philosophy of career education, the rationale for its development, its components and contributions and basic steps for its implementation. The career-education texts specific to the early stage of career development provide curriculum goals and guidelines that can allow for the integration of the content of career education into the elementary-school curriculum.

In *Career Education and the Elementary School Teacher,* for example, Hoyt and others (1973, pp. 41 – 42) identify six career-education concepts that should be integrated into the elementary school curriculum. These concepts relate to (1) the role of work in life and society, (2) the nature of the world of work, (3) work values, (4) education and the world of work, (5) career development and career decision making, and (6) work habits. The following illustration of the content of one area is taken from Hoyt and others (1973, pp. 41 – 42).

Concepts Related to Education and the World of Work

1. Education and work are interrelated.
2. Different kinds of work require varying degrees and types of educational preparation.
3. Basic education enhances job performance.
4. There are both specific and general knowledges for each career area.
5. There are many training routes to job entry.
6. Workers may need vocational retraining several times in the course of a lifetime.
7. Knowledge and skills in different subjects relate to performance in different work roles.

While Hoyt and others (1973) do not supply detailed lesson guides, they do provide a wealth of specific examples of ways to incorporate career information into the elementary curriculum to improve career awareness. They discuss simulated work experiences, field trips, and ideas for resource visitors, and they describe exemplary programs.

Specific models and programs, which may include lesson plans and other resources providing detailed instructions for the integration of career information into career education and for the implementation of career education, have been developed at the national, state, and district levels. Tiedeman and others (1976), in *Key Resources in Career Education,* summarize information on numerous national programs and models (pp. 152 – 176), as well as state and district models and programs (pp. 176 – 273). Their descriptions generally consist of title, length and date of publication, address of sponsoring organization, population affected by the program, and related information, and in many cases include more extensive data, such as the purpose and contents of the resources. What follows is an excerpt from Tiedeman and others (1976, pp. 186 – 188).

SUBJECT:	State models (Arkansas)
	The six publications whose bibliographic citations follow are described as a group at the end of the citations.

A

TITLE:	*Career Awareness: Elementary Teacher's Guide, What Shall I Be?*
ORGANIZATION:	Arkansas Department of Education, Little Rock, AR
DATE:	1972
NUMBER OF PAGES:	280
POPULATIONS:	All

B

TITLE:	*Career Awareness Units, Magnolia Public Schools, Grades 1 – 7*
ORGANIZATION:	Magnolia Public Schools, AR

AVAILABILITY: Magnolia Public Schools, Magnolia, AR 71753, $15 for complete set of 37 units including postage; also ED 117 538

LEVELS: Grades K – 12

POPULATIONS: All

C

TITLE: *Career Education . . . Concepts and Bulletin Board Ideas*

ORGANIZATION: Arkansas Department of Education, Little Rock, AR

NUMBER OF PAGES: 65

AVAILABILITY: ED 117 539

LEVELS: Grades K – 12

POPULATIONS: All

D

TITLE: *Communicative Skills-9. An English Course For Career-Oriented Students*

ORGANIZATIONS: Little Rock Public Schools, Little Rock, AR: Arkansas Department of Education, Little Rock, AR

DATE: 1973

NUMBER OF PAGES: 237

LEVELS: Grades K – 12

POPULATIONS: All

E

TITLE: *Drop-In Mathematics, Teacher's Manual*

ORGANIZATION: Arkansas Department of Education, Little Rock, AR

DATE: 1972

NUMBER OF PAGES: 145

AVAILABILITY: ED 080 329

LEVELS: Grades K – 12

POPULATIONS: All

F

TITLE: *A Digest of Resource Activities for Career Education*

ORGANIZATION: Arkansas Department of Education, Little Rock, AR

DATE: September 1973

NUMBER OF PAGES: 142

AVAILABILITY: ED 118 758

LEVELS: Grades K – 12

POPULATIONS: All

A – F

MODEL: The Arkansas material includes a variety of sources geared toward teacher use in fusing career education into the existing curriculum.

The *Digest of Resource Activities* is a primary example of this, offering career education material developed by teachers in the State. This *Digest* lists activities used to fuse career education into the regular curriculum and is intended to stimulate elementary and secondary teachers to modify, add on, and develop new activities using this digest as a model. The activities cover kindergarten through high school and their variety extends from units on "How to Use Tools" to "Money in the Bank." *Career Awareness* similarly lists areas such as the "home" and presents concepts, activities, resources, and references linked to the regular curriculum.

COMMENT: The value in the Arkansas material comes from its development by teachers actively engaged in career education in the classroom. The variety of information is of value to classroom teachers in particular.

Beginning in 1976, summaries of projects funded through the Office of Career Education, U.S. Office of Education, are described in an annual publication entitled *Profiles of Career Education Projects* (Buffington & Associates, 1978; Pacific Consultants, 1976). The publication does not include specific materials but provides addresses of major sources of information. A review of the two- to four-page summaries of each project funded during the previous fiscal year will generally allow the reader to determine whether materials will meet his or her needs. As in the case of the Tiedeman and others (1976) publication, the resources described include those appropriate to all ages. Many will apply to persons who are beginning to explore work in relation to themselves.

Career-information textbooks

Career-information and career-counseling textbooks (Herr & Cramer, 1972, 1979; Hoppock, 1976; Isaacson, 1977; Norris, 1969; Norris, Hatch, Engelkes, & Winborn, 1979; Tolbert, 1974; Whiteley & Resnikoff, 1978) can also provide useful concepts and methods for using career information in promoting occupational awareness and conceptualization.

Of the above, the textbook by Willa Norris (1969) entitled *Occupational Information in the Elementary School* is the only occupational information textbook specific to our career-exploration period. This book is a beginning effort to incorporate occupational information into the elementary school curriculum and is divided into two parts: (1) Theory and Methods and (2) Resource Materials. Although the theory and resource components are significantly outdated, the very complete resource unit includes certain materials not available from any other information source. For example, in Section 5, "Occupational Songs by Industry" (pp. 234–239), more than 100 songs are organized by field of work. A table allows the user to determine quickly the industry and grade level for which the song is appropriate and the page number and music publication from which it was taken. The resource materials also include occupational books and pamphlets, occupational films and filmstrips, and occupational recordings. Most of these resources are organized by industry.

The most useful components of this book are Chapters 3 and 4, which deal with projects and activities through which occupational information is presented. The focus in the primary elementary curriculum (K–3) is on information that relates to careers in the home, school, and community. During the later elementary years (4–6) the focus is on the broader work world, including the child's state, the nation, and other countries. The occupational information program following the sequence suggested by Norris (1969, p. 56) is as follows.

> *Kindergarten.* The child learns about the work activities of mother, father, and other members of child's household.
> *Grade 1.* The child learns about work in the immediate environment—child's home, school, church, and neighborhood.
> *Grade 2.* The child learns about community helpers who protect and serve the child as well as about familiar stores and businesses in the community.
> *Grade 3.* The child studies the expanding community. Emphasis is placed on transportation, communication, and other major industries.
> *Grade 4.* The child learns about the world of work at the state level, including the main industries of the state.
> *Grade 5.* The child's studies broaden to cover the industrial life of the nation. Major industries of the various sections of the United States are selected for study.
> *Grade 6.* The child's program is expanded to include the entire western hemisphere. Life in Canada and South and Central America is contrasted with life in the United States.[1]

Dozens of occupational information projects and activities as they relate to each grade in the above sequence are provided. These activities consider the increased ability of the students to expand their radius of awareness and to think abstractly. They include role plays and dramatizations, poems and songs, murals, reports, resource persons, games and riddles, field trips, scrapbooks, interviewing workers, and readings.

Herr and Cramer (1972, pp. 127–130; 132–134) suggest sample objectives to facilitate career development at various educational levels, the activities to attain the objectives, and the evaluation methods as they relate to the objectives. Not only do the objectives broaden the base of occupational awareness and conceptualization but they are also keyed to different levels of affective and cognitive domain (Bloom, Engelhart, Furst, Hill, & Krathwohl, 1956; Krathwohl, Bloom, & Masia, 1964). The appropriate use of career information is central to the accomplishment of the majority of their objectives. For example (p. 132), the behavioral objective "In a flannel board presentation, the student can label on the basis of their tools and clothing ten different types of workers found in his community" is keyed as a cognitive-knowledge objective. Sample

---

[1]From *Occupational Information in the Elementary School,* by Willa Norris. ©1963 (revised 1969), Science Research Associates, Inc. Reprinted by permission of the publisher.

activities to attain the objective could include "class visits to police and fire stations, etc." or "reading books on different occupations within the local community—grocer, minister, policeman, etc." (p. 132). Obviously career information is also central to the activities for attaining the objectives.

In another section of their text, Herr and Cramer (1972, pp. 149–159) provide a variety of strategies and activities that relate to the use of career information in the elementary school. Isaacson (1977, pp. 430–436) also has a very useful section related to the development of broad, basic knowledge of the world of work.

Career-related journals

Career periodicals, particularly *The Vocational Guidance Quarterly* and *Elementary School Guidance and Counseling,* contain articles related to broadening young children's awareness and conceptualization of the work world. Many of the articles provide suggestions as to the content of projects or activities designed to improve youngsters' abilities to understand the broad differences separating one group of occupations from another and to begin a simulated involvement with the work world.

One of the most significant sources is a column entitled "Career Guidance in the Elementary School," which has been a regular feature of the journal *Elementary School Guidance and Counseling* since December of 1971. This feature has as its purpose "to discuss, describe and disseminate information regarding career guidance principles and practices in the elementary school" (Leonard, 1971, p. 124). Descriptions of creative activities suggested by this column include:

1. A simulated popcorn factory, in which students, under the direction of a teacher and a counselor, become a board of directors, company supervisors, foremen, and workers, including poppers, butterers, baggers, counters, delivery-truck drivers, and clean-up crew. Arithmetic, spelling, reading, and writing are all required as the factory employees develop stock certificates, advertise, and exchange money both in selling shares in the company and in selling popcorn. The foreman selects employees on the basis of their job applications (Hedgepeth, 1972).

2. An activity called "living in a medieval town," which includes group discussion about jobs available and kinds of equipment used in medieval towns, conducting a medieval town fair, visiting modern-day craftspeople whose trade was active during medieval times (such as glassblowers and cabinetmakers), and related activities (Leonard, 1972b).

3. An elementary-school employment service that involves the students in completing job applications and interviewing for positions such as safety patrol member, future teacher, lunchroom helper, custodian's helper, and library staff

member. On the basis of the job openings available and the students' abilities to meet job requirements, applicants are either hired, put on a waiting list, or not hired for a given position (Jackson, 1972).

4. A hat exhibit that includes headgear from a variety of workers. Included below each "hat" are printed materials describing the occupations represented. Class discussions and a video component are built around the exhibit (Forsyth, 1972).

5. A "career pyramid" activity in which information about a job-related local event, such as construction of a new building, is placed at the top of a bulletin or chalk board. This becomes the top of the pyramid. Through class discussion, students determine the various occupations that are currently involved in the event and those that will be involved in the future. As occupations are suggested, they are grouped into general categories according to worker functions, such as planning, operation, maintenance, and so forth. These become the base of the pyramid, and each category is then used to start a discussion focusing on the interrelatedness of the occupations and on what might happen if one group of occupations failed to do its job (Rost, 1973).

6. An "on-the-job illustrations" activity, for which students are asked to find and bring in pictures representing people at work. The pictures are arranged on the floor and group members each choose two that appeal to him or her. In small groups they then discuss what they found appealing and what they believe is good in the work represented (Wubbolding & Osborne, 1976).

7. A "Career Dress-Up Day," on which students dress up to depict an occupation that interests them. In addition, they develop scrapbooks that illustrate their selected occupations (Anderson & Ramer, 1976).

8. A "classified ad" activity, in which the children write a classified ad to sell a toy or other article they no longer need. The ads are placed in a class-made newspaper and circulated throughout the classroom or school. A discussion of advertising, newspaper publishing, sales, and other occupations can relate to this activity (Coombs & Sklare-Lancaster, 1978).

While all of these activities provide an increased awareness of work, some require the active participation of children in work roles (Hedgepeth, 1972; Jackson, 1972) and thus allow for the comparison of self to different jobs. These job try-outs facilitate an increased awareness of one's own interests and capacities as they relate to work in general, as well as to specific jobs.

Bender (1973), who has also proposed a type of school employment service, recommends that job applications be used as a tool to facilitate children's personal understanding of work. Job applications, which become increasingly complex as grade levels progress, are used for assigning students to a variety of work activities.

Kaback (1960, 1966) provides a detailed description of a variety of sequential activities designed for gradual increase in children's awareness of work. They include simple activities such as a discussion of the tools, processes, and materials needed to fix a broken leg on a toy chair, an interview with parents to discuss their occupations, and a discussion focusing on the surnames of different children in the class. More complex activities appropriate to older children include children's spending part of the day with their parents at work and inviting minority workers to speak about the special hardships that they may have faced in entering employment.

Laramore and Thompson (1970) suggest 13 career-exploring activities, including a few not yet discussed in this chapter. Among their suggestions are:

1. Ask students to fantasize about their future jobs as adults. Request that they do research about the occupations and then pantomime them in class. Let others guess what they are doing.
2. Encourage students who have interesting hobbies to describe them. Relate different occupations to these hobbies.
3. Upper-grade students with part-time jobs can present their jobs to your class, emphasizing the skills required and the satisfactions gained from the jobs.
4. Ask the students to prepare a résumé of jobs that they can do. Focus on how they can sell their skills in their neighborhoods.
5. Have students draw pictures showing occupations with which they are familiar. Ask them to describe the meaning of their pictures.

Bank (1969) emphasizes the expansion of student occupational awareness through the use of role models. Using an adaptation of the grade-level concept of Norris (1969) outlined earlier in this chapter, Bank developed nine job families and found corresponding vocational role models. These models came to school dressed in "on-the-job" working clothes and were interviewed by students. Bank also provides preinterview activities to prepare for the interviews and postinterview activities to reinforce the learning from the interviews. The activities include drawing and collecting pictures about the jobs and writing stories about parental and other occupations.

Commercial publications

Commercial publishers have begun to develop materials for use in assisting youngsters to develop career awareness. Guidance Associates (1973) has produced a sound filmstrip series entitled *First Things* for use in grades K–4. For one primary reason sound filmstrips are useful in presenting career information: they are as vivid as films in providing individuals with the sounds and sights of occupations, yet they allow the pace of the presentation to be controlled by holding a scene as long as necessary to facilitate discussion.

Career Kits for Kids, developed by Encyclopaedia Britannica (1974), is designed to facilitate career awareness in children during the early elementary years. The kits contain six units: Barney the Baker, Freddy the Fireman, Mary the Letter Carrier, Maxi the Taxi Driver, Nellie the Nurse, and Rusty the Construction Worker. These units can provide the basis for involving children in activities related to the occupations, such as baking, plastering, and so on (Schmidt, 1976).

Effectiveness of career-awareness strategies

In the last ten years significant numbers of resources and strategies have been designed to facilitate career awareness and occupational conceptionalization. The opinions of the developers and users of the various strategies, as reported in the literature, are consistently and unanimously positive. There is a consensus among these sources that the activities are useful for the purpose of initial career expansion. Unfortunately, at the present time these highly subjective evaluations are the primary source of input about the effectiveness of career-awareness strategies. Occasionally journals, particularly the *Journal of Vocational Behavior, Measurement and Evaluation in Guidance,* and *The Vocational Guidance Quarterly,* provide evaluative research regarding the effectiveness of career-information strategies.

Fortunately, a few studies that compare different strategies in terms of their effectiveness in imparting career information at the awareness and conceptualization stage have been reported. Edington (1976) evaluated three methods of using resource people in helping kindergarten students to become aware of the world of work. The three treatments, all involving ten occupations, were (1) an interest center with ten mannequins dressed to represent ten different occupations, the tools of the occupation, and a tape recording about the occupation; (2) a field trip to each of ten sites representing the occupations; and (3) a visit to the class by a representative of each of the occupations. A picture test designed to measure the level of information acquired about the ten occupations was used to evaluate the treatments. While all the treatments showed significant gains, the children who were exposed to the field trip showed the most significant gain in information from pre- to posttest. Exposure to the interest center resulted in gain of least information. The administration of the picture test two months later showed that the gains persisted over time.

The task of overcoming occupational sex stereotyping in elementary schools has been the focus of two studies. Harris (1974) attempted to expand the career awareness of five sixth-grade girls using counseling sessions that involved role playing, discussions, and career-oriented exercises. This treatment did not result in significant changes in the girls' number of sex-typed occupational choices, perhaps because none of the activities was directly related to sex-typed thinking.

The problem of sex-typed occupational thinking in children, as the stereotypes relate to both men and women, was studied by Vincenzi (1977). An experimental group and two control groups, each with 59 subjects, were involved in the study. The treatment to which the experimental group was exposed for two 30-minute sessions per week over ten weeks included:

1. a review and discussion of magazine articles depicting men and women in nontraditional occupational roles;
2. a discussion of stereotyping as a general concept;
3. presentations by seven women who worked in traditional male occupations.

The number of sex-typed occupations, as measured on a scale of occupational sex stereotyping adapted from Schlossberg and Goodman (1972), was significantly reduced in the experimental as compared to the control groups. The author feels that the female speakers may have been the major influencers of the results.

The importance of children's having contact with live occupational models is supported strongly by the results of the Edington (1976) and Vincenzi (1977) studies. The common practices of conducting field trips and scheduling class speakers appear to be a significant means of broadening career awareness in children.

SUMMARY

This chapter focused on the major career resources and strategies designed to facilitate client abilities to become aware of the broad spectrum of work and to conceptualize the relationships among occupations. Career-education materials, career information, and counseling texts and journals were presented as major sources of activities and information designed to achieve that objective. The few studies that have evaluated the effectiveness of imparting information to broaden career awareness in children suggest the importance of children's having contact with live occupational models.

RECOMMENDED READINGS

Elementary School Guidance and Counseling. American Personnel and Guidance Association.

This journal has published a column entitled "Career Guidance in the Elementary School" as a regular feature since December of 1971. It is an excellent source of information and activities designed to enhance career awareness and conceptualization in children.

Herr, E. L., & Cramer, S. H. *Vocational guidance and career development in the schools: Toward a systems approach.* Boston: Houghton Mifflin, 1972.

This text provides a comprehensive overview of the principles and activities related to career development in the schools and is an excellent resource for ideas and activities to facilitate children's career awareness and conceptualization.

Hoyt, K. B., Pinson, N. M., Laramore, D., & Mangum, G. L. *Career education and the elementary school teacher.* Salt Lake City: Olympus Publishing Company, 1973.

This textbook identifies career-education concepts, defines curriculum goals based on the concepts, and provides specific examples of means to achieve the goals. Ideas for simulated work experiences, field trips, class visitors, and other resources are provided.

Norris, W. *Occupational information in the elementary school.* Chicago: Science Research Associates, 1969.

Though significantly outdated with respect to concepts and theory, this book is exceptional in its presentation of projects and activities related to the development of career awareness and conceptualization in younger children.

LEARNING ACTIVITIES

1. Interview a child between the ages of 6 and 12, focusing on the work-related activities the child has completed in school or at home over the previous two or three days. How did these activities enhance the child's understanding of various occupations?
2. Recall your own observations of television, movies, and other mass media. How do the media affect children's perceptions of occupations?
3. Ask two children between the ages of 5 and 12 what jobs they want to have when they grow up. Explore with them the information sources that have affected their plans. Compare your findings with those of other class members.
4. Visit an elementary school that has implemented a career-education program. Observe the students in a career-related activity and interview a teacher and a counselor regarding their opinions of the effectiveness of the program.
5. Select an activity designed to improve the career awareness of children from either Norris (1969), the journal *Elementary School Guidance and Counseling,* or another resource and complete it with a group of children. Make an oral or written report on your activity.

CHAPTER SEVEN

CAREER UNDERSTANDING: RESOURCES AND STRATEGIES

THE UNDERSTANDING STAGE

As children move from elementary school to junior high or middle school, they refine and strengthen the basic cognitive and manual skills acquired at an earlier age. They are involved in the task of becoming a person independent of their peers and families. The task of sorting out who they are in relation to others reflects the significant emphasis on transition during these years. The transition from childhood to adulthood is reflected in increased demands from home and school. During the transition from acquiring broad skills and knowledge in elementary school to preparing for the more specialized skills to be acquired in senior high school, the child finds that activities in school more clearly represent "real work." The relationship between school and work takes on new significance as the person begins to recognize that decisions about curriculum choice will affect later educational and occupational levels (Katz, 1963).

As part of this activity of separating self from others, individuals begin to look more specifically at their own abilities, interests, and personalities. Improved awareness and ability to conceptualize the broad structure of work and increased exposure to occupations allow youngsters to begin viewing occupations as specific entities (Edwards, Nafziger, & Holland, 1974). The process of differentiation among occupations permits a more accurate comparison of self to work and becomes the basis of the individual's making tentative choices about preferred later work activities.

As the child matures, the basis of decision making moves from interest to capacity to a consideration of needs, interest, capacities, values, and opportunities taken together (Super, 1953). Choices that were very tentative become more realistic as time progresses and as the youngster becomes more aware of self and environment.

Certain decisions may be more significant than others during this time. For example, a decision to enter a vocational-technical high school rather than an academic high school program generally has more long-term career implications than a selection of consumer math over algebra in the ninth grade. However, the decision to take consumer math may expose the student to the teacher whose presentation of consumer issues inspires the student to view consumer law or consumer relations as a potential future occupational choice. As counselors, we must be cautious to remain flexible and open toward such decisions. While we may make general statements about the significance of certain decisions, we must consider the unique characteristics of the individual to whom those decisions relate before prognosticating about their impact.

While some decisions may seem more significant than others, it is important to remember that all career-related decisions contribute to shaping the individual's career. Decision making, in this context, is viewed not as a single decision to enter a certain field of work but as a continuum of choices made over time that ultimately define the career.

During the periods of differentiation and decision making, individuals become more dependent on career material that supplies detail to their broad concepts about work. Exposure to part-time work, such as newspaper routes or baby-sitting, provides concrete exposure to and information about work. Having a newspaper route, for example, exposes a youngster to specific tasks and information that relate to bookkeeping, sales, and public relations. It requires the development of skills such as planning, punctuality, and politeness and may encourage attitudes such as responsibility and respect for work and money.

Performing regular chores in the home or assisting Mom and Dad with household tasks provides another avenue for gaining specific information, attitudes, and skills that relate to later decision making. For example, helping Dad build a porch provides significant exposure to many of the tasks of carpentry. Helping Mom start flowers indoors and later plant them in the garden provides considerable information that relates to the occupation of greenhouse worker.

Observing the parents' behavior while working or when discussing work yields information regarding their attitudes about work. Modeling parental behavior, an effective means by which children learn, is a significant resource and one of which counselors must be cognizant. Parental attitudes of dissatisfaction, boredom, or competitiveness regarding work are transmitted as readily as attitudes regarding their satisfaction, enthusiasm, and cooperation.

RESOURCES AND STRATEGIES FOR UNDERSTANDING

A variety of career information resources is available for assisting individuals to differentiate among occupations and to begin the process of career decision making. Resources include government publications, particularly the *Dictionary of Occupational Titles* (DOT) (U.S. Department of Labor, 1965, 1977) and the *Occupational Outlook Handbook* (U.S. Department of Labor, 1978). The DOT provides descriptions of thousands of individual occupational titles and provides classifications that organize occupations in useful ways. The *Handbook* disseminates information about job duties and trends in approximately 800 occupations. Dozens of commercial publications also carry job-related information. The last ten years have also seen the development of innovative simulation experiences designed to supply career information and facilitate career decision making. These methods include computer simulations of career counseling, kits that simulate various occupations, and games that provide occupational information and simulated exposure to career decisions. There is also a variety of audiovisual modalities for conveying career information appropriate to the career-understanding stage.

The United States government, through the Department of Labor, has an intensive interest in providing accurate, current, and comprehensive career information for the purposes of career counseling and guidance. For more than 30 years the Labor Department's Bureau of Labor Statistics has conducted research and provided extensive information about occupations and industries. Two major products of this effort are the *Dictionary of Occupational Titles* and the *Occupational Outlook Handbook.*

Dictionary of Occupational Titles

The *Dictionary of Occupational Titles,* commonly referred to as the DOT, is a significant career-counseling tool. There is a Canadian counterpart of the DOT entitled the *Canadian Classification and Dictionary of Occupations.* The DOT does not provide certain kinds of information available in the *Occupational Outlook Handbook,* such as the employment outlook, places of employment, advancement tracks, earnings, and similar information for 800 or so *major* occupations. It does contain information not available in the *Handbook* or from any other source, such as definitions of more than 20,000 occupations and occupational classifications that group occupations by fields of work and on the basis of worker qualifications. Because it provides general descriptions of practically *every* occupation in North America, the DOT is a very useful tool for career counselors.

Four editions of the DOT have been published. The first edition, published in 1939 and revised in 1949, is currently outdated and of limited utility in career counseling. The third edition of the DOT, published in 1965, and the fourth edition, published in 1977, will both be discussed extensively as valuable tools in current use. The third edition contains particulars not yet available in the fourth regarding the qualifications of workers in specific occupations. Pending publication of a supplement, now in preparation, the fourth edition is not currently as useful as the third for purposes of job-placement activities. It is also very likely that many counselors will not have access to all components of the fourth edition, particularly the *Guide for Occupational Exploration* (U.S. Department of Labor, 1979a), published late in 1979.

The third edition

The third edition of the DOT consists of Volume I, *Definitions of Titles;* Volume II, *Occupational Classification;* and two supplements. Volume I is an alphabetical listing of 21,741 separate occupations with brief descriptions. Volume II classifies these occupations by nature of the work (Occupational Group Arrangement) and by requirements of the workers (Worker Trait Arrangement) according to assigned six-digit codes. The supplements to the third edition list the types of physical demands, working conditions, and training time for each occupation defined in Volume I.

Volume I: Definitions of Titles. All 21,741 separate occupations in Volume I are arranged in alphabetical order. Alternate titles, other names by which the occupations are known, are included in alphabetical order along with the base titles. There are 13,809 alternate titles, bringing the total number of occupations defined to 35,550. The job titles are alphabetically arranged on the basis of a letter system—the entire title, regardless of number of words, is considered as one word for purposes of alphabetizing. For the most part, titles are worded as they are commonly used, except in cases where they have been inverted so that a distinguishing word can be used to form the alphabetical guide. This inversion has taken place when (1) the same base word can be used for discriminating among several related occupations (a spray painter would be listed as *painter, spray*), (2) titles of jobs are followed by modifiers that qualify them according to rank, size, color, and so on (a second baker would be listed as *baker, second*), or (3) arbitrary modifiers have been used to distinguish one occupation from another (a flower salesperson is listed as *salesperson, flower*). Since many of the titles have been inverted, inexperienced users often have difficulty locating certain titles.

In addition to the definition, each listing in the DOT includes the industry to which the occupation belongs and a six-digit DOT code. It may include an alternate title. The definition of *architect* from Volume I appears as Figure 7-1 for illustrative purposes. In this definition, *architect* is the main job title; *profess. & kin.* (professional and kindred) is the industrial designation; *001.081* is the occupational code; and the remainder of the entry, which describes the occupation, is the definition.

The industrial designation indicates which of 229 industries is the usual industrial location of the occupation. In general it follows the designations in the *Standard Industrial Classification Manual* (U.S. Executive Office of the President, 1972). Each occupation is assigned one or more industrial designations, except that, if an occupation is one of a group that occurs in several industries and retains its nature, it keeps its own designation. Clerical and professional occupations are examples of exceptions: regardless of the industry in which clerical and professional persons work, their industrial designations in the DOT

ARCHITECT (profess. & kin.) 001.081.
Plans and designs private residences, office
buildings, theaters, public buildings, factories,
and other structures, and organizes services
necessary for construction: Consults with
client to determine size and space requirements, and provides information regarding
cost, design, materials, equipment, and estimated building time. Plans layout of project,
and integrates structural, mechanical, and
ornamental elements into unified design. Prepares sketches of proposed project for client.
Writes specifications, and prepares scale and
full size drawings and other contract documents for use of building contractors and
craftsmen. May specialize in a particular type
of structure or project. May confer with other
consultants to develop feasibility studies, financial analyses and arrangements, site selection, and land assembly.

FIGURE 7-1. Sample definition from the *Dictionary of Occupational Titles
(3rd ed.), Volume I: Definition of Titles. (U.S. Department of Labor, Washington, D.C.: U.S. Government Printing Office, 1965.)*

remain *clerical* and *professional,* respectively. When the number of industries in
which an occupation occurs is too large to be conveniently listed, the occupation
is assigned the designation *any ind.* (any industry). A tractor-trailer truck driver is
an example of such an occupation.

The occupational code consists of a group of six digits. The code relates each
occupation to the two major classifications in Volume II. The three digits preceding the decimal point (001. in *architect*) identify the occupation and relate it
to similar ones by the type of work done (Occupational Group Arrangement).
The last three digits (.081 in *architect*) identify the occupation and relate it to
similar ones by the level of complexity of what the worker does in relation to
data, people, and things (Worker Trait Arrangement). The occupational codes
and related classification systems will be discussed further in the section entitled
"Volume II: *Occupational Classification.*"

The body of the definition usually consists of two or three parts: a lead
statement, a number of task-element statements, and a "may" item. The first
sentence in the definition, followed by a colon (:), is the lead statement. It offers
the user essential information in an overview of the occupation. Read the lead
statement in *architect.*

The task-element statements indicate the specific tasks that the worker performs in completing the overall job described in the lead statement. These
statements begin with action verbs and usually describe what the workers in the
occupation do, how they do it, and why they do it. Reread the definition of
architect and note the manner in which the task-element statements describe the
what, how, and *why* information.

Many definitions include one or more sentences beginning with the word *may*. They describe duties required by some employers but not by others. Note the "may" items in the definition of *architect*.

Volume II: Occupational Classification.   All occupations defined in Volume I have been incorporated into two classification systems. The Occupational Group Arrangement classifies occupations on the basis of the type of work done. The Worker Trait Arrangement classifies occupations on the basis of the requirements of the occupation for the worker. The six-digit code assigned to all occupations allows the user to identify where in each of the two classifications a specific occupation fits.

In the Occupational Group Arrangement, occupations are classified according to one or more of the following: the purpose of the worker action; the materials, products, subject matter, and services produced *or* used; the industry and/or field of work. The first three digits of the code reflect this arrangement. All occupations are grouped into one of nine broad "categories" (first digit), which then break up into 84 separate "divisions" (first two digits). These divisions, in turn, separate into 603 homogeneous "groups" (first three digits).

The nine occupational categories, as reflected in the first digit of the occupational code, are:

0 1	Professional, technical, and managerial occupations
2	Clerical and sales occupations
3	Service occupations
4	Farming, fishing, forestry, and related occupations
5	Processing occupations
6	Machine trade occupations
7	Bench work occupations
8	Structural work occupations
9	Miscellaneous occupations

The two-digit divisions into which the category 0/1 is broken up are shown below.

00 01	Occupations in architecture and engineering
02	Occupations in mathematics and physical sciences
04	Occupations in life sciences
05	Occupations in social sciences
07	Occupations in medicine and health
09	Occupations in education
10	Occupations in museum, library, and archival sciences
11	Occupations in law and jurisprudence

12   Occupations in religion and theology
13   Occupations in writing
14   Occupations in art
15   Occupations in entertainment and recreation
16   Occupations in administrative specializations
18   Managers and officials, n.e.c.[1]
19   Miscellaneous professional, technical, and managerial occupations

The three-digit groups into which the division 00/01 (occupations in architecture and engineering) is subdivided are as follow.

00
01   Occupations in architecture and engineering

001. Architectural occupations (Architecture)
002. Aeronautical engineering occupations (Aeronautical engineering)
003. Electrical engineering occupations (Electrical engineering)
005. Civil engineering occupations (Civil engineering)
006. Ceramic engineering occupations (Ceramic engineering)
007. Mechanical engineering occupations (Mechanical engineering)
008. Chemical engineering occupations (Chemical engineering)
010. Mining and petroleum engineering occupations (Mining and petroleum engineering)
011. Metallurgy and metallurgical engineering occupations (Metallurgy and metallurgical engineering)
012. Industrial engineering occupations (Industrial engineering)
013. Agricultural engineering occupations (Agricultural engineering)
014. Marine engineering occupations (Marine engineering)
015. Nuclear engineering occupations (Nuclear engineering)
017. Draftsmen, n.e.c. (Drafting and related work)
018. Surveyors, n.e.c. (Surveying and related work)
019. Occupations in architecture and engineering, n.e.c. (Architecture and engineering, n.e.c.)

Note that *architect,* with an initial three-digit code of 001, belongs in the professional, technical, and managerial category (0/1); the architecture and engineering division (00/01); and the architectural occupations group (001). The occupational categories, divisions, and groups shown can all be found on page 1 of Volume II of the third edition of the DOT.

The Occupational Group Arrangement, beginning on page 33 and extending through page 213 in Volume II, not only classifies all occupations within their specific group but also provides definitions of each of the nine categories, 84

[1] The abbreviation *n.e.c.* means *not elsewhere classified.*

00 OCCUPATIONS IN ARCHI-
TECTURE AND ENGINEER-
ING

This division includes occupations concerned with the practical application of physical laws and principles of engineering and/or architecture for the development and utilization of machines, materials, instruments, structures, processes, and services. Typical specializations are research, design, construction, testing, procurement, production, operations, and sales. Also includes preparation of drawings, specifications, and cost estimates, and participation in verification tests.

001. **Architectural Occupations**

This group includes occupations concerned with the design and construction of buildings and related structures, and/or floating structures, according to aesthetic and functional factors.

001.081 ARCHITECT (profess. & kin.)
ARCHITECT, MARINE (profess. & kin.)

architect, naval
naval designer

001.168 SCHOOL-PLANT CONSULTANT (education)

901.281 DRAFTSMAN, ARCHITECTURAL (profess. & kin.)

Draftsman, Tile and Marble (profess. & kin.)

FIGURE 7-2. Sample portion of the Occupational Group Arrangement from the *Dictionary of Occupational Titles (3rd ed.), Volume II: Occupational Classification. (U.S. Department of Labor, Washington, D.C.: U.S. Government Printing Office, 1965.)*

divisions, and 603 groups. Part of the first page of the Occupational Group Arrangement is reproduced in Figure 7-2.

Read the description of the division and the group and note that *architect* is included within this occupational group. In general, the occupations within the three-digit groups are arranged in decreasing order of complexity required in the performance of their duties. Note the position of *architect* within this group.

Since the Occupational Group Arrangement is an ordinal scale, the location of each occupation in this arrangement is as straightforward as counting once the code is located. Note the first three digits of *draftsman, architectural,* in the occupational group above. The 901 code, rather than an exception to the above rule, is a typographical error in the DOT. It should read 001.

The Worker Trait Arrangement is based on worker functions: the various abilities, traits, and other characteristics required of workers in carrying out occupational activities. The 114 unique worker-trait groups are indicated by the last three digits of the DOT code. This classification system assumes that each job requires the worker to be involved to some degree with data (information and/or instructions), people (the public, fellow workers, and/or supervisors), and things (equipment, products, and/or material). The fourth digit of the occupational code reflects the relationship of the occupation to data, the fifth to people, and the sixth to things.

The worker functions listed on page 649 in the third edition of the DOT are:

Data (4th digit)	*People* (5th digit)	*Things* (6th digit)
0 Synthesizing	0 Mentoring	0 Setting Up
1 Coordinating	1 Negotiating	1 Precision Working
2 Analyzing	2 Instructing	2 Operating—Controlling
3 Compiling	3 Supervising	3 Driving—Operating
4 Computing	4 Diverting	4 Manipulating
5 Copying	5 Persuading	5 Tending
6 Comparing	6 Speaking—Signaling	6 Feeding—Offbearing
7/8 No significant relationship	7 Serving	7 Handling
	8 No significant relationship	8 No significant relationship

The worker functions in each category are arranged in descending order of complexity: as the numbers increase, the levels of complexity within that category decrease. Each successive function, going from higher numbers to lower ones, assumes the ability to complete the simpler functions and excludes the more complex functions. Thus the last three digits of the occupational code for *architect* (.081) reflect an occupation that requires the highest level of complexity in working with data (synthesizing), the lowest level of complexity in working with people (no significant relationship), and a very high level of complexity in working with things (precision working). The most complex occupations would have a terminal three-digit code of .101 and the least complex code would terminate in .887 or .878. The .101 codes signify occupations in surgery; the .887 and .878 codes indicate manual-labor activities and personal-service work. Definitions of each of the levels in the data, people, and things categories are included in Appendix A of Volume II of the DOT (page 649).

While in theory there are more than 600 combinations into which the terminal three digits of the DOT code can be arranged, the third edition organizes them into fewer than 100 combinations. These combinations do not adequately express the complex relationships of a worker to data, people, and things, particularly since the code may reflect "no significant relationship" when in fact such a relationship may exist, even if on a low-frequency basis. As an example, let us look again at the terminal code for *architect,* which is .081. Although the 8 denotes "no significant relationship" with people, we know that architects normally do meet with clients to confer about their designs. Fortunately, this problem of ambiguities has been greatly reduced in the fourth edition of the DOT.

The last three digits have been organized into 114 worker-trait groups, which are included in the Worker Traits Arrangement under 22 broad areas of work (DOT, Volume II, page 214): Art; Business Relations; Clerical Work; Counseling, Guidance, and Social Work; Crafts; Education and Training; Elemental Work; Engineering; Entertainment; Farming, Fishing, and Forestry; Investigating, Inspecting, and Testing; Law and Law Enforcement; Machine Work; Managerial and Supervisory Work; Mathematics and Science; Medicine and Health; Merchandising; Music; Personal Service; Photography and Communications; Transportation; and Writing.

The titles of the areas are the guide to locating the specific worker-trait groups. For example, one might correctly surmise that *architect* would be included under the area of *Engineering.* Within the 22 areas there is a varying number of worker-trait groups. The following is the list of worker-trait groups included under the area of *Engineering* (third edition, page 370):

Engineering

.081   Engineering Research and Design
.151   Sales Engineering
.168   Engineering, Scientific, and Technical Coordination
.181
.281   Drafting and Related Work

.181
.281   Technical Work, Engineering and Related Fields

.187   Engineering and Related Work
.188
.288   Industrial Engineering and Related Work

.188
.288   Surveying, Prospecting, and Related Work

.188
.288   Technical Writing and Related Work

Although each of these nine worker-trait groups falls under *Engineering,* the titles show that they are distinctly different groups. The small amount of variation in their terminal codes indicates the similarity of these groups in their relationships to data, people, and things and, therefore, in the requirements that they pose for workers. Note that, in general, the more complex occupations appear higher in the listing and the less complex appear lower. This arrangement is typical of all the groupings of worker-trait groups under areas of work.

Three of the worker-trait groups in this listing have identical final codes of .188/.288 and two have identical codes of .181/.281. This confusing duplication of terminal digits exists throughout the Worker Trait Arrangement. Identical codes indicate worker-trait groups that relate to data, people, and things at the same level of complexity, although in different fields.

In scanning the worker-trait groups under *Engineering* one may be unsure whether *architect* would be included under *Engineering Research and Design* or *Drafting and Related Work*. Remembering that the terminal code for *architect* is .081 points to the worker-trait group *Engineering Research and Design,* coded .081, as the correct choice.

For each of the worker-trait groups, a fact sheet briefly describes (1) the work performed, (2) the worker requirements, (3) clues for relating the applicants and requirements, and (4) training and methods of entry into the occupations included within the worker-trait group. A section entitled "Related Classifications" lists worker-trait groups similar to the worker-trait group being described. A "Qualifications Profile" that provides a general description of the qualifications required for average successful performance in the occupations making up the worker-trait group is also included. Figure 7-3 is a sample of the worker-trait group for *Engineering Research and Design.*

To decode the Qualifications Profile, refer to Appendix B in Volume II of the third-edition DOT (pp. 651 – 656). The profile suggests certain levels of attainment required in engineering research and design occupations within the worker-trait components of general educational development (GED), specific vocational preparation (SVP), aptitudes (Apt), interests (Int), temperament (Temp), and physical demands (Phys. Dem.). On the page or pages immediately following the fact sheet, all occupations included within each worker-trait group are arranged numerically according to their six-digit occupational codes. This arrangement by occupational group allows the user to compare occupations having similar worker requirements within and across specific fields of work.

In addition to the contents already described, Volume II contains other useful information, including an arrangement of DOT titles within different industries and a glossary defining many technical terms used in the definitions found in Volume I.

DOT supplements. The first supplement to the third edition is called *Selected Characteristics of Occupations (Physical Demands, Working Conditions, Training Time)* (U.S. Department of Labor, 1966). It contains selected information regarding all occupations defined in Volume I. The occupations are located by code numbers, which are listed in numerical order. To locate a specific job listing in the first supplement, the user must first locate the occupational code through Volume I or another source. The occupational information is

ENGINEERING RESEARCH AND DESIGN
.081

Work Performed

Work activities in this group primarily involve using and adapting earth substances, properties of matter, natural sources of power, and physical forces to satisfy human needs and desires. Typically, workers are engaged in conducting analyses and experiments of materials and systems by application of known laws and relationships; in conceiving and designing new structures, machines, tools, precision instruments, and other devices; in devising and constructing cooling, heating, lighting, communication, transportation, and other productive systems; in developing the most practical forms of new techniques, processes, and products; in performing structural, functional, and compositional tests of materials and parts; and in preparing technical reports of investigations.

Worker Requirements

An occupationally significant combination of: Ability to learn and apply basic engineering principles and methods; good visual acuity with respect to graphic representations; creative talent or imagination; ability to perceive or visualize spatial relationships of plane and solid objects; logical mind; organizational ability; and facility in mathematics.

RELATED CLASSIFICATIONS

Sales Engineering (.151) p. 373
Engineering, Scientific, and Technical
  Coordination (.168) p. 375
Engineering and Related Work (.187)
  p. 381
Technical Work, Engineering and
  Related Fields (.181; .281) p. 379
Industrial Engineering and Related Work
  (.188; .288) p. 383
Drafting and Related Work (.181; .281)
  p. 377

Clues for Relating Applicants and Requirements

Level of attainment in language and mathematics as indicated by scores on aptitude tests and grades in educational courses.

Previous drawings or sketches produced, either freehand or mechanical.

Kind of literature read (whether scientifically or technically oriented).

Clear, coherent verbal expression.

Interest in scientific and technological developments.

Training and Methods of Entry

A bachelor's degree in engineering is usually the minimum educational requirement for entrance into this field. However, some draftsmen and engineering technicians having extensive experience together with some college-level training may qualify for entry.

Most employers require either advanced graduate degrees or significant experience on the basic engineering level for entry into research work.

Students interested in engineering should acquire a strong background in mathematics and the physical sciences.

QUALIFICATIONS PROFILE

GED: 6
SVP: 8 7

Apt:	GVN	SPQ	KFM	EC
	111	124	333	54
	22	23		

Int: 7 8
Temp: 4 0 Y
Phys. Dem: S L 4 6

FIGURE 7-3. Sample portion of the Worker Trait Arrangement from the *Dictionary of Occupational Titles (3rd ed.), Volume II: Occupational Classification. (U.S. Department of Labor, Washington, D.C.: U.S. Government Printing Office, 1965.)*

presented in seven columns: (1) DOT code number, (2) page number in Volume II for the worker-trait group in which the job appears, (3) industrial designation, (4) DOT job title, (5) physical demands, (6) working conditions, and (7) training time, including general educational development and specific vocational preparation. Information regarding physical demands, working conditions, and training time is provided through a coding system explained in three appendixes to the supplement. A description of training time and the scale for rating general educational development are reproduced in Chapter 8 of the present text.

In addition to providing specific information about selected occupational characteristics, the first supplement is useful in locating worker-trait groups in Volume II, since the appropriate page numbers are listed for each title in the DOT. Often it is more efficient to locate a worker-trait group through the first supplement than to use the areas-of-work method discussed earlier.

The second supplement to the third edition, *Selected Characteristics of Occupations by Worker Traits and Physical Strength* (U.S. Department of Labor, 1968), was published in 1968. It includes the same information in columnar form as does the 1966 supplement, except that the first two columns have been reversed. Entry into the second supplement is by page number of the worker-trait group in which the occupation appears in Volume II. Essentially, the supplements provide the user with specific information on selected characteristics for each job title in the DOT, as compared to the general information provided for a group of occupations through the qualifications profile from the worker-trait groups in Volume II.

The second supplement, organized by page references to worker-trait groups, facilitates the user's comparison of occupations with respect to their required physical demands, working conditions, and training time. This cross-referencing is particularly useful when the issue is a client's possible transferability from one occupation to another while retaining the fullest possible application of his or her occupationally significant characteristics, experience, and remaining functional capacity. For example, physical disability might prevent a worker from continuing in a job for which he or she is otherwise qualified; the counselor could identify potential occupations within the same worker-trait group as the worker's previous job. In other situations, the cross-reference may assist individuals in finding jobs that use the skills acquired on previous jobs; help in the transition from military to civilian jobs and vice versa; redirect workers displaced because of technological change; and guide decisions regarding the kind and extent of rehabilitation and retraining necessary. Both supplements caution that the information provided is based on a composite description of requirements through job analysis and that it does not prevent the same occupation from having different requirements in situations not studied.

The fourth edition

The fourth edition of the DOT, published in 1977, maintains the same basic structure as the third edition, with significant modifications to enhance its usefulness for counselors and others. Probably the most significant change in the 1977 edition is the updating of job-definition material. On the basis of more than

75,000 job analyses, 2100 new occupational definitions have been added and 3500 obsolete definitions deleted. All other job definitions have been verified or revised. Titles with age or sex referents have been eliminated. Other significant changes in the fourth edition have taken place in format, coding, and worker-trait-group structure.

Format. The fourth edition incorporates much of the occupational classification data from Volumes I and II of the third edition into a single volume. The resulting large volume includes chapters presenting instructions for use, occupational definitions listed by Occupational Group Arrangement, a glossary, an alphabetical index of occupational titles, a listing of occupational titles by industry designation, and an industry index. A supplement entitled *Guide for Occupational Exploration* is a drastic modification of the Worker Trait Arrangement of the third edition. Another supplement, similar to the supplements for the third edition, is currently in preparation and will be useful as a guide to careers for disabled workers.

The most significant change in format is that the Occupational Group Arrangement, which makes up more than 900 pages of the 1369-page document, now incorporates updated occupational definitions in addition to occupational titles. These definitions are organized by Occupational Group Arrangement and therefore by DOT numerical code in ascending order. Including definitions within the Occupational Group Arrangement provides a better integration of occupations with the occupational groups to which they belong, thus helping the user to identify closely related occupations. This format is most useful in gaining a broad perspective on the interrelationship of occupations and career ladders. It also serves as a guide to job transfers and advancements.

To appreciate the differences between the 1977 DOT and the third edition, compare the new Occupational Group structure in Figure 7-4 with the third edition's occupational definition of *architect* (Figure 7-1) and the third edition's Occupational Group Arrangement (Figure 7-2). In comparing the samples from the two editions, note the updating that has occurred in the definition of *architect*.

The alphabetical index of occupational titles is identical in format to the listing of occupations in Volume I of the third edition, except that it does not contain descriptions of the occupations. Since it provides DOT codes for the occupations listed, it facilitates the user's locating the title and definition desired in the Occupational Group Arrangement. Since the most frequently used materials are incorporated into a single volume, flipping between volumes is for most purposes eliminated. However, this reorganization is not without problems. Since the Occupational Group Arrangement now occurs before the alphabetical listing of occupations and also incorporates the definitions of occupations, users of the earlier editions may see it as organized backwards.

A new glossary provides definitions of technical terms, which are italicized in

00/01 OCCUPATIONS IN ARCHITECTURE, ENGINEERING, AND SURVEYING

This division includes occupations concerned with the practical application of physical laws and principles of engineering and/or architecture for the development and utilization of machines, materials, instruments, structures, processes, and services. Typical specializations are research, design, construction, testing, procurement, production, operations, and sales. Also includes preparation of drawings, specifications, and cost estimates, and participation in verification tests.

001 ARCHITECTURAL OCCUPATIONS

This group includes occupations concerned with the design and construction of buildings and related structures, or landscaping, and/or floating structures, according to aesthetic and functional factors.

001.061-010 ARCHITECT (profess. & kin.)

Provides professional services in research, development, design, construction, alteration, or repair of real property, such as private residences, office buildings, theaters, public buildings, or factories: Consults with client to determine functional and spatial requirements and prepares information regarding design, specifications, materials, equipment, estimated costs, and building time. Plans layout of project and integrates engineering elements into unified design. Prepares scale and full size drawings and contract documents for building contractors. Furnishes sample recommendations and shop drawing reviews to client. Assists client in obtaining bids and awarding construction contracts. Supervises administration of construction contracts and conducts periodic onsite observation of work in progress. May prepare operating and maintenance manuals, studies, and reports.

FIGURE 7-4. Sample portion of the Occupational Group Arrangement from the *Dictionary of Occupational Titles (4th ed.). (U.S. Department of Labor, Washington, D.C.: U.S. Government Printing Office, 1977.)*

DOT definitions, for easy identification of terms that may not be found in a standard dictionary.

Coding. In reading the fourth-edition entry for *architect* you may have noted a nine-digit DOT occupational code instead of a six-digit code. Updating of the DOT has resulted in the addition of the seventh, eighth, and ninth digits, significant modifications in the fourth, fifth, and sixth digits (Worker Trait Arrangement), and minor and infrequent modifications of the first three digits (Occupational Group Arrangement).

The final three-digit code, known as the suffix code, provides a unique code for each title. While certain occupational titles may have the same initial six-digit code, none will have the same suffix code. The full nine digits provide each occupation with an individualized code suitable for computerized operations. Note the suffix code for *architect*.

Due to a revision in the worker-function scale, an attempt to have the middle three-digit code reflect what the worker actually does, and the elimination of worker-trait groups based on this code, there are significant differences between the third and fourth editions in the second three-digit codes for most occupations. The revised worker-function scale, taken from page xviii of the fourth edition, is as follows:

Data (4th Digit)	*People* (5th Digit)	*Things* (6th Digit)
0 Synthesizing	0 Mentoring	0 Setting Up
1 Coordinating	1 Negotiating	1 Precision Working
2 Analyzing	2 Instructing	2 Operating—Controlling
3 Compiling	3 Supervising	3 Driving—Operating
4 Computing	4 Diverting	4 Manipulating
5 Copying	5 Persuading	5 Tending
6 Comparing	6 Speaking—Signaling	6 Feeding—Offbearing
	7 Serving	7 Handling
	8 Taking Instructions—Helping	

Note that there are no longer categories of "no significant relationship" at low levels of relationship to data, people, or things. Because all occupations relate to data, people, and things at some level, even if at low rates of frequency, the current worker-function scales more accurately reflect what workers do.

Since the third edition used fewer than 100 combinations from the worker-function scale for purposes of grouping occupations into worker-trait groups, the complexity of the relationships of workers to data, people, and things was inadequately expressed. In the fourth edition, relationships can be more accurately represented because worker-trait groups are not organized by the second three-digit code. Note the differences between the worker-function ratings (middle three digits) for *architect* in the third edition and in the fourth. The code of .061 more accurately reflects the relationship of *speaking* with people (clients), as compared with .081, which denotes "no significant relationship" with people. Also note the increased emphasis in the fourth-edition definition of *architect* as the work relates to people.

Worker-trait-group structure.   The Worker Trait Arrangement classification has been extensively revised and is the only major component of the third edition not currently included in the single volume of the fourth edition. Instead, it appears as a supplement entitled *Guide for Occupational Exploration* (U.S. Department of Labor, 1979a). In combination with the material included in the main volume, it is useful as a counseling tool for occupational exploration and understanding. Because of its simpler format and clearer instructions, it can more easily be used by clients than the worker-trait groups in the third edition.

The revised *Guide* continues the useful organization of information around a worker rather than a product or industry. The bases for the work groups are also similar to those in the third edition; that is, occupations in each work group include workers with similar qualifications. More specifically, the groups are based on the following types of worker qualifications: (1) level of development in language and mathematics (General Educational Development), (2) amount of specific training related to the occupation (Specific Vocational Preparation), (3) types of activities preferred by workers (Interests), (4) ability to adjust to different types of working situations (Temperament), (5) aptitude levels, (6) physical capacities, and (7) level of complexity required of the worker in relation to data, people, and things.

The *Guide for Occupational Exploration* organizes 66 work groups within 12 interest areas. Each work group may contain from one to 32 subgroups. In addition it contains an index, which assigns each occupation included in the fourth edition to one of the 348 subgroups. This index is particularly helpful when clients desire general information about the requirements of a specific occupation and other occupations related to it. The 12 interest areas correspond to interest factors that were identified through research in interest measurement by Droege and Hawk (1977). The interest areas and their two-digit code numbers are:

01. Artistic
02. Scientific
03. Plants and Animals
04. Protective
05. Mechanical
06. Industrial
07. Business Detail
08. Selling
09. Accommodating
10. Humanitarian
11. Leading/Influencing
12. Physical Performing

Within each career area there are varying numbers of work groups. In general, the work groups listed first usually require the most education, training, and experience. The worker groups included in career area 05., *Mechanical,* follow. Note their four-digit identifying codes.

05.01 Engineering
05.02 Managerial Work: Mechanical
05.03 Engineering Technology
05.04 Air and Water Vehicle Operation
05.05 Craft Technology
05.06 Systems Operation

05.07 Quality Control
05.08 Land and Water Vehicle Operation
05.09 Materials Control
05.10 Crafts
05.11 Equipment Operation
05.12 Elemental Work: Mechanical

Each work group contains two major parts: a description of the group and a list of sample occupations within the group, organized within subgroupings. Each subgroup has its unique six-digit code and title. Within each subgroup specific occupations are arranged in clusters by the industry in which they are located. The reduced number of worker-trait groups from 114 in the third edition to 66 in the fourth means that the fourth edition provides less specific information than the third. The orientation toward more general information, step-by-step instructions, and the simplified format make this *Guide* a helpful tool for clients to use in exploring occupations. It does have the drawback of being more limited for use by counselors in direct job placement activities, particularly when transferability of skills is involved, primarily because it does not provide a qualification profile.

A forthcoming supplement to the fourth-edition DOT should be more useful for purposes of job placement. A publication that should be similar to this supplement, entitled *The Classification of Jobs According to Worker Trait Factors,* is currently available (Field & Field, 1980). This publication contains four classifications:

Section 1: Profiles of Jobs by Worker Trait Factors Arranged by DOT Code.
Section 2: Jobs Arranged by Guide for Occupational Exploration (GOE) Code.
Section 3: Jobs Arranged by Data/People/Things Code.
Section 4: Group Profiles by Worker Trait Groups on General Educational Development, Specific Vocational Preparation, and Aptitudes.

The first section of this publication organizes information in a manner similar to that of the supplements to the 1966 DOT. Both provide information regarding the physical demands, working conditions, and training time required of workers in all occupations included in their respective editions. However, the publication also provides information regarding the aptitudes, temperaments, and interests required of workers in different occupations. This updated information is similar to that previously included in the Qualifications Profiles of the Worker Trait Group in the 1966 DOT, except that the information previously supplied for groups of occupations is now specific to each occupational title.

This definitive information allows for the comparison between the assessed characteristics of individuals and the requirements of jobs. Comparisons should be made cautiously, however, because the worker-trait requirements in this classification are frequently based on estimates and because considerable variance in these data may exist from job to job within the same occupation. Another major difficulty in such uses of worker-trait information is that assessment methods linking an individual's traits to occupational requirements have not yet been adequately developed. This difficulty exists because the same concepts are rarely used to describe and assess occupational trait requirements and individual characteristics (Droege & Padgett, 1979). The United States Employment Service (USES) is attempting to overcome the problem by developing instruments such as the USES Interest Inventory (Droege & Hawk, 1977), which measures 12 interest factors corresponding to the 12 interest areas in the *Guide for Occupational Exploration*. Unfortunately, these interest factors are not the same ones to be included in the new addendum. The General Aptitude Test Battery, an assessment tool that has long been in service, does directly correspond to the aptitude requirements presented in the addendum.

The remaining three classifications in the addendum are totally new. One classification arranges occupations by *Guide for Occupational Exploration* (GOE) code and provides information such as the DOT code, job title, and the data/people/things code for all sedentary and light occupations. This information allows the user the opportunity to locate sedentary and light jobs that are related to each other by similarities on dimensions such as job activities performed and worker requirements.

Another classification that arranges all sedentary and light jobs by the data/people/things codes allows the user to compare the various trait requirements for occupations requiring similar levels of interaction with data, people, and things. This information can provide a potentially useful approach to the transferability of skills between related work groups.

A third classification organizes sedentary and light jobs by the 66 worker groups in the *Guide for Occupational Exploration* and provides mean data on training time and aptitude requirements for each group. This global information may be useful in assisting clients who are interested in exploring the training and aptitude requirements of different work groups or in comparing the requirements of work groups to those in which they have been employed.

Perhaps the greatest utility of the information in these classifications is the contribution they make to understanding the vocational history of individuals who have been employed, since they provide a general idea of the requirements of the jobs in which people are or have been employed. Assuming that individuals can perform the same or similar requirements in future jobs allows counselors to assist them in locating other jobs for which they may be qualified. Assisting in the transfer of skills from one occupation to another is potentially most useful with experienced workers who have become handicapped and/or unemployed. Counselors-in-training are encouraged to locate and become familiar with this addendum.

Occupational Outlook Handbook

The *Occupational Outlook Handbook* contains information about job duties, places of employment, educational and other requirements, advancement, employment outlook, earnings, working conditions, and sources of further information for more than 850 occupations and 35 industries. This information is provided through 300 occupational briefs, grouped into 13 clusters of related jobs, and 35 industry briefs. The occupations described account for about 95% of salesworkers; 90% of professional, craft, and service workers; 80% of clerical workers; 50% of machine operators; and smaller proportions of managers and laborers. Although the information from the *Handbook* is generally the most detailed available for the occupations included, it may be necessary to use the *Dictionary of Occupational Titles* for descriptions of occupations not included in the *Handbook.*

The organization of the occupational briefs into 13 clusters facilitates the review of a variety of jobs in a specific field. A review of any single cluster allows the individual to review a large number of occupations within a specific field of interest whose training and skill requirements are at varying levels. This organization improves an individual's understanding of the work world, as well as permitting a person to study future occupational opportunities within selected fields.

In addition to the occupational and industrial descriptions, the *Handbook* includes four introductory chapters, which act as a guide to the *Handbook.* These chapters also provide sources of further career information and projections about tomorrow's jobs. They are an invaluable resource for counselors and clients who wish to remain current regarding employment and related trends. In combination with the Employment Outlook sections related to each of the 300 occupational and industrial briefs, they represent the most current information available on future job opportunities. The information in the *Handbook* about the requirements of occupations, nature of the work, and the employment environments allows individuals to compare occupational characteristics and requirements to personal strengths, limitations, and interests. The additional information concerning the availability of jobs affords significant input to individuals who are in the process of career decision making.

The occupational brief for electrotypers and stereotypers shown in Figure 7-5 illustrates the content of the *Handbook.* This brief is one of the shorter of the 300 briefs included in the *Handbook* and does not contain the detailed data available in many of the longer briefs.

To facilitate its use the *Handbook* contains a number of indexes. In addition to an index organized alphabetically by occupation and industry, the *Handbook* provides a DOT index, which lists *Handbook* occupations by DOT code number. This index is included because career-information centers and libraries frequently use DOT codes for filing occupational information. It also facilitates

ELECTROTYPERS AND STEREOTYPERS

Nature of the Work

Electrotypers (D.O.T. 974.381) and *stereotypers* (D.O.T. 975.782) make duplicate press plates of metal, rubber, and plastic for letterpress printing. These plates are made from the metal type forms prepared in the composing room. Electrotypes are used mainly in book and magazine work. Stereotypes, which are less durable, are used chiefly for newspapers. Electrotyping and stereotyping are necessary because most volume printing requires the use of duplicate plates. When a large edition of a magazine or newspaper is printed, several plates must be used to replace those that become too worn to make clear impressions. Also, by having duplicate plates, printers can use several presses at the same time and finish a big run quickly. Furthermore, many big plants use rotary presses, which require curved plates made by either electrotyping or stereotyping from flat type forms.

Electrotypers make a wax or plastic mold of the metal type form. They then coat the mold with chemicals and place the mold into an electrolytic bath that puts a metallic shell on the coated mold. Electrotypers then strip the shell from the mold and fill the back of the shell with molten lead to form a plate. After removing excess metal from the edges and back of the plate, electrotypers inspect the plate for any defects.

The stereotyping process is simpler, quicker, and less expensive than electrotyping, but it does not yield as durable or as fine a plate. Stereotypers make molds or mats of papier-mache instead of wax or plastic. The mat is placed on the type form and covered with a cork blanket and a sheet of fiberboard. The covered form is run under heavy steel rollers to impress the type and photoengravings on the mat. Then the mat is placed in a stereotype casting machine which casts a composition lead plate on the mold. In many of the larger plants, automatic machines cast stereotype plates.

Some electrotypers and stereotypers do only one phase of the work, such as casting, molding, or finishing. Others handle many tasks.

Places of Employment

About 4,000 electrotypers and stereotypers were employed in 1976. Many electrotypers work in large plants that print books and magazines. Most stereotypers work for newspaper plants, but some work in large commercial printing plants. Electrotypers and stereotypers also are employed in service shops that do this work for printing firms.

Jobs in these trades can be found throughout the country, but employment is concentrated in large cities.

Training and Other Qualifications

Nearly all electrotypers and stereotypers learn their trades through 5- to 6-year apprenticeships. Electrotyping and stereotyping are separate crafts and relatively few transfers take place between the two. The apprenticeship program of each trade covers all phases of the work and almost always includes classes in related technical subjects as well as training on the job.

Apprenticeship applicants must be at least 18 years of age and, in most instances be able to pass physical examinations that usually are given to prospective apprentices. Due to the decline in demand for electrotypers and stereotypers, however, very few apprenticeships have been offered in the last several years. Many experienced electroplaters and stereotypers are now being retrained as plate makers in offset and press operators.

Employment Outlook

Job opportunities for electrotypers and stereotypers are expected to be scarce through the mid-1980's. Despite the anticipated increase in the volume of printing, employment of electrotypers and stereotypers is expected to decline because of labor-saving developments. For example, automatic plate casting eliminates many steps in platemaking. The use of plastic printing plates also requires less labor because such plates are more durable and reduce the demand for duplicate plates. Furthermore, the greater use of offset printing reduces the need for electrotype and stereotype plates, which are not needed in offset printing.

Earnings and Working Conditions

Based on a union wage survey, it is estimated that in 1976, union minimum wage rates in 69 large cities averaged $7.23 an hour for electrotypers and $7.88 an hour for stereotypers in book and commercial printing shops. Both averages were considerably higher than the average for all nonsupervisory workers in private industry, except farming.

Much of the work in these trades requires little physical effort since the preparation of duplicate printing plates is highly mechanized. However, some lifting of relatively heavy press plates occasionally is required.

Nearly all electrotypers and stereotypers are members of the International Printing and Graphic Communications Union.

Sources of Additional Information

Details about apprenticeship and other training opportunities may be obtained from local employers, such as newspapers and printing shops, the local office of the International Printing and Graphic Communications Union, or the local office of the State employment service.

For general information on electrotypers and stereotypers, write to:

American Newspaper Publishers Association, 11600 Sunrise Valley Dr., Reston, Va. 20041.

Graphic Arts Technical Foundation, 4615 Forbes Ave., Pittsburgh, Pa. 15213.

International Printing and Graphic Communications Union, 1730 Rhode Island Ave. NW., Washington, D.C. 20036.

Printing Industries of America, Inc., 1730 N. Lynn St., Arlington, Va. 22209.

FIGURE 7-5. Sample occupational brief from the *Occupational Outlook Handbook (U.S. Department of Labor, Washington, D.C.: U.S. Government Printing Office, 1978.)*

locating an occupational brief in the *Handbook* after using the DOT to locate an occupation and writing down its DOT number.

Since the *Handbook* is revised every two years and since much of the data is acquired through extensive, large-sample research by the Bureau of Labor Statistics, the *Handbook* is the most current and accurate occupational-information resource available. In fact, the *Handbook* is suggested as the criterion for determining the accuracy of other sources of occupational information (Isaacson, 1977, p. 361). While its projections regarding employment outlook have generally been shown to be valid, they should not be viewed as factual; they are based in part on assumptions about future conditions such as energy supply, avoidance of war, or reduced unemployment that may prove false.

In our opinion, the *Handbook* is the most useful career-information resource available for counseling persons who wish to understand themselves in relation to work. It is particularly attractive because of its low cost ($8.00 in 1979) in comparison with commercially developed resources.

To supplement the use of the *Handbook* for career counseling, the Department of Labor provides other materials and services. For example, all sections of the *Handbook* are available as low-cost reprints. Individuals may thus review information about the occupations and industries in which they are interested without carrying around the complete *Handbook,* which is more than 800 pages long.

The *Occupational Outlook Quarterly* (U.S. Department of Labor, 1980) is designed to keep readers current regarding occupational and industrial information, particularly trends. It complements the *Handbook* by including articles on matters such as summer jobs for students, problems of older and female workers, and related topics. The *Occupational Outlook for College Graduates* (U.S. Department of Labor, 1979b) is an abridged form of the *Handbook* appropriate to the named population. These publications and other low-cost occupational resources available from the federal government are described in the last few pages of the *Handbook*.

The DOT and *Handbook* as career-counseling tools

The DOT and *Occupational Outlook Handbook* are significant career-counseling tools. The DOT is the most comprehensive source of information about individual occupations currently available. It also provides two useful systems for organizing information about occupations. The *Handbook* furnishes information regarding employment trends, working conditions, and other information for major industries and occupations. While significant resources, these tools cannot supply career counselors with all the information they need. For example, the DOT and *Handbook* do not contain information about sources and locations of educational and vocational preparation for careers such as is found in college or vocational-school guides. They do not identify local sources of information that may be necessary for entry into an occupational field. However, even without a multitude of other resources, the DOT and *Handbook* can provide counselors and clients with a significant means of improving their occupational knowledge.

For example, the definitions in Volume I of the third edition and in the Occupational Group Arrangement of the fourth edition can be useful in assisting clients to understand the tasks required of workers in various occupations. This awareness may be most helpful to them while they are in the process of exploring preferred occupations prior to studying them in more depth, either through further reading of the *Handbook* and other materials, observing and interviewing workers, or other means. The definitions can also be helpful in assisting clients to recall the tasks that they have performed in previous jobs and may facilitate client recognition of strengths that relate to other jobs.

The Occupational Group Arrangement in both the 1965 and 1977 editions can be valuable in aiding clients to understand the relationships between individual occupations and groups of occupations. Because occupational groups adjacent to one another are more similar with respect to the tasks involved than occupational groups disparate from one another, the user can identify closely related occupational groups by the tasks the jobs entail. Within each occupational group, occupations are listed in decreasing order of complexity, with occupations requiring most education and experience listed first. While this arrangement provides useful information to the never-employed client who is interested in exploring the relationships among occupations of interest, it is perhaps most helpful to clients with previous work experience. By locating occupations in which they have had prior training and/or experience within an occupational-group arrangement, they are able to find other occupations with similar tasks to which their previous strengths as workers are optimally transferable. Because the worker groups and occupations within the Worker Trait Arrangement of the third edition and the *Guide for Occupational Exploration* of the fourth are arranged in similar fashion, the above procedures can also be used with these classification systems.

The worker-function scales in both editions can provide general information to users on the relative demands of occupations with respect to data, people, and things. Clients who prefer occupations demanding more in one area than in another can locate information about occupational options that match their preferences by using either the data/people/things codes assigned each occupation in both editions or the codes related to the worker-trait groups in the third edition. The organization of similar occupations by their relationships to data, people, and things in the Worker Trait Arrangement of the third edition makes it easier to use for this purpose. Reading the definitions and the information provided in the worker-trait groups enables the user to learn more about preferred occupations.

For detailed information regarding worker requirements such as the aptitudes, interests, preparation, and physical demands of occupations or groups of occupations, users may refer to the worker-trait groups in the third edition and work groups in the fourth. While the information in the third is more detailed and specific and is, in general, more appropriate for placement purposes, the information in the fourth edition has the advantage of being more current and more easily used and understood by clients. Its organization by interest areas helps clients identify and explore occupations in which they have the most interest. The organization of the worker-trait groups in the third edition by the three-digit data/people/things code helps clients locate and investigate occupations that relate most to their preferences of working with either data, people, or things. By exploring these groups and the occupations within them, clients can determine if one or more appear to suit their interests and qualifications better than others.

When the supplement to the fourth-edition DOT is published, there will no longer be any advantage to using the third edition for the majority of purposes, except perhaps to locate obsolete DOT titles when completing a client's vocational history or relating DOT titles to an assessment instrument such as the Ohio Vocational Interest Survey or Jewish Employment and Vocational Service work-sample system. The proposed supplement, which will contain detailed information about worker requirements for occupations now covered in the supplements and Worker Trait Arrangement of the third edition, will provide more current and usable information. An appropriate substitute for that supplement, *The Classification of Jobs According to Worker Trait Factors* (Field & Field, 1980), is currently available and is recommended. Except in cases where the user does not have the Field & Field or similar substitute, and has a need for specific data about occupational requirements, the fourth edition is definitely preferred and should be used.

The utility of the DOT, *Handbook,* or other tool is obviously dependent on the nature of clients' situations. Lacking information about jobs, clients will generally benefit from counseling methods designed to provide them with information. Clients whose problems extend beyond a lack of information will need other resources and methods.

Clients in need of expanded career knowledge may have a variety of difficulties for which they seek assistance. Some may be totally undecided and uninformed regarding career directions. Others may have several general areas in which they have knowledge and interest, but little more than that. Still others may be generally well informed about many occupations but undecided among a few areas and may wish assistance in deciding. The DOT and *Handbook* can be useful in assisting with a great number of career-counseling situations when there is a need for improved knowledge about occupations and the structure of the work world. For the counselor to help, he or she must have a "hands-on" knowledge of the contents of the DOT and *Handbook.* An understanding of the organization of the DOT and *Handbook* contents is essential prior to guiding clients in its use.

A process that can be useful in helping clients to expand their information about occupations and to start thinking of possible choices is presented below. It can be applied in a group or individual context, but each client's unique needs should be considered. Recognize that some clients may need more time than others in proceeding through the steps. Either the third or the fourth edition of the DOT may be used, but because of its updated occupational definitions the fourth (most recent) edition of the DOT and its supplements are recommended. The same is true for the *Handbook.*

1. Locate the summary listing of occupational categories, divisions, and groups found in the early pages of the Occupational Group Arrangement (pages 1–24 in Volume II of the third edition or pages xxxiv–xli in the fourth edition).

2. Ask clients to select from this listing and write down the names of categories of work (page 1 in the third edition; page xxxiv in the fourth) in which they have some interest.

3. Request that for their categories of interest they read the definitions found in the Occupational Group Arrangement itself (pages 33–213 in the third edition; pages 15–946 in the fourth) rather than the summary listing. Categories are arranged in ascending numerical order by the first digit of the occupational code.

4. Ask the clients to scan the occupational divisions listed in the summary listing (pages 1–2 in the third edition; pages xxxiv–xxxv in the fourth). Have

them select and write down the names of those occupational divisions in which they have some interest. Do not restrict the clients to selecting divisions from the categories they had previously selected. If the clients express interest in occupational divisions that were not subsumed under a previously chosen category, ask them to write down the names of newly selected categories.

5. Request that the clients read the definitions of the occupational divisions in which they expressed interest. These definitions are part of the Occupational Group Arrangement itself (pages 33 – 213 in the third edition; pages 15 – 946 in the fourth) and are arranged in ascending numerical order by the first two digits of the code.

6. Ask the clients to scan and write down the names of occupational groups in which they are interested. They are also in the Occupational Group Arrangement and are listed below the divisions in which they expressed interest.

7. Have them read the definitions of those occupational groups.

8. Explain to the clients that those groups represent major fields of work in which they have some interest and that within the groups are included occupations requiring different levels of skill and ability.

9. Select a group and, using the Occupational Group Arrangement, show that in general the occupations within groups are listed in descending order of complexity in relation to the skills and knowledge required of workers: higher-listed occupations require more skills and knowledge than those listed lower.

10. Request that the clients select and write down occupational titles of interest from the listing below each occupational group.

11. Ask the clients to read the definitions of those titles that interest them. They are located in Volume I of the third edition and together with the occupational titles themselves in the Occupational Group Arrangement of the fourth edition.

12. At this point, the client and counselor may choose to continue the process by looking at what the occupation offers the worker or what the occupation requires of the worker. If the client is interested in what the occupation offers the worker, reading about the occupation in the *Occupational Outlook Handbook* generally provides appropriate information. If the client's interest is in what the occupation requires of the worker, the worker-trait arrangement in Volume II, the supplements to the third edition, the supplements to the fourth edition— *Guide for Occupational Exploration* (U.S. Department of Labor, 1979a) and/or *The Classification of Jobs According to Worker Trait Factors* (Field & Field, 1980)—are generally useful. The *Worker Trait Group Guide* (Winefordner, 1978) is also a helpful tool for such reference, since it provides a qualifications profile for each work group.

13. For clients interested in what the occupation can offer them, locate the occupation in the *Occupational Outlook Handbook* by using the DOT code-number index in the back portion of the *Handbook*. Ask the clients to read those portions of the *Handbook* brief that are of interest.

14. For clients interested in the requirements that the occupation places on

the worker, locate the worker-trait groups to which the occupations of interest belong. They are found in Volume II of the third edition or in either the *Guide for Occupational Exploration* or the *Worker Trait Group Guide.* For specific information regarding worker requirements for each occupation selected, use either Supplement I of the 1966 DOT or Section 1 of *The Classification of Jobs According to Worker Trait Factors.* These specific data are classified by DOT code. Compare the worker qualifications described with the information that the clients have about their own abilities, interests, and personalities.

15. Ask the clients to select those occupations that fit best with their interests, abilities, and personalities and to explore them further through reading, discussion, observation, and/or tryouts. Obviously this step and the preceding one can be a long-term process.

Although this process is described in a mechanical fashion, the counselor is advised to be creative in its application. Further information and exploration using other resources and strategies should be provided according to clients' needs during the process.

Other sources of career information

Information that helps persons to differentiate among occupations and aids in the process of decision making is available from a variety of other sources, both public and commercial. The information may relate to one or more of a variety of important categories of career information. Some sources provide occupational information such as trends in certain occupations, a description of the occupation, a brief statement about preparing to enter the occupation, and similar information. Other approaches use simulation games designed to provide either an analogue or a vicarious exposure to specific career areas. The resources in all the above areas may be printed or represented through audiovisual media or by electronic means, such as computers.

Table 7-1 presents a sampling of resources that provide occupational descriptions. Many of these sources contain information similar to that in the *Occupational Outlook Handbook.* All the resources included in this chapter are discussed in Hoppock (1976), Isaacson (1977), and/or Norris and others (1979); page references are given in the table.

Table 7-2 presents a sampling of resources that simulate various occupations or provide a model of the occupational decision-making process.

Use of career information

The use of information sources is essential on account of the tremendous amount of information available and the limited capacity of counselors' memories. It is impossible for counselors to retain the vast amount of information

TABLE 7-1. Resources providing occupational information

Name	Description	Publisher	Further information*
Career's Desk Top Kit	Highly portable, condensed supplement to the regular occupational file containing brief sketches of a wide range of occupations.	Career, Inc. P.O. Box 135 Largo, FL 33540	I: 380
Career Information Kit	A coded filing system providing 600 pieces of current literature filed alphabetically by job families and cross-referenced to the Dewey Decimal System.	Science Research Associates 259 E. Erie St. Chicago, IL 60611	I: 379–380
Career Planning Program	Career materials organized around 6 job clusters and 25 job families. Partly based on the theoretical concepts of Holland and interest-inventory research.	American College Testing P.O. Box 168 Iowa City, IA 52740	I: 227–228, 250, 475
Concise Handbook of Occupations	Presents concise information about 300+ jobs, arranged in alphabetical order.	Doubleday & Co. 1818 Ridge Rd. Homewood, IL 60430	N: 361
Encyclopedia of Careers and Vocational Guidance	Two volumes, one discussing career planning and choice, the other providing facts about 650 occupations in 71 major fields.	J. G. Ferguson Co. 6 N. Michigan Ave. Chicago, IL 60602	N: 360
Occupational Library	More than 600 occupational briefs, filed by DOT occupational code and supplemented by microfiche and viewdecks.	Chronicle Guidance Publications Moravia, NY 13118	H: 58

*Key: H = Hoppock, 1976; I = Isaacson, 1977; N = Norris, Hatch, Engelkes, & Winborn, 1979.

that relates to the array of career directions their clients may take. In spite of this recognition, our experience shows that most career counselors do not make good use of career-information resources, nor do they make good use of the research related to the dissemination of career information.

A major problem in the use of career information relates to counselor and client motivation. Motivation to use career information is viewed by Herr and Cramer (1979, p. 300) as being "based on a person's attempt to satisfy a career-related need. In other words, no need, no action, no action, no career-related learning."

Various authors have suggested methods to enhance motivation for using career information. Hollis and Hollis (1969) suggest that information be "personalized." By this they mean that it be individualized to meet the unique needs of the client. Another suggestion that has received considerable support from research is the use of behavioral techniques to increase career-information-seeking behaviors (Aiken & Johnston, 1973; Borman, 1972; Krumboltz & Schroeder, 1965; Krumboltz & Thoresen, 1964). In general, this approach

TABLE 7-2. Resources providing simulated occupational experiences

Name	Description	Publisher	Further information*
Decision-Making for Career Development	Activities permitting students to analyze decisions through role-play situations. Contains four audio cassettes and student response book.	Science Research Associates 259 E. Erie St. Chicago, IL 60611	N: 361
Job Experience Kits	20 kits, each containing simulated work tasks similar to those found in one occupation. Designed to provide occupational exploration opportunities for students in grades 8–11.	Science Research Associates 259 E. Erie St. Chicago, IL 60611	I: 410 N: 390
Life Career Game	Simulation designed to improve career decision making through the selection of education, leisure time, marriage, scholarship, and occupational activities.	Bobbs-Merrill 4300 W. 2nd St. Indianapolis, IN 44268	I: 409 N: 366
Occupational View-Deck	Allows students the opportunity to explore 605 occupations and compare the occupations to their own interests, temperaments, education, physical capabilities, and preferred working conditions. Microfilm mediated.	Chronicle Guidance Publications Moravia, NY 13118	N: 360, 389

*Key: H = Hoppock, 1976; I = Isaacson, 1977; N = Norris, Hatch, Engelkes, & Winborn, 1979.

suggests that verbal reinforcement of client information-seeking responses results in an increase in external career information seeking.

Another way in which behavior-oriented counselors have contributed to the acquisition of career information has been their development of occupational simulations. Krumboltz and his associates (Hamilton & Krumboltz, 1969; Krumboltz, 1967) have developed a series of *Job Experience Kits,* which provide clients with the opportunity to explore briefly a variety of occupations that serve as a basis for further exploration. These kits are particularly useful for many young people who have lacked the opportunity to develop occupationally relevant interests because of limited exposure to occupations. Research results reported by Hamilton and Krumboltz (1969) found that one of these brief simulated experiences was enjoyed by participants and generated a desire for further information. Johnson (1971) found that the simulated experiences generated interest in general career exploration as well as in the specific occupations simulated. These *Job Experience Kits* are now commercially available and are described in Table 7-2.

Multimedia approaches combining audio and visual modes of transmitting information have been developed to overcome problems that may occur in sustaining motivation and improving retention of information when a single mode is used. Research by Sankowsky (1973) and Johnson, Korn, and Dunn (1975) suggests that many learners, particularly adults and those described as atypical (low motivated, disabled, disadvantaged, and so on) are more receptive to multimedia approaches than to traditional modes of information transmittal, particularly aural or written approaches. Sankowsky (1973) found that a slide-tape format was the technique preferred by staff of rehabilitation facilities to provide specific information to their clients. Johnson and others (1975) found that their clients, who were "reluctant learners" in high school, were more receptive to a slide-tape presentation than to a written or audiotaped presentation and gained more occupational information from it.

Evaluating career information

Prior to deciding on the purchase and/or use of career information resources, the materials should be evaluated in terms of quality. Probably the most significant criterion in their selection is the applicability of the information for the purpose intended. Although the descriptive material provided by publishers may be helpful in this decision, be careful, since much of the descriptive literature is intended primarily to promote sales and may not be completely accurate.

Certain resources are expensive, and equivalent or better resources may be available from nonprofit or governmental sources at much lower cost. This difference applies particularly to resources providing occupational information similar to that available from the *Occupational Outlook Handbook*. In fact, the *Handbook* is suggested by Isaacson (1977, p. 361) as the criterion for determining whether a commercial publication is accurate.

Another significant factor closely related to the accuracy of career information is its currency. In a rapidly changing world, career information may quickly become outdated. Resources more than a few years old may be obsolete in describing certain occupations or the preparation for entering them. It is important for career counselors to avoid personal obsolescence by keeping current with information across the broad scope of the work world. Reading widely about world events and specifically about occupational and educational trends affecting careers, as well as maintaining contact with employers and community members, is an important way for counselors to stay current.

Another important consideration in the selection and application of career information is the appeal of the information to users. The manner in which the material is packaged and presented may be significant. As we have already indicated, multimedia presentations of career information may be more effective than printed or aurally presented material for some learners.

A major tool that can be helpful in evaluating career information is "Guidelines for the Preparation and Evaluation of Career Information Literature," published by the National Vocational Guidance Association (1980). These guidelines provide detailed recommendations for the content (nature of occupation, entry preparation, advancement outlook, licensing, and so forth) and style and format (including vocabulary, illustrations, revisions, and freedom from bias) of films, filmstrips, and printed material. The guidelines can be useful as a checklist for evaluating a variety of material. Each issue of *The Vocational Guidance Quarterly,* also published by the National Vocational Guidance Association, reports on the quality of a variety of career information resources using these guidelines. In addition, this association publishes the *NVGA Bibliography of Current Career Information* every two years, presenting these evaluations in one volume.

SUMMARY

In this chapter the resources and strategies available to assist persons in differentiating between occupations and deciding among occupational options were presented. During the career-understanding stage, more accurate comparisons of self to work are developed by individuals. Therefore, there is greater reliance than before on career information that provides more detail and concreteness to broad concepts about work.

Fortunately, the resources available to assist in the process of differentiation and decision making are vast and varied. They include governmental publications such as the *Dictionary of Occupational Titles* and the *Occupational Outlook Handbook,* as well as commercial publications, including innovative simulation experiences. While the emphasis of this chapter is on governmental publications and their use, commercial publications were also discussed. The use of various strategies to enhance client motivation to use career information resources was presented, as were suggestions and resources for evaluating career information.

RECOMMENDED READINGS

Appalachia Educational Laboratory. *Career Information System.* Bloomington, Ill.: McKnight Publishing, 1978.

This comprehensive system provides for the organizing, indexing, and filing of career information. Based on the fourth-edition DOT, it organizes information by worker trait groups, allowing clients to explore occupations according to what they know about their abilities, interests, and values. The components relating school subjects to work groups are particularly useful.

Herr, E. L., & Cramer, S. H. *Career guidance through the life span: Systematic approaches.* Boston: Little, Brown, 1979.

This text, which focuses on the systematic delivery of career-helping services, has two chapters (7 and 8) that are particularly relevant to career-information resources and strategies used in junior and senior high schools.

National Vocational Guidance Association. Guidelines for the preparation and evaluation of career information literature. *The Vocational Guidance Quarterly,* 1980, *28,* 291–296.

These guidelines, which are designed for both publishers and consumers of career-information literature, present the National Vocational Guidance Association's view of what constitutes high-quality career literature. The guidelines form the basis for ratings of career literature that appear in each issue of *The Vocational Guidance Quarterly.*

LEARNING ACTIVITIES

1. Interview three youngsters between the ages of 13 and 17 years old, focusing on the work-related activities they have completed at home, in school, or in the community over the preceding few days. How did these activities enhance their understanding of various occupations?

2. Visit a junior high, middle school, or high school that has implemented a career-education program. Observe the students in a career-related activity and interview a teacher and counselor regarding their opinions of the program's effectiveness.

3. Using the newspaper's "want ads" and the State Employment Service, identify the part-time jobs available in your community for junior and senior high school students. Consider how these jobs provide opportunities to try out different skills and knowledge relevant to possible future occupational choices.

4. Use the DOT and *Handbook* exercise on page 144–146 to assist a client in expanding his or her information about occupations and to begin thinking about possible choices. Evaluate the success of the activity on the basis of whether your client's understanding of possible occupational choices was enhanced and whether the process was interesting to you and your client. Note: You may wish to try out the exercise on yourself before you try it out on someone else.

5. Select an occupational brief from the *Occupational Outlook Handbook* and compare it with one describing the same occupation from the resources in Table 7-1. What are the primary differences between the two briefs? Using the "Guidelines for the Preparation and Evaluation of Career Information Literature," evaluate both briefs.

6. Select an occupational simulation from Table 7-2 and carry it out by yourself or with classmates (depending on the nature of the experience). Evaluate it, considering the degree to which it improved your understanding of various occupations and/or the decision-making process.

CHAPTER EIGHT

CAREER ACTION: RESOURCES AND STRATEGIES

THE ACTION STAGE

Following the decision to enter an area of work, persons generally begin preparation for entry. After preparation or during the latter stages of preparation, job seeking usually starts. If the job seeking is successful, persons become employed. The time spent preparing for and seeking work can vary significantly, depending on the occupation chosen and, particularly in job seeking, on personal factors such as motivation for work and geographical area.

In looking at the vast array of occupations, think of those that require least preparation for entry and those that require most preparation. In general, occupations that demand more physical ability, are tedious, and allow for little discretion in how they are carried out do not require extensive preparation time. Occupations that entail less physical and more mental ability, are more interesting, and allow for considerable independent judgment in execution usually require more time for preparation.

Whereas the time spent in preparing for occupational entry is somewhat consistent for individual occupations, personal factors such as willingness to relocate, interviewing skills, motivation to work, and an understanding of what one wants from work affect the time spent in seeking work. If we assume (and this is a big assumption) that those personal factors can be held constant, then the amount of time spent in job seeking would depend very much on the occupation chosen.

Now think of those occupations whose great need of workers leads to large-scale recruitment campaigns. Then consider those occupations in which it is extremely difficult to locate employment. You may have selected occupations that require at least a college education as those with least entry problems and those requiring a high school diploma or less as occupations in which it is more difficult to find work. Although statistical evidence indicates that, in general, lifetime earnings increase and unemployment rates drop with years of school completed (U.S. Department of Labor, 1978), being highly educated, in and of itself, does not assure easy entry into the work force. For example, in 1980, individuals with bachelor's degrees in mining or petroleum engineering typically did not have a difficult time locating a job, whereas persons with bachelor's degrees in art history did.

You may also have selected occupations requiring considerable physical strength, such as general-labor occupations, as difficult areas in which to locate jobs. While this impression may be accurate, in a general sense, it is important to recognize that there are considerable differences within the category of less-skilled work. For example, a roustabout (general laborer) in the oil-drilling industry will have a better-than-average chance of finding work, as compared with a general laborer in the house-construction industry, who will have a poorer-than-average chance (U.S. Department of Labor, 1978).

You may have noticed that in both of these examples the high-demand occupations are located in the energy field. In 1980 and undoubtedly throughout the 1980s, most persons prepared to work in the area of energy will have little difficulty finding employment. Factors that contribute to the change in occupational structure and affect the number of persons entering and leaving occupations will be discussed further in this chapter.

RESOURCES AND STRATEGIES FOR ACTION

Educational preparation for work

The educational preparation for work can be considered in a variety of ways. One way is to differentiate by the setting in which the education is acquired. Did preparation occur in a school setting or outside the conventional educational system, such as through on-the-job or related experiences? In many of its publications, including the DOT and *Handbook For Analyzing Jobs* (U.S. Department of Labor, 1972), the U.S. Department of Labor recognizes these two paths and views them as serving somewhat separate purposes in preparing for work.

A person's in-school activities relate in most cases to what is called *general educational development*. This concept includes "those aspects of education which contribute to the workers' (a) reasoning development and ability to follow instructions; and (b) acquisition of 'tool' knowledges such as language and mathematical skills" (U.S. Department of Labor, 1972, p. 209). This educational preparation is general in nature and does not have a specific occupational objective. Ordinarily, this education is obtained in elementary school, high school, or college.

General educational development is made up of three major components: reasoning development, mathematical development, and language development. It is assumed that as persons move through their general education they progress from more elementary to more complex, theoretical levels within the three areas. A scale of general educational development has been devised to measure these levels. It is reproduced in Table 8-1.

Specific vocational preparation is the term used to describe "the amount of time required to learn the techniques, acquire the information, and develop the facility needed for average performance in a specific job-worker situation" (U.S.

TABLE 8-1. General educational development

Level	Reasoning development	Mathematical development	Language development
6	Apply principles of logical or scientific thinking to a wide range of intellectual and practical problems. Deal with nonverbal symbolism (formulas, scientific equations, graphs, musical notes, etc.) in its most difficult phases. Deal with a variety of abstract and concrete variables. Apprehend the most abstruse classes of concepts.	Apply knowledge of advanced mathematical and statistical techniques such as differential and integral calculus, factor analysis, and probability determination, or work with a wide variety of theoretical mathematical concepts and make original applications of mathematical procedures, as in empirical and differential equations.	Comprehension and expression of a level to —Report, write, or edit articles for such publications as newspapers, magazines, and technical or scientific journals. Prepare and draw up deeds, leases, wills, mortgages, and contracts. —Prepare and deliver lectures on politics, economics, education, or science. —Interview, counsel, or advise such people as students, clients, or patients, in such matters as welfare eligibility, vocational rehabilitation, mental hygiene, or marital relations. —Evaluate engineering technical data to design buildings and bridges.
5	Apply principles of logical or scientific thinking to define problems, collect data, establish facts, and draw valid conclusions. Interpret an extensive variety of technical instructions, in books, manuals, and mathematical or diagrammatic form. Deal with several abstract and concrete variables.		
4	Apply principles of rational systems to solve practical problems and deal with a variety of concrete variables in situations where only limited standardization exists. Interpret a variety of instructions furnished in written, oral, diagrammatic, or schedule form.	Perform ordinary arithmetic, algebraic, and geometric procedures in standard, practical applications.	Comprehension and expression of a level to —Transcribe dictation, make appointments for executive and handle his personal mail, interview and screen people wishing to speak to him, and write routine correspondence on own initiative. —Interview job applicants to determine work best suited for their abilities and experience, and contact employers to interest them in services of agency. —Interpret technical manuals as well as drawings and specifications, such as layouts, blueprints, and schematics.
3	Apply common sense understanding to carry out instructions furnished in written, oral, or diagrammatic form. Deal with problems involving several concrete variables in or from standardized situations.	Make arithmetic calculations involving fractions, decimals and percentages.	Comprehension and expression of a level to —File, post, and mail such material as forms, checks, receipts, and bills. —Copy data from one record to another, fill in report forms, and type all work from rough draft or corrected copy. —Interview members of household to obtain such information as age, occupation, and number of children, to be used as data for surveys, or economic studies. —Guide people on tours through historical or public buildings, describing such features as size, value, and points of interest.
2	Apply common sense understanding to carry out detailed but uninvolved written or oral instructions. Deal with problems involving a few concrete variables in or from standardized situations.	Use arithmetic to add, subtract, multiply, and divide whole numbers.	

TABLE 8-1 General educational development (continued)

Level	Reasoning development	Mathematical development	Language development
1	Apply common sense understanding to carry out simple one- or two-step instructions. Deal with standardized situations with occasional or no variables in or from these situations encountered on the job.	Perform simple addition and subtraction, reading and copying of figures, or counting and recording.	Comprehension and expression of a level to —Learn job duties from oral instructions or demonstration. —Write identifying information, such as name and address of customer, weight, number, or type of product, on tags, or slips. —Request orally, or in writing, such supplies as linen, soap, or work materials.

From *Dictionary of Occupational Titles (3rd ed.), Volume II: Occupational Classification,* U.S. Department of Labor. Washington, D.C.: U.S. Government Printing Office, 1965, p. 652.

Department of Labor, 1972, p. 209). This training is most frequently acquired through (1) apprenticeship training, (2) in-plant training given by the employer in the form of organized classroom study, and (3) on-the-job training given to a trainee by a qualified worker. Training can also be acquired in a school or college setting through a curriculum oriented toward specific occupational objectives such as vocational and technical education, commercial high school programs, art schools, and related programs. While specific vocational preparation is usually acquired while performing the typical job in the community, it may be attained through military training or through government-related programs developed as a result of legislation such as the Comprehensive Employment and Training Act (CETA).

An understanding of the requirements of occupations and the means by which prospective employees can prepare to meet them is essential for the career counselor. The DOT and *Occupational Outlook Handbook* are the two most useful publications for determining the requirements of occupations. In some cases, because the DOT and *Occupational Outlook Handbook* provide general information about occupations and may lack specific information about a particular job, it may be necessary to carry out a job analysis. Job analysis is the process of observing a worker carrying out a job and reporting pertinent facts about the job, such as the relationship of the work to data, people, and things, the requirements of the worker, and a step-by-step description of what the worker does. The *Handbook for Analyzing Jobs* (U.S. Department of Labor, 1972) provides explicit instructions for carrying out job analyses.

Counselors should also be aware of the services within their communities that provide opportunities for preparation to meet occupational requirements. In general, counselors appear to be aware more of facilities offering general educational development than of programs offering specific vocational preparation, particularly those that are smaller and/or less visible, such as on-the-job training

and related training. Counselors should develop all possible contacts with educational and training opportunities in their communities and maintain a file of
education and training sites and the particular services offered.

There is a substantial number of publications, summarized in Table 8-2, that
describe the available avenues of educational preparation. Most of these resources list colleges, universities, vocational schools, and other sources of preparation for entry into occupational areas and provide information about their
programs of study. They are particularly useful for assisting clients to make
tentative choices regarding a place for preparation. Other resources relate school
subjects to careers; they are more useful for clients who are in the process of
deciding on programs of study.

Personal preparation for work

Employability.   Movement through a career involves acquiring the skills
and knowledge necessary to get a job, keep a job, and enhance one's career
through upgrading. In order to become successfully employed, a person must
first have an appropriate work-role identification. Oetting and Miller (1977, p.
30) view work-role identification as having at least four components: seeing
work as valuable, perceiving oneself as a worker, perceiving one's social environment as including an expectancy of work and working, and expecting work
to be rewarding. In addition to appropriate work-role identification, persons
should have vocational goals commensurate with their abilities, interests, and
personalities (Super, 1969); that is, goals that they have the skills and knowledge
to achieve and that meet their needs. Without appropriate work-role identification and vocational goals, people are not *employable.* Their work-role identification and/or vocational goals need to develop or change. Change in work-role
identification is difficult, for it requires a change in work values and social milieu.
As Oetting and Miller (1977) suggest, a person's orientation toward work sometimes changes under the influence of someone with significant personal impact
and traditional work-role identification. Selecting an occupational goal that fits is
also difficult for many people. Counseling, education, work experience, maturity, luck, and other factors can contribute to people's selecting occupations that
they can both perform and also find satisfying.

Even with appropriate work orientation and occupational goals, people are
not *placeable* if they are unable to interview appropriately or do whatever else is
necessary to compete for a job, such as locating jobs, filling out applications, and
so forth. Fortunately, job seeking is something that can be effectively learned
(Azrin, Flores, & Kaplan, 1975; Azrin & Philip, 1979; McClure, 1972). However,
job-getting skills are helpful only to people who are employable and job ready. A
major difficulty with job placement programs is that they have not always served
employable persons.

A more difficult problem rests with people who are oriented towards working and have appropriate skills and job-getting behavior but cannot find work in the geographical areas in which they live or are willing to live. This problem is particularly prevalent in rural areas of the country that have seen the departure of major industry. It is difficult for persons who know and share only the culture immediately surrounding them to move to areas that they perceive as strange and threatening. Choosing alternatives such as supporting oneself from the land and accepting secondary work such as school-bus driving and wood cutting are often necessary to survive. Unfortunately, the motives for such choices may be misunderstood and individuals may be labeled "lazy" or "freeloading." Service agencies may bar these individuals from benefits by regulations such as those requiring them to accept any job they can do, regardless of pay or geographic location.

Advancement and adjustment.   Once people are hired for a job, they should be able to maintain their employment and eventually enhance it by progressing up a career ladder. As Oetting and Miller (1977, p. 31) point out, maintaining a job requires a number of basic behaviors, including (1) comforming in attendance, dress, punctuality, language, and other factors, (2) meeting entry-level performance requirements, such as listening to and following directions, working steadily, and attending to the task, (3) maintaining appropriate interpersonal relationships with fellow workers and supervisors, and (4) performing higher-level functions, such as taking initiative, developing good decision-making skills, and working independently. Counseling techniques can help clients to overcome some problems in maintaining work; for example, simulation exercises, such as role play of supervisee/supervisor interactions, may be useful. However, some clients—particularly those who are alienated from work or are chronic job changers—may need long-term, intensive work-adjustment programs prior to employment (Campbell, 1971). Other persons, particularly those who become bored in tedious jobs, may need assistance in selecting jobs more commensurate with their interests, abilities, and personalities.

Career enhancement typically occurs after workers have shown themselves to be useful and productive for an employer. Career upgrading has payoffs for both employers and employees. Employees generally acquire increased pay, prestige, independence, and satisfaction as a result of upgrading. Employers benefit by having a worker who is stable and who performs well at a higher-level position. To upgrade, employees must (1) develop a viewpoint that sees promotion or change as desirable and possible, (2) be aware of available opportunities matching their own skills, (3) seek and successfully compete for the position, and (4) continually upgrade to maintain the high-level performance required by the new position (Oetting & Miller, 1977, p. 34).

Unfortunately, many individuals, particularly those who are unskilled and work in menial jobs, cannot upgrade because there is virtually no career ladder

TABLE 8-2. Sources of information about educational preparation

Publication Title	Description	Publisher	Further Information*
American Universities and Colleges	Provides information for more than 1500 bachelor's-degree-offering institutions that are accredited by a professional association or regional accrediting body.	American Council on Education 1 DuPont Circle, N.W. Washington, DC 20009	I: 277, 282 N: 195
American Junior Colleges	Provides information such as history, buildings, characteristics of teaching staff, financial aid, etc., on junior colleges with at least regional accreditation.	American Council on Education 1 DuPont Circle, N.W. Washington, DC 20009	I: 282
Barron's Guide to Two Year Colleges	Volume I provides information about admission requirements, enrollment figures, financial aid, academic programs, etc., for two-year colleges. Volume II arranges information in tabular form by program of study.	Barron's Educational Service 113 Crossways Park Dr. Woodbury, NY 11797	I: 281–282 N: 194, 363, 364
Barron's Profile of American Colleges	Volume I provides descriptions such as campus environment for approximately 1500 regionally accredited colleges and universities. Volume II arranges this information in tabular form by program of study.	Barron's Educational Service 113 Crossways Park Dr. Woodbury, NY 11797	I: 274–275 N: 362
Barron's Handbook of American College Financial Aid	Source of information about financial aid for students of four-year colleges and universities.	Barron's Educational Service 113 Crossways Park Dr. Woodbury, NY 11797	I: 270
Barron's Handbook of Junior and Community College Financial Aid	Source of information about financial aid regarding junior and community colleges.	Barron's Educational Service 113 Crossways Park Dr. Woodbury, NY 11797	N: 222
The Bluebook of Occupational Education	Lists and briefly describes vocational and technical schools across the U.S.	CCM Information Corporation 909 Third Avenue New York, NY 10822	N: 197
College Guide for Students with Disabilities	Describes the architectural accessibility of buildings at various colleges, support services for handicapped students, etc.	Abt Publications 55 Wheelan St. Cambridge, MA 02138	N: 196
Comparative Guide to American Colleges	Provides description of colleges and universities with programs less than two years in length up to the baccalaureate degree.	Harper & Row, Publishers 10 East 53rd Street New York, NY 10022	I: 278 N: 210, 216
Directory of Accredited Private Trade and Technical Schools	Institutions approved by the National Association of Trade and Technical Schools. Revised annually.	National Association of Trade & Technical Schools 2021 L Street, N.W. Washington, DC 20036	N: 197
Directory for Exceptional Children	Information on schools for the mentally retarded, emotionally disturbed, and physically handicapped, including day and boarding schools.	Porter Sargent Publisher 11 Beacon Street Boston, MA 02138	N: 199

Title	Description	Publisher	Reference
Directory of Post-Secondary Schools with Occupational Programs	Provides information regarding accredited sources of occupational preparation on a state-by-state basis providing name of training site, address, programs, etc. Has useful index relating occupational areas to sites where training can be acquired.	U.S. Department of Health, Education & Welfare Washington, DC 20204	N: 203
Directory of Private Home Study Schools	Annual listing and brief description of correspondence schools accredited by the National Home Study Council.	National Home Study Council 1601 18th Street, N.W. Washington, DC 20009	N: 203
Guide to Independent Study through Correspondence Instruction	Listing of subjects offered through correspondence or independent study by the 200 member institutions of the National University Extension Association.	National University Extension Association Suite 360, 1 DuPont Circle Washington, DC 20036	N: 203
Handbook of Private Schools	Annual publication describing boarding and day schools for young children, the college bound, vocationally oriented students, and students needing remedial work.	Porter Sargent Publisher 11 Beacon Street Boston, MA 02108	N: 199
Lovejoy's College Guide	Provides descriptive material for more than 3600 American institutions of higher education, including colleges and universities; junior colleges, technical institutions, and special schools.	Simon & Shuster 630 Fifth Avenue New York, NY 10020	I: 275–277, 281 N: 195, 362
The National Guidance Handbook	Describes 146 vocational/technical programs and relates the training to occupational fields.	Science Research Associates 259 E. Erie Street Chicago, IL 60611	I: 285
The New Guide to Study Abroad	Listing and description of academic offerings from secondary school to graduate level, work-study programs, and educational tours offered abroad.	Harper & Row, Publishers 10 E. 53rd Street New York, NY 10022	N: 195–196
Non-Traditional College Routes to Careers	Describes methods and colleges with unusual schedules and degree programs.	Julian Messner 1230 Avenue of the Americas New York, NY 10020	N: 196
Scholarships, Fellowships, and Loans	Information about aid available from business, industry, governmental, and other sources. Frequently updated.	Bellman Publishing P.O. Box 146 Arlington, MA 02174	I: 269–270 N: 223

*I = Isaacson, 1977; N = Norris, Hatch, Engelkes, & Winborn, 1979.

and thus nowhere for them to climb (U.S. Department of Health, Education and Welfare, 1973). Some individuals overcome this problem by acquiring additional saleable skills or educational credentials that allow them to switch careers by changing jobs.

The acquisition of the skills and knowledge necessary to select appropriate vocational goals, get jobs, maintain employment, and enhance careers should be viewed as a developmental sequence through which people progress during their careers. In order to progress to higher levels in this developmental procession, a person must first master earlier behaviors. For example, an individual cannot upgrade his or her employment without having selected a vocational goal and secured a job in earlier life. Table 8-3, which is adapted from a figure by Oetting and Miller (1977, p. 30), summarizes the levels through which persons move in their successful adjustment to work. It also includes the behaviors necessary to be successful at each level and the behavior that generally indicates successful achievement of each level. It can be helpful as a checklist in determining the adjustment of clients to work.

ENTERING THE WORK WORLD

Although there is frequently much emphasis by authors, educators, and counselors on clients' selecting an appropriate vocational objective, all too seldom is there adequate emphasis on job seeking and maintenance (Vandergoot & Engelkes, 1977). In large part, this shortcoming may be related to the belief that the appropriate selection of a vocational goal will automatically lead to successful job

TABLE 8-3. The hierarchy of work adjustment

Level and required behaviors	Successful outcome
(A) Acquisition Group	
Level I—Work Orientation	Motivated to seek work.
1. Wants to work and sees work as valuable.	
2. Identity includes self-perception as a worker.	
3. Perception of social environment includes an expectancy of work and working.	
4. Expects work to be rewarding.	
Level II—Job Readiness	Applies for job.
1. Has a vocational goal that	
a. person can do.	
b. meets personal needs.	
c. is available in the community.	
Level III—Job Getting	Obtains job.
1. Knows sources of job leads.	
2. Seeks work frequently enough.	
3. Has appropriate interview behavior:	
a. can present assets.	
b. can account for obvious deficits.	
c. shows enthusiasm about working.	
d. free of negative mannerisms.	

TABLE 8-3. The hierarchy of work adjustment (continued)

Level and required behaviors	*Successful outcome*
(B) Maintenance Group	
Level IV—Job Conformance and Adaption	Not fired and does not
1. Attends work regularly.	quit in the first few
2. Attends work promptly.	days.
3. Conforms to dress, hygiene, safety, and other requirements of the job.	
Level V—Entry Level Performance	Still employed beyond usual
1. Quantity and quality of work performance is adequate.	probation period.
2. Works steadily.	
3. Listens to and adequately follows directions.	
4. Attends to task at work station to appropriate degree.	
5. Sustains effort and shows adequate stamina.	
Level VI—Interpersonal Relationships	Long-term employment.
1. Maintains interpersonal relationships with coworkers that are pleasant and supportive.	
2. Maintains interpersonal relationships with supervisors that show acceptance of subordinate role and do not require excessive attention.	
Level VII—Skilled Performance and Job Satisfaction	Permanent employment except for job changes.
1. Works independently without supervision.	
2. Takes initiative when appropriate.	
3. Exercises good decision-making skills.	
(C) Upgrading Group	
Level VIII—Orientation for Change	Motivated to seek improvement.
1. Sees promotion or change as possible and desirable.	
Level IX—Advancement Readiness	Applies for promotion or job.
1. Aware of opportunities available.	
2. Knows requirements of jobs considered.	
3. Recognizes how skills fit these jobs.	
Level X—Job or Promotion Getting	Gets promotion or
1. Actively seeks position.	better job.
2. Successfully competes for position.	
Level XI—High-Level Job Maintenance	Satisfactory and satisfied
1. Upgrades work skills and output.	in new position.
2. Improves interpersonal skills.	

Adapted from "Work and the Disadvantaged: The Work Adjustment Hierarchy," by E. Oetting and C. D. Miller. In *Personnel and Guidance Journal,* 1977, *56*, p. 30. Reprinted by permission of the American Personnel and Guidance Association.

placement. The belief may be warranted in some cases; however, our current high level of unemployment, particularly for youth (U.S. Department of Labor, 1978), the dramatic changes in the structure of occupations, and the difficulty for handicapped, minority, disadvantaged, and/or marginally skilled persons of locating and maintaining work heighten the importance of systematic approaches to job seeking and maintenance for many segments of our population.

In order to be successful in assisting clients to locate jobs, the counselor needs an awareness of the changing occupational structure and the factors contributing to that change. In addition, effective methods for locating job leads, preparing résumés and employment applications, and preparing for the employment interview are essential.

Changes in occupations

The world is constantly changing, and with it the occupations of the world. This change is evident when we consider the occupations of the past that are almost non-existent now but that linger in occupational surnames such as Millers, Coopers, and Smiths. What factors contributed to the decline of the grain miller, the barrel maker, and the blacksmith? Technological change, particularly automation, comes to mind as do changing cultural patterns—our lives are different now from what they were when millers, barrel makers, and blacksmiths thrived. As our society has grown more complex, so have the reasons for occupational change. In fact, it has become so complex that a thorough discussion is beyond the scope of this book. We will, however, look at certain of the significant factors that contribute to change.

In our current society, technological change and changing life patterns continue to influence occupations. Other factors also play an important role. These include national and international policy and events, calamities and disasters, the birth and death rate, and the need to replace workers who retire, die, or change jobs.

National and international policy and events play an increasingly significant role in occupational change. For example, the decision by the oil-producing countries to control the price and flow of oil was the major reason that the United States developed a policy to become energy self-sufficient by the 1990s. This policy contributed to the increase of jobs in the energy field. Other international events, such as the Russian grain deal and disarmament proposals, affect employment and the structure of occupations in the agricultural and defense industries. During the 1960s and 1970s, a national policy and legislation to require equal opportunity in employment without regard to sex, age, race, religion, or handicapping condition has contributed to enlarging the numbers of women and minority group members in certain occupations, particularly professional, managerial, and technical ones. An increased social consciousness on the part of employers that all persons have a right to equal employment opportunities is also a major contributor to this growth.

Technological change is also important and often interfaces with national goals. Our national policy to reduce environmental pollution often clashes with the policy to be energy self-sufficient, as many of our domestic fuels are polluting. As technology is developed to extract and use energy resources without damaging the environment, totally new occupations could be developed. Our current efforts to convert high-sulfur coal, an extensive polluter, to a cleaner burning gas or liquid is an example of how this change could occur. These changes obviously have impact on the occupational structure. Coal-mining occupations would increase and new occupations in coal liquefaction and gasification would be created.

Automation is another aspect of the technological change affecting the occupational structure. Faunce (1968) defines automation as the automatic, centralized control of an integrated production system. While much of American production is not at this advanced state of automation, mechanical, electrical, and electronic systems have taken over much of the production of goods and services once provided through human, animal, water, wind, or steam power.

The effects of this takeover have been dramatic. While some contend that there has not been a loss of jobs due to automation, Snyder (1964) argues that automation has eliminated, and will continue to eliminate, many jobs for workers. An HEW task force on *Work in America* (U.S. Department of Health, Education and Welfare, 1973, p. 20) states: "It is an illusion to believe that technology is opening new high level jobs that are replacing low level jobs." Perhaps a more significant problem than unemployment is that automation may be resulting in the stagnation of workers in dead-end jobs. To quote *Work in America* again, "Many workers at all occupational levels feel locked in, their mobility blocked, the opportunity to grow lacking in their jobs, challenge missing from their tasks" (pp. xvi–xvii). Ferkiss (1970) also believes that automation and the resulting specialization robs workers of meaningful jobs. He suggests that workers "are likely to be lonely, bored, and alienated, often feeling less the machine's master than its servant" (p. 123). Business, labor, government, and academic institutions must work together to overcome these significant technological threats.

A change in life patterns also affects occupational change. Expanded leisure time as a result of a shorter work week, improved transportation systems, and the widespread use of labor-saving devices, particularly in the home, has resulted in a dramatic increase in service occupations, especially in relation to recreational and other personal services. Our growing urbanization, rising incomes, and living standards contribute further to an increase in service-producing industries. In fact, the service sector of our economy has grown faster than the goods-producing sector since World War II. During the next decade, this industry is expected to show more growth than any other (U.S. Department of Labor, 1978). Perhaps the extensive inflation of the late 1970s will affect our way of life to reduce this need for services.

Calamities, or events believed to be calamities, can also have significant impact. The Three Mile Island nuclear incident has, at least in the short term, affected the development of occupations in the nuclear-energy field. Wars often create significant change in a short period of time, as the mobilization of industry after Pearl Harbor exemplifies. Industries producing goods for use by the general public quickly switch to goods needed to meet the war effort. Their expansion and the shortage of male workers due to service in the Armed Forces contribute significantly to the entry of women, handicapped persons, and other minorities into the work force.

The birth rate and death rate are also important considerations. The current concern among academicians over a possible decline in college and university enrollment during the 1980s is one reflection of this change. The declining birth rate affects all aspects of our educational system, from nursery school to adult education. Obviously, occupations involved in supplying goods and services are also affected by the declining birth rate. If the number of births in a given year significantly declines, the effect is immediate on occupations in the manufacture of baby clothing and diapers, infant formula and foods, and baby furniture, and in services such as diaper service and baby-sitting. The reduced number of babies born has a significant and somewhat predictable effect as time progresses. Five years later, goods and services for five-year-olds show a decrease. This impact lessens as goods and services become less related to human development and chronological age. For example, there is much more similarity among the goods and services needed for 30 to 40-year-olds than among those needed by 1 to 10-year olds.

Another factor relating to occupational change is death or mortality rate. As people live longer, more people become employed in businesses catering to the needs of older persons. The need to replace workers who retire, die, or seek employment elsewhere also has an important effect on occupational change. The average age of workers in different occupations varies greatly (U.S. Department of Labor, 1978). If the average age of workers in a given occupation is generally low, the need to replace those workers will be lower than if the average age of workers were high.

Because new jobs are created and eliminated every day, counselors should maintain an awareness of occupational and labor market changes. Regular reading of newspapers and news magazines helps in this task. There is probably no better resource for keeping abreast of occupational change than the *Occupational Outlook Handbook* (U.S. Department of Labor, 1978). The chapter on changing jobs and the "Occupational Outlook" sections of the individual occupational descriptions in the *Handbook* are particularly useful. The *Occupational Outlook Quarterly,* the annual *Manpower Report of the President,* and the monthly publications *Manpower* and *Monthly Labor Review* are other useful government resources published by the U.S. Department of Labor. State employment services frequently publish monthly, quarterly, and annual reports providing information regarding labor market and industrial changes within their local jurisdictions.

Locating jobs

Job-seeking behavior is an interesting phenomenon. Most of our adult population has been involved in it at one time or another, and advice from friends, associates, and relatives abounds. A large number of paperback books focusing on job finding are easily obtained at local bookstores (Bolles, 1979; Garrison, McCurdy, Munson, Brolie, Saunders, Sims, and Telis, 1977; Marshall, 1976; Rust, 1979; Yeomans, 1979). In general, these books provide information on such things as where and how to look for jobs, how to prepare applications, cover letters, and résumés, and how to interview properly. While courses of this type can provide helpful hints, the methods that they advocate are not generally based on systematic research or on a systematic technology of job finding. Fortunately, such research has begun, and a systematic technology is developing. For example, considerable empirical documentation exists on methods that are successful in locating job openings (Granovetter, 1974; Jones & Azrin, 1973; Rungeling, Smith, & Scott, 1976; U.S. Department of Labor, 1975a, 1975b); questions that commonly appear on employment applications (Gregory, 1966); résumé content and format desired by personnel managers (Dipboye, Wibach, & Fromkin, 1975; Feild & Holley, 1976; Stephens, Watt, & Hobbs, 1979); the purpose, content, validity, and reliability of letters of reference (Muchinsky, 1979); factors contributing to successful job interviewing (Clowers & Fraser, 1977; Dipboye & Wiley, 1977, 1978; Forbes & Jackson, 1980; McGovern & Tinsley, 1978; Wiener & Schneiderman, 1974; Young & Beier, 1977); and programs that have been successful in assisting clients to receive employment (Azrin & Philip, 1979; Azrin, Philip, Thienes-Hontos, & Besalel, 1980; Keith, Engelkes, & Winborn, 1977). In spite of this documentation, the majority of job seekers and persons assisting them are unaware of the findings and resources available.

Most job searches comprise simple informal methods, such as direct application to an employer and consultation with friends, relatives, or business associates. These informal methods account for approximately two-thirds of jobs landed, according to a 1974 review by Granovetter of 12 published studies. Since his review, at least four additional published research studies support those results (Jones & Azrin, 1973; Rungeling et al., 1976; U.S. Department of Labor, 1975a, 1976). The more formal methods (answering or placing want ads in newspapers and using the public employment service or private agencies, union, and other placement services offered through a school placement office or community action organization) matched approximately one-third of workers to their jobs. To a great degree, these same studies indicate that the methods that are most successful in locating jobs are the ones used most frequently in finding them. Table 8-4 compares the frequency of use and effectiveness of the various methods reported in five studies.

The results of these studies strongly suggest that contact with friends and relatives and direct application to employers are the most desirable methods of finding jobs, regardless of the type of work sought. Brown (1967), in his nationwide study of college professors, found personal contact methods to be the major means of locating jobs, with direct application ranked a distant second. Granovetter (1974), in his study of professional, technical, and managerial workers in a suburb of Boston, found very similar results. Granovetter (1979,

TABLE 8-4. The frequency of use and effectiveness of job-seeking methods

| | Study sample | | | | | | | | | | | | | | | | | | | |
| Method used | Urban (U.S. Dept. of Labor, 1975a) | | | | Urban (U.S. Dept. of Labor, 1976) | | | | Master's degree graduates (Jones & Azrin, 1973) | | | | Rural (Rungeling, Smith, & Scott, 1976) | | | | Blue collar—Small city (Sheppard & Belitsky, 1966) | | | |
	% Used	Rank	% Suc.	Rank	% Used	Rank	% Suc.	Rank	% Used	Rank	% Suc.	Rank	% Used	Rank	% Suc.	Rank	% Used	Rank	% Suc.	Rank
Friends, relatives, and associates	78	1	26.1†	2	65	2	30.7	1	*	*	66	1	54.8	2	26	2	77	3	56	1
Direct employer application	66	2	34.9	1	82.1	1	29.8	2	*	*	15	2	76.0	1	59	1	72	4	14	2.5
Answering newspaper ads	57.6	3	14.0	3	47.5	3	16.6	3	*	*	5	4	*	*	*	*	88	1	4	6
Public employment agencies	33.5	4	5.1	5	27.6	4	5.6	4.5	*	*	8	3	30.8	3	6.3	3	84	2	14	2.5
Private employment agencies	21.0	5	5.6	4	14.5	6	5.6	4.5	*	*	2	6	*	*	*	*	17	7	*	*
Union	6.0	7	1.5	6	6.2	7	1.4	7	*	*	N/A	N/A	*	*	*	*	20	6	5	5
Other activities	23	6	4.2	7	15	5	3.4	6	*	*	4	5	21.5	4	8.3	4	45	5	7	4

*Data not provided.

†Does not include business associates.

pp. 87–88) suggests that personal contact is the major method of locating jobs because the cost of the information is low (no agencies, no fees) and employers view the information as being of better quality than that from formal sources, which cannot always be trusted. While the informal method is effective for job hunters, employers who hire primarily on the basis of personal contact may be violating Affirmative Action legislation if they fail to consider broader qualifications or exclude other applicants by filling positions without advertisement. The more widespread and intensive application of Affirmative Action programs may reduce the impact of personal contact on hiring.

The state employment service may be less successful than other methods for a variety of reasons. It may be, as Zadny and James (1976) suggest, that employers use direct applications to fill job openings before turning to the employment service. Granovetter (1979) suggests that the reason for this pattern is that employers distrust agencies of all kinds. Since the employment service has assumed, as a primary function, the provision of services for the hard-to-employ (U.S. Department of Labor, 1975b), its significance as a job locater for the general population may be somewhat diminished. The results of a study by Schiller (1975) showed that the effectiveness of the public agencies—employment service and work-incentive program—in finding disadvantaged clients jobs was superior to contacting friends and relatives or making direct application.

The findings of most studies that initial leads for most jobs are provided by friends, relatives, and work associates led both Granovetter (1974, 1979), a sociologist, and Jones and Azrin (1973), behavioral psychologists, to advocate methods for capitalizing on this informal job-information network. An obvious method is to consider whether family, social, or business contacts can help locate jobs. Granovetter (1974, p. 61–62) suggests that the chain of contact between the person who initially supplies the information (the employer) and the person subsequently taking the job be kept small. In his research, most job procurement occurred when there was no intermediary or when one person acted as an intermediary between job seeker and employer. These findings suggest that the primary sources of information should be persons who are closest, either socially or professionally, to the employer. Listing all social or work friends and acquaintances and using their potential links to employers may be the most productive way to move into the job-information network.

Jones and Azrin (1973) have made slightly different use of their findings that 66% of job leads were from friends, relatives, or acquaintances. Usually, the supplier of information about a job opening to a friend, relative, or associate is motivated by social reinforcers. Jones and Azrin (1973) have provided economic reinforcers for supplying such information. They placed a newspaper ad offering $100 for information about job openings that resulted in placements of at least three weeks' duration. Response to this ad was compared with response to a similar ad of the "position desired" type that offered no monetary reward. The reward ad produced more calls (14 versus 2), more reports of job openings (20 versus 2), more interviews for applicants (19 versus 1), and more applicants' employment for at least one month (8 versus 1) than the nonpaying ad. Jones and Azrin (1973, p. 352) note that all eight placements and 17 of 20 job leads came through persons who either had the hiring responsibility or were socially or occupationally related to the employer. The authors cite the cost-effectiveness of this procedure as a significant factor in advocating its use. The reward-ad procedure is viewed as supplementary to capitalizing on the client's contacts with employed persons and the development of new social contacts for gaining information about job leads. The considerable research evidence indicating the significance of personal contact as a major hiring influence certainly provides support for these suggestions.

In their study of job seeking, Sheppard and Belitsky (1966) found that those workers who used a "wide-ranging" technique tended to be more successful in their job search than those who used a "prior-awareness" technique. In the wide-ranging approach, workers applied for positions in firms without being aware that they had job openings. Prior-awareness users applied for positions only when they were aware of job openings. Sheppard and Belitsky (1966) also found that job-hunting success, as measured by number of jobs acquired, was increased if workers started the job hunt as quickly as possible and used a variety of job-seeking methods. This finding makes intuitive sense, so we are not surprised that it is supported by research.

Certain occupational groups may, because of their special characteristics, have methods of locating work that are not available to the general working public. For example, many persons who are in trade occupations and have strong union affiliations locate their jobs through union halls. While it is possible to obtain the same information through a literature search (U.S. Department of Labor, 1976, p. 58), the career counselor's understanding of the job-hunting techniques and other career-related characteristics of varying occupational groups can be acquired by talking with workers and employers representing those groups. This information is vital to success as a counselor.

Capitalizing on the finding that direct application to employers is a successful means of locating jobs, Ugland (1977) has developed a systematic approach to job seeking. His materials, known as Job Seeker's Aids, included the following components:

1. Industry Lists, which provided background data on local business and industry. These lists were organized so that job seekers with telephone skills could telephone the individuals with responsibility for hiring in all companies within a target industry in a short period of time.

2. Industry Maps, which pinpointed the locations of business and industry and also provided public transportation routes so that the job seekers could use the most cost- and time-efficient means for the job search.

3. The Job Seeker's Guides, which were reference cards that provided brief

instructions on the most efficient means of planning a day's work in employer contact. The reverse of the card was used to record the results of daily contacts.

4. The Feedback System, which used the job-contact information from the reverse of the job seeker's guide card as a basis for ongoing job-search planning between counselor and client and for indicating where openings were occurring that could benefit other clients.

On a number of job-seeking dimensions, rehabilitation clients who used the job-seeking aids in addition to regular rehabilitation-agency placement services exceeded similar clients of the same agency who did not receive the job-seeker's aids. Those using job-seeking aids made more than twice as many employer contacts (428 versus 183), placed nearly three times as many applications (172 versus 63), and reported more than four times as many job openings (62 versus 15). While nearly twice as many of the clients using the aids found employment as did the regular clients (17 versus 10), this result was not used as a measure of effectiveness, since job leads were shared among all clients. It appears that the systematic exploitation of direct employer contact is worth the effort in increasing the productivity and efficiency of the job searcher. Since direct employer application seems to be a more successful job-seeking method in rural areas where the social network of friends, relatives, and associates is more widespread than in urban areas (Rungeling et al., 1976, p. 123), the systematic approach may be even more effective in rural areas than in the urban area where the program was implemented.

There have been numerous other methods used successfully to develop job leads. An advisory committee made up of a high proportion of businesspersons with hiring influence has been used advantageously by local committees on the Employment of the Handicapped and by other rehabilitation agencies and facilities (Zuger, 1971). Job fairs, which resemble the exhibits at national meetings of professional and trade associations, have also been widely used (Musselman, 1969; Poor & Delaney, 1974; Souther, 1972; Wilstach, 1962). In addition to exposing clients to a wide variety of occupations in a short time, fairs can provide an opportunity to develop contacts between employers and job seekers and result in placement (Poor & Delaney, 1974; Souther, 1972).

APPLYING FOR JOBS

Locating potential job openings is an important step in becoming employed. It is also important for clients to be able to present themselves to employers in a positive manner, so that they will enhance their chances of being hired. Most jobs require that self-presentation be in writing, by way of a job application or résumé, and, in many instances, in person, through job interviews. Letters of recommendation, although not originated by job seekers themselves, are also a means by which job applicants are presented to employers.

In preparing for this presentation of self to employers through applications, résumés, and/or interviews, many job seekers rely on the judgment of others regarding practices that have worked. The seekers may also rely on the many job-hunting books whose suggestions are most frequently based on opinion and tradition. While this area of job seeking is not as thoroughly researched as others, such as resources used to locate jobs, empirical data exists on the format and content of résumés, as well as the ingredients of successful interviews. Ideally, a combination of the empirical data and the experience- and tradition-based information would be used by job seekers as guidelines.

Self-presentation on paper

The importance of the job application and résumé in job seeking is based on the opinion that "if relevant information is presented to employers in a preferred manner, the chances of a favorable response to the candidate are improved" (Stephens et al., 1979, p. 26). For this reason, considerable attention should be paid to the content of information presented in job applications and the content and format of the information in résumés.

Prior to completing applications or résumés, and as preparation for the job interview, it may be useful for clients to identify and review their positive attributes in relation to employment. This identification process results in asset lists, which Carkhuff, Pierce, Friel, and Willis (1975) call *Education and Work Fact Sheets* and the Human Resources Center (1977) terms *Feature Reviews*. Carkhuff and his associates suggest that a review be organized around the following questions: Can the applicant do the job? Is the applicant dependable? Does the applicant get along with others? Carkhuff and his associates believe, and we agree, that these are important areas of concern to employers regarding the workers they hire.

To facilitate review, clients should be instructed to list all strengths that fall into the categories indicated by the questions. Factors related to getting the job done could include such things as grades, honors, course work completed, job-related skills, output and efficiency on previous jobs, and similar items. Under dependability, attendance and promptness on previous jobs or in school, level of responsibility in previous schooling or work, and other related factors would be important to include. A review of relationships with teachers, supervisors, and peers, as well as participation and leadership in organizations, could provide useful information related to one's ability to get along with others. This information should be written and kept by clients so that it can be referred to when necessary.

Counselors may wish to carry out an interview with clients in order to assist them in reviewing these features. If, following this review, job seekers' strengths do not appear to relate to selected job objectives, it may be important for clients to rethink their objectives or review their education and work-related experiences more thoroughly to uncover job-related assets (Human Resources Center, 1977, p. 33).

Job applications. Numerous individuals have suggested that counselors and teachers use actual job applications to improve the ability of clients to present themselves appropriately and thereby influence the job-hiring decision in their favor (Hoppock, 1976; Human Resources Center, 1977; Norris et al., 1979; Warren, 1955). In general, this procedure consists of acquiring employment applications from local employers and asking clients to complete them. Following this, clients typically compare their application forms with one another or allow counselors to review them and provide feedback. In general, this procedure is thought to improve markedly the quality of clients' completed applications.

Some clients, particularly those with poor writing and reading skills, may need to be taught exactly what to write in each blank. A form containing information requested on most applications can be completed for these clients and they can be taught to copy the information from their application to that of the employers.

The most easily available applications, however, are not necessarily typical of the ones generally encountered by job applicants. Fortunately, Gregory (1966) has provided the basic data from which a standardized or composite application can be developed. Gregory received applications from 80 firms in upstate New York believed to be representative of those in the United States in composition of occupations, industries, and labor force. He then determined the frequency of appearance of the various items on the applications. Table 8-5 is a composite application based on Gregory's findings. The number in parentheses after each question indicates the frequency (percentage) of the item's use on the application blanks reviewed.

Bear in mind that these data were collected during the 1960s, when questions of a personal nature were asked that are no longer permitted on applications or in job interviews unless they are shown to be job related. Clients should be aware of their legal rights in this regard when seeking employment. Numerous laws require equal employment opportunities for job seekers. The Civil Rights Act and Equal Employment Opportunity Act prohibit discrimination in employment practices because of race, color, sex, or national origin. Public Law 90-202 prohibits discrimination because of age for persons between the ages of 40 and 65. Sections 503 and 504 of the Rehabilitation Act of 1973 require nondiscrimination toward handicapped persons by most employers receiving federal grants and contracts. All of this legislation precludes employers from asking questions that are not job related: questions such as date of birth, sex, weight, height, marital status, number of children and other dependents, dates of school attendance, disabilities, arrests, imprisonments, and similar items. These questions can be asked if the employer can show them to be related to the job applied for. On our composite application, these items are in italics.

A major difficulty for job seekers is that many employers continue to use applications that ask illegal questions. Frequently, these questions relate to such difficulties as previous arrests, incarcerations, mental illness, and similar problems. Some authors (Anderson, 1968; Human Resources Center, 1977) re-

TABLE 8-5. Composite Job Application Blank

Date _____ (96)

PERSONAL

Name _____ (100)   Soc. Sec. No. _____ (98)

Present Address _____ (100)
           No.   Street

Telephone No. _____ (100)

_____
City

Sex _____ (75)

_____
State   Zip Code

Marital Status

☐ *Single*   (96)

Date of Birth _____ (90)

☐ *Married*   (96)

Weight _____ (89)

☐ *Divorced*   (85)

Height _____ (89)

☐ *Separated*   (75)

U.S. Citizenship (82) _____ yes _____ no

☐ *Widowed*   (88)

If no, specify country _____

No. of children _____ (79)

Do you own your own home? (50) _____ yes _____ no

No. of dependents _____ (60)

Disabilities: _____ (59)

EDUCATIONAL DATA

School	Name and address of school	Dates of attendance (74)	Course of study (70)	Did you graduate? (72)	List degrees
Elementary (88)				_____ yes _____ no	
High (86)				_____ yes _____ no	
College (89)				_____ yes _____ no	
Other				_____ yes _____ no	

MILITARY SERVICE

Have you served in the military? (65) _____ yes _____ no   *Dates of service* _____

Branch of service _____ (65)   Rank at discharge _____

Describe your duties: _____

PAST EMPLOYMENT

List all past employment below, beginning with your most recent job.

Employer & address (100)	Dates of employment (98)	Describe the work you did (99)	Job title (100)	Last weekly salary (89)	Reason for leaving (90)

PERSONAL REFERENCES

Do not use relatives or employers.

Name (71)	Address (71)	Occupation (54)	Phone

POSITION APPLIED FOR

Position(s) applied for _____

Expected salary _____ (64)   Previous employment with us? (65) _____ yes _____ no

Date available for work _____   If so, when? _____

List any relatives or friends working for us (69) _____

Whom may we notify in case of emergency, should we hire you? (68) _____
                                                                    Name

_____   _____   _____   _____
Street   City   State   Telephone

_____
Signature of applicant (89)

(For office use only)

Interviewer (59) _____

Based on Gregory (1966).
Note 1: Number in parentheses denotes frequency (in percentage) with
        which item was included on applications reviewed by Gregory.
Note 2: Items in italics may be discriminatory.

commend that applicants leave these questions unanswered and explain them to employers during interviews. The guidelines in Table 8-7 regarding responses to questions about personal deficits may assist with this explanation. This alternative seems better than lying or answering bluntly when it appears that the information, if provided, would preclude a later interview and subsequent hiring. Pointing out to employers that they are asking illegal questions would probably not facilitate being hired. However, clients who believe that they have been discriminated against in hiring because of such information should be informed of their right to file a complaint with an Equal Opportunity Officer or Human Rights Officer through the state or federal Department of Labor or Human Rights Office.

The Human Resources Center (1977, pp. 34−35) offers a number of useful suggestions for completing an application:

1. Type or print legibly on the application.
2. Avoid crossing out responses.
3. Be honest, but use acceptable reasons for leaving previous employment: more pay, returning to school, laid off, career goal change, mutually agreed-upon resignation, and so forth.
4. Use influential people as references—supervisors, teachers, clergy, and the like.

Anderson (1968) suggests that providing too much information, particularly that which may be irrelevant, is a problem for many job seekers. He suggests that information irrelevant to the job applied for and not requested by the employer be omitted. Clients who need assistance should be instructed in completing the application blank similar to the one in Table 8-5.

Résumés.   While résumés have not traditionally been submitted by job seekers for nonprofessional positions, they are now being widely recommended for all persons, regardless of the type of work sought (Azrin et al., 1975; Flannagan, 1977; Human Resources Center, 1977). The primary reason for this shift of viewpoint is the résumé's unique capability of presenting a person's distinctive and positive characteristics in a manner that increases the possibility of getting the attention of an employer. Since job seekers have a great deal of control over the information presented in a résumé, as compared to an application, résumés allow job seekers to take the initiative and direct attention toward their strongest assets.

Execution and timing are significant considerations in using the résumé. Azrin and his associates (Azrin et al., 1975, p. 20) suggest that the résumé be used for each contact, regardless of whether it was requested by the employer. These times include: "(a) before an interview; (b) as an attachment to application forms if an interview was unobtainable; (c) with letters of inquiry about openings; or (d) when applying to a help-wanted advertisement or a telephone interview."

The logic behind these suggestions seems to be that since résumés present the strongest attributes of job seekers, opportunities that maximize an employer's chance of seeing them should be taken.

Job seekers have two major considerations in developing résumés: content and format. Résumé content focuses on *what* should be included in the résumé. It is the informational component. Résumé format focuses on *how* the information should be organized. It is the organizational or structural component of the résumé. Ideally, content and format should be integrated in the manner most likely to improve the person's chances of being hired.

Rather than depending on opinion and tradition to guide résumé preparation, researchers have surveyed employers regarding their preference for the content and format of résumés (Dortch, 1975; Feild & Holley, 1976; Huggins, 1977; Stephens, et al., 1979). Of these, two studies stand out as being very helpful in guiding the job seeker: those of Feild and Holley (1976) and Stephens and others (1979). Their strength, in large part, is based on the recency of their information and the emphasis on using the results in practice.

Feild and Holley's (1976) primary focus was on the content or informational component. Using a questionnaire, they received information from 205 personnel directors regarding their preferences for the cover letter and résumé. Based on their findings (p. 232), the following suggestions can be made to job seekers regarding the cover letter:

1. Cover letters should be typed and short (no longer than one page).
2. Photocopying and photo-offset printing are acceptable, but not preferred to typed letters.
3. The most significant items to be included in the cover letter (in rank order of importance) are:
   a. position the applicant is seeking;
   b. applicant's job objective;
   c. applicant's career objectives;
   d. reason applicant is seeking employment;
   e. indication that the applicant knows something about the organization.

Other factors generally considered important in cover letter preparation were supported by their findings. For example, personal cover letters suggesting an interest in a specific company rather than those of the "shotgun" variety were considered very favorably. Specificity of information, particularly as it related to job and career objectives, was also of considerable importance. While specificity is important, job seekers should be careful not to be overly restrictive, thereby ruling out jobs that may meet their career needs. Statements that cannot be supported by later investigation should be avoided. While it is appropriate to exclude weaknesses, since résumés should emphasize assets, an exaggeration of strengths is unfair to employers and may have deleterious effects if uncovered by the employer at a later date.

The research findings of Feild and Holley (1976) suggest that the following be incorporated into the résumé:

1. It should be typed or printed. Photocopies, although a second choice in their findings, are appropriate if they are high quality.
2. It should be two pages or less in length.
3. Rather than give a biographical history, it should highlight significant activities relating primarily to employment and education.
4. Personal data is less important than data relating to work skills and educational accomplishments.
5. Specific skills (for example, statistics, foreign languages, or computer programming) are of less importance in a general résumé than in one designed to fill a specific job opening requiring such skills.

On the basis of their findings, Feild and Holley (1976) designed a checklist (Table 8-6) to assist individuals in selecting appropriate content items and at the same time keeping the résumé brief. To be applicable to workers from fields other than professional, this checklist needs slight modification. Rather than emphasizing college preparation, as is suggested in Item 4, nonprofessional workers should emphasize educational achievements most relevant to their job and career objectives. Membership and leadership activities in any organization that have a bearing on job and career objectives should be provided in Item 6, professional activities.

While personnel officers may generally prefer résumés of two pages, preferred résumé length may vary by occupation. In general, résumés used by professionals, particularly in academic settings, are longer than those used by technicians or persons employed in business or industry. Advice about résumé length appropriate to a specific occupation may be best obtained by asking an experienced worker in that occupation.

In addition to gathering information about the résumé-format preferences of 57 personnel officers (selected from 100 companies on the Fortune 500 list), Stephens and others (1979) do an excellent job of reviewing the literature relevant to résumé format and integrating that information with their findings. These findings provide the following guidelines for structuring the résumé:

1. The presentation of education and work experience information is preferred early in the résumé, with information regarding awards and achievements, affiliations, and references preferred later. The preferred position for personal data is either first or next to last.
2. The positioning of résumé information on the page is not a significant factor in the selection decision, although there is a slight preference for ample margins and left headings. Crowding information should probably be avoided.
3. Clean corrections, neatness, correct spelling, and proper English are highly

TABLE 8-6. Checklist of item content in résumé construction

Clusters of résumé content	Résumé items
1. Personal data	Current address Permanent address Date of availability for employment
2. Job and career objectives and goals	Specific job objectives Specific career goals
3. Previous experience	Past work experiences (include description of duties) Tenure on previous jobs Military experience
4. Educational and academic background	Major in college Minor in college Grades in college major Grades in college minor Colleges and universities attended Overall grade-point average Class standing Years in which degrees were awarded Awards and scholarships received Sources for financing college studies (percent of money earned for college)
5. Physical health	Specific physical limitations Overall health status
6. Professional activities	Membership in professional organizations Offices held in professional organizations
7. Miscellaneous	Salary requirements Travel limitations Specific skills Spouse's willingness to relocate References Job-location requirements

From "Résumé Preparation: An Empirical Study of Personnel Managers' Perceptions," by H. S. Feild and W. H. Holley. In *Vocational Guidance Quarterly*, 1976, *24*, p. 236. Reprinted by permission of the American Personnel and Guidance Association.

preferred. The use of abbreviations had no effect on the hiring decision by a sizeable portion of the personnel directors (78%).

4. The use of bond paper was not significant in affecting the chances of employment. Colored paper elicited a mildly negative response.

5. The use of italics, underlining, and capital letters is not a major factor in deciding to accept or reject applicants.

6. The use of gimmicks in the résumé was looked upon negatively, while a unique approach was considered positive by the personnel managers. Stephens and others (1979, p. 32) suggest that a "uniqueness continuum" exists whereby a résumé that stands out from the rest is perceived positively up to the point where the "unusual is no longer viewed as attractive, but is perceived as being bizarre and obnoxious."

Some caution must be exercised in using the findings of these studies of résumé content and format. The research solicited the opinions of personnel directors; in larger firms the directors may not be the persons who are making the screening decisions, but rather, entry- or intermediate-level employees whose opinions may differ from those of the directors. However, directors generally provide the policy and guidelines for their departments, and most have probably functioned at the entry and intermediate levels in personnel; accordingly, their views may be the most valid.

Perhaps a more serious consideration is the applicability of these findings to job seekers who are not classified as professional workers. All research located and reviewed with respect to the résumé and cover letter was oriented toward job seekers with college degrees. We suspect that personnel workers are less vigorous in their review of the credentials of the nonprofessional worker, but acknowledge that this is an empirical issue which to the best of our knowledge has not yet been studied. Until further guidance is available, we believe that the findings and suggestions provided will be helpful to job seekers of all types.

Earlier in this chapter, we discussed the importance of understanding the different means by which persons in different occupational groups locate job openings; the same statement can be applied to the manner in which job applicants present themselves in writing to employers. An understanding of the variability among occupational groups is important knowledge for the career counselor to have.

Letters of reference.   Letters of reference are the least-researched component in the job-seeking process, although 82 – 99% of employers who have responded to various studies use some type of reference check as part of their hiring process. Muchinsky (1979) makes this interesting observation based on his thorough review of the purpose, desired content, reliability and validity, and legal aspects of letters of reference. Muchinsky's major findings are as follows:

1. The primary purpose of reference checks is to verify information given on applications and to obtain additional information about the applicants, particularly negative information.

2. The majority of employers appear to prefer information relating to the personality of applicants (Peres & Garcia, 1962; Sleight & Bell, 1954).

3. Responses among raters of the same applicant are not very reliable (Mosel & Goheen, 1952, 1959). Muchinsky (1979) suggests that this may be expected; different raters base their evaluations on differing perspectives of the applicant. In general, references were most valid (predicted performance best) when they were completed by the applicant's immediate supervisor (Browning, 1968; Mosel & Goheen, 1959). Even in this situation, the predictive validity is modest.

4. Caution should be used in requesting and providing information about applicants, particularly when that information is subjective and relates to personality characteristics (Wangler, 1973). Not many legal problems have arisen as a result of references (Levine & Rudolph, 1977).

Muchinsky's (1979) review suggests that job applicants select individuals to provide references from those who view the applicants favorably and would not provide negative information about them. In addition, it suggests that applicants select immediate supervisors as one of their references. Since reference letters are frequently used as a validity check on the data provided in the application and résumé, it supports our earlier statements about the importance of honest responses on these devices.

Applicants may have unresolved questions regarding letters of reference: "Outside of immediate supervisors, whom should I ask to write letters of reference for me? What are the advantages and disadvantages of requesting a copy of the reference from the reference writer?" Unfortunately, the research literature appears to offer no answers to these questions or to some others that arise.

Self-presentation in person

Assuming that they survive the screening of their job applications or résumés, the majority of job hunters will present themselves to their prospective employers through employment interviews. Although applications, résumés, and/or testing are frequently used for screening purposes, job interviews appear to be the primary method by which employers make hiring decisions (Spriegel & James, 1958). Because of the significance assigned to the interview in worker selection, it is important that career counselors and job seekers understand the key elements of the interview. Knowing these elements can guide the design of programs to improve job-interviewing skills.

Fortunately, numerous research studies have contributed to an improved understanding of the employment-interview process. Clowers and Fraser (1977), in their review of the employment literature from 1969 to 1976, located 24 data-based studies. Mayfield (1964), Ulrich and Trumbo (1965), Wagner (1949), and Wright (1969) had previously reviewed dozens of research studies of the selection-interview process. In general, the empirical investigations have studied the relationship of two major variables to the hiring decision: desirable applicant characteristics and the interview process itself. We hope that this information can contribute to the typical purposes of coaching for the job interview—the reduction of anxiety and the improvement of one's general interviewing skills (Keil & Barbee, 1973; Prazak, 1969).

A major problem with the literature in this area is its focus on the job applicant with a college degree, as opposed to the job seeker who would be entering nonprofessional fields. We noted a similar problem when we discussed the résumé.

Applicant characteristics. Perceptual factors such as the appearance, communication skills, and perceived personality characteristics of job interviewees seem to be more critical variables in hiring decisions than objective

background information such as education, work history, and related information (Clowers & Fraser, 1977; Lumsden & Sharf, 1974). Clowers and Fraser
(1977), in their review of the research, tabulated the frequency with which
applicant-related factors were identified as significant to the hiring decision and
found the perceptual factors to be significant to hiring in more than twice as
many instances as the more objective data (47 compared to 22). The most
important perceptual factors and the number of times cited as significant to the
hiring decision were: appearance(8), motivation for upward career mobility (6),
sociability (6), ability to interact with the interviewer (6), and speech (4).
Academic standing/grade-point average (8) and work experience (4) were the
most significant of the objective data. These factors would appear important to
consider when interviewing.

Interview process. Interview-process variables that have been found to be
important in job interview decisions include the favorable first impression
(Drake, Kaplan, & Stone, 1972), appropriate nonverbal behavior (Forbes &
Jackson, 1980; McGovern & Tinsley, 1978; Young and Beier, 1977), conversation flow (Svetlik, 1973), and information assimilation and decision making
(Farr, 1973; Springbett, 1958; Wagner, 1949; Webster, 1964; Wiener &
Schneiderman, 1974). In general, the research literature supports the importance of applicants' making a good first impression. This finding suggests that
interviewers using unstructured interviews tend to make an overall evaluation of
the job seeker early in the interview, usually within the first four minutes
(Springbett, 1958; Webster, 1964). More recent research indicates that when a
structured-interview format requiring an accumulation of decisions is used, this
evaluation decision is made toward the end of the interview (Farr, 1973).

There is some question about what constitutes the positive first impression.
Drake, Kaplan, & Stone (1972) found that the appearance and mannerisms of
job seekers were the most significant factors in creating a good first impression.
Contrary to popular opinion, the handshake itself was not nearly as important.

Researchers generally agree on what constitutes appropriate nonverbal interview behavior. In their study of judgments made in real-life interviews, Forbes
and Jackson (1980) found that interviewees accepted into an engineering-
apprenticeship program displayed more eye contact, smiling, and head nodding
than did individuals who were rejected. More active nonverbal behavior presented by interviewees has also been found to be rated higher than more passive
behavior (minimal eye contact and low energy level) by personnel representatives (McGovern & Tinsley, 1978).

The conversation flow of the interview is another element that job seekers
need to understand. Svetlik (1973) studied previous research and found that
interviewers talk about two-thirds of the time and applicants about one-third of
the time during the interview. Svetlik recommends that interviewers spend much
less time talking and encourage the applicant to talk the majority of the time.

Clowers and Fraser (1977, p. 20), in consideration of this trend, suggest that counselors assist applicants to "carry the interview conversation." Clients should learn to initiate topics and be spontaneous and creative in the interview.

Research regarding the decision-making process of the interviewers can provide significant guidance to job seekers with respect to the presentation of positive information and the control of negative information in the interview. Webster (1964) and Wiener and Schneiderman (1974) have found that employment interviewers tend to assimilate negative information more accurately than positive information. This tendency may be due to the extensive use of interviews to screen out applicants rather than screen them in. In consideration of these findings, Clowers and Fraser (1977, p. 21) suggest that clients point out positive job-related knowledge and skills frequently during the interview. Being as informed as possible about the requirements of the position and presenting information in relation to those requirements would appear to enhance the chances of being perceived positively. The nature of the position applied for also appears to affect interviewer decision making. Dipboye and Wiley (1977, 1978) found that applicants demonstrating moderately aggressive interview behavior were evaluated more favorably for a supervisory position than for an editorial assistant position.

Preparing for interviews. To a great degree, the Job-Interview Skills Sheet and Rating Scale (Table 8-7) incorporate these research findings. These tools can be helpful in structuring a job-interview training program. They are also useful for providing feedback to clients in mock interviews, particularly when those interviews are audio- or videotaped. Certain of the components of the Job Interview Skills Sheet and Rating Scale were adapted from previous work by Anthony (1973), Carkhuff and others (1975), and the MultiResource Center (1971). The latter two references are commercially available and are suggested as useful resources for planning and undertaking job-interview skills training. In general, the sequence of skills on the sheet is in the chronological order of the interview process.

TABLE 8-7. Job-interview skills sheet and rating scale

Skills Sheet[a]
1. Appropriate material
   _____ Carry appropriate material (notebook, pen, résumé, and open letter of reference) into the interview.[b]
2. Appropriate appearance
   _____ Be neat and clean.[b]
   _____ Wear clothes appropriate for interview.[b]
3. Appropriate entry to the interview
   _____ Walk in briskly.[b]
   _____ Give a firm handshake.[b]
   _____ State name and reason for being there.

TABLE 8-7. Job-interview skills sheet and rating scale (continued)

4. Appropriate attending behavior
   _____ Maintain appropriate eye contact with the employer.
   _____ Face the employer squarely.
   _____ Lean slightly forward in the chair.
   _____ Use appropriate nonverbal behavior (head nodding, smiles, etc.).
   _____ Listen to the employer carefully.
   _____ Refrain from exhibiting nervous mannerisms.

5. Responding with strengths
   _____ Present statements to support job choice, focusing on concrete work-related skills/abilities acquired through work experience, vocational training, or general education, or skills related to personal abilities, hobbies, etc.
   _____ Present at least three such statements during the interview.
   _____ Present strong skills statement during the first five minutes of the interview.

6. Responding to interviewer's questions
   _____ Respond to interviewer's questions, particularly to ambiguous questions, by presenting work strengths.
   _____ Respond to questions regarding personal deficits (physical disabilities, emotional hospitalization, prison record or arrest, poor job history, lack of education, age, etc.) by identifying the liability in nonstigmatizing terms and ending with a positive statement or demonstration related to one's ability to do the job. If the deficit is not related to the job, respond providing one or more ways that it is an asset in some area of life.
   _____ Respond to questions about past, present, and future vocational/educational decisions by expressing verbally how these decisions are or have been based on greater opportunities for personal, educational, or employment-related growth.

7. Initiating in the interview
   _____ Mention an obvious disability (physical handicap, age, etc.) to the employer within the first few minutes, if the employer has not previously initiated. Do so using nonstigmatizing terms and end with a positive statement or demonstration related to one's ability to do the job.
   _____ Ask specific questions about the job or the employer to show interest in the job.
   _____ Ask employer if he has questions about you that he has not yet asked.

8. Appropriate exit from the interview
   _____ Summarize important strengths.
   _____ Request permission to contact the employer by a certain date regarding the hiring decision.
   _____ Thank interviewer for interview.
   _____ Shake interviewer's hand firmly.[b]
   _____ Walk out of interview briskly.[b]

Rating Scale[c]
1. Interviewee *does not present* the skill and should have. Interviewee presents the skill, but for one or more reasons (brevity, clarity, timing, etc.) it is *inaccurate* or *detracts noticeably* from the interview.
2. Interviewee *presents* the skill *accurately;* however, it is only minimally effective because the skill presentation is *mechanical* and *unspontaneous,* possessing a rehearsed quality. It does not add or subtract markedly from the interview.
3. Interviewee *presents* the skill *accurately* and *spontaneously.* Interviewee's voice quality and other personal characteristics show him to be quite involved in the skill presentation. It adds significantly to the interview.

---

[a]Based in part on Anthony (1973); Carkhuff, Pierce, Friel, and Willis (1975); and Multi-Resource Center (1971).

[b]Rated yes or no. All other skills rated using the Rating Scale.

[c]Adapted from a job-interviewing skill rating scale developed by W. A. Anthony in an unpublished manuscript. Copyright 1980 by William A. Anthony. Reprinted by permission.

JOB-SEEKING SKILLS TRAINING PROGRAMS

There are a number of training programs designed to teach clients job-seeking skills (Azrin et al., 1975; Azrin & Besalel, 1979; Carkhuff et al., 1975; Human Resources Center, 1977; Keith et al., 1977; MultiResource Center, 1971). In general, these programs provide information about completing the job search, application, résumé, and the interview. They are described in Table 8-8.

Two of these programs, the Minnesota Job Seeking Skills Program (Multi-Resource Center, 1971) and the Job Club (Azrin et al., 1975; Azrin & Besalel, 1979), have been exposed to empirical research that strongly suggests that these comprehensive group-training formats emphasizing structured-learning activities enhance success in entering the job market (Azrin & Philip, 1979; McClure, 1972). While these two programs appear useful for all types of job seekers, their comprehensiveness and organization enable them to be especially appropriate for helping persons who may have more difficult job-getting problems, particularly socially disadvantaged and mentally or physically handicapped persons.

The Job Seeking Skills Program developed by the MultiResource Center (1971) was the first major program of this type. It provides clients with two days of instruction on finding job leads, completing job application blanks, and job interviewing. There is an emphasis on preparing for job interviews. Clients are instructed in answering problem questions and receive group and instructor feedback on role-play interviews, which are generally video recorded.

McClure (1972) compared the effectiveness of the Job Seeking Skills group with that of the normal state rehabilitation-agency placement procedures. Within 90 days of completing training, 50% of the Job Seeking Skills group members (19 of 38) received employment and maintained it for 30 days. Only 24% of the group handled according to conventional placement procedures (9 of 38) achieved and maintained employment. Those who completed job-seeking training required significantly less counselor time, due to the group format, than clients who were not in the group training. McClure (1972, p. 194) concludes: "Use of the job-seeking-skills class appears to be a more *effective* and *efficient* approach to placement than conventional placement procedures." We agree.

Azrin and his associates (Azrin & Besalel, 1979; Azrin et al., 1975) have developed a Job Club model similar in some ways to the Job Seeking Skills program but emphasizing behavioral-counseling methods and supervised practice in job seeking. Also important in their approach is the emphasis placed on mutual support among the Job Club members, achieved, in large part, through the group format, which allows peer and instructor feedback on résumé construction, telephone practice, and role play of interviews. Job leads are shared, and members provide one another with encouragement through the group process. A buddy system whereby clients are paired off with one another allows more individualized, as well as group, advice and encouragement. Transporta-

TABLE 8-8. Job-seeking skills training programs

Name	Publisher	Description	Further information
Employment Seeking Preparation and Activity	Robert D. Keith Lansing Psychological Associates 601 Abbot Road East Lansing, MI 48823	Comprehensive guide to job getting, with an emphasis on locating jobs. It includes useful information and a number of innovative activities and forms.	Keith, Engelkes, and Winborn (1977)
Get a Job	Human Resource Development Press Box 863, Dept. M3 Amherst, MA 01002	A systematically organized book focusing on the specific information, skills, and strategies needed in job getting, with a focus on developing job leads, preparing a résumé, and job interviewing.	
Job Club Counselor's Manual	University Park Press 233 East Redwood St. Baltimore, MD 21202	A comprehensive model of job finding that views the process as a series of complex skills learned through structured activities in a group format. Provides supervised practice in job seeking during the course of training.	Azrin, Flores, and Kaplan (1975); Azrin and Philip (1979)
Minnesota Job Seeking Skills Program	MultiResource Center 1900 Chicago Ave. Minneapolis, MN 55404	Two-day group-training approach that focuses on locating job leads and completing job applications, with an emphasis on job interviewing. Materials include a job-seeking skills workbook for the job seeker, a job-seeking skills reference manual, and an instructor's manual.	Anderson (1968); Azrin and Philip (1979); McClure (1972)
Modular Placement Training Program	Human Resources Center Albertson, NY 11507	Innovative job-placement training approach for rehabilitation professionals, divided into twelve 2½-hour multimedia presentations covering topics such as evaluating work readiness, working with employers, and self-placement. A participant's handbook provides a continuing resource of job-seeking information.	

tion to employers is also frequently shared between buddies or among group members.

The Job Club emphasizes that the job search is a full-time activity, and group counseling sessions are arranged on a five-day work-week schedule. Kemp and

Vash (1971) suggest that supervised practice in job seeking is necessary to insure an effective job-placement program. The manual for the program describes in detail the many other significant components of the Job Club (Azrin & Besalel, 1979).

The Job Club method has been exposed to more empirical study than any other method of job hunting. It has been found to be successful with a general group of unemployed persons (Azrin et al., 1975). Within three months of completing the program 93% of the Job Club members located full-time employment, as compared to 60% of a control group who did not receive Job Club counseling services. Job Club members also started work in fewer days (14 versus 53), obtained higher hourly starting wages ($2.73 versus $2.10), and acquired better types of jobs.

A subsequent application of the Job Club method to 1,000 welfare recipients resulted in an 85% placement rate, compared with 55% of clients who received regular agency services (Azrin et al., 1980). Jobs were obtained more quickly and the salaries and job types were comparable or better for the Job Club clients.

Other recent research has compared the Job Club with an alternative method based on the Minneapolis Job Seeking Skills program, using 154 clients with physical, emotional, intellectual, or social handicaps or long-term unemployment (Azrin & Philip, 1979). Six months following the completion of training, the Job Club members had been more successful than the Job Seeking Skills group members on the percentage of jobs obtained (95% versus 28%) and had taken less time to locate them (10 days versus 30 days).

While these results suggest greater effectiveness of the Job Club, they should not be interpreted to suggest that the alternative method based on the Minnesota Job Seeking Skills program is ineffective; it has been shown to be more successful than regular rehabilitation-agency placement practices (McClure, 1972). Azrin and Philip (1979) suggest that the comparative success of the Job Club may be due to its comprehensiveness and intensity. They also found that continued participant attendance and effort were necessary for success.

State vocational rehabilitation agencies in Illinois, Michigan, and Wisconsin (and probably in other states) have incorporated Job Seeking Skills and Job Club models in their programs (Jewish Vocational Service, 1976). Probably the most extensive agency placement program is that of the Michigan Vocational Rehabilitation Service, which has integrated a state-wide system of relationships with employers and Job Club/Job Seeking Skills groups into a comprehensive placement model (Jewish Vocational Service, 1976, pp. 20–30; Molinaro, 1977). In the employer-contact component of this program, all rehabilitation counselors are responsible for establishing and maintaining employer accounts and contact with companies in their area. Counselors in charge of accounts offer consultation to employers with respect to troubled employees, Affirmative Action, worker's compensation, awareness training of rehabilitation services and needs, meeting manpower needs, and related concerns. The focus in using this concept goes beyond "take my client" to "what can I do to meet your employment needs?" (Molinaro, 1977, p. 125).

Job openings were developed through the procedure and were provided to a central job bank (Job Central). Counselors in agency offices would review job orders, select appropriate clients, and call Job Central to discuss the applicability of the positions to their clients. Skill banks, which provided an updated list of job-ready clients, were used to refer workers to employers who had manpower needs. In general, subjective evaluations of the program suggest that it has resulted in better-paying and more varied jobs for clients (Jewish Vocational Service, 1976, p. 20).

Counselors and other human-service providers interested in the process of job placement should pay close attention to journals and other resources in the rehabilitation-counseling field. Of the counseling specialties, rehabilitation counseling has most emphasized job seeking. This emphasis is due primarily to legislative mandates, in addition to the traditionally difficult job-seeking problems of handicapped persons.

SUMMARY

This chapter focused on the resources and strategies designed to assist persons in preparing for and entering occupations by carrying out job-seeking activities. Educational preparation for employment was viewed in terms of two paths: in-school preparation and out-of-school preparation. Resources that describe the available avenues of preparation were listed and summarized.

Success in assisting clients in job seeking requires counselors to be aware of the changing occupational structure and effective methods of assisting clients to locate jobs and present themselves to employers both in writing and in person. Strategies suggested for locating jobs, writing résumés and letters of reference, and interviewing for jobs were primarily research based. Systematic programs designed to enhance job-seeking skills were reviewed and evaluated.

RECOMMENDED READINGS

Azrin, N. H., & Besalel, V. B. *Job Club Counselor's Manual: A behavioral approach to vocational counseling.* Baltimore: University Park Press, 1979.

This manual serves as a guide to using what is probably the most comprehensive, systematic, and effective job-seeking approach currently available. Recommended for practitioners who will assist clients in finding jobs.

Clowers, M. R., & Fraser, R. T. Employment interview literature: A perspective for the counselor. *The Vocational Guidance Quarterly,* 1977, *26,* 13–26.

On the basis of their thorough review of data-based studies published from

1969 to 1976, the authors provide numerous suggestions to counselors for improving clients' job-interviewing behaviors.

Feild, H. S., & Holley, W. H. Résumé preparation: An empirical study of personnel managers' perceptions. *The Vocational Guidance Quarterly,* 1976, *24,* 229–237.

Following a survey of 205 personnel managers, the authors provide suggestions as to the desired content of the résumés and cover letters of job seekers.

Muchinsky, P. M. The use of reference reports in personnel selection: A review and evaluation. *Journal of Occupational Psychology,* 1979, *52,* 287–297.

Recommendations related to the purpose and desired content of reference letters are suggested by this thorough review.

Oetting, E., & Miller, C. D. Work and the disadvantaged: The work adjustment hierarchy. *Personnel and Guidance Journal,* 1977, *56,* 29–35.

This interesting and well-written article provides a useful context for understanding the work-related problems of adults and youths.

Stephens, D. B., Watt, J. T., & Hobbs., W. S. Getting through the résumé preparation maze: Some empirically based guidelines for résumé format. *The Vocational Guidance Quarterly,* 1979, *28,* 25–34.

The résumé-format preferences of 57 personnel managers are summarized in this article. In addition, the authors do an excellent job of integrating the results of an extensive literature review with their findings.

Vandergoot, D., & Worrell, J. D. (Eds.). *Placement in rehabilitation: A career development perspective.* Baltimore: University Park Press, 1979.

This excellent book provides a useful model for integrating career placement within a career-development perspective. It contains an outstanding collection of original chapters illuminating both the theory and practice of career placement.

LEARNING ACTIVITIES

1. Interview workers from at least two different occupations—one representing professional and managerial kinds of work, the other representing clerical, trade, semiskilled, and related occupations. Note the differences in educational preparation required of the various occupations. Ask the workers whether they believe their preparation to have been typical for their occupations.

2. Using the *Handbook for Analyzing Jobs* (U.S. Department of Labor, 1972), analyze a job that interests you or someone you know who is seeking work.

3. Become familiar with at least two of the sources of educational preparation summarized in Table 8-2. If possible, use these resources with someone who is planning some educational preparation beyond high school.

4. Using the Hierarchy of Work Adjustment (Table 8-3) as an interview guide, evaluate someone's current work adjustment. What behaviors in this developmental sequence have been successfully acquired and which have not been? What recommendations can you make to improve this person's work adjustment?

5. Ask at least five persons who are employed how they first heard about their current jobs. Compare your findings with those presented in Table 8-4.

6. Using the information discussed in the section on locating jobs, assist someone to locate potential job openings.

7. Assist someone to complete an application and/or résumé using the suggestions provided in the sections on completing job applications and résumés.

8. Using the recommendations provided in the section on job interviewing, assist someone to prepare for an interview.

CHAPTER NINE

COUNSELING FOR CAREER ADJUSTMENT

An examination of the therapy-oriented literature of the disciplines of psychiatry and clinical psychology reveals a dearth of references to the issues of work and career adjustment. Yet most practitioners are aware that job dissatisfaction and the inability to cope with ordinary work frustrations are common themes among client problems. Within the counseling and guidance discipline, the literature on career counseling and career development has emphasized the issue of career decision making and has largely ignored the treatment of career-maladjusted individuals. As discussed in the previous chapters, career counseling is viewed by most practitioners as a specialty that promotes adaptive educational and/or career decisions at any appropriate point in the life span. In this chapter, however, we will advocate another form of career counseling: one less specialized than the process of assisting career decisions, but career-oriented by virtue of its focus on the emotional well-being of the client as it relates to his or her involvement in work and the pursuit of a satisfying career.

CONTEXT FOR CAREER-ADJUSTMENT COUNSELING

In many counseling-practice settings, clients do not come for help in considering career options or, for that matter, to complain specifically about work-related problems. They come because they are experiencing psychological pain and they seek its alleviation through treatment. The presenting pain typically comprises negative affect states, principally those of anxiety, depression, frustration, or unsatisfactorily managed hostility.

Initially, the relationship between these negative affect states and career issues is evidenced in one of two ways: either the emotional condition is a direct consequence of unfavorable work conditions or the emotional condition is a function of conditions external to the job or occupational choice, but extra work conflicts could arise from another adjustment factor, such as marital difficulty, or some aspect of the person's personality that generates maladaptive emotional reactions. In either situation, the counselor must work therapeutically with career or work issues. In the case of younger people, schooling can be legitimately viewed as the traditional "job" of the adolescent, and these perspectives still apply.

189

The negative affects that require therapeutic intervention are distinguishable from those negative responses many have to career and work. As Wool (1975) points out, there is considerable disaffection with work among lower- to middle-income workers. With continuing economic hardship and little intrinsic satisfaction accruing from work, aversive reactions among most of those employed are more commonplace and normal than the types of reactions that bring individuals to counseling. One will feel career dissatisfaction because much in the working world is not very satisfying. To live and work is at times to feel disappointed, angry, frustrated, and so forth. The anxiety and depression that warrant counseling are more severe than the kind of dissatisfaction that, though uncomfortable, does not seriously impair performance. The working client who requires psychological treatment not only complains about work but also manifests such conditions as the excessive use of alcohol, psychophysiological symptoms, and other problem states and behaviors. In many cases maladjustment on the job prompts a crisis in the marriage and leads to real and serious physical impairments.

In this chapter we deal first with adult clients suffering from externally induced stress originating in their job settings. We then discuss how work often provides the occasion to amplify faulty coping because of characterological deficits. The concept of character in clinical use is almost interchangeable with the concept of personality (Hinsie & Campbell, 1970): both refer to the complex of cognitions and behaviors regularly available to a person in coping with daily life. A character deficit is the existence of repetitious, self-defeating thought and/or behavior, or the absence of a performance-related competency.

It can be argued that the interaction of personal makeup (character) and work setting (environment) is needed for an accurate understanding of career-related adjustment (Lofquist & Dawis, 1969). As discussed in Chapter 2, Holland's theory of career development (1973) applies to the issue of career dissatisfaction as well as to career choice. This theory aids in the understanding of mismatches between personality and work environment. Attempts to distinguish these constructs discretely will never be completely successful, of course. From the life sciences we have learned that every organism flourishes under a set of conditions favorable to its makeup. In turn, even a healthy organism cannot withstand for long a situation in which vital processes are not supported. In recent generations, prisoners of war have dramatically exemplified this principle in the social psychological domain. Thus, we acknowledge the interdependence of these factors but will examine them here as distinct entities in order to simplify the discussion.

THE EFFECT OF WORK SETTING

Many of us have had direct experience with persons who appear to be reasonably adaptable individuals but who at a period in their lives experience significant levels of psychological pain; on such occasions we conclude that the situations in which they live are inhospitable, at least in part, generating negative responses that otherwise would not be present. In some such cases the individuals may benefit from a generally supportive family and community apart from the employment setting; they express few complaints other than those specifically related to work. The stress reaction may derive from a negative view of a job by comparison to previous employment. For example, an individual in a vocationally stable career pattern may have, for reasons of income and advancement, changed employers several times and found only the most recent position unsatisfactory.

In actuality the problem is broader than this example indicates: job stress and work-related anxieties are worldwide problems requiring much more effort by the allied helping professions than has been made up to now (Srivastava, 1977). Continuing and increasing investigation of the problem of coronary heart disease reveals that occupational sources of stress, even more than smoking tobacco and consuming animal fat, play a primary etiological role (Cooper & Marshall, 1976).

Much of the misery individuals experience due to the conditions under which they work is not portrayed very vividly by the statistics of research reports. The objective of this discussion is not advocacy for those so distressed but the demonstration of the situation's appropriateness for counseling intervention. The case of Marie and Arnold Black may support this point of view.

A career example

Marie Black was referred to a psychiatric-outpatient clinic at a university medical center by her family physician because of continuing depression. The doctor had tried with only moderate success to treat the condition through mild antidepressive medication. During the initial interview, Marie explained that for the preceding 22 years she and her family had lived in numerous communities in several countries because of her husband's military career. Col. Arnold Black had graduated from one of the military academies and was described as fully committed to a service career, but had prematurely retired because of knowledge that his ambition to achieve the rank of general would not be fulfilled. He had received an unsatisfactory rating from his last superior, sealing his fate. In disappointment he retired to take a management position in his younger brother's company. The latter's business involved a chain of franchised muffler-repair centers in small towns dispersed over a rather large geographic area.

As Mrs. Black described her condition, she detailed the tension at home, especially during the dinner hour and evening following her husband's return from work. A rather passive and unassertive woman, Marie would begin by midafternoon to worry about her husband's mood, expecting him to return home and shout at the teenage children about insignificant things, sulk through dinner, and finally retire to the den to watch TV, rarely to attend to her for the rest of the evening. These data and other intake information were eventually construed as signs more of a family/marital crisis than of a personal one for Marie; her mood was essentially a meter or manifestation of the former. From this perspective, she was informed of the counselor's hypotheses and asked to bring her husband to the next session.

Much of the second session involved Col. Black's description of his military career, its disappointing termination, and his decision to work for his brother. His new job was described as a disastrous situation. Although handsomely paid initially to do management work similar to what he had done in the military, he soon found that his brother was not willing to permit him any decision-making power. Rather, his brother oversaw all his activities, having even publicly humiliated him on several occasions. He felt he must control his rage over this situation, since two children in college and a new home filled with new furniture had put him heavily in debt. He believed he had little opportunity to escape from the situation in which he found himself with his brother.

In marital counseling he admitted he was difficult to live with, having become increasingly impatient and demanding. While over the next four sessions Marie's mood gradually improved (for example, she regained enough self-confidence to drive a car and was able to sleep through the night), a dramatic change in the family occurred as a consequence of a new job opportunity for her husband.

Prior to his retirement Col. Black's principal responsibilities in the military of dealing with computer technology and a data retrieval system had been transferred to a private corporation. Upon finalizing the contract with the government, the corporation made contact with him, proposing in essence a return to his old duties as a civilian with a general's salary. Being a retired officer, of course, allowed him military privileges at the installation as well. The effect of this fortuitous offer was indeed dramatic in terms of enhanced well-being for both wife and husband. In fact, it exemplifies clearly how a job change may have more positive consequences than the self-knowledge achieved from counseling.

A school example

The college counselor may also verify instances in which a school setting appears, just as work may, to be the primary source of difficulty for an otherwise normal and adequately functioning student. It is not uncommon, for instance, for a student to select a college major consistent with her or his personality but a school to which he or she cannot adjust. The fact that sizeable differences exist among particular schools is evidenced by the number of transfers requested to other schools. Some institutions, just like individual homes, are more hospitable than others. Other factors besides those related to career satisfaction and choice seem to affect a student's reaction to a particular campus. Prevailing attitudes of materialism among fellow students, sexual standards, and so forth contribute to pressure beyond tolerance for some students. Although satisfied with their course of study, they may for other reasons be sufficiently unhappy to seek the assistance of a counselor or dorm advisor. These students, as did Col. Black and others, experience significant emotional improvement as a consequence of a change of work or educational setting.

STRESS AND WORK

In recent years much interest has been directed toward stress and stress-management strategies. For the career counselor, stress is an important topic because occupational factors are major contributors to people's stress levels. Since the precise meaning of this variable is often misunderstood, we will describe stress in general prior to discussing it in a career context.

The nature of stress

Hans Selye (1976), an endocrinologist and winner of a Nobel Prize, is the person most responsible for our current understanding of stress. Selye (1976) defines *stress* as "the nonspecific response of the body to any demand." The stimulus that precedes this response is called a *stressor*. This terminology is different from an engineer's use of the terms *stress* and *strain:* Selye's *stress* is the engineer's *strain*.

Stressors can be objective (actual environmental events) or subjective (perception of events). The stress response can be determined by observing the activation of the endocrine system in the body, particularly the presence of various adrenal secretions (hormones) in the bloodstream. Without the presence of these adrenal secretions, by definition there is no stress. This response distinguishes stress from anxiety and nervous tension. When people "feel tense," more than likely they are stressed. However, stress can be present even when a person is not aware of tense feelings or emotional pressure. People can become so accustomed to working while stressed that they do not realize the strain their bodies are enduring. Stress is potentially damaging, especially when it continues over a period of time.

Selye (1976) further describes stress as reflecting the rate of "wear and tear" of life. Stress reactions are equal to what Selye calls the General Adaptation Syndrome (GAS). The GAS has three stages: alarm, resistance, and exhaustion. To represent these stages, we will describe one of Selye's animal experiments (1976). In this study, a group of laboratory rats were moved from indoors to the cold roof of the building housing the laboratory. When initially placed in the cold environment, the rats became agitated (alarmed). After a period of time their behavior returned to normal, with the appearance that they had adapted to the cold (resistance). After a period of time, however, the rats died (exhaustion). Even though for a while they seemed to adapt, the stressor (cold) became too much to endure.

To explain the GAS, Selye (1974, 1976) hypothesizes that every organism inherits its biological equipment with a differential capacity to tolerate stress. The capacity is governed in part by a reservoir of inherited adaptation energy. This energy has nothing to do with caloric intake; it is a "deep" resource on which the organism draws to meet threats or challenges. When one uses up all one's adaptation energy, death results. For Selye, adaptation energy is not renewable. This energy theory is only a theory at present; since it does not deal with observable data, it will remain difficult to support.

Connected with adaptation energy are Selye's views of aging—the "wear and tear" theory. The demands of life call for response; we use up adaptation energy and continue to wear out various parts of our bodies. The weakest body system, subjected to the most stress, wears out first.

When stress is present, the adrenal secretions are present. These secretions produce bodily changes associated with the organism's preparing for what is commonly called "fight or flight." Heart rate and blood pressure increase along with other changes. Under prolonged stress, increased cholesterol levels and further changes result. One can see how coronary heart disease is linked to stress (Cooper & Marshall, 1976). For the organism itself as for the heart, repeated preparation for muscular activity (fight or flight) over prolonged periods without eliminating the stressors results in organ damage (Fröberg, 1972). In fact, various sources (for example, McQuade & Aikman, 1974) estimate that up to 80% of all illness is related to stress. Stress thus becomes extremely important as a major health problem. It is linked not only to heart disease but also to arthritis, allergies, cancer, increased susceptibility to infection, and general aging (Selye, 1976).

Occupational stressors

In recent years the counseling profession has become increasingly aware of the fact that environmental or situational factors need careful consideration in the understanding of social-emotional problems. Many believe that in the past practitioners were too inclined to identify "intrapsychic factors" or the client's personality as the chief origin of adjustment problems. In order to understand general health problems, researchers have now begun to establish information systems to study the relationship between occupational stressors and worker health. For example, Colligan, Smith, and Hurrell (1977) in Tennessee examined admissions records of mental-health centers to see if the incidence of certain diagnoses was related to major occupations in the state. While the data on such relationships are not conclusive at present, such investigations help to develop the methodology needed to study these phenomena.

In general, there is increasing support for the view that factors contributing to stress and to emotional problems are in the nature of most occupations. Cunnick and Smith (1977) investigated the effects of occupational stress, in part, by reviewing suicide rates over the past 50 years. They concluded that emotional problems seem on the increase among younger males and females and among middle-aged females. Incidence rates of older persons and middle-aged males seem to have stabilized. Cunnick and Smith's data suggest that most of the difficulties that are evidenced at the workplace are specifically related to work. Important psychological stressors that are work related include loss of employment, conflicts over policy, procedures, results, and the like, frustration of unfulfilled expectations, rapid change, role conflicts among women, male "menopause," and relapsing psychiatric disability.

To this point we have treated occupational stressors in direct connection with negative emotional reactions. Increasingly counselors are becoming concerned about the general health of workers and its relation to working conditions, which include not only physical factors such as presence of excessive noise but also organizational ones such as work overload. Drawing from several general references on occupational stress (Cooper & Payne, 1978; Klein, 1971; McLean, 1974; Stellman & Daum, 1973), we have randomly listed important physical and social-psychological occupational stressors in Table 9-1.

The occupational stressors listed in Table 9-1 are not considered to represent all potential stressors within the work setting. We listed factors randomly because no valid way currently exists of ordering occupational stressors according to their potency or importance to workers.

It is impossible for human beings to avoid stress. While stress remains a major health problem, not all stress is bad. Selye (1974, 1976) classifies stress as either *distress* (negative and damaging) or *eustress* (positive and enjoyable). One can recognize the flow of adrenaline by the burning sensation that occurs in the abdomen after an experience such as narrowly escaping an auto accident. The same sensation often occurs before being reunited with loved ones while waiting

TABLE 9-1. Occupational stressors

Physical	*Social-psychological*
Physical danger	Closeness of supervision
Noise	Little social interaction
Excessive heat	Employer performance standards
Excessive cold	Self-performance standards
Pollution	Job security
Monotonous tasks	Impersonal/disinterested management
Repetitive tasks	Worker role conflict
Vibration	Worker role ambiguity
Motion	Changes at work
Wind	Expense of making mistakes (monetary & career)
Radiation	Work overload: quantitative (too much),
Magnetic fields	qualitative (too difficult)
Atmospheric pressure	Overpromotion
Reduced oxygen	Underpromotion
Excessive travel	Mismatch of formal/actual power
	Responsibility for others
	Frequent decisions

for them to appear on an airport concourse. Eustress is often our response to self-actualizing life challenges. This may use up adaptive energy, but as it does it fills life with meaning and purpose. Counselors might assist people to conserve energy by avoiding needless exposure to distress so they can invest it in meaningful and satisfying encounters.

COUNSELING FOR OCCUPATIONAL DISTRESS

Diagnosis

To determine whether a client's distress is largely the result of an unhealthful work setting, consider the answers to the following questions.

1. Does the client evidence a history of poor adjustment, or does it appear that the client's distress is of recent onset, with little prior occurrence of similar difficulties?
2. Is there any information that the client's co-workers are experiencing unusually high levels of dissatisfaction? Does available information suggest that members of the client's occupation as a group have high levels of emotional and/or physical problems?
3. Does the client appear to have an operational support system (family and friends) that could be expected to assist in weathering the usual disappointments and frustrations associated with work?
4. Does the client personally verbalize dissatisfaction with the work setting, attributing to it the major source of the problem?

If the client seems to have been reasonably adaptive in the past, can document that his or her dissatisfaction and stress are shared by other workers in a similar situation, is supported by friends and family, and can document (at least verbally) the relationship between emotional pain and working conditions, the counselor can be reasonably assured that situational concerns are the chief factors in the case.

Suggested treatment

If the problem is determined to be largely situational in nature, treatment is usually not very complicated. The client ordinarily has insight into the problem, which, being external, is nonthreatening for the client to discuss. The client may become anxious during the discussion, however, as the consequences of a lost job are imagined, especially its financial repercussions. Not being able to cope with the situation can bring a loss of self-esteem if the client believes, "I should be able to tough this thing out."

Supportiveness. Since feeling victimized and entrapped are common reactions, supportive, relationship-oriented counseling seems to be a wise choice, especially early in the process. The empathy and warmth of a counselor will help to energize the discouraged client. As vitality increases, so also will action taking increase.

A common error made by counselors is to move too rapidly into concrete action steps oriented toward changing the work setting or relocating through an employment change. It often seems so clear to the counselor what must inevitably be done that it is hard for the counselor to remember the courage it takes to execute the obvious steps. Discouraged people, suffering loss of self-esteem, are seldom decisive in doing something about their misery. Those who are able to take quick control of an unsatisfactory situation rarely come for counseling.

An additional way to aid in vitalizing the client for the inevitable effort to make a job change is to bring the family into direct contact with the client's pain. This can be done in two ways, either by arranging a family session or by reviewing and rehearsing how the client is to make the rest of the family aware of the problem. As the family becomes more fully aware of the client's distress, it can more completely mobilize support and encouragement. Routine but troublesome issues and demands at home may be ignored temporarily, further relieving tension for the client. In fact, the simple matter of the family's knowing that a member is troubled enough to seek professional help can make a positive difference. Burke and Weir (1977) demonstrate how one marital partner can be helpful in moderating the stress the other partner experiences at work. The key to the impact of this is the perception of the troubled worker; he or she must be satisfied with the means the spouse selects in attempting to be helpful. Such a supportive situation at home can facilitate positive consequences whether or not the worker makes a job or career change on the way to gaining greater tolerance of the work situation.

Therapeutic strategies. With the advent of many "technique-oriented" approaches to counseling, training for many counselors seems recently to have omitted a full understanding of the real potency of the counseling relationship. Such counselors fail to realize that the "core" conditions (Rogers, 1957) of therapy or counseling provide enormous value in that they help to generate psychological energy. To vitalize a discouraged person is far more valuable than making suggestions for alternative action, especially if the fuel to sustain action is lacking, as is usually the case with discouraged and confused individuals. Troubled persons do not seem to have the energy and confidence to sustain the action taking that others might see as reasonable.

In some counseling cases the client may need to have instances identified in which his or her negative affect appears to be increased by dwelling on the disagreeable aspects of a job. Such approaches as Rational-Emotive Therapy (RET) may offer the practitioner some useful strategies for helping the client understand and better control tendencies to exaggerate or amplify the discomforts of an already unsatisfactory situation. Ellis (1973) is very clear in describing how cognitions can exacerbate emotional reactions. Again, though, it is important to recall past criticism of counselors and other helping professionals for unrealistically advocating personal control over reactions to stress. We emphasize the need for views that balance self-responsibility for feeling states and realistic appraisals of stress within an environment. Many current views, as supported by literature cited in this section, document the distinct likelihood that factors external to an individual may be beyond the finite coping ability of that individual. Most regard the person in such a condition not as in need of corrective therapy but as in need of diminished stress.

As the client experiences the concern of counselor and family, revitalization occurs, and decision making and action taking tend to increase. Many of the sessions midway in the process will involve cognitive review of the week's events and plans for the future. At this point the counseling process may resemble one or more of the decision-making strategies discussed in Chapter 3.

In some cases a decision to change jobs is not the outcome of counseling. As both client and counselor explore the problem, and as the client experiences the empathic understanding of the counselor, the client may gain in tolerance of others on the job and hence create conditions conducive to improved interpersonal relationships. Making an effort to understand the frame of reference of a stress-inducing supervisor, for instance, may help to reduce the client's stress. The perceptual change, then, becomes the key to improved adaptation to the job. Patterson (1969) describes this process well in the context of client-centered therapy.

Much of what we have discussed as counseling strategy for the relationship and cognitive therapist is systematized in some of the more recent behavioral strategies. From Meichenbaum, Turk, and Burstein (1975), for example, and from the senior author in particular, has come what is called *stress inoculation training*. This approach involves an educational phase in which the client is provided with a conceptual framework for understanding the way in which he or she responds to a stressful event. Next, in the rehearsal phase, the client collects information on coping strategies, learns how to arrange escape routes from the stress, learns how to relax, and in general learns adaptive self-statements to replace negative ones. In what is largely a cognitive phase, the client is trained to develop the capacity for self-reinforcement. Finally, the client receives application training, in which what was learned is tested out in practice and evaluated. Similarly, Feinberg, Stabler, and Coley (1974) report a behavior-therapy case study in which relaxation and systematic desensitization were applied to a 49-year old female suffering from work-related situational anxiety. Six 45-minute sessions did reduce the subject's measured anxiety. The authors also report no symptom substitution.

Dealing with stress. It is unfortunate that counseling psychology, the applied discipline most directly associated with the study and treatment of normal people who have to cope with stress, has not been more oriented toward the study of the area of work. Goldman (1976) has been frequently cited for his widely held view that most of the published research is rather meaningless and that important adjustment issues have not been examined. The late Ralph Berdie (1973) had identified the same issue. He noted that many special populations have gone unnoticed in favor of laboratory or analogue studies on counselor training. It is hardly surprising that little of a concrete nature is available to the practitioner in dealing with stress tolerance among clients; little is even available in dealing with occupational stress among practitioners. Riggs and Kugel (1976), in *Social Casework,* do describe a situation in which mental health workers had to adjust to work in a rural community after being part of a very large urban practice. In being part of a small community, practitioners experienced the loss of personal privacy and the accustomed anonymity and formality of the therapist; for them this loss was described as a significant stressor. The issue of "counselor burnout" is currently a popular one in professional meetings; by the time the present book is in print, we hope there will be a better understanding of stress in counseling practice and how to cope with it. In the future, that understanding may extend to clients.

With the situation as it is, we conjecture that the preferred mode of treatment for coping with stress remains supportive therapy, in which counselor warmth and understanding help to fortify and energize the client. As mentioned earlier, counselor empathy seems to engender client empathy or understanding of others. Understanding develops tolerance; with greater tolerance of others usually comes greater tolerance of self. In learning to live with the idiosyncrasies of work mates, the client begins to take herself or himself less seriously. Work ambition, for example, can be explored and redefined in a more acceptable way; overzealousness can be moderated. Recall that the clients we are discussing are not disabled by pathological levels of such characteristics; they are normal human beings, with human imperfections, in whom the work setting has encouraged some kind of acute stress response. This response, while often not very adaptive, can be understood realistically by such clients. Counseling reaffirms the strengths in the individual's personality, balancing it for better coping with undesirable elements of the job setting.

Counseling outcomes. The balancing effect of the counseling process ultimately puts work in clearer perspective among the client's involvements. The client can become able once again to appreciate family, friends, and community. These outcomes relax the client, reduce the stress, and put the client in a position to cope better with a less-than-desirable work setting. The greater emotional stability also enables the client to recognize more clearly and to capitalize on safe opportunities to make a job change; he or she is better able to think and perceive. This result forms an interesting paradox: as clients begin to need a job change less, they become more able to make one.

Although seldom discussed in the professional literature, an experience not uncommon in counseling is to see a case such as we are describing change from a stress-tolerance situation to a form of growth or actualization therapy. On coming to grips with what they cannot change, some clients recognize what parts of themselves they would like to change, not merely because coping requires it but because the changes will more fully develop them as people. Then what may have begun as either a frustrating or a routine case for the counselor becomes a situation with great potential for gratification and even personal growth for the counselor.

Inexperienced practitioners and those who are involved in structured group practice or consultation might consider further study of such practices as stress inoculation training. An approach such as this has the advantage of organizing the intervention process in a manner that is easy to understand and execute. Developing a program to offer training to groups of employees or students may provide the counselor with experience that is applicable to one-to-one practice.

PERSONAL PROBLEMS AFFECTING WORK EFFICIENCY

Under this heading we depart from the topic of client distress associated directly with the work setting. Instead we will examine client problems in which something other than work precipitates the acute and situational negative affect. Despite the origin of the stress, if the client is troubled, work efficiency may be reduced; gratification from work may be lessened; job security may even be threatened.

Disruptions in primary relationships, illness and other physical problems, and financial setbacks constitute three important categories of events eventually affecting work efficiency. Clients become consumed by the immediate threat and pain associated with the circumstance, not being able to attend fully to the demands of their occupation. It may be argued that this reponse is adaptive in that mobilization occurs with respect to the most immediate threat. The career counseling task in such circumstances, however, is to help maintain the client's adequate functioning on the job while the principal effort in counseling is directed toward the source of disturbance.

Primary-relationship problems

One of the most significant general areas of personal difficulty is that of love relationships, which may for one reason or another go through a period of turmoil and in many cases eventually dissolve. This category includes a breakup between single persons, separation and divorce for married persons, and other kinds of disruption in very important interpersonal relationships. Bloom, Asher, and White (1978) have provided a comprehensive review of the impact of marital disruption in a multitude of personal areas. They report that in 1976, for example, 3,000,000 persons in this country were directly involved in a broken marriage. Such data certainly document that relationship problems are widespread and suggest that they can be expected to appear frequently among persons seeking supportive intervention. For instance, school counselors will probably deal with affected children and mental-health counselors will likely treat one or both the partners—those who are damaged enough from the breakup to require professional assistance—or the remnants of a separated family.

College counselors will also invariably be sought out for relationship breakdowns. Girlfriend and boyfriend problems are frequently brought into counseling. On a college or university campus, with two- to four-month grading periods, even short-term emotional disablement can affect scholastic achievement to the point of jeopardizing the student's academic future.

In some cases clients come into treatment while the relationship breakdown is still in progress. In other cases the process has concluded in a final dissolution. In the former, the mood is characterized by confusion and anxiety; in the latter, grief is predominant. Often counselors deal with clients through both phases.

While we will deal with counseling strategy in detail after we review other situational problems, we believe it important now to emphasize that the main effort in counseling is directed toward the primary-relationship problem. The time spent discussing work is intended to help reduce further damage to the client resulting from the consequences of lowered work efficiency.

Illness-related problems

Many counselors with little training in the life sciences often fail to understand and appreciate fully the psychological consequences of a physical disability or illness and how it affects work adjustment. Rehabilitation counselors may constitute an exception to this statement; their training includes careful consideration of the psychological consequences of disability. In rehabilitation-counselor preparation programs there is usually one course devoted to the psychological effects of disability, but the emphasis is on permanent or chronic disability. Our present concern is with persons whose illness is more acute, time-limited, and more likely to have responded to medical treatment with some degree of success; for example, the young person who has had lower back problems, or a recent "mild" heart-attack victim. In such cases most would assume that the client had been successfully rehabilitated, having been released from the hospital and put on follow-up medication presumed to be effective in alleviating any remaining pain or other symptoms. Some clients may even have been completely discharged from medical treatment. Most people who are in contact with this person will assume that he or she is "healthy" again. From this assumption follows the expectation that the person will function at levels similar to those prior to the onset of the physical disability. The client also may have similar self-expectations.

Problems both at home and at work persist for many such people, however, largely because they continue to be depressed. Both the clients and their associates begin to believe that the depression is a product of the person's character or personality. While many clients are indeed characterologically depressed, and we will discuss them later in this chapter, we are still talking about those who are essentially adaptive individuals; they do not reflect a history of maladjustment.

Blinder (1977) discusses cases in which the depression is rather pronounced. Initially the client is most likely to seek assistance from a medical-treatment setting. Individuals whose depression is less severe, however, may seek help at a center not primarily medical in nature. In such cases the counselor has in fact no treatment for what may be an emotional state related to the aftermath of a medical problem. The counselor's role is then usually one of referral agent, which requires the awareness that such consequences do occur from what appears to be an adequately treated physical problem. It is important as standard procedure to inquire about physical illness when clients with no significant history of repeated episodes of the condition seem to reflect emotional problems of fairly recent onset. In this regard, other factors warrant similar investigation. For example, Blinder (1977) notes that depression may follow a period of severe dieting. Increasingly, the allied helping professions are recognizing the important effect diet or nutrition has on human behavior. While counselors are not adequately trained to evaluate diet and recommend changes, general awareness of possible side effects related to poor nutrition may increase the counselor's ability to at least participate through referral in a remedial effort.

Direct treatment by the counselor will generally consist in supportive counseling involving the client's reevaluation of personal goals and values in light of recent events, including the recent illness. The counselor can be helpful by pointing out that being depressed may be a natural continuation of the physical problem presumed to be resolved. The counselor should probably advise the client, on the basis of the client's history, to expect improvement within a relatively short time as a result of the counselor's and the client's combined efforts. If depression continues, a medical or psychiatric consultation may be warranted.

Financial problems

Such recurring economic problems as recession and inflation at times create enough stress for otherwise vocationally and emotionally well-adjusted people that they seek out a counselor. These individuals might ordinarily be satisfied and suited to their occupations; they express dissatisfaction with their work primarily because they do not earn enough money to meet expenses. While at one time this problem was more characteristic of blue collar workers, more and more white-collar, middle-income families experience similar financial problems. When economic conditions are unfavorable, all ages are affected, including retired and other persons on more or less fixed incomes.

Counseling a client who is experiencing job dissatisfaction in terms of economic stress can be difficult: if the problem is essentially a consequence of broader social problems related to the economy, the solution is beyond the scope of counseling; if the problem is the client's personal inability to handle money, the counselor must be confident of special competence in helping the client to become a better money manager. Most counselors we know have little systematic training in this area and will need to refer persons with such problems.

Some individuals may come to a career counselor expressing an interest in making a career change for the primary reason of making more money. They may be well suited to their current position and need little of what was described in Chapter 3 as counseling for career decision making; they simply need to achieve better financial conditions. We do not view such situations as warranting counseling. Acknowledgement of the problem as such, with referral to a financial-management source, may be the best a counselor can do.

PERSONALITY AND CAREER ADJUSTMENT

We have described job factors that, classified as stressors, are sufficiently disabling to require counseling assistance. We take the balanced view that career issues are complex in nature. Problems related to adaptation to work seem clearly to be culture-, person-, and situation-specific. In this section we will treat how the formation of one's personality and its attributes affect the way an individual copes with occupational stress. While generally recognized in the literature (Cooper & Marshall, 1976), those personality dimensions that provide a poor prognosis for work adaptation have not been examined systematically. This section will be devoted to such problems and their treatment. To demonstrate the breadth of the topic, we will begin with a serious cultural problem and hence a common work-related problem: the problem of alcoholism, its effect on a career, and its treatment.

Alcoholism

Scope of the problem.   Management in business and industry has been very concerned with the problem of alcoholism and has often sought assistance for its workers from counselors and therapists. In many ways alcoholism stands out as a clear example of how work and the economy of a culture can be affected by social and psychological factors.

Alcoholism is a problem of considerable magnitude. It affects an estimated 4.5 million workers (Trice & Roman, 1973), and drinking problems not classified as alcoholism probably affect millions more. It pervades all social classes, from presidents of corporations through the ranks to unskilled workers.

Alcoholism, while defined in many ways, is most commonly understood as the use of alcohol to the degree to which it injures one's health and/or social and economic functioning. Excessive use of alcohol is our concern as career counselors since it seriously impairs worker performance. Clearly a career-related problem, it usually develops over a 7- to 10-year period, during at least part of which the person is working. As the problem develops, its chronicity becomes manifest; loss of function is also evident. For the alcoholic, disablement is not limited to periods of intoxication. Even when sober the alcoholic may divert his or her attention from other pursuits to the concern of securing liquor, hiding the problem from others, and so forth.

Not all clients with drinking problems are labeled *alcoholics.* Wolberg (1977, p. 882) describes what he terms the *anxiety drinker,* who is not a chronic alcoholic but a neurotic person who uses drink to help control negative feelings. When the coping ability and mood of an anxiety drinker improves, the drinking will generally moderate. Vogler, Weissbach, Compton, and Martin (1977) describe the *problem drinker,* who, unlike the alcoholic, still has an intact family, lives in the community, has regular employment, and enjoys some sense of self-esteem: characteristics that do not typify the alcoholic.

Etiology of alcoholism.   The work of the counselor in treating drinking problems has been difficult. Part of the reason is that there are many different kinds of alcoholics and many different kinds of problem drinkers. Milt (1969) substantiates the view that alcoholism is not a unitary disease; Sherfey (1965) argues for the position that there exists no measurable "alcoholic personality."

Theories on alcoholism abound, each accompanied by some supporting evidence. Differences in alcoholism rates among different ethnic groups provide support for cultural factors. Convincing arguments also exist that explicate alcoholism as a learned response. Cahn (1970) examines alcoholism as a disease or illness, as a product of one's personality, as learned behavior, and other interpretations; he concludes that deviant drinking rarely occurs in isolation from other problems. The use of *alcoholism* in the diagnosis of psychiatric patients probably occurs more frequently in conjunction with other diagnostic labels than any other; that is, when both primary and secondary diagnoses are made using the American Psychiatric Association diagnostic system, alcoholism occurs more often than any other label as part of the compound diagnosis. Clearly, drinking problems are associated with complex human functioning, and are themselves complex and multifactorial in nature. It is thus understandable that as a group alcoholics are difficult to treat successfully.

To crystallize the factors that are said to cause alcoholism, we will examine

Milt's (1969) representative point of view. For him alcoholism has its roots in a culture that condones alcohol use and in people who, with a physiological constitution susceptible to alcoholism, use alcohol to cope with psychological distress. With continued use, drinking becomes habitual (a learned avoidance response), in addition to being physically addicting.

Practitioners have a special interest in the personality characteristics the individual brings to counseling. In this regard, Cahn (1970, p. 104) mentions an investigation in which personnel from 20 special clinics for the treatment of alcoholism were asked to identify the personality of problem drinkers. In rank order, these are the characteristics identified: (1) dependency, (2) immaturity, (3) anxiety, (4) hostility, (5) depression, (6) compulsiveness, and (7) self-deprecation. We list these characteristics only to suggest what the alcoholic client may be like, not to describe an "alcoholic personality."

Treatment of alcoholism. Alcohol-treatment programs often go beyond the domain of one professional group. The physical deterioration that occurs, sometimes to life-threatening degrees, often necessitates hospitalization, which is frequently followed by vitamin and dietary regimen. During in-patient and out-patient treatment, various drugs are often used. Antabuse (Disulfirian) is a drug prescribed to help a detoxified person maintain remission. A prophylactic dosage of Antabuse will prompt violent illness on the ingestion of alcohol. Awareness of this consequence discourages drinking and supports abstinence. Some counselors still view Antabuse as a controversial treatment. Since alcohol is often used to control anxiety, prescription of various minor tranquilizers helps many to moderate or abstain from drinking. Counseling or psychotherapy is often provided in conjunction with use of Antabuse or other medications.

Well known for its success in the treatment of the problem is Alcoholics Anonymous (AA) for alcoholics, Alanon for family members, and Alateen for teenagers with alcoholic parents. Counselors have learned much from these organizations about treating the alcoholic. Furthermore, since the record of counseling in the treatment of alcoholism is unimpressive, counselors might consider a referral to Alcoholics Anonymous as standard procedure. Some believe that the religious elements in AA make it inappropriate for nonbelievers. Counselors should be aware of the religious overtones of AA and be prepared to give the referred client an objective description of the organization's approach.

Personality and career maladjustment

We noted earlier that counselors and other mental-health practitioners have been criticized for too often underestimating the stressors related to work and overemphasizing personal characteristics that supposedly enable individuals to cope with work stress. This point is worth repeating, for it is only recently that practitioners have begun to understand the negative consequences of work stress. Still of interest, however, is how worker personality interacts with occupational stressors.

In the present section we will discuss some significant maladaptive traits that are not usually associated with hospitalization and subsequent reentry into work and the community.

The concept of personality disorder.   Counselors, especially those working in a medical setting, observe and come to recognize certain forms of maladjustment that are known as *personality disorders*. Typified by certain behavior patterns that are understood to have developed early in life, they produce a persistent, usually lifelong constriction in a person's gamut of responses (Detre & Jerecki, 1971, p. 242). Understanding such response tendencies and their cognitive and emotional components can help practitioners to understand why some of their clients spend much of their work time in conflict with fellow employees, how they may be having difficulty in accepting supervision, and so forth.

Personality disorders are many in number and belong as part of traditional psychiatric diagnosis and technology (American Psychiatric Association, 1968, 1979). Although career counselors are wise to be familiar with such classification systems, the systems will not be adequate for the present discussion of the role of worker personality in career maladjustment. The categories of personality type (for example, histrionic, compulsive, paranoid, and schizoid) are viewed by many as too general for real utility, representing such a diffuse view of a personality that they provide little concrete direction for actual treatment. Moreover, the diagnostic label initially applied tends to follow an individual thereafter, despite change or possible error in original diagnosis. Finally, such descriptions of personality as that of John Holland may be closer to the traditions of vocational counseling than these classifications and thus more digestible for the old-timers in the profession.

Certainly some characteristics associated with the classic personality disorders have some potential for explaining maladaptive work behavior. For example, the following character traits may increase the likelihood of poor work adjustment:

1. the tendency to overdramatize and exaggerate (histrionic);
2. excessive attention-seeking (histrionic);
3. playing of sexual "games" (histrionic);
4. the tendency to withdraw from human contact (schizoid);
5. suspiciousness (paranoid);
6. the tendency to be oversensitive or easily hurt (schizoid);
7. the excessive need for perfection (compulsive);
8. the need to be in constant control (compulsive);
9. the inability to tolerate ambiguity (compulsive);
10. the tendency to project blame on others (paranoid).

We plan to avoid in our discussion the general diagnostic labels in favor of the more generic characteristics leading to poor work adjustment, in the belief that these generic tendencies lead more directly to appropriate intervention. Thus, instead of discussing compulsive traits, we will investigate the inhibiting features of perfectionistic tendencies and how they relate to work adjustment. If a counselor were required by job definition to assign a traditional diagnosis, he or she could readily associate the generic tendencies with a particular classification.

Complaints of the work maladjusted. Other than people who are in a mid-career crisis or who are work phobic, adults who have not adapted well to work are unlikely to come for counseling help with negative feelings toward work. As we mentioned in Chapter 2, feelings of failure are virtually universal among those in the mid-career period. Overly ambitious people experience them intensely, even at times to the point of being suicidal, especially if they lack sufficient interpersonal support and perceive themselves as having failed in other phases of their lives as well as work. For the most part, though, the typical adult client will be motivated to seek counseling for the following primary reasons:

1. marital problems;
2. difficulty in dealing with an adolescent child;
3. problem drinking;
4. general depression;
5. ritualistic/compulsive behavior;
6. referral due to a peptic ulcer, colitis, or other psychophysiological problems.

One large group of prospective clients who seldom seek counseling either independently or by referral is that of coronary victims. If referral occurs at all it is usually after serious physical damage has occurred. Many such patients have been studied in relation to their ability to endure work stress. The work of Friedman and Rosenman (1974) has dominated the study of coronary-prone (Type A) behavior; we shall discuss this further at the end of this chapter in a section dealing with overwork.

The categories of typical client complaints are not mutually exclusive. For example, a marital partner anticipating a divorce is often depressed. Ritualistic/compulsive behavior and gastric problems are often part of the profile of the work-phobic person. Important in accurately assessing such situations is the recognition of the client's approach to work and its effect on somatic symptoms and other problems in living.

Defining mental health. Awareness of the characteristics of the adaptive, well-functioning worker contributes to an understanding of characterological or personality deficits as they affect career adjustment. Among the many existing definitions of mental health, we have selected the one posited by Kornhauser

(1965) in an extensive investigation of worker mental health in the automobile industry. To understand a worker's healthy adaptation to employment, Korn-hauser used the following as indexes of mental health:

1. level of manifest anxiety and emotional tension;
2. level of self-esteem;
3. level of hostility—trust and acceptance of people;
4. sociability and friendship versus social withdrawal;
5. overall satisfaction with life;
6. personal morale versus anomie, social alienation, despair;
7. purposive striving (goal orientation) in work and nonwork activities.

It is evident that some of the factors listed will have existed in a person's makeup prior to employment. For example, people may begin work filled with anxiety, having chronic self-esteem problems, suspiciousness, and a tendency to withdraw from human contact. They could be involved in ritual without a sense of purpose other than to escape feared situations and feelings. These charac-teristics certainly portray a person unlikely to cope well with the everyday frus-trations and disappointments involved in work. Such a person may seek counseling, beginning treatment on account of one or more of the typical com-plaints listed earlier.

Poor candidates for career-adjustment counseling

Not all clients with disabling personality dimensions will benefit from the kind of treatment a career-oriented counselor is likely to give. Some will have deficits not remediable during more or less short-term treatment conducted by school counselors, counseling psychologists, and similar mental-health counselors. By short-term counseling we mean 20 or fewer interviews. As discussed by Strassberg, Anchor, Cunningham, and Elkins (1977), counselors believe that an unfavorable cost/benefit ratio begins after this duration of treatment; what is likely to be achieved has usually been accomplished by then.

Problem behavior of persons who have serious difficulty resulting from early developmental deficiencies cannot be treated effectively in the short term. As documented by the famous Menninger Foundation Psychotherapy Research Project, such developmentally disabled individuals seem to respond only to an "uncovering" form of therapy. Sometimes these people are described in psy-chiatric circles as suffering from a *borderline state:* they do not manifest the ego strength required for the more cognitive and supportive forms of counseling. Kernberg (1976) and Giovacchini (1979) provide material on how borderline patients are understood and treated. These references assume a background in psychoanalysis and ego psychology and may not be useful for counselors with little knowledge of these theoretical systems.

For practitioners without that background, we will take time briefly to discuss the concept of ego strength. To benefit from counseling, clients must have certain personal-management competencies that add to ego strength. At a minimum there must be contact with reality (perceptions similar to those of others), which allows the person to separate personal identity and experience from those of other persons. Reality contact includes the ability to make plans, to compromise, and to delay self-gratification. We could expect clients with such characteristics to be able to keep their side of a treatment contract, to attend scheduled appointments, and to be amenable to influence by logic and by other people.

A practical way to determine ego strength is to use as an indicator the empathic capacity of the client in the immediacy of the counseling situation. The client likely to improve with short-term counseling usually can be sensitive to a counselor's feelings and understand the counselor as a person who lives a life much like other normal people's. The client assumes that counselors have a home, get sick, need to bathe, and so forth. Low-ego-strength clients have little recognition of a therapist as a normal person and are often surprised, even disappointed, if they learn, for example, that their counselor may have to apply for a loan at a bank.

Ego strength has been at least partially operationalized by Barron (1953) in the scoring of selected items on the Minnesota Multiphasic Personality Inventory (MMPI). In an early investigation, Crites (1960) observed a positive relationship between ego strength and well-defined interest patterns, as measured by the Strong Vocational Interest Blank.

Counselors working in mental-health centers will encounter clients who cannot function on their own but are part of a symbiotic relationship with a parent or spouse. *Symbiotic* is an accurate way to describe this relationship, in that a psychological umbilical cord supports the client. The other member of the relationship "fills in" by assuming some of the adaptive (ego) functions of the client. The practitioner can expect recurring contact with both individuals because the lack of adaptability on the part of the client will be chronic. Brodsky and Byl (1976) note that people with serious work problems often manifest them in medical complaints or exaggerated physical problems. Such somatizations provide the means for avoiding the work to which they have been unable to adapt.

For many beginning counselors it is difficult to accept the fact that counseling will not help all the clients assigned to them. To some degree a misconception may be perpetuated in their preparation programs by an occasional subtle implication that a select, very skilled group of practitioners do have the technology to achieve significant gains where others have repeatedly failed. While the possibility may always exist that unexpected results will occur, it is at times difficult to determine realistic expectations in isolation. Thus it is extremely important for practitioners to seek case consultation with colleagues as a way to ensure the development of accurate diagnosis and balanced counseling goals.

Having discussed clients with a low probability for favorable outcome, we can begin to identify some factors that lead to more favorable counseling outcomes. In this regard we shall discuss several types of clientele who may respond to counseling.

Prime candidates for career-adjustment counseling

Clients most likely to benefit from career-adjustment counseling are those individuals with whom counselors usually prefer to work. The acronym YAVIS has been used to represent this type of client (Goldstein, 1971): young, attractive, verbal, intelligent, and successful. Further, the most promising outcomes in counseling can be expected with clients who are able to establish and maintain interpersonal relationships, enjoy the process of introspection, and generally manifest psychological openness rather than a rigid, defensive cognitive style (Schofield, 1964).

We will describe several types of clients who are assumed to have some of the above characteristics but are noteworthy because of a characteristic cognitive and/or interpersonal style by which they can be identified. The client types discussed illustrate the need to approach problems in career adjustment in a varied and flexible fashion. Essentially, counseling strategy will fluctuate in light of dominant client traits. The client illustrations to be given exemplify rather than exhaust the diversity of client traits important in the process of work adjustment.

It is important to recall at this point that the specific objectives of counseling in the present context relate to work and career adjustment, not to some generalized personality change. We hope to achieve better adjustment to work, not to mold a different person, if that were even possible. From this perspective, career-adjustment counseling with the clients in the subsequent illustrations would be directed toward the following outcomes:

1. reduction of work-related complaints;
2. reduced negative affect on the job;
3. reduced cognitive intrusions (dreams, images, and the like) reflective of unresolved conflict at work;
4. reduced escapist behavior (questionable absences, drinking, and so forth) related to work;
5. a more positive worker self-image and more positive self-references as a worker.

Related to improved work and career adjustment could also be improved job performance, reduced general anxiety and irritability, improved family and co-worker relationships, and better physical health. One would expect that an improved sense of well-being resulting from better work adjustment would generalize to other life situations and relationships. However, these overall improvements need not be mandated when one embarks on counseling for career adjustment.

It is always risky to talk about counseling goals when of necessity the discussion is about general counseling issues and procedures. Counseling practitioners have been conditioned to accept the necessity of specific, often observable outcomes. Specificity of objectives is frequently valuable, especially in evaluating the counseling process. However, to cast specific goals for work adjustment requires specific counseling situations. Such objectives are subordinate to some of the general goals herein described and could therefore be subsumed under them.

As we indicated earlier, distinctions between work/career adjustment and corrective personal change may not always be easily made; the complaints brought to counseling may relate to matters other than work issues. Thus counseling for career adjustment may occur in the context of a more global treatment. In such situations it is common that multiple problems will eventually be expressed by the client, and priorities must be set according to relative levels of distress or chances of resolution (Karoly, 1975, p. 205). When this happens, work-related problems may receive priority, and hence counseling begins with a focus on career adjustment.

A representative situation is that of a middle-aged man who comes for counseling under pressure from his spouse. She threatens separation or divorce unless he does something about his drinking problems, increased irritability, and subsequent, although infrequent, physical abuse of family members. In the course of the initial series of interviews, problem exploration and identification might suggest occupationally related stress as an important contributor to the home problems. Thus in the beginning, to set goals, the counselor might say: "Over the past few weeks we have explored a number of important problem areas. It seems that when things go bad at the office, things at home also become worse. I think we ought to attend first to some of the work problems; they may be the key to improving your overall situation."

If some of the pressure is reduced through helping the client to cope better with occupational frustrations, the phase of counseling for career adjustment may end and family-oriented counseling may begin. This latter effort may include the entire family, spouse, or just the client. New goals would emerge related to increased harmony within the family. Obviously, in such situations the boundaries between family and career will not be absolute, and counseling will frequently overlap them. Even if counselors would prefer to keep various problems separate in treatment, for the duration of counseling the client will require assistance at least to survive within both contexts. Effective treatment recognizes this need and concurrently monitors client adjustment in these different life situations.

The perfectionistic client. It seems paradoxical that individuals concerned with order and precision should become candidates for work problems, exhibit a poor work record, and eventually seek counseling: paradoxical because the "ideal" employee is so often described as being well-organized and orderly, setting high personal standards for performance, and so forth. Having perfectionistic tendencies would seem desirable, at least at first glance. A company will, in fact, truly benefit from the work habits of a conscientious, ambitious employee. As we shall discuss later, however, many highly responsible employees pay a personal price in terms of coronary heart disease and other stress-related ailments.

The obvious problem with perfectionism is the "no win" situation it fosters; generally it leads to intolerance of self and others and can be a negative influence on interpersonal relationships. Besides being excessively demanding and hence alienating family and potential friends, perfectionistic individuals encounter problems in work performance. Perfectionistic strivings become noticeably dysfunctional when a person spends more time preparing to be effective than actually being so. Most of us have had experience with a roommate, for instance, who spends the evening organizing his or her desk to study but never actually accomplishes any studying. Most people become increasingly ineffective as they overemphasize making lists, measuring, and planning without performing. Behavior becomes ritualistic and repetitive. As it progresses it reveals itself as a means of protecting self-esteem and controlling anxiety rather than completing a task.

Excessive perfectionism leads to more than compulsiveness; it can be a basis for procrastination and indecision (Barnett, 1972). To be perfect is to avert mistakes; to prevent error requires deliberation. Overdeliberation can impede effective decision making. A perfectionist delays or avoids decisions and tends to make last-minute decisions impulsively in order finally to escape the increasing anxiety evoked by the pending decision. Thus deliberateness at times breeds its opposite. In addition, deliberateness entails careful scrutiny of some features in a situation but often a neglect of other features. Such selective attention can cause critical errors in the process of managing complex problems.

The defeating quality of such behavior is manifested in extreme degree by the work phobic. Perfectionism and conscientiousness are frequently the obstacles for those having difficulty getting to work. Such workers never measure up to their own standards and thus resort to self-criticism and feelings of failure. They become sensitive to criticism from supervisors. Radin (1972) discusses work phobia and describes how such individuals become obsessed about losing their jobs even though the level of job performance is generally acceptable.

Counseling strategy with such clients can be approached in a number of ways. For example, two general themes can become salient in the process. The counselor may attempt intellectually to persuade the client to abandon the inordinate need for perfection and control by pointing out the dysfunctional nature of such beliefs and strivings; and the counselor may help the client to recognize his or her dependency needs and thirst for intimacy not being fulfilled by compulsive behavior.

In counseling for career adjustment these two themes are examined specifically in the context of the work setting. One would expect the perfectionistic client to describe overwhelming elements of the job and to describe the insensitivity of supervisors and peers. Specific complaints will likely rotate from session to session among various irritants without much expression of emotion or much personal interpretation of the events being symbolized (Horowitz, 1976, pp. 155—157). Consequently, some of the goals for career-adjustment counseling include the following:

1. helping the client to understand and accept the complex emotions evoked by the work setting and other workers, thereby to diminish the need to defend against such emotions;
2. helping the client to assemble various isolated perceptions into a more complete perceptual Gestalt of the work setting, which would permit greater cognitive mastery of the work experience;
3. aiding the client in accepting the value of his or her specific career achievements and the tangible contributions made during work while diminishing the need to be universally competent;
4. increasing the client's tolerance of self and other workers' imperfections and limitations;
5. aiding the client in understanding the process of decision making and in developing more consistency in making actual job-related decisions;
6. increasing the client's ability to accept and verbalize the importance of intimacy and the real social need to be on good terms with work colleagues.

If a client is willing to undertake the last goal, even to verbalize it, the counselor can be justifiably optimistic about the eventual outcome of counseling. Often, however, the client may not be able to make such a disclosure, for to do so would be too intense a threat to self-esteem.

Perfectionistic clients may evidence a tendency to externalize blame. Their tendency toward harsh criticism of others often inclines less-experienced counselors to issue reminders too quickly and too severely of each person's responsibility for his or her own reactions. This type of confrontation delivered prematurely merely produces an increasingly defensive client. Modeling of tolerance and careful timing of interpretations are critically important counseling strategies in such cases. In fact, the counselor might be wise in early sessions to utilize reflective and clarification statements even when an interpretation might be given. Whenever possible the counselor would be safer to credit the client with important insights rather than taking personal credit: to make summations that enlarge on the client's statements, making it appear that the client's statement had been as complete as the counselor's subsequent one. This approach promotes less resistance; perfectionistic people often become stubborn or overly submissive in the face of powerful and highly competent people.

As counseling progresses and the client becomes less guarded and increasingly willing to accept some of the counselor's interpretations, it may be appropriate to suggest that there are alternatives to ritualistic ways of coping with anxiety. Many sessions may follow that explore alternative means of anxiety control. Some therapists would see such clients as excellent candidates for systematic relaxation techniques. Horowitz, (1976, p. 190), however, believes that the treatment may not be appropriate for this type of client, who may have difficulty in associating the right emotion with the right image. The most practical resolution for such problems may be to examine each case cautiously before making treatment decisions. Because effective counselors seek solutions to individual problems rather than offering packaged solutions in the hope that they apply to a given problem, any technical intervention, such as relaxation techniques, must follow accurate problem identification.

A collateral consultation with the client's family is also recommended to determine its level of annoyance with its probable subjection to a series of excessive demands by the client. Family members may need to develop an understanding of when they have shown enough disapproval. When the client has become more stable emotionally, they may take the opportunity to ventilate some negative feelings they have contained. Improved communication between client and family indicates that noteworthy improvement has occurred.

The unassertive client.   In many respects, shy, unassertive clients are the perfectionists' opposite. In contrast to the rigidity of the perfectionist, these individuals are lacking in defenses. Instead of externalizing blame for disappointments, they readily blame themselves. The cumulative effect of their behavior is low self-esteem and a transparent lack of self-confidence. Often they sell themselves short and subsequently miss opportunities to achieve gratification. Such clients often fail to realize how high they stand in others' regard. They tend to focus excessively on a thoughtless remark or criticism, becoming easily hurt and overly sensitive to the comments of others. They often complain of loneliness. They may in reality have above-average interpersonal relationships, but they feel as though they do not fit in.

At work such clients can become dissatisfied when they see less competent, less conscientious colleagues receive promotions, sometimes through political means. Unassertive persons attempt to control anger and to avoid verbalizing it in fear of further alienation. In reality they themselves withdraw, actually bringing about what they fear from others. If in such cases low self-esteem is the principal issue, the reason for seeking counseling often will be depression. If increasing resentment of perceived mistreatment predominates, psychophysiological problems may be the presenting complaint.

Optimism in such cases is partially a function of the overall attractiveness of the client. If he or she has some physical and intellectual potential, then the outcome of counseling will likely be favorable. Some clients have highly visible reasons for self-devaluation.

In general, counseling with a client of the unassertive type has the following goals:

1. raising self-esteem and incorporating accurate and more positive elements into the client's self-concept;
2. increasing emotional energy;
3. encouraging greater assertiveness in interpersonal relationships.

At the core of shy, unassertive people seems to be low self-esteem (Cooper-smith, 1967), and the most common approaches to treatment seem to be both supportive and insight-oriented therapy. Eisenberg (1979, pp. 26–30) identifies client-centered and Rational-Emotive Therapy as useful choices for clients with rather mild self-doubt. Popular in recent years has been the use of behavioral and cognitive behavior modification (Meichenbaum, 1977), called *assertiveness training,* which frequently includes well-developed materials to aid counselors in structuring its practice (for example, Lange & Jakubowski, 1976).

Low-esteem and shy clients respond well to the counselor's warmth and empathy and will quickly acknowledge accurate interpretations made by the counselor. They often subscribe to the mistaken idea articulated by Albert Ellis (1962) that it is necessary to be loved and approved by virtually everyone.

The dependency needs of these clients, both overtly and covertly expressed, are obvious in counseling and can become an important issue. Counselor trainees are often cautioned to be wary of client dependency—to be sure not to promote it. Counselors know, however, that all clients are dependent on their counselors in the beginning and that all successful treatment is marked by increased autonomy of the client toward termination (Heller & Goldstein, 1961). It is important to deal directly with dependency but to avoid suggesting that it is in some way illicit. When the clients come to accept their dependent nature and realize that dependence is a universal human characteristic, they can begin to see how their need for others can be organized so that those others satisfy their dependency in return. Once clients learn that dependent people can be interdependent, they learn that their personal dependency need not be parasitic in nature. This realization opens a new view of human relations, one based on equality rather than submissiveness.

In career-adjustment counseling, the counselor who models empathy shows the client how better to understand supervisors and peers. Those other persons come to seem more human in the client's view and consequently less threatening. This is not to say that increased assertiveness is attained only indirectly or is merely a by-product of enhanced self-esteem. The counselor usually can be confident that, once a strong alliance develops in counseling, on-the-job relationships can be discussed directly, followed by examination of alternate ways of relating interpersonally. By this time in counseling the client should readily agree with such statements as, "I think you need to stand up for your rights as a person," or, "You can express how you feel without being aggressive and alienating others." While timing may not be as important with a shy client as with a perfectionistic one, it still seems practical to recognize that counseling makes greater advances, as does normal development, when one understands and utilizes the notion of "critical periods." During the course of counseling, the client passes through optimal times for assimilating information or interpretations. Recognizing these periods of readiness magnifies the impact of what the counselor has to say.

In judging positive outcome with shy clients it is useful to attend to physical appearance. Attempts at weight loss and other cosmetic changes are positive signs even if ultimately unsuccessful. These clients may also come to renewed appreciation of features of their lifestyle that they had ignored while focusing on disappointments. Thus the client may not become more successful at work but may come to suffer less from work problems and to speak more positively about other nonoccupational pursuits.

An example of this kind of resolution is a case involving a college professor who complained of depression. This individual was only moderately productive as a research biologist but was an excellent teacher, having received several awards for his instruction and his development of creative teaching materials. The incoming chairman in his department was a rather stiff and demanding man who apparently was interested in reworking the department, creating openings by applying pressure on several faculty members, including the client.

As the chairman repeated vague threats in the context of a generally cool attitude toward the client, the client withdrew, becoming despondent and spending time at work only when necessary. As his spirits improved during counseling, he discussed his difficulties for the first time with other professors in his department, receiving some valuable emotional and professional support. In the end he was able to weather the problems with his superior, who fell further and further out of favor with the dean and subsequently reduced his inappropriate intervention in the affairs of faculty. The client was able more fully to appreciate his own ability as an instructor. This development was followed by a change from doing minor research to assuming an active and rewarding role as consultant to the university's television series for high school biology students.

The attention-seeking client. Some people become candidates for career-adjustment counseling because their personalities comprise characteristics compounding the problems related to their attention-seeking. Frequently they are highly dependent, overemotional, and prone to making catastrophes out of everyday difficulties. They manifest the cognitive style of an hysterical person in that their ideas are not well developed and that they are given to premature conclusions.

In the world of work, attention-seekers often have little difficulty achieving employment; they generally do well in job interviews by virtue of their typical charm and well-groomed physical appearance. Being the center of attention often demands physical attractiveness and a good sense of humor. These same workers, however, get into trouble on the job as a consequence of their seductive behavior and noncompliance with regulations. They are often late for work, are disorderly and tend to avoid the more mundane tasks. In general their relationships with other workers are superficial. However, they usually do not get along well with colleagues of the same sex and often play "games" with those of the opposite sex. It is not unusual for someone to gain special status with a supervisor through sexual means and in the process antagonize coworkers. Boredom is very painful for attention seekers. Thus, to keep things exciting at work, they often gossip and spread rumors, have emotional outbursts and confrontations with other employees, and greatly dramatize their complaints about company management and fellow employees. Sometimes they alienate other employees by taking undeserved credit for results.

The complaints of such clients entering counseling can be quite varied, but general anxiety is common. In describing their problems at work they tend to externalize blame and represent themselves as powerless to correct unsatisfactory situations. While they may offer dramatic descriptions, they often omit details; the picture is often impressionistic rather than crisp and factual. Another sort of initial presentation may occur instead: the client appears dazed and unresponsive. If the counselor feels the urge to coax and protect, but is a little suspicious of the client's authenticity, it is a good bet that an attention-seeking client is present.

During a client's description of the problem situation, the counselor's task is often to help the client represent the situation more accurately—to take vague statements and reconstruct them into workable and more concrete descriptions. A reflective, clarifying style of interviewing works well during this period. While a more confrontive style may provide the client with more excitement, it usually discharges too much superfluous emotion, delaying the understanding of problems and the working toward solutions. Early in the interviews it may be helpful to recognize that what the client says about an event is often a reaction to a visual image he or she has in mind. The counselor might say, "I think you have a picture of the situation in your mind—let's see if we can put that picture into words." Such statements encourage the client to talk as verbal labels are attached to the experiences. The cognitive understanding this device produces enables the client to cope better with the work-related conflict by facilitating better control of the emotions. In addition, this process counters the tendency to draw premature conclusions.

As counseling continues and the client becomes more secure in response to continued support, the counselor could teach the client about attention-seeking and hysterical behavior. By this time the counselor should be able to give examples of how the client has perceived situations to be worse than they really were and has overreacted without sufficient justification. Because such clients tend to be self-centered, appealing to social interest is usually ineffectual. Rather, the counselor presents self-control and forethought in terms of the client's self-interest and as a means to increased gratification. If these clients reflect or think more before they react, they will likely adjust better to their careers.

These issues generally comprise the goals of counseling for attention-seeking clients. It is unlikely that such individuals will drastically change their style of reacting; we hope they will, however, adjust better to their work and general life situation. We must note that some self-centered clients gauge their need for counseling on their feelings. If some of the pressure at work and at home is alleviated, they will probably feel better and may thus feel less in need of counseling. Ultimately they may terminate counseling before counselors believe it appropriate.

A case illustration.   Diane had come to the university counseling center as the spouse of an assistant professor recently appointed to the college of education. Diane expressed a desire for career counseling because she wished to reenter school and pursue course work that would enable her to become more employable. At the time she was 32 years old and the mother of twin ten-year-old daughters. Diane explained that throughout her marriage she had had to do without many things because of the very modest income of her husband, first as a student, then as a school teacher, again as student, and finally as a college professor. She quickly added that she had become pregnant in the first month of her marriage and been "forced" to be homemaker and mother during most of her marriage. Three years earlier, when her husband had returned to school to earn his doctorate, she had worked in a nursery, but could not tolerate so many "screaming kids." She now wanted to work full time, but believed that her undergraduate degree in child development from a school of home economics was insufficient. Since the university was located in the state capital, she hoped eventually to secure professional employment in one of the state agencies.

Diane also explained that she and Tom, her husband, were not getting along well and that her reentry into full-time employment would be crucial if she and Tom separated. She said that they argued frequently and that she was frankly envious of his enthusiasm for his new job.

To underscore the attention-seeking nature of the client, we might mention that Diane called the director of the center to question whether or not the doctoral-student intern assigned to her was able to deal with some of the complexities of her situation. Familiar with such clients, the director assured her that the intern was indeed competent and that he himself was supervising the student, in which case a person such as she would be getting "two counselors for the price of one." On hearing that information, Diane giggled and indicated that she was satisfied with the arrangement, but in her distress she needed reassurance that her counselor was a capable person.

As treatment progressed the counselor had hoped to work on the identification and exploration of career alternatives with the client. But in order to do so it seemed important to stabilize her situation at home and to provide interim career adjustment prior to a life change. This case thus reflects the frequently unclear boundaries between career decision, career adjustment, and marital counseling.

During counseling, Diane appeared to recognize that Tom's preoccupation with work competed with her own need for attention from him. Furthermore, her tendency to deal with the competition by instigating arguments was having the reverse effect of what she intended, since it seemingly encouraged her husband to spend even more time away from her. Her boredom was explored in the context of her interest profile to establish a basis for her educational decision.

Toward the end of this rather brief interim phase of counseling, Diane's husband participated in two sessions. During these meetings, he reassured her that he was entirely devoted to her, that there were no other women in his life, and that he totally approved of her desire to seek a new career. Tom suggested that since he did teach several evenings each week, it would be very appropriate for him to arrange his daytime schedule and use of the family car to coordinate with her class schedule at the university and the school day of their daughters. While Diane seemed to be suspicious of these proposals, it appeared that she was concealing real delight over them.

During the final individual sessions with Diane, the counselor reinforced the calming effect of Tom's verbalized interest, as well as reemphasizing her strong need for his attention. Diane was able to verbalize her tendency to react without thinking and to exaggerate the seriousness of situations. When counseling terminated, she informed her counselor that she had decided to delay a career decision. Instead she would seek personal enrichment as a special student, enrolling in some courses she had always wanted to take in the humanities.

The value of client stereotypes revisited

As we conclude our illustrations of the effect of personality characteristics or types on career adjustment, it may be useful to consider again the value of such stereotypes. Certainly much debate still exists in the counseling profession regarding the value of typologies. For many, their generalizations are believed to mask the unique characteristics of individual clients, leading to stereotypic counseling strategies. The equally popular rebuttal to this position states that a discussion of personality types recognizes the commonality among people and enables counselors to generalize to current cases what was learned in the past. It may be that client models or stereotypes serve counselors in much the same way that, as Holland suggests, occupational stereotypes aid clients in making career decisions (see Chapter 2). Such representations of characteristics attributable to a group of people, if accurate, provide in part the closure needed to make decisions. In the task of deciding on counseling strategy, counselors may be more confident of their intended efforts when they view them as consistent with important and stable client characteristics. People do seem to have much in common, and, as the counseling profession matures, these commonalities are becoming increasingly recognized.

THE "DISEASE" OF OVERWORK

The topic of overwork provides an interesting contrast to themes commonly discussed in career guidance, which emphasize the problems associated with "underwork." Most middle-class parents, teachers, and counselors talk of the satisfaction involved in working. They stress the self-esteem one can derive from doing a job well. While this perspective is appropriate in many cases, overinvolvement in a career can have undesirable social and biological consequences.

One may wonder why we call overwork a "disease." It is not a disease entity by traditional definition, but overwork can be and is a health problem in our culture. What do we mean by *overwork?* Simply defined, overwork is involvement in one's occupation to the point that it becomes destructive to one's physical health and primary interpersonal relationships. A description of overwork generally assumes that the person has the choice to work less—that the person controls the degree to which he or she invests energy in a career. We assume that overworkers are driven to a point at which they ignore their need for rest and diversion by some internal factor rather than by external pressure from a superior.

Who is susceptible to overwork? According to Rhoads (1977), people are more likely to be victimized by overwork if they are in open-ended occupations. Included in this category are business executives, lawyers, physicians, accountants, clergy, housewives, and probably students. These individuals are always in a position to view their work day as incomplete; there is always one more parishioner for the priest to see, a little more trial preparation for the lawyer, and so forth. It is interesting that information regarding overwork in an occupation is rarely included in the information assembled for career exploration.

It should be clear that not all accountants and housewives overwork. In addition to involvement in an open-ended occupation, certain personality characteristics seem to predispose particular persons to be overworkers. To date little is known regarding such contributory personality factors.

What has been studied is the susceptibility of workers to both coronary heart disease and mental ill health. Cooper and Marshall (1976) provide a thorough review of the literature. Since coronary heart disease remains our number-one health problem, the research of Rosenman, Friedman, and their colleagues (Rosenman, Friedman, & Jenkins, 1967; Rosenman, Friedman & Strauss, 1964, 1966) in this area has received much attention. In their study of business executives in high-stress positions, two groups of subjects emerged. One group seemed to weather the stressors of the job well and had a low risk of coronary heart disease (Type B), while the other group was prone to coronary heart disease (Type A).

Type-A persons had behavioral traits that seemed to make them overworkers. As a group they were described by the following traits: restlessness, high competitiveness, achievement orientation, a feeling of urgent time pressure, explosiveness in speech, a sense of pressure from responsibility, aggressiveness, and impatience. Of all these, time consciousness seems to capture most succinctly the traits of the Type A person.

How can counselors help the overworker and possibly the Type-A person before it is too late? If Jenkins (1971) is correct, these potential clients are likely to be so deeply involved in work that they will have neglected other aspects of their lives. We might postulate that a spouse may signal the overworker through such problems as drinking and depression. Problems of teenage runaways, truancy, and others regarded in the past by the courts as status offenses may also signal overwork of a parent.

Once an overworker is identified, how can the person be helped? No adequate research has been done regarding the treatment of overworkers. Physicians often recommend enforced rest and relaxation along with medication once high blood pressure is discovered. Counselors might help, as Rhoads (1977) suggests, by enabling people to become aware of their physical and emotional needs—of the value of balance in their lives between vocational and avocational pursuits.

Dealing with stress is a popular topic and includes the recognition that work contributes much to human stress. Articles in magazines and paperbacks recommend numerous means to slow down, reduce stress, enjoy life, and live longer. Some commonly recommended strategies are running, meditation, biofeedback, and counseling. Because of the widespread need for assistance in this area, career-adjustment counseling can indeed become an important treatment in the future.

SUMMARY

This chapter was concerned with career-counseling issues that arise after job placement. Occupational-adjustment problems were discussed as consequences of unhealthful work conditions, problems in other life situations affecting work performance, and worker personality. Career adjustment was presented as a personal developmental challenge that often demands a variety of interventions, including at times intense personal counseling.

The need for work adjustment likewise was understood broadly as indicating more than mismatches between workers and jobs or faulty personality characteristics. Sources of occupational stress were examined with the realization that much of employment can be stressful and produce much disaffection among workers. When these factors interact with worker attitudes and behavior, further complications in work adjustment arise. Since personal perceptions, attitudes, and behavior affect worker adjustment, counselors skilled in effecting changes in these factors become a potential source for individuals learning how to change and better adapt to work.

RECOMMENDED READINGS

Cooper, C. G., & Marshall, J. Occupational sources of stress: A review of the literature relating to coronary heart disease and mental ill health. *Journal of Occupational Psychology,* 1976, *49,* 11–28.

A review of interdisciplinary literature relating medical evidence to stress at work. Included is a model for understanding the relationship of stress to coronary heart disease and emotional problems.

Crites, J. O. A comprehensive model of career development in early adulthood. *Journal of Vocational Behavior,* 1976b, *9,* 105–118.

An initial attempt by the author to explain career satisfaction and adjustment. One of the few articles to treat this area of adult development.

Lofquist, L. H., & Dawis, R. V. *Adjustment to work.* New York: Appleton-Century-Crofts, 1969.

The classic trait-factor explanation for work adjustment.

Terkel, S. *Working.* New York: Avon Books, 1975.

The paperback version of a bestseller in which the author interviews and writes about a cross-section of American workers.

LEARNING ACTIVITIES

1. Describe how adverse working conditions can contribute to worker stress and other emotional problems. Demonstrate how even ordinarily adaptive workers can be victimized by employment conditions.
2. Interview a person you know who is not satisfied with his or her employment. Using the list of occupational stressors supplied in this chapter, identify factors that might contribute to this dissatisfaction. Compare this with the job-satisfaction theories surveyed in Chapter 2.
3. Working with several others, generate an initial interview outline that might be used in diagnosing work-adjustment problems.
4. How is Holland's theory helpful in understanding career adjustment? What issues in career adjustment are not answered by this theory?
5. List several personality characteristics that seem to impede career adjustment. How do these characteristics also lead to other life-adjustment problems?
6. Describe how a worker's family can help or hinder career adjustment.
7. Working with several others, imagine that your group had been hired by

a small electronics company that was interested in the physical and emotional health of its employees. How would you study those health issues?

8. Describe how a community mental-health center aids people with career-adjustment problems.

9. Briefly recall your own theory of or approach to counseling. How does your theory explain career-adjustment problems? What procedures or techniques does it advocate in dealing with these problems?

10. During what periods in adult development are work adjustment problems most likely?

11. Explain how college students and their common problems may be parallel to full-time workers and their employment problems.

CHAPTER TEN

CAREER CONSULTATION

The foundry management had been expecting one of the counselors from the local mental-health agency to discuss plans for a field trip that would involve area social-service and school personnel. The plan was to make local school and agency counselors more aware of employment opportunities and job characteristics at the foundry. In the course of discussions, management observed that better awareness of work conditions and expectations might improve the quality and commitment of young employees in their plant. The counselor was curious about this last statement and asked for elaboration. The foundry personnel identified absenteeism as one of their major work problems: "Some of the workers are very unconcerned about whether they miss days, and with the resulting drop in productivity, the financial loss has been substantial this past year."

Originally, the counselor's plan had been to function in the role of community-oriented consultant, to develop better linkage between education, mental health, and business. Her purpose was to develop more effective career placements and greater work satisfaction for both employers and employees. Now the counselor saw an opportunity to function in the added capacity of an organizational consultant. By directly assisting the foundry with a work-related problem she hoped to establish the area counselors as valuable resources to local business.

The counselor asked about the procedure followed when employees returned to work after missing a day or more. According to management, the workers simply picked up their time cards from the rack at the front gate and punched in. The counselor pointed out that in the school setting, students returning from an absence often had contact with a counselor or a teacher. In a brief interview the contact person conveyed an awareness of the student's absence, showing concern about the reason and welcoming the student's return.

"There is probably even greater potential in a large industrial complex for workers to feel unimportant and unnoticed," the counselor observed. "They may not think that anyone is even aware they have missed a day. Might it be possible to remove the time cards of absent employees from the rack and give them to the foreman or supervisor of their section? On returning, the workers would pick up their cards from the supervisor before they could punch in. This would give the supervisors a chance to ask about any problems and to indicate that they were glad to see the workers back. It would give the workers a greater sense of individuality and, in a nonpunitive fashion, let them know that they would be at least informally accountable for their absence. It makes it more difficult to rationalize an absence based on the belief that no one notices or cares!"

This rather simple observation, based on the psychological concepts of reinforcement and social modeling and made by a counselor who was alert to opportunities to be a resource to the community at large, resulted in a savings of many thousands of dollars for the corporation the following year. The company had never thought of this approach. Not only did management reduce absenteeism, with a substantial resultant savings, but it modified other personnel practices in accordance with basic human-relations strategies.

This was not a chance event; the counselor had initiated the contact to explore ways of collaboration for the mutual benefit of all parties—business, agency, client, student, worker: the general community. The outcome just described was not specifically anticipated but was the kind of outcome that frequently occurs as a result of establishing collaborative, sharing relationships. Those relationships represent one type of career consultation.

The overall program goals initially described were also achieved, and the total effect of all these events was a great deal of very positive publicity through community media about the results of this cooperative venture. Additionally, the business community provided financial support of other collaborative "career awareness" activities involving counselors, teachers, prospective employees, and students. The example illustrates Mann's (1971) concern for cooperation among business, personnel, and social scientists with regard to implementing organizational change and Arensburg and Niehoff's (1964) findings that the best change results occur when the consultee rather than the consultant identifies the need. Business and industry in the community thus can become partners with, and strong supporters of, local career counselors, educators, and mental health personnel.

PERSPECTIVE ON CAREER CONSULTATION

Background

Consultation pertaining to career development is closely tied to the concept of work, the satisfaction of the worker, and the constellation of life experiences related to a career. Its roots are in the *organizational development* movement, which began as early as 1924 with the early research dealing with effects of various working conditions on worker functioning and productivity (Homans, 1950; Roethlisberger and Dickson, 1964). This research was conducted at the Hawthorne Works of the Western Electric Company, and when the results indicated that productivity increased no matter how specific working conditions were manipulated, at least partly as a result of the phenomenon of being part of an experimental group, the now well-known "Hawthorne Effect" originated.

Organizational development is defined by Hornstein, Bunker, Burke, Gindes, and Lewicki (1971) as a process of cultural change, or in some cases the creation of a culture, that seeks to institutionalize the use of behavioral-science knowledge and intervention strategies in order to "regulate . . . behaviors related to organizational decision making, communication, and planning" (p. 343). Organizational development in the late 1940s heavily emphasized human-relations training for managers and supervisors (Mann, 1971). While many follow-up studies raise serious questions (Mahler & Monroe, 1952) or negate the long-term effectiveness or impact of this approach (Harris & Fleishman, 1955), they do point out the importance of considering the total work climate or environment when initiating change. More recently, Sarason (1967) has pointed out the importance of the worker/system relationship in the process of advice giving and advice seeking. Any attempt at change will meet with limited success if the interactive system is not understood and accommodated. In short, it is extremely difficult to achieve substantial and long-term change without considering the environmental dynamics and the roles of others with whom consultees have significant relationships.

The research and development of training strategies for industry set the stage for current thinking about the consultation process. Consultation applied to mental-health and counseling situations emerged in the 1950s with emphasis provided by the National Training Laboratory (1953) and other key educational and mental-health professionals (Bettelheim, 1958; Bordin, 1955; Caplan, 1959; Faust, 1968; Lippett, 1959; Newman, 1967; Schwab, 1968). The field gained form and substance during the 1960s with the passage in 1963 of the Community Mental Health Act and a 1964 role statement for secondary counselors by the American School Counselor Association (ASCA). In 1966 the ASCA issued a joint recommendation with the Association for Counselor Education and Supervision (ACES) that consultation be considered one of the three major service areas for elementary school counselors.

Caplan (1970), with his emphasis on mental-health consultation, set the standard for the emergence in the last decade of consultation as a recommended major tool for the counselor. Consultation probably occurs informally in mental-health and educational settings to a much greater degree than may be realized. It has the potential for being extremely effective as a formal systematic strategy in career development (Herr, 1979).

Definition

Career consultation is simply the indirect facilitation of career-development experiences for individuals and groups. The career consultant assists people in acquiring the knowledge and skills they need to provide career-developing experiences for others.

While the term *counseling* usually indicates direct client service, consultation generally refers to indirect service to a client. The consultant usually does not have direct contact with a client, but works through a consultee, who is in turn working with the client. Frequently, the consultee has identified a problem experienced in working with a client or clients and has initiated contact with the consultant (Caplan, 1970). For example, a teacher identifies poor linkage between curriculum and the requirements of the working world, a problem resulting in absenteeism and dropouts. When the counselor-consultant has provided a career-awareness program that integrates curricular activities with job characteristics, it is then the teacher's responsibility to work directly with the students. The teacher is the consultee in this instance, and the students are the clients. Career consultation extends the impact of the counselor far beyond what could be expected from direct-contact services.

In this illustration, the teacher and the counselor share the responsibility of developing and implementing strategy. An essential characteristic of consultation is the collaborative nature of the relationship (Lambert, 1974). This equality is essential to the process, for the consultant usually has no authority over the consultee. The consultee who has had an active role in developing a program or intervention will be likely to have an incentive to implement that activity.

Function. In career consultation, as in other areas of consulting, consultants have an educative function. They facilitate the consultee's acquisition of problem-solving skills and provide knowledge necessary for further problem solving. The knowledge required belongs both to the specific area of careers and career development and to the general area of psychological information. In the case illustration at the beginning of this chapter, the consultant provided basic information concerning the principle of reinforcement and how it was used in another setting and an example of how it might work in the factory situation. The counselor-consultant, in working with the classroom teacher, may suggest specific career-awareness activities or resources that require drawing on specific vocational and career information. When providing information, always remember that the principles of collaboration and awareness of the constraints and characteristics of a particular system must be followed. The consultee is not required to accept the information provided, and, if not relevant to the particular setting, it will probably go unheeded. As a case in point, a novice consultant in an agency setting had correctly determined that the staff had certain skill deficiencies that prevented them from being totally effective with clients involved in the career-change process. The consultant identified a very effective and relatively inexpensive short-term training opportunity for the staff in a neighboring state the following month. Although totally accurate in assessment of need and having the concurrence of the manager and staff, the plan would fail because the consultant was naïve with regard to the bureaucracy of the system. The consultant had forgotten to familiarize himself with all the characteristics of the agency, particularly those related to approval of out-of-state travel (two-person limit) and lead time for processing requests (60 days).

Like other aspects of career guidance, career consultation can be very broad, ranging from the more traditional activities already illustrated to assisting individuals with the productive use of leisure time, including recreation, volunteer work, adult education, and cultural activities (Edwards & Bloland, 1980).

Terminology. The terminology of consultation is basic to all content areas. In all discussions of consultation, the *consultant* provides assistance to the *consultee,* who is the primary contact or recipient of consultation or prescription and who, in turn, serves the *client.* The client is the end recipient of the consultant's activity through the intermediary of the consultee. On occasion the consultant may have direct contact with the client without working through the consultee, but in most cases the consultation contact is indirect.

The use of the terms *direct* and *indirect* refers to the nature of client contact. If consultants work primarily through the consultee, then any contact or impact that they might have with regard to the client would be indirect. In our opening illustration, the consultant's contact was not with the workers whose absentee behavior was targeted for change; the consultee, or foundry management, had the direct contact. If, at the request of the consultee, the consultant meets with the client, engages in diagnosis, and provides the intervention or treatment without working through the consultee, then the consultant/client contact would be direct.

In our opening case, reference was also made to an external consultant. The terms *external* and *internal* or *inside* and *outside* refer to the origin of the consultant. A consultant who is an employee regularly working within the system would be an internal consultant. One who is not a regular employee of the system but comes in from outside specifically for the purpose of consultation is external. In career-guidance counseling, outside consultants frequently come from settings similar to the consultation settings, such as mental-health, educational, or health services.

The career-consultation process focuses on work-related and career-development problems. Personal-emotional needs are a focus only if they are work related. When the terms *task process* and *interpersonal process* are used, the former usually refers to problem-solving activities, problem definition, and data collecting, while the latter refers to communication style or problems, leadership conflicts, and related breakdowns in interpersonal relations.

CONSULTATION APPROACHES

The career consultant will be involved in a variety of settings, with different goals and client groups, and will probably use a fairly wide range of techniques. Consultation approaches can be conceptualized as extensions of counseling and counseling theory. Consultation is a tool.

Approaches to consultation essentially take two forms: that of the expert, who tells others what to do or provides specific information, and that of the process facilitator, who assists others in solving problems for themselves (Schein, 1978). Between these two apparently distinct forms, the dividing line is unclear. In career consultation, many situations will call for a content expert but will also require the process function. Consider the junior high school teacher who sought the counselor's assistance in creating a more reality-oriented curriculum through integrating career-awareness activities with academic tasks. To be of assistance with this problem, the counselor must explore with the teacher what goals or outcomes are important to achieve, decide with the teacher which career ac-tivities and materials are most appropriate to those goals and the curricular area, and explore how best to utilize the materials. The counselor is required to be an expert in the content of career guidance and materials, as well as skilled in process facilitating. Apart from the counselor's expert content knowledge, the relationship is heavily collaborative in nature. The responsibility for the project is shared between counselor and teacher.

The case/administrative model

Gerald Caplan (1970) has created one of the most complete models of con-sultation of those currently in use in mental-health and school settings. Caplan identifies two categories of consultation—case and administrative—and each is further divided into a client, or program, emphasis and a consultee focus.

Case approach. The case approach, which is client-centered, represents a traditional content-expert or diagnostic-prescriptive model. The consultee is un-able to manage a particular case and requests that the consultant examine the client and determine a treatment strategy. At this point, the consultant, at the consultee's discretion, can either implement the strategy as direct treatment or present it to the consultee as a treatment recommendation.

The consultee-centered case approach has as its goal the instruction or tech-nical improvement of the consultee. Although the objective for this type of consultation is the remediation of a consultee's inability to manage a particular problem for a specific client, the expectation is that the consultee will be better able to handle similar client problems in the future. If the emphasis is on tech-nical advice and information, then we have a content-expert orientation. If the emphasis is on technical improvement through a collaborative process of exploring alternatives, then the orientation, while still requiring some consultant expertise, is primarily the shared process. An example of this distinction might be a special-education teacher's request for career information for a special popula-tion. The consultant might provide a listing of appropriate job opportunities for students with certain types and degrees of disability. Alternatively, the consultant might identify resource material that codes work activities in terms of physical or intellectual limitations and assist the teacher in using them. In the first instance, the teacher may be satisfied with the information provided; however, if it does not exactly fit the student group, or when the class mix changes the following year, the teacher will need to repeat the request. The teacher is dependent on the consultant. In the second case, the teacher has learned how to acquire the information and practiced using it; feeling more secure with the material, the teacher is able when necessary to modify or collect information to assist a different handicapped population. The teacher can deal effectively with similar situations in the future. While both approaches have application, the collaborative-process strategy has very definite advantages.

Administrative approach. Caplan's (1970) administrative models evidence similar distinctions. In program-centered administrative consultation, the primary goal is program analysis and remediation or prescription. A consultant designing and implementing a career-development program for a secondary school is an example of program-centered administrative consultation.

Consultee-centered administrative consultation has as its primary goal consultee education with regard to program management or development. A request for assistance in career-program development using this approach would require the consultant to instruct school or agency personnel in the processes of needs assessment, goal identification, establishment of priorities, identification of in-house and community resources, and other activities related to program design and implementation.

Caplan's case and administrative categories reflect the distinction between content and process and the importance of matching consultation style to situational characteristics that are echoed in almost all major systems of consultation (Blake & Mouton, 1976).

Other content/process models

Behavioral consultation also differentiates content and process approaches. Direct aid is the solving by the consultant of specific problems, while the instructional method teaches problem-solving skills (Moore & Sanner, 1969). While behavioral consultation generally uses a problem-solving approach (Bergan, 1977), consultant activities may range from content-expert instruction to process facilitation (Russell, 1978). To facilitate change the consultant may choose any intervention or strategy as long as the condition of empirical validation of change in target behavior is met (Gambrill, 1977; Krumboltz & Thoresen, 1969, 1976). The process of behavioral consulting, like most other major approaches, emphasizes the consultant-consultee-client triad.

An example of validation of behavior change is the case of a major corporation and a local school system that together desired to provide students with an understanding of employment environments. The major goals were to provide first-hand experience with the work setting, to permit exposure to people in industry who could serve as career models, and to promote understanding of how academic skills are used in industry. The consultant, working in collaboration with business and school personnel, identified the student experiences necessary to achieve the desired goals. Additionally, the consultees were advised of new behaviors that could facilitate the desired goals. The industry provided worker models who could demonstrate procedures and work attitudes. Teachers created classroom assignments that tracked the work experience and planned follow-up discussions and assignments. At the end of a four-week program, students shared their reactions with teachers and the counselor-consultant. They described work attitudes essential for successful employment and demonstrated their knowledge of specific job functions and necessary skills. While these outcomes represent one approach to empirical validation of change in the target behavior, the ultimate test is the students' performance in the related classroom assignments and their post-high school employment record.

Another exponent of the content/process theme of consultation is Schein (1978), who describes both the content-expert approach and a process model. The content-expert approach is appropriate in a situation where service personnel are not available or where only information or specific solutions are wanted. The process approach is appropriate for situations involving interpersonal or intergroup dynamics, as well as affective, valuing, and cultural elements.

In Schein's (1969) process model, there are two strategies: the catalyst model and the facilitator model. In the catalyst approach, the consultant does not know the solution to the problem but uses his or her skills in problem analysis, problem solving, and facilitation to assist the consultees to determine their own solution. The consultant using the facilitator model does have some idea about the problem and possible solutions but determines that the learning process and outcome can be better served by helping consultees or clients to develop their own solutions. The process approach assumes that the consultee initiates the contact for assistance. The counselee need not know exactly what the problem is, since the consultant will help to discover and clarify the need (Schein, 1969, p. 5).

The facilitator model is of particular interest for career consultation. This approach suggests the integration of the content expert and process facilitator. Counselors engaging in career consultation will be expected to be content experts and may logically be requested to develop or design career-guidance systems. They must also have the type of collaborative relationship with the consultee that will provide essential information about characteristics of the setting for identifying appropriate solutions. Only with this relationship can one be sure of the consultee's positive intent and ability for problem solving. The consultee is also the one person who knows what type of solution is personally acceptable and likely to work in the given setting. The consultee must have a strong commitment to the problem solution or intervention, with the vested interest of one who helped develop the solution.

In summary, the major approaches generally agree on the use of indirect over direct client contact and the emphasis on enhancement of consultee learning or problem-solving skills as an important goal. Most consultation approaches share some additional common elements. The consultant is required to demonstrate flexibility in approaching the consultee and the consultee's setting. In general, consultation in response to a voluntary, consultee-initiated contact has the most effective results.

Most approaches agree that the ideal product of most consultations is an independent, skilled problem solver who could in turn consult with others encountering similar problems. Both content and process approaches can be collaborative in nature, and both are necessary for effective career consultation. Borrowing from Caplan's model, and incorporating the facilitator-process approach from Schein, provides a desirable balance for the career emphasis—content/facilitative consultation.

CONSULTATION GOALS

All consultation approaches stress the importance of clearly stated and defined goals, cooperatively identified by consultant and consultee. Most acknowledge the implications of being an inside or an outside consultant for assessing information that will produce accurate goals (Dinkmeyer & Carlson, 1973; Kurpius & Brubaker, 1976; Lippitt & Lippitt, 1978). While inside consultants may have a better sense of system history and dynamics, the outside consultant may find it easier to develop acceptable goals and be viewed as credible—the "prophet in his own country" effect.

Problem reduction and increased consultee ability to solve future problems are goals acknowledged without exception. The most simple and direct statement of goals that seems to apply to all approaches suggests three areas for behavior change: client-behavior change, consultee-behavior change, and the promotion of change in the social organization in which the client and consultee are functioning (Bergan, 1977).

Client-behavior change

The most important goal of career consultation is to effect change in client behavior. When a school system and local industry seek to develop a program to link curriculum with a better understanding of employment environments, as in the foundry case already cited, the school expects better classroom performance, and industry looks for a change in work behavior for new employees. The counselor who consults with specialty-area teachers to develop career-oriented activities within vocationally oriented clubs such as Future Teachers of America or science clubs is seeking to improve interviewing skills, interpersonal skills, or career-planning and self-placement competencies (Brown, Wyne, Blackburn, & Powell, 1979; Gysbers & Moore, 1975).

Consulting for client change may focus on remedial skills as well as development of further skills and knowledge. Consistently with Schein's (1978) process model, the career consultant does not focus on the interpersonal process per se, except as deficiencies in the interpersonal area are blocking problem solving or hindering development of necessary career-related skills.

Consultee-behavior change

In career consultation the emphasis on changing consultee behavior closely follows client behavior in importance. Providing consultees with new or additional competencies may well affect the quality of their relationship and effectiveness with clients (Caplan, 1970). The development of consultee professional skills resulting in the ability to deal more effectively with problem solving is a good investment in future generations of students and workers (Binderman, 1964). As an example, the intended goal of a training project for inner-city elementary teachers was development of career-related games. These could be linked to curricular areas both to instruct children in career opportunities and the nature of certain jobs and to provide a built-in motivation for completing school and homework assignments through the gaming model. As the teachers discovered more and more career opportunities for minority youngsters to explore and developed creative vehicles for presenting career information, their own attitudes about work and vocational options changed. The children in their classes sensed this new excitement and the belief that new and varied opportunities were possible. Teachers and students worked together to seek out minority role models and many of the children realized for the first time, through the teachers' behavior and attitudes, that there were aspirational possibilities that they had never imagined. Completion of school work increased remarkably, and at the end of a five-year period the drop-out rate at the junior level had markedly decreased (Leonard, 1968a; Leonard, Jeffries, & Spedding, 1974; Leonard & Vriend, 1975). Similarly, a consultant's efforts to provide job-placement skills for rehabilitation counselors not only increased their number of successful placements, thus changing client behavior and self-concept for those placed, but changed their attitudes about the possibilities for placing severely handicapped individuals. In many instances, difficulty with placement of the handicapped and the resulting distress experienced by themselves and their families are a function of counselor skill deficiency or lack of knowledge. The consultant has facilitated the placement process through improving consultee skills and, as a result, changed their attitude toward the placement process.

Organizational change

For the third goal—changing the social organization—the emphasis is on creating a more facilitative or supportive environment for the client and consultee (Messing & Jacobs, 1976; Robbin, 1971; Sarason, 1967). The high school that experiences a successful job-site visitation program and later initiates a work-study or cooperative work-experience program would be an example of organizational change.

A larger-scale example is that of the counseling staff of several large senior high schools; they were experiencing problems both with job placement of graduates and with a weakening guidance image in the community. Working with an outside consultant from a nearby university, they decided to involve local business and industry personnel in the solution of the problem. The counselors identified one source of difficulty in their own lack of information concerning work settings in the community. During exploration of options with the consultant, the suggestion arose that the counselors visit selected employers and discover the requirements and characteristics of jobs to which high school graduates would most likely have access. Job information collected by the counselors during employment-site visitations was developed into career "packages" that could be used by students not only to learn about work and local work settings but to match their personal characteristics and interests against the requirements of specific jobs. The project received widespread publicity, as well it should have, considering the key local employers involved. Two problems were solved: Career guidance, supported by the counselors' newfound knowledge, materials, and enthusiasm—they were now visible local professionals involved in an exciting community experiment—experienced a dramatic upsurge in effectiveness; and the community image of the school and the counselors, for similar reasons, markedly improved. Furthermore, the school organization had changed its curriculum, incorporating essential academic components for work preparation on the basis of feedback from business and industry.

Two primary components of organizational change—communication and problem solving (Bergan, 1977)—are illustrated by this example. Normally, communication refers to facilitating effective styles and channels of message transmission and information exchange within the organization. In this instance, it connected the school and the community, the school and local industries. Problem solving was effected through improved skills in problem identification, identification of possible solutions, selection and implementation of a solution, and the achieved outcome. Other changes also occurred. The clients (students) involved came to view work in a more realistic and knowledgeable fashion and the counselors to master new counseling tools as a result of new information. In this case, however, the system change was essential to maintaining a supportive or encouraging environment for both counselors and students.

In a similar project linking career counseling and educational activities with work settings and requirements (Messing & Jones, 1980), handbooks and audio visual materials illustrating work characteristics of local industry were developed and placed in local libraries. School counselors were available to discuss those materials with community members. The use of libraries as career-information centers for adults is described in recent studies by Ironside and Jacobs (1977), Harrison and Entine (1977), and Jacobson (1979).

It should be obvious that another major theme running through career consultation is utilization of community resources. The career consultant, possibly more than any other type of consultant, needs to develop such resources.

DEVELOPING A CAREER/CONSULTATION APPROACH

Counselors are encouraged to develop a personalized approach to consultation that best reflects their own beliefs, theoretical orientation, cognitive style, and method of personal interaction—in short, a "minimum change" approach to development of a consultation style: an approach that is comfortable and natural. McBeath (1980) observes that counselors' preferences for various consulting models differ according to their particular counseling situations and their individual philosophies and trainings. If already subscribing to an Adlerian or behavioral counseling system, a counselor might use the corresponding consulting approach. The particular characteristics of career consultation as already described tend to support a content-facilitator model. This approach recognizes the need for content expertise and process facilitation required by many career-development situations.

Table 10-1, "Consultation Dynamics," provides another system for visualizing the process. This chart organizes the consultation process around work settings, the nature of consultant-consultee contact, goals, and consultation strategies. These are the settings: school, including both elementary and secondary; parents, an area which represents the unique family setting; college, including most forms of post-secondary training; agency, both mental health and rehabilitation; and business, including the corporate and industrial settings. While there is some overlap in goals and activities among all these settings, they represent the general structure of career consultation.

Initiation of consultation

The table, while providing some recommendations for a content-expert strategy, is heavily oriented toward the content-facilitator and process approaches. The initiation of consultation is about evenly divided between consultee- and consultant-initiated contacts. Most consultants favor the consultee-initiated contact whenever possible. A distinguishing characteristic of career consultation is the need in certain situations to use a consultant-initiated contact. In most of the examples discussed so far, the contact has been consultee initiated, a factor that has already been cited as important to consultation success. This consultant-initiated emphasis is very similar to the change-agent approach described by Walz and Benjamin (1978) and to Kurpius's (1978) mediation mode.

While prospective consultees may make an initial contact on the basis of the consultant's visibility and established expertise in the area of career development

TABLE 10-1. Consultation dynamics

Setting	Contact initiation	Client contact		Goals/objectives	Consultation strategy
School	Consultant initiated	Direct	Change in consultee	Consultee awareness of career-guidance activities and methods through direct service to students	Content expert or content facilitator
		Indirect	Change in consultee	Teacher involvement/training	Content facilitator
			Change in system	Curriculum change to accommodate career development	Content expert
			Change in client	Career awareness through curriculum	Content facilitator
	Consultee initiated	Direct	Change in client	Program development and provision of career guidance	Content expert
		Indirect	Change in consultee	Teacher involvement/training to eliminate sex stereotyping	Content facilitator
			Change in system	Employer/community involvement in placement	Content facilitator or process*
			Change in client	Develop career decision-making skills	Content facilitator or process*
Parents	Consultant initiated	Indirect	Change in consultee	Parent education	Content facilitator
			Change in system	Develop parents as career program resources	Content facilitator
	Consultee initiated	Indirect	Change in consultee	Understanding of child/career development	Content facilitator
			Change in client	Skill training in facilitation of child's career development	Content facilitator or process*
College/ Post-secondary	Consultant initiated	Direct	Change in client	Job-seeking skills	Content expert or content facilitator
			Change in client or change in system	Develop student career-resource groups	Content facilitator
		Indirect	Change in consultee	Staff skill development	Content expert
			Change in client or change in system	Career-orientation program development	Content facilitator or process*
	Consultee initiated	Direct	Change in client	Career-decision groups	Content expert
		Indirect	Change in consultee	Faculty involvement in career awareness linked to curriculum	Content facilitator or process*
			Change in system or change in client	Program development	Content facilitator

Setting	Initiation	Approach	Goal	Activity	Role
Community rehabilitation agency	Consultant initiated	Indirect	Change in system	Program development and evaluation	Content expert
			Change in consultee and in client	Staff development (career awareness and related skills)	Content facilitator
	Consultee initiated	Direct	Change in system or change in consultee	Staff skill development	Content facilitator
			Change in client	Adult education (skill training)	Content facilitator or content expert
		Indirect	Change in system	Program development	Process*
			Change in consultee	Staff development (training needs)	Content facilitator or process*
			Change in client	Employer education (e.g., effective placement or utilization of disabled)	Content facilitator
Business/industry	Consultant initiated	Direct	Change in client	Career planning and guidance workshops	Content expert or content facilitator
			Change in consultee and system	Employee assessment (motivation and skills)	Content expert
		Indirect	Change in client	Facilitate career program and workshop development	Content facilitator
			Change in consultee and system	Employer education	Content facilitator
			Change in client and consultee	Identification of resources for employee career planning	Process* or content facilitator
	Consultee initiated	Direct	Change in client	Career planning and guidance workshops	Content facilitator
			Change in consultee	Employee assessment (motivation and skills)	Content facilitator
			Change in system	Modification of work environment	Content facilitator
		Indirect	Change in client	Facilitate career workshop or seminar development	Content facilitator
			Change in consultee and system	Employer education	Content facilitator or process*
			Change in client and system	Identification of resources for employee career planning	Process*

*The process approach can be more readily used when the consultation is consultee initiated.

and guidance, frequently a basic consultation goal is to educate prospective consultees to the need for effective career systems. The establishment of visibility and the creating of an awareness of need within an organization or community may be closely linked together. Through teaching, publication, and the use of local media in which the need for career guidance in certain settings is promoted, counselors create an awareness both of the problem and of themselves as a resource. When the design of career programs is a primary function, the consultant's role is most often that of expert resource rather than process facilitator. When counselors are engaged in convincing the school or agency of the wisdom of developing career programs, they are basing part of the appeal on their own status within that setting or their knowledge of the career area. It is very difficult to maintain a low profile and function solely in the process mode once that step has been taken. The use of the needs-assessment approach is an alternative to the hard sell and accomplishes much the same result of creating an awareness of career-guidance or programming needs. Needs assessment is a data-collecting activity that identifies the perceived or expressed needs of a group or organization. It defines the gap between what is and what is wanted (State University of New York, 1976). Further discussion of needs assessment will occur in Chapter 11. The advantage of this approach is its involvement of the client or consultee system in generating the issues and allowing the counselor-consultant to respond in a process-expediting fashion. This approach still has action- or consultant-initiation characteristics but allows for greater role flexibility if a balance between the content expert and facilitator is desired.

Direct and indirect client contact

In both the consultant- and consultee-initiated situations, the nature of the contact can be direct service to the client or indirect service through the consultee. In several instances cited in Table 10-1, only indirect client contacts are described; the nature of the setting or clientele would generally not require a direct client contact.

An example of consultant-initiated indirect intervention is the Born Free project, developed to create educational environments that facilitate student exploration and pursuit of a wide range of career and lifestyle options (Hansen & Keierleber, 1978). The project also educates or sensitizes teachers, as student influencers, to the attitudes they have that may affect the way career development is presented. This goal assumes that sex bias greatly limits those options; the project compensates for this limiting by bringing students into contact with broadening materials and experiences. The field-based school staff, identified through its stated interest in this concept and through being key influencers in their systems, cooperated with university personnel in developing materials and methods that would constitute part of the intervention strategy.

A particularly interesting aspect of the Born Free project is the use of a consultation system within a system. The university staff function as external consultants to the project's field staff by providing them with both theoretical and applied information in areas such as the effects of sex-role stereotyping on student career development. The university staff function as expert resources, as well as collaborators in identifying common concerns and characteristics of each setting that may affect interventions. The combined effect of this interaction is the identification of specific school-based problems and development of appropriate intervention strategies.

At a second level of consultation, the field-based project staff, initially the consultees, now function as internal consultants with teachers in their schools, who now constitute the consultee system. The students now become the client system and will benefit from the collaboratively developed interventions to improve career-exploration service delivery.

Goals and objectives

The goals and objectives section in Table 10-1 refers to the primary activity of the consultant. The goals are Bergan's (1977) three change goals of consultation, as described earlier. The objectives are suggested as illustrative of the goals. For example, "teacher involvement and training" could be illustrated by an activity such as the Open Door project in New York City: Teachers attended career-guidance workshops to promote development of creative classroom guidance materials and, acting as investigative reporters, produced a book dealing with the experience of working in New York City. They also developed a curriculum package for career and community exploration (National Manpower Institute, 1978). Teachers developed new skills through training and increased their career-guidance involvement. The consultant functioned as a content facilitator by providing the initial structure, offering ideas, and then working collaboratively with the teachers to identify the task and develop materials. In the elementary school setting, consultee awareness can be created through the consultant's working directly with children in the classroom and modeling career-exploration activities and group facilitation for the teacher.

In working with parents, the goal is usually to educate the parent. While direct child contact may be used to illustrate or demonstrate a concept in the area of career development, the direct contact would be very limited. In the agency settings, a consultant-initiated contact would most often be for training or program-development purposes and not to assume responsibility for an individual client. For instance, a consultant might provide limited service to a client group to demonstrate career exploration or the values-development process. Career guidance of adults is taking many new forms and is attracting national attention and priority (Herr & Whitson, 1979). Mental-health agencies are providing new counseling services to this population in order to create adult awareness of occupational opportunities and decision-making skills and to meet their need for educational and leisure-time information (Farmer, 1977). The career consultant working in the agency setting can facilitate staff training and program development that will result in delivering this information to the adult working population of a community.

Consultation strategy

Finally, the table indicates consultation strategy. *Content expert* and *content facilitator* should be familiar terms. The use of the general term *process* suggests that any process approach would be potentially appropriate. In addition to the consultee-oriented process models from Caplan (1970) and Schein (1969, 1978), several other approaches warrant attention. A system that is similar to Schein's process model has been described by Kurpius (1978) and uses the term *collaboration* to describe the activity. Kurpius also uses the terms *provision mode* and *prescriptive mode* to describe the content-expert approach generally. The Adlerian approach described by Dinkmeyer and Carlson (1973, 1977) provides a good parent- and school-oriented process that favors the small-group model. Russell (1978) describes a behavioral approach that emphasizes the triad interaction process among consultant, consultee, and client.

A final note about the content-expert approach is in order. A situation may arise that calls for a role strongly oriented toward content expertise. The consultant will need to be satisfied that certain conditions are met before adopting this model. Before undertaking any consulting activity, consultants should determine that their strengths are in the requested area, the consultee's understanding of the problem is accurate, the consultee is adequately committed to the project, and the necessary resources for project success have been identified and are available. Additionally, the consultant should ask the following questions:

1. Is the consultee's system or organization receptive to an external (or internal) consultant, and does the consultee concur with the stated need?
2. Does the content approach have an advantage over the process approach for improving the quality of the system or the consultee's potential for planning or decision making?
3. Is there an advantage in time, money, or personnel utilization in the consultant's taking the content-expert role and assuming major responsibility for requested services?

If the answer to any of the preceding three questions is no, or even maybe, then a process approach should be considered instead.

An example of a situation that conforms to the above conditions is consultation for increasing career mobility or enhancement of present work effectiveness. A large agency specializing in human services had recently been awarded a contract to perform specialized services. The agency requested a consultant to evaluate their capacity for performing these tasks and recommend additional skill-building experiences when and if appropriate. The project provided funds for training activities, and the awarding of the contract was not contingent on the consultant's conclusions. Although the agency did not want its employees to relocate, it believed that the options provided by increased competency and the ability to move up in the organization would be major inducements to participate. The consultant was a university professor familiar with training programs and the competency areas represented by the agency. Although an external consultant, the professor was known to many of the staff through past training and research programs and professional meetings. The professor realized the accuracy of the projected need for consultation from his familiarity with the agency staff and the contracted project.

The consultant's first step was to conduct a staff-training needs assessment (Nida & Messing, 1979) to gather more precise information concerning specific competencies of staff and staff's perception of the proposed activities. The needs assessment provided consultee (agency manager) and client (agency staff) input and was expected to increase their feeling of participation and involvement in the project. At that point, the question concerning the appropriateness of any consultation had been answered affirmatively: The consultant's expertise was suitable, both the consultee and the clients concurred in the problem statement, and the process and the resources to effect change through training existed.

The next step after processing the results of the needs assessment was to meet with the consultee and clients as a group. As an additional check on perception of task and commitment, the group was asked to discuss both the current program and the revisions necessary to deliver the contracted services. The group meeting provided a useful diagnostic tool allowing the consultant to observe group interaction and preparing him for the individual interviews to follow. The group meeting also provided the staff with expectations for the individual sessions. It was then that the answer to the second of the three preliminary questions became somewhat clouded. One of the group members indicated that identification of training activities related to desired staff competencies was one of his assignments, and a monthly calendar was prepared and circulated. Only on determining that there was no specific attempt to match training with the specific contract task needs and that significant resources were not identified did the consultant conclude that a content rather than process approach was still appropriate. The consultant could provide unique content, whereas a process model would not substantially improve agency planning. The individual interviews emphasized staff members' past training and experience and provided an opportunity for the consultant to assess their skill and knowledge levels in selected areas. The consultant also enlisted the staff persons' ideas about desirable training experiences.

Following further discussion with the primary consultee, the third question could be answered and the case for the content expert was intact: Timing was important, and information about available training experiences or specially designed training was needed immediately. Maximal personnel utilization could not be realized unless individualized training plans could be developed and completed within several months. Facilitating consultee skills in this area was unrealistic, in terms of both time and future need for large-scale repetition of the activity. The consultant also discovered that there were advantages to being an external consultant with this agency (something the consultee had known from the start!). Authorization for training and related travel could be more easily expedited by the recommendation of an outside "expert" than from within.

CAREER-CONSULTATION PROCESS

The content-expert example just described points out several dynamics that represent steps or stages in the career-consultation process. This process comprises five stages: establishing working relationships, information gathering and diagnosis, exploration of possible solutions, intervention implementation, and evaluation and reduction of involvement.

Establishing working relationships

Once initial contact has been made, the consultant's task is twofold: developing the interpersonal relationship process and establishing expectations. Consultants must determine what the consultee wants and communicate what service they, as resources, can provide. Part of building the initial relationship may be the collaborative establishment of goals and expectations. This shared activity goes a long way toward demonstrating a frank, yet open and flexible, relationship, which is the keystone of effective interpersonal process. The consultant is both a resource and a partner in responding to the consultee's needs. Schroeder and Miller (1975) emphasize the importance of establishing an effective emotional climate early in the consulting process. This initial climate greatly affects the success of what is to follow. In the example, the consultant's initial needs-assessment activities and processing of information with the consultee illustrate this first stage. Frequently the problem is not clearly defined, and the identification process and establishment of relationship require several contacts. Gaining the support of key individuals through involving them in the initial process of determining needs or clarifying the problem is a very important element of this climate-setting stage.

Information gathering and diagnosis

In this stage, further problem clarification occurs along with additional climate-setting activities. An end result of the stage is a goals or objectives statement of desired outcomes. A needs-assessment or personnel survey can be conducted using interview, instrumentation, and document-review (vitas or transcripts) techniques. In the content-expert case, all three procedures were employed. Using all three procedures is a good system not only for obtaining problem- or need-related information but also for familiarizing the external consultant with the staff and setting, some of which has naturally occurred in the first stage. This is the time for establishing or selecting an entry into the consultee system through persons who are in critical positions for making a program or treatment successful and effectively maintaining an established system. Ideally, consultants look for cognitively open or flexible persons receptive to new ideas, but they may need to be prepared to promote some openness in important members of the consultee system.

In our example, the consultant used information gathered in a variety of ways to confirm the presenting problem. Frequently, the initial problem turns out to be only part of the actual need or is misperceived completely by the consultee. Misidentification can be a result of having incomplete information or of responding to symptoms of a larger problem as if they were themselves the problem. In these instances, the consultant will need to collect further data to clarify the problem. Try to involve as many of the consultee's personnel as possible in the information-gathering and diagnostic process. Consider in this process the relationships and communication patterns within the consultee system, as was done in the large group meeting described in the example. Give particular attention to relationships between the primary consultee and the rest of the system. These patterns may explain resistance or the misinterpretation of data and provide insight into system dynamics that could affect successful interventions. Schein (1969) points out that data collection is a type of intervention. Many times individuals will change their attitudes or behavior as a result of being included in or excluded from the process. Informal discussions with participants in the consultee system prior to formal assessment frequently provide cues to sensitive areas and individuals.

Exploration of possible solutions

One of the most frequently described activities at this stage is brainstorming. This is an important diagnostic tool and an intervention in the same sense as is data gathering. It is also an excellent device for temporarily removing situational constraints and beliefs that limit the generation of options. Both the large group meeting and individual interview provided this opportunity in our content-expert case. At this point, check again to be sure that the problem is clearly stated in terms of desired outcomes or goals, so that solutions can be precisely directed toward specific targets. Involvement of the consultee and others who will be immediately affected in the consultee system is extremely important. The best determination of whether a solution is feasible is the beliefs of those who will be affected by it or responsible for it. A decision against feasibility of a solution does not necessarily mean that it is not good but does indicate that it probably will not work, given the current beliefs of the persons in the consultee system. If a solution is rejected, the consultant will have to decide whether to explore other solutions or to engage in activities that influence beliefs so that the solution becomes more credible or attractive. The consultee is the best source of information about the predicted consequences of a particular solution, especially for the external consultant. Not to be overlooked in exploring possible solutions is the identification of resources in support of specific interventions. Knowing the available resources for problem solving is one of the first steps in determining feasibility. Fortunately, the agency consultant in the case we described was aware of appropriate training programs prior to the time of the consultation and had established that funds for training were available.

Intervention implementation

In the implementation stage, it is important for all participants to understand their responsibilities, resources, and time lines. Schein (1969) points out the value of providing some theoretic input prior to intervention to create both readiness and an increased sensitivity to the process. The best method may be to distribute article reprints concerning application and evaluation of a particular system or procedure in a comparable setting. Articles describing the rationale behind a certain intervention are also useful.

Feedback, based on results of surveys and needs assessment, is helpful in creating readiness. Additionally, suggestions concerning more effective communication or interpersonal processing can improve implementation skills and increase the chances of success for the intervention. An interpersonal-process group meeting that focuses on interactive dynamics and how they may affect the intervention is one procedure for making these suggestions in a collaborative atmosphere. It should be noted that intervention and evaluation are not entirely separate activities; evaluation may require ongoing contacts with the intervention activity as it is occurring. The monitoring of intervention provides another type of feedback that serves to create involvement. If monitoring indicates deficiencies in the intervention, then additional problem-solving activity on the part of the consultee is required.

In our illustrative case, the individualized training programs constituted the primary intervention. The training plans were designed to accommodate the clients' special needs, time and travel constraints, and further formal academic goals. Consideration of those factors would facilitate implementation of the training program by the consultee. In that case, the consultant did not necessarily have to provide any actual training.

An example of a situation that would require provision of training is the educating of teachers to characteristics and effective interactive practices for special groups. If teachers are to be involved in classroom career-guidance activities for minority or handicapped populations, they will frequently need help in identifying goals and developing strategies that are appropriate for a distinctive group (Campbell, 1975).

Evaluation and reduction of involvement

As indicated in the discussion of intervention implementation, evaluation is partly the monitoring of the ongoing intervention or treatment process. This activity provides a system for continuous feedback and allows consultant and consultee to make decisions about the appropriateness of the process and identify problems very quickly. The second part of the evaluation process is the product or outcome assessment. Outcome evaluation deals with the degree to which the solutions or goals related to the problem statement are realized. In our illustration, assessment of the extent to which contracted services could be performed, or performance was improved as a result of the individualized training programs, would constitute outcome evaluation. One aspect of the training was to prepare certain individuals in the agency to perform training and consultation activities. Schroeder and Miller (1975) emphasize the importance of training personnel within the consultee system for maintaining a program or service when its continuation over an extended period of time is desired. The alternative is continued dependence on the consultant or possible failure of the program after consultation activity is reduced or terminated.

The reduction of consultation involvement can begin with the evaluation process. The consultee is assisted in learning to process feedback to lead to decisions concerning the appropriateness of the solution. If the solution is not effective, redesign of the treatment or provision approach may be required. Additional training or identifying resources will be necessary if maintenance of the system or treatment is desired. Within the process-consultation model (Schein, 1969), consultant/consultee contact does not immediately terminate but gradually diminishes through small interactive or supportive efforts. Reduction and termination are mutually agreed on in view of both consultant's and consultee's assessments of outcome and continued need. As in any other helping relationship, the consultation contact may be reinstated at any time.

The efficiency and power of providing indirect service through affecting the client's environment are well established. The particular theory or consultation approach selected is a function of the individual's beliefs about the learning process and an assessment of the setting dynamics and needs of the consultee and client population. The content-facilitation approach discussed in this chapter provides a great deal of flexibility in a multitude of settings and with a wide range of materials. It is an approach that recognizes the content of career development as being technical and specific and the collaborative process as essential for realistic problem identification and strategy implementation. This approach requires not only content expertise but personal objectivity and skill in interpersonal and group dynamics, since the consultant frequently serves as a model (Quinn, 1978) for the desired attitudes and behaviors to be realized as a result of consultation.

SUMMARY

In this chapter the concept of career consultation has been advanced and defined. It represents an emphasis in consultation and an approach to delivery of career guidance that, although new, are more than justified by the limitations on counselors' time and the need for greater community involvement in career issues.

The application of consultation to human-service areas draws on the organizational-development movement in business and industry, which was briefly reviewed along with the basic consultation approaches. The major approaches can be generally categorized under content and process consultation. The work of several theorists in the area of consultation process has been summarized and examples of application with career content provided. For the serious student of consultation, additional reading and skill development are essential.

A suggested approach to career consultation has been described that brings together the relevant concepts from both the content and process models. Five stages are involved in the development of the career-consultation process. Counselors must consider their particular theoretical dispositions and interaction styles as well as the setting and goals when selecting a consultation-intervention approach. Several illustrations of the selection procedure have been included.

RECOMMENDED READINGS

Bergan, J. R. *Behavioral consultation.* Columbus, Ohio: Charles E. Merrill, 1977.

This book is a description of behavioral consultation theory and techniques. Part one (pp. 3 – 27) provides a good overview of consultation roles and goals.

Blake, R. R., & Mouton, J. S. *Consultation.* Reading, Mass.: Addison-Wesley, 1976.

The authors have developed a set of constructs that they feel best account for the dynamics of the consultation process. These constructs are organized into a three-dimensional model called the Consulcube.

Caplan, G. *The theory and practice of mental health consultation.* New York: Basic Books, 1970.

This is a basic reference in mental-health consultation and one of the first comprehensive reviews of the process. Chapters 6 and 7 (pp. 109 – 150) present the concepts of client- and consultee-centered consultation as applied to a variety of human-service situations.

Kurpius, D. J., & Brubaker, J. C. *Psychoeducational consultation: Definition – functions – preparation.* Bloomington, Ind.: Indiana University, 1976.

A very readable basic introduction to the consultation process. The emphasis is on educational settings, and the authors present the five most-often-encountered consultation models.

Mann, F. C. Studying and creating change: A means to understanding social organization. In H. A. Hornstein et al. (Eds.), *Social intervention: A behavioral science approach.* New York: Free Press, 1971.

The content, although slightly dated, provides an excellent understanding of the change process as it operates within social organizations. Understanding and effecting change are critical to successful consultation.

Personnel and Guidance Journal, Special Issues. Consultation I & II, Nos. 6 & 7, 1978, *56.*

These two special issues provide an excellent overview and review of the major consultation models and their application in public-school, college, and mental-health settings. Number 6 reviews models and procedures, while number 7 emphasizes specific uses of consulting techniques.

Schein, E. H. *Process consultation.* Reading, Mass.: Addison-Wesley, 1969.

A basic description of both expert, or content, and process consultation, but, as the title suggests, emphasizing the latter. While this work focuses on the business community, its application to human services can be readily discerned.

LEARNING ACTIVITIES

1. In a group discussion consider the characteristics of individuals who have been of assistance to you in providing relevant advice or knowledge. What are the important qualities, characteristics, or conditions of that individual or relationship?

2. Accurate or precise communication—identification of the problem, posing relevant questions, and so on—is an important skill in consultation. Identify one member of your group whose task it will be to design and build a structure that depends on hidden structural elements for support or strength. A suspension bridge constructed of paper, string, and cardboard tube is a popular choice. Depending on the size of the group, each member may try to reproduce the structure using the visible materials, or this may be a group project. In a group setting, one member must be chosen to communicate with the "master builder." Questions concerning construction can be posed to the "builder" by that individual, but the group must agree on the question and it must be answerable simply with a yes or no. If working individually, each person is responsible for formulating his or her own questions, and the element of competition as opposed to cooperation is introduced.

3. Consider your current beliefs concerning counseling theory and technique: (1) Of the consultation approaches described, which most closely approximates your preferred theory? (2) What are the key elements or factors involved? (3) What are your personal-interaction characteristics that might cause this consultation approach to be more or less effective?

4. Think about your work setting or anticipated work setting. Identify one area of change that would provide more effective career decision making or could increase client or employee potential for work satisfaction. If currently employed, you may wish to discuss this with colleagues.

5. Identify the types of career consultation you might be able to provide within your work setting or anticipated work setting. Identify a need or problem experienced in that setting. What are some of the additional skills or knowledge that you might need?

6. If employed, do you believe an internal or external consultant would be more effective in your setting? Why? List the dynamics, relationships, or regulations that would be important for a consultant to know about your agency or setting. (If not employed, your answer could be about your school environment.)

7. Establish contact with a counselor or the equivalent at a local school or agency and discuss the activities in which that individual is currently engaged that could be considered consultation in general and career consultation in particular. Can the person suggest activities other than those currently under way? Are all the activities described clearly consultation, or would some be considered either counseling or coordination?

CHAPTER ELEVEN

COMPREHENSIVE CAREER GUIDANCE

The various theories, techniques, and resources that constitute the fabric of career guidance have been presented in the preceding chapters. The design of the integrated product is now our final concern. Much has been presented to suggest the nature and requirements of career-guidance programming. This chapter will discuss program-development procedures, necessary counselor competencies, and important program characteristics.

To promote career guidance under a federal grant entitled "Legislative Provisions for the Improvement of Guidance Programs and Personnel Development," the National Center for Research in Vocational Education established the following criteria for the design of comprehensive career-development programs:

1. The program must serve all clients.
2. It is based on identified needs.
3. It provides service and programs appropriate for the particular setting.
4. It provides written objectives for staff and clients.
5. It uses a variety of strategies to assist clients in attaining objectives.
6. Strategies are evaluated for effectiveness.
7. Feedback is provided for management decisions.

In an effort to meet such criteria, programs require concentrated effort on the part of many professional and paraprofessional personnel. Fortunately much of the initial work in conceptualizing and structuring essential program components has already been done through early efforts, mostly funded by the federal government. This conceptual base helps to organize a community's effort to plan and execute a career-guidance program directed toward its unique needs. In this chapter we describe the philosophy behind program planning and treat aspects of the shared conceptual framework for comprehensive career guidance.

Comprehensive programs that promote career development are represented by two generic efforts: one is called *career guidance;* the other, *career education.* As we mentioned in Chapter 1, we recognize differences between the two; however, each helps us to conceptualize the meaning of a comprehensive program and the roles counselors play in promoting career development, especially in conjunction with other professional personnel. We will therefore enlarge on our earlier discussions of career education in order to give it full credit for its contribution to career-development programming. And we will devote separate attention to concepts and procedures specific to career guidance.

CAREER EDUCATION REVISITED

Reviewing some of the earlier discussions of career-related terms, we think of Hoyt's (1975) statement that career education is the composite of "activities and experiences through which individuals prepare themselves for and engage in work—paid or unpaid—during their lives" (p. 304). Career education differs from vocational education in Hoyt's view by including a broader base of activities, such as awareness of career opportunities, exploration, decision making, career preparation, entry, and advancement. Vocational education predominantly focuses on the career-preparation component. By virtue of its inclusive nature, career education is for all persons, while vocational education has the traditional image of concentrating on vocational-technical training in preparation for work that does not require the baccalaureate degree. A final distinction that Hoyt (1975, 1977a, 1980) and others (Bottoms & Sharpe, 1973; Gysbers & Moore, 1975; Mangum, Becker, Coombs, & Marshall, 1975; Munson, 1978) point out is the emphasis of career education on both paid and unpaid work and the productive use of leisure.

It is important to think of career education as a process rather than a specific plan of study (Shertzer, 1976; Super, 1976). It focuses on learning experiences related to self-understanding, educational endeavors, and career potential. Career education, as a curriculum innovation, is a part of all school subjects, from kindergarten through grade 12 and throughout higher education. Since one's career and education continue through retirement, career education must span the entire life cycle.

CAREER-EDUCATION MODELS

Because career education is a systematic attempt to increase individual career options, alternative models within the general concept of career education are necessary in order to deliver the necessary exposure to the maximum number of people. In trying to conceptualize the possibilities for career education, consider your own community. The school is an obvious source for career-related knowledge and experiences, and not so long ago the home was too. The local employers represent the experiential or on-the-job opportunities, and community or state agencies normally serve the crisis-situation or "problem" client. Typically these various units work independently of one another, though they need not. All represent a potential base for organizing career information, and collaboration is both possible and desirable. Corresponding to these sources are four career-education models, developed under the supervision of the National Center for Research and Development and later transferred to the National Institute of Education:

1. the school-based or comprehensive career-education model;
2. the employer-based model;
3. the home-based model;
4. the residential-based model.

School-based model

According to Marland (1972a, 1974), the school-based model reshapes and focuses the curriculum from kindergarten through junior college on the concept of career development. The school is closely tied to activities of local community, business, and industry. Of particular importance in this model is the role played by parents and counselors in shaping the student's career choices. Since sources outside the school strongly influence the student's choices, the model emphasizes development of effective relationships with those sources, particularly parents, who help students to set their own values and make decisions. As we have previously stated, values and decisions are not imposed on the student. Given this external source of input, the school-based model can be combined with adult education and with programs for educationally disadvantaged populations.

The Developmental Career Guidance Project (Leonard, 1968a) in Detroit is one example of the school-based model in action. It focuses on broadening career awareness for inner-city children, primarily in elementary and junior high schools. Classroom techniques such as career games linking career information with school subjects were combined with career materials developed specifically for Detroit-area employment. Parents were oriented to vocational-training and educational opportunities in the community and instructed in techniques for encouraging the children in their educational and career development. This program depicts a K−12 approach to career development. Each school's guidance team consists of a guidance worker, a community career aide, students who function as peer advisers to other students, and parents. The community provided major support: each participating school was sponsored by a local company. The five-year project realized major success in decreasing the junior and senior high dropout rate in those schools and in increasing student employability on high school graduation (Leonard, 1972b, Leonard & Vriend, 1975).

The school-based model also represents an excellent design for handicapped or special populations. Brolin and Gysbers (1979) have recommended programs developing daily-living, personal/social, and occupational guidance and work-preparation skills that require family, school, and community involvement and support. These skills are organized under the categories of career awareness, career exploration, career preparation, and career placement and follow-up. They provide the framework for a K−12 program appropriate for both handicapped and nonhandicapped students alike. Certain activities included under each category, such as the daily-living skills of caring for personal needs or getting around the community (mobility), may need to be modified for selected groups. Others, such as maintaining good interpersonal skills and knowing and exploring occupational possibilities, are applicable to all children. This integrated approach is in fact highly desirable for realizing the goals of mainstreaming and, as Beane and Zachmanoglou (1979) recommend, assisting special individuals to become a part of, rather than apart from, society. The school-based model is equally appropriate for all populations and settings.

The school-based model requires coordination among the various grade levels. Activities must be sequenced, with awareness of developmental readiness at various grade levels, and not simply independent and nonlinked experiences.

The school-based model is intended to provide students with:

1. a comprehensive awareness of career options;
2. a concept of self that is in keeping with a work-oriented society and includes positive attitudes about work, school, and society, and a sense of satisfaction resulting from successful experience in these areas;
3. personal characteristics such as self-respect, initiative, and resourcefulness;
4. a realistic understanding of the relationship between the worlds of work and education, which assist individuals in becoming contributing members of society;
5. the ability to enter employment in a selected occupational area and/or to go on for further education (Goldhammer & Taylor, 1972, p. 7).

Employer-based model

Primarily developed and housed within the business community, the employer-based model also requires cooperation and support from the schools. In 1974 the National Institute of Education modified this concept to be more encompassing: originally known as employer-based career education, it now uses the initials *EBCE* to stand for experience-based career education. EBCE still emphasizes the community as the primary resource. The program provides services for individuals in the 13–20 age range who have left school without obtaining the proper skills and knowledge for successful career and personal development. General education, vocational training, and selected work experiences are combined in such a way as to maximize career-development possibilities (Sexton, 1977). Individuals would have the option for several types of part-time jobs in various settings, such as construction, parks, laboratories, hospitals, hotels, or restaurants, to allow them to elect an occupational area of choice rather than being restricted to a single possibility. Of Studs Terkel's interviewees in his book *Working* (1975), many who expressed lack of interest and gratification in their jobs, and who indicated a feeling of being vocationally trapped, never having had any options, represent the high-school-age target population of this approach. The EBCE model responds to the issues of academic curriculum relevance, the crisis of values, aspirations, and recognition of human diversity (Coleman, 1971, 1974; Cusick, 1973; Faure, 1969). It focuses on corrective and remedial basic skills and is instructionally centered away from traditional learning facilities at sites such as civic centers, performing arts centers, and government or recreational facilities (Elseroad & Hensley, 1976; Jenks, 1976). The student can complete graduation requirements while learning through work experiences.

The EBCE concept, using four slightly different programs, was evaluated in the early 1970s at four sites: The Appalachian Education Laboratory, in Charleston, West Virginia; The Far West School, in Oakland, California; The Academy for Career Education, in Philadelphia, Pennsylvania; and the Tigard, Oregon, Community Experience for Career Education (Goldhammer, Gardner, Heilman, Mokma, Libby, & Rietfors, 1975; Hewett, Warner, & Wolff, 1975). The four programs deal with high-school-age youngsters working in both learning centers and community work settings. They emphasize experiencing subject matter, including life skills, basic skills, and career development, through investigative activities and projects in community employment settings.

The Oregon program was specifically called a community-based model, although all four programs used community resources to a major degree. Community persons were used for tutoring when necessary, and employers conducted seminars on the "world of work" (Northwest Regional Education Laboratory, 1974). All four programs were judged effective (A comparison . . ., 1976) in terms of students graduating and gaining employment.

Coordination of the experience-based model could come from a consortium of business and industry or from specialists employed by the school system (Barlow, 1978; Hoyt, 1976). Support for the program could be recruited from labor unions, parents, PTAs, Chambers of Commerce, and other business and professional groups. The community-based classroom approach encourages year-round employment opportunities and open entrance and exit of students.

Home-based model

The home/community-based model is designed to develop educational delivery systems for the home and the community and to provide new career-education programs for adults. The model also develops a guidance and career-placement system to assist individuals in occupational and related life roles and enhances the quality of the home as a learning center (Goldhammer & Taylor, 1972, p. 9). It is particularly valuable for women, who are moving in increasing numbers from the home into the work force (Campbell, 1975; Vetter, 1975). This model can provide them with new skills and broader vocational horizons.

Ironside and Jacobs (1977) point out that adult counseling and information services are being provided in many nontraditional settings and utilizing a variety of media and technologies. Herr and Whitson (1979) found home services provided through telephone counseling, information hot lines, and mobile vans equipped with career information, assessment resources, and counseling personnel (p. 115). Television is a particularly effective medium for the home-based model. Schools and industry can combine efforts with the federal government to develop educational programming that conveys both local career options and necessary basic skills, as well as nationally oriented information about work opportunities. Video packages for public television that suggest techniques for combining occupational and homemaker roles and teach communications skills could be central elements of such programming. Additional audio- or video-cassette instruction could be provided by the local school system, allowing the student to complete a competency examination in a given career area and qualify for placement.

It is possible that for many adult populations a combination of the experience-based model and the home/community approach would be most effective. Herr and Whitson (1979) note that public libraries, among other resource centers, are a major source of information. They also point out that adult career-guidance services within a given area are typically not coordinated and do not meet the diverse needs of women, the poor, the physically handicapped, and racial minorities.

Residential-based model

Disadvantaged individuals and rural families are targeted by the residential-based model. Its purpose is to provide remedial education, counseling, health information and services, family skills, community services, and placement information for the entire family. This program differs from the other three models in that the family or individual relocates to the residential training center. Employment would be guaranteed to each family by the home state on completion of the residency. The residential-based model requires the greatest commitment from both the individual and the sponsoring state, and for that reason it may be the most difficult to develop. Relocation of the disadvantaged or rural family has many social and psychological implications that will need to be studied and will probably prove difficult to manage successfully.

An alternative for providing services to rural families would be the use of school, television, and mobile units, as described in the home-based approach. The Rural America Series distributed through the National Center for Research in Vocational Education is the most extensive and well-developed community/school-curriculum-based approach available at this time (Axelrod, Korfhage, & Whitson, 1977; Bagby & Kimmel, 1977).

These four models together represent the first comprehensive approach to a career-education system for all Americans throughout their lifetimes. In summary, career education is an evolving concept. It is an attempt to bring occupational relevance to the academic curriculum at all grade levels. It is a focus on self-awareness in relation to careers and an opportunity to explore a number of occupational possibilities (Blocher, 1973). Career education is a lifelong process, giving individuals the option to upgrade their skills and knowledge later in their careers and to retrain for a new job if desired. Career education requires collaboration between the school and business sectors and within the community.

CAREER GUIDANCE

Career guidance, like career education, is an organized, systematic program to help the individual develop self-understanding, understanding of societal roles, and knowledge about the world of work. Whereas career education is the lifelong totality of experiences through which one prepares to engage in work, career guidance is one aspect of the preparation; it entails active assistance with the development of decision-making skills and the framing of occupational and educational plans. While there is some overlap between career education and career guidance, career education stresses direct experience and activities related to occupational skills and attitudes (Hoyt, 1977b). Career guidance emphasizes the process of planning, decision making, and implementation of decisions.

Characteristics of a comprehensive program

A comprehensive career-guidance program usually refers to the range of services provided by an individual counselor, agency, or group of counselors in the same setting. It often implies a team concept: various counselors having complementary specialties, as well as certain common or general skills and knowledge, work together.

The advantages of comprehensive programs are fairly obvious when one considers both the possible range of client needs as a group and the range of needs presented by any given client. The ability to provide information services, career counseling (individual and group), assessment, consultation, and placement means that the client does not have to seek out other services and the school or agency does not have to make referrals. Not only does this approach offer greater convenience to the client but it allows the service providers to enjoy greater effectiveness and impact through control of the entire process. In the school setting, the unified program allows for integration of career information and decisions with other curricular experiences. For example, one comprehensive school-based career-guidance program, involving teacher and counselor teams, developed curriculum activities organized around five career-development themes: problem solving, understanding self and others, understanding the world, obtaining skills and experience, and achieving identity (self, social, and functional) (McKinnon & Jones, 1975).

Follow-up and evaluation are most readily accomplished when all services are provided by a single staff. The evaluator does not have external service providers to account for and involve in processing feedback and expediting program changes. Provision of comprehensive services by diversified staff, each member specializing in an area of career guidance that complements the others', may result in a substantially higher quality of service.

When considering specialization, guard against overspecialization. Compartmentalizing information, rather than linking it to or integrating it with other relevant career processes, may narrow rather than broaden experiences and choice options. Specializing in career information but excluding the decision-making process, for example, is like providing tools without giving instructions on how to use them.

Since staffing a comprehensive program may be difficult in some settings, requiring services to be provided from several sources, coordinating those programs or services is most important. Frequently secondary schools use local vocational-rehabilitation personnel to provide vocational assessment. With the passage of special-education legislation (PL 94-142), both schools and agencies will be relying on vocational rehabilitation for information concerning career opportunities and placement for special students. While being able to staff a comprehensive program has many advantages, other community resources must not be overlooked. Training or employing personnel whose field of expertise is duplicated elsewhere in a school system or community disregards the reality of economics. Comprehensive services can be provided by careful coordination of available resources between schools and agencies.

A factor to consider with regard to program articulation among grade levels is the developmental nature of career choice. A secondary or elementary school cannot provide all the career-development experiences that will be required by an individual during the lifelong process. Elementary, middle, or secondary school personnel need to coordinate their program development efforts carefully. The prerequisites for the career-development process in the middle school years must be provided in the elementary grades. This cumulative experience should merge with the skills and knowledge associated with the goals of the secondary-level career-guidance program. External services from community agencies must be articulated and integrated with the school activities to provide an even and logical flow. Agencies need to be aware of the career-development activities in the schools, the better to understand the background experiences of working adults in the community. The cooperative planning and availability of personnel and expertise from one educational setting to another should enrich the entire career program for all.

Business applications

Mid-career change or the "second" careeer is an emerging theme (Thomas, 1979) that points out the importance of career guidance in settings other than the schools. Sheppard (1977) indicates that the second-career phenomenon is represented by "mostly men in professional and business positions, who have made drastic leaps from one type of occupation to another seemingly unrelated one" (p. 335). Business and industry are discovering the necessity of assisting employees in problem solving and decision making with regard to careers. Employee productivity and satisfaction can be greatly enhanced through a system of planned guidance.

Brewer, Hanson, VanHorn, and Moseley (1975) see the pressure and anxiety associated with contemporary work settings and requirements as related to personal and institutional problems. Personal problems are of two types: those related to career potential, such as the inability of a job to support a certain lifestyle or standard of living, and those problems not directly related to career, such as family problems or dissatisfaction with a particular geographic location. Clearly, there may be overlap between these two areas, as in the case of marital problems due to a lack of sufficient income to support a desired standard of living. Institutional problems are usually related to dissatisfaction with working conditions, conflict with fellow employees or supervisors, lack of interest in job-related activities, or lack of real or perceived opportunities for professional growth.

In order to minimize these conflicts and the resulting symptoms, Brewer and others (Brewer et al., 1975) suggest a career-planning and guidance process involving employee, management, and an employee development division. This process focuses on communication between employee and employer and on planning for and assessment of work activity and goals. The program provides an orientation to employee development and the value of the career-guidance program for employees. Career-planning workshops and a self-guided planning manual provide experiences with career values, definition of goals and objectives, decision-making skills, and an analysis system for determining personnel potential. Motivated skills and individual strengths and interests related to effective work placement and training experiences are assessed, and a career-materials center provides information sources. Both peer and professional counselors are provided to facilitate the guidance process.

Response to changing needs

The comprehensive view of career development and career guidance is necessitated by several patterns in society that reflect changing personal and vocational needs. Changing lifestyles and goals, unique needs of special populations, the expanding age range of populations served, and increased numbers of individuals recognizing mid-life career crises or moving into the work force for the first time are some of the forces requiring a comprehensive programming approach to careers (Miller & Benjamin, 1975). The comprehensive approach requires several steps, which produce career-guidance programs that reflect the needs of the individuals to be served. Miller and Benjamin (1975, p. 94) have identified and ordered four basic steps: (1) needs assessments, (2) development of goals and objectives, (3) identification and selection of guidance strategies (methods and resources), and (4) program evaluation.

The following approach to program development places needs assessment in a key position. It is the tool for organizing the entire development process. Needs assessment functions as a preorganizing activity, the method for data collection and analysis, the organizer for goals and objectives, and at least one method of evaluation.

NEEDS ASSESSMENT FOR CAREER GUIDANCE

One of the primary considerations in preparing to develop a career-guidance program is the identification of client needs. The assessment of client needs must precede the establishment of goals and objectives, which in turn govern counselor behaviors. The term *need* in this context refers to the discrepancy between an individual's current situation or knowledge level and a desired skill or knowledge level. It applies not only to the psychomotor and cognitive areas but also to the affective domain.

Needs assessment, while viewed primarily as a source of data to determine program priority areas and enable the development of goals and objectives, also serves an awareness function. Frequently, students or prospective clients and staff will become aware of a problem or unmet need as a result of the assessment activity. Sometimes the counselor intends this effect in order to expedite mental readiness for activities to follow, including planning or goal-setting sessions. If not, the counselor must at least be aware of the effect and its possible impact on the surveyed population. The wording of items, instructions, organization of items, and number of questions focusing on a particular area are all factors influencing perceptions of the activity.

The assessment process can be both a data-collecting activity for purposes of program planning and decision making and an ongoing process that provides continual updating on changing needs and priorities. This feedback function provides a method for determining the impact of program planning and intervention activities on the target population's perceived needs. Assessment can also provide a vehicle for public relations, as well as a method of involving teachers, parents, students, and community in planning.

An example of the intentional multiple use of needs assessment is a survey conducted with an inner-city junior high school population to identify career-information needs and beliefs concerning accessibility of certain jobs (Messing, 1964). Job titles had previously been identified as familiar to the students, and they were used to construct a short job-title listing. When asked to indicate jobs they would be interested in if they could do anything they wanted, the students chose a representative cross-section of semiprofessional and nonprofessional activities, with some professional choices. When asked further to indicate jobs that they thought would actually be accessible to them, the students chose only nonprofessional, domestic, and labor or maintenance activities. The exceptions were military jobs. When asked to indicate jobs about which they would like more information, the students primarily indicated areas consistent with their beliefs about accessibility. Given their predominant minority and low economic background, one could point out that this differentiation indicated good reality perception. However, given the goals of increasing career awareness, which includes awareness of the expanding work opportunities for all individuals, and increasing the accessibility of various careers through educational programs, this assessment indicated a need not only for information but also for activities related to self-concept and beliefs. It also provided information about cognitive readiness and the types of guidance activities that might best create a readiness for exploring new possibilities or accommodating alternative notions about job availability. In this instance, the needs assessment was a data-collection activity, as well as a diagnostic tool and treatment device.

Components of needs assessment

Any needs-assessment process should include three general activities: system mapping, issue identification, and clarification and statement of needs (Brown & Wedel, 1974). *System mapping* refers to the development of an understanding of the area being assessed and the setting in which the activity takes place. In the school setting, mapping would involve identification of the important characteristics of the school, including the students and faculty and the relationship between those groups. It would also be important to understand the current curricular focus and what is being tried in the area of career development and guidance. In the junior high school illustration just mentioned, the socioeconomic background of the students, key staff in policy-making or decision-making positions, curricular offerings, and current guidance activities were all relevant mapping data.

Issue identification refers to the recognition of concerns that emerge during the mapping process. The issues that emerge may be symptoms of a more basic problem or a direct indication of the fundamental concern. In a school setting, issues could be high dropout rate, large number of retentions, absenteeism, high teacher turnover, or resistance to a guidance program. In an agency, the issues could be a high number of client "no-shows," large staff turnover, or a high frequency of long-term client contacts.

Clarification and *statement of needs* arise out of the issues identified. In either of these phases, an instrument can be developed and administered that involves the system's personnel in the process of selecting the major or highest-priority needs. In career guidance as in consultation, it is possible for a system to identify its own area of need; the assessment task is then to clarify and refine the need. If the need area is not well defined, the system-mapping activities should be sufficient for general issue identification. Specific needs or patterns of need can then be established through record review, individual and group interviews, and assessment instruments. The end result is a clearly stated need or set of needs and, very possibly, some specific suggestions or ideas concerning how to meet those needs.

A needs-assessment procedure

Another view of the needs-assessment process is provided by a publication of the State University of New York, Bureau of Guidance of the New York State Education Department (1976). This publication provides a good listing of resource material and instrumentation and discusses needs assessment as part of a program-planning approach. The following breakdown of needs-assessment activities takes into consideration the position of this aspect in the larger program-planning process. This listing of phases or activities is drawn both from the New York State publication and our own experience.

1. Obtain approval from governing group (board of education, advisory board, chief administrator).

2. Involve interested persons (teachers, parents, staff, students, clients) in discussion groups to identify program philosophy, general goal statements, and desired outcomes. At this point, additional information needs may be identified concerning the current status of the program and the setting in which the program is conducted.

3. Summarize opinions from discussion groups concerning current program adequacies and needs.

4. Identify areas and populations to be assessed. On the basis of discussion-group information, a general area of need and populations affected can be determined.

5. Identify sampling procedures. Depending on the size and nature of the population, one of four sampling approaches may be used. If the population is smaller than 100 in number, the entire group could be surveyed. For larger groups, simple random sampling draws names randomly from the entire population. Stratified random sampling draws samples separately from various subgroups, whose members have an equal chance for selection. Cluster sampling allows people who live near each other to be selected (State University of New York, 1976, p. 13).

6. Information gathering. The assessment activity begins with four questions: What do we want to know? Why do we want to know it? Who knows it or has the information? and How can the information be most economically, efficiently, and accurately collected? (State University of New York, 1976, p. 10).

a. Identify assessment instruments and approaches. Although standardized assessment devices are available, frequently an instrument will need to be developed to fit the area and special population in question. Other sources of information can be interviews, follow-up study reports, organizational records or annual reports, and other test results from standardized testing programs.

b. Perform pilot testing of instruments. A check of the integrity of an instrument can be achieved by field testing with a small group similar to the larger intended population. This step provides an opportunity to check the clarity of questions, appropriateness of focus, and sequencing. Usually the members of the pilot population are encouraged to discuss their reactions to the instrument, including their beliefs about its intent.

c. Collect assessment data. Surveys can be conducted individually, through direct contact, in small groups, and via telephone or mail. The individual or small-group contact can take either a structured interview or "paper and pencil" form. The interview structure should be clear and replicable for all surveyed. For a self-administered written survey, the format should be simple, with clear instructions and examples. The mail contact has the risk of lowest return rate, and some combination of self-administered mail form and telephone follow-up should be considered. A self-addressed return envelope always improves mail response.

7. Score responses and edit for internal consistency. The scoring procedure is usually determined by the item design, such as a closed or open response item. The closed or objective response (yes/no), while easier to manage, does not provide the expressive freedom of the open-ended response.

8. Process and analyze results. Separate responses from different populations and identify required statistical procedures.

9. Interpret. Identify discrepancies between the existing program or student (client) status and the desired status, and prioritize results.

10. Compare results with previous assessments in the same setting or in similar settings.

11. Establish goals and objectives. Goal statements are subdivided into objectives and activities to be accomplished to facilitate goal attainment. Student/client objectives are behavioral objectives, and staff objectives are called operational objectives (State University of New York, 1976, p. 7).

12. Identify resources and staff responsibility. Resources necessary to carry out the program include personnel who will be responsible for segments or phases of the program.

13. Maintain ongoing assessment activities. Identify a plan, with time lines, for implementing the program goals. Ongoing feedback is necessary for maximum

staff and clientele involvement and for determining effectiveness of intervention activities. Feedback can also identify changing needs, which may require new goals or strategies.

At some point in this process, if major program reorganization is involved, an advisory committee should be formed of members of the early discussion groups. Formation could occur at step four, nine, or eleven.

It is frequently a good idea, once discrepancies have been identified, to analyze the amount of time service personnel are spending on certain related activities. It is then possible to determine whether the priorities as indicated by time investments are consistent with the prioritized identified needs.

Alternate strategies

One can see from our discussion that execution of needs-assessment strategies can be costly. In some situations the pressure to activate a program may necessitate abbreviating parts of the process. Efforts to assess needs and outcome should nevertheless continue concurrently with program development. If necessary, planners can refer to needs-assessment efforts of others. Since people and communities have many common career-development concerns, results from similar populations should generalize across those groups. Thus reports available in state agencies, Educational Resources Information Center (ERIC) and other clearinghouses may provide important data of a needs-assessment nature. For that matter, reports may already exist in one's own community that contain up-to-date information about residents' career-development needs.

COUNSELOR INVOLVEMENT IN CAREER EDUCATION

A tenth-grade boy—one of the counselor's clients, no less—had stolen the driver-education car: for the counselor, just one more crisis to round out a typically challenging day. It was not just that there had been so much to do but that so much was left undone. The counselor thought about the various role statements she had seen and the lists she had compiled during her graduate work. Totally unrealistic, she thought, and yet I'm trying to accomplish most of those tasks! Of those things I do or might do, what really makes a difference?

The counselor believed that the students were her primary concern, and in the high school setting crisis counseling certainly took its toll of time. After that, though, there were the everyday concerns with course work, values, lifestyles, self-concepts, interpersonal relations, vocational decisions—all things that seemed to fall under the general heading of career guidance. As she thought about the day's activities of consequence, tasks related to career education certainly assumed major proportions. Much of her time had been spent either working directly with students in careeer-awareness and decision-making groups or working on career projects with teachers in the classroom. While she did not spend her time exactly that way every day, the apportionment was quite representative. Job-placement programs with juniors and seniors, while requiring substantial contact time with employers earlier in the year, were running smoothly by then. Placement was a good investment of time, she thought, since it also provided her the opportunity for good contacts with the business and industrial community. The contacts were productive ones; the video materials in the career library had been provided by two of the largest employers of the school's graduates.

The career activities in the chemistry class had gone very well that morning, particularly the experiments that simulated procedures at a water-purification plant. Some time had been spent in discussion with administration concerning a career-guidance plan for the year. The counselor felt it was important for administration to understand her career role. The balance of the morning had been spent in two career decision-making groups dealing with values clarification.

This would probably be the longest day of the week, since the counselor still had a meeting with parents of special students that evening. In some respects, that might be the most gratifying and most challenging activity of the day. Mainstreaming had brought to the front the tremendous need for, and lack of, career-education material for the handicapped. The following day would require spending time with the college-admissions program and drug education. Even though not every activity related to careers, the counselor could not help thinking that drug education related to lifestyle. The career theme certainly seemed dominant. She remembered the tenth grader with the driver-education car and thought with a note of irony, I wonder if he's planning to explore a used-auto-parts career?

The counselor's reflections about her role and her involvement in career education are certainly consistent with contemporary professional role statements. In 1975, the American Personnel and Guidance Association adopted a policy statement concerning the function of guidance personnel in career education (American Personnel and Guidance Association, 1975; Association for Counselor Education and Supervision, 1976). Two general categories of leadership and participatory functions were further elaborated later the same year through a U.S. Office of Education seminar. That program, held at Ohio State University, enlisted the aid of school counselors to generate specific ideas and activities related to "School Counselors and Career Education." In general, these activities can be organized into five categories: implementation of career education in the classroom, liaison between school and business/industry/labor community, parent understanding and involvement in career education, direct assistance for students in career decision making and the total career-development process, and job placement and follow-up (Hoyt, Evans, Mangum,

Bowen, & Gale, 1977, p. 365). The counselor is a key member of the career-education team, along with teachers, administrators, paraprofessional and support personnel, parents, and representatives of the business and labor community. Kilby (1980) observes, "Counselors might make other educators aware of what is currently known about the career development process, both theoretically and empirically, and make sure that the career education program is providing students with activities and experiences developmentally appropriate for each age group" (p. 119).

The counselor's leadership function in career education includes six areas of activity; there are seven participatory functions.

Leadership functions

1. Provide leadership in the identification, classification, and use of self-, educational, and occupational information. The counselor should provide and disseminate career-education materials and activities to teachers, along with counselor evaluation of the materials. In order to avoid duplication of career-education materials and activities, it is important for the counselor and the teacher to work together on a regular basis. An additional caution: teachers need more than a listing of occupations related to their subject areas to be successful in relating subjects to career. The counselor must help teachers understand careers in relation to their instructional areas. A math teacher needs to know more than the fact that insurance actuarial work is a related field; the teacher may need information about how actuarial problems could be used to illustrate a particular concept. The biology teacher can indicate to the class that marine science is a related field, but it is more effective to illustrate the relationship through an experiment showing the effects of oil pollution on vegetation and marine life in an aquarium setting.

A career-education resource center could serve both currently enrolled students and graduates. Hoyt and others (Hoyt et al., 1977, p. 383) illustrate two ways in which a centralized resource serving an entire school district could function: "(1) as a central physical facility to which students from throughout the school system are sent when in need of career guidance and counseling; or (2) as a central clearinghouse serving each school in the system, but with the basic career guidance function being decentralized in each school."

2. Provide leadership in the identification and programmatic implementation of individual career-development tasks. The counselor is a recruiter in the sense of identifying teachers who are receptive to implementing career information into their curricula. The counselor/teacher relationship in this area differs from the strict sense of "leadership function" in that encouraging the teacher to infuse career information into course work is better accomplished on an individual basis, using a "sharing" rather than a "telling" approach.

A counselor may teach a specific course dealing with self-awareness or values, or may teach a unit or module within a subject-matter course. The better counselors function as teachers, the more influence they will have with teachers. These counselor/teacher-shared activities will help teachers understand their responsibility for vocational-skills training and career awareness.

3. Provide leadership in the assimilation and application of career decision-making methods and materials. The counselor can construct homemade career-education materials (filmstrips or slide-tape presentations) for teachers' use in the classroom and serve as a role model and in-service trainer of teachers who are interested in teaching decision making and values clarification. Shared teaching activities are excellent vehicles for role modeling and generating teacher interest for in-service training. If the decision is made that the teachers, once trained, be solely responsible for values-clarification or decision-making instruction, the counselor should periodically follow up on those activities to maintain the resource contact and to keep channels open for sharing new materials and techniques.

4. Provide leadership in emphasizing the importance of, and carrying out, the functions of career counseling. The counselor should ensure that administration understands the nature and importance of career guidance. Yearly career-education plans, including reaffirmation of the guidance role and allocating blocks of time for both individual and group counseling contacts, should be prepared. An additional counselor responsibility could be the provision of in-service education to teachers who want to use group process with classroom career activities.

5. Provide leadership in eliminating the influence of both racism and sexism as cultural restrictors of opportunities available to minority persons and to women. Clearly, the counselor has the responsibility for implementing this modification function through participating in curriculum revision. Content of course materials, or even access to the course itself, can reflect bias. The counselor should be especially diligent in reviewing career materials for references or stereotypes that are sexist or racist.

6. Provide leadership in expanding the variety and appropriateness of assessment devices and procedures required for sound personal, educational, and occupational decision making. The counselor may participate in the selection and development of career-education evaluation instruments.

Participatory functions

1. Participate in efforts to monitor and assess operations, and communicate the results of those activities to other practitioners and clientele, as appropriate. The predominant theme of participatory function is program evaluation and counselor accountability. An additional concern is the encouragement of interaction between academic and vocational-education teachers for the purpose of emphasizing the necessary link between the two areas and the educational requirements for work, whether unskilled, skilled, or professional. The counselor also performs the monitoring function by facilitating the articulation of career guidance activities among elementary, junior high or middle school, and high school career-guidance programs.

2. Participate in curriculum revision. In order to be effective curriculum consultants, counselors must not think of vocational education as the logical alternative for students who cannot succeed in the academic curriculum. This image makes vocational education an unattractive option for some and a stigma for others. Many students, sometimes those going on to four-year college, have need of certain vocational skills, such as drafting and machine skills for the engineering student and welding skills for the aspiring artist. Frequently such programs are either not available, available only for limited enrollment, or offered at times that conflict with so-called academic offerings. The counselor must be able to influence curriculum change in order to create the greatest variety of resources for the greatest number of students.

An additional source of curriculum-revision information is the placement program. As part of the follow-up and educational/job-placement program, the counselor has a valuable source of feedback concerning the adequacy of student preparation for entry into work or college education. Mathematical and language skills are two areas most frequently criticized by employers and colleges alike, and yet infrequently is there any vehicle for systematic feedback to the school system.

3. Conduct career-guidance needs-assessment surveys. Student needs must be identified and conveyed to all curriculum planners. Collecting self-report data from students, teachers, and administrators as part of a career-needs assessment is an essential part of a systematic approach to career education and guidance (Ryan, 1974).

4. Organize and operate part-time and full-time educational, occupational, and job-placement programs. Frequently, job-getting skills (interviewing, vita development, communications skills, and so forth) are taught in conjunction with placement programs (Hartz & Kosmo, 1977; Goeke & Salomone, 1979). Interpersonal skills, assertiveness training, and similar "seeking and holding" skills could come anywhere in the guidance curriculum.

The "teacher-adviser" system for career education identifies teachers from each curriculum or specialization area who can advise students concerning career options in their areas. They should be available at least one period each day and are, in effect, the career counselors for careers related to their particular subjects. This program could also fall within the in-service education area of counselor responsibility, since most teacher-advisers need some training in information-processing and exploration techniques.

If the school system employs a work-experience coordinator, the counselor may not assume the placement function. Placement is, however, a legitimate and necessary function, and a logical role for the counselor is expediting client movement from developing a career plan to implementing that plan through job placement (Cheek, 1977; Fielding & Fielding, 1976).

5. *Serve as liaison between the educational and community resource groups.* Organizing and carrying out field trips gives the counselor valuable contacts with the business/labor community. It not only affords the counselor experience and contact with the working world but provides positive visibility in the community for the guidance program. Field trips offer the opportunity to make contacts with business-community resource persons who can be useful in the career-guidance program. When possible, both counselor and teacher should participate. If the entire class is not involved in the trip (small-group field trips, with specific job-search tasks, are becoming quite popular), a parent or paraprofessional could be used to monitor the balance of the class. The counselor does not always have to be present on field trips and may function most effectively in preliminary and follow-up activities with both teachers and the community.

6. *Conduct follow-up, follow-through, and job-adjustment activities.* The counselor can collect self-report data on community-based work-study placements and postgraduation employment. The career-resource center, as described earlier, would serve out-of-school youth and adults. As a community-based career-guidance center, it could provide a valuable link between schools and business/industry. It could also serve as a feedback and evaluation unit for career-education programs in the individual schools and a source of career counseling for adults seeking assistance with mid-career change and problems of reemployment.

7. *Participate in efforts to involve the home and family in career education.* Parental expectations that are inconsistent with students' interests, abilities, or needs frequently present difficult and constraining situations for the counselor trying to assist with the process of career decision making. Working to change parental attitudes and beliefs about the world of work, in order to bring about support for the goals of the career-education program, is a top priority. This relationship is not one way, however, and counselors should also solicit parental input to help create or validate program goals. Portions of this function can be closely related to the home/community-based career education model described earlier in this chapter.

Defining the counselor's role

While all the leadership and participatory functions are recommended, limitations on time or resources may not permit a counselor to function effectively in all thirteen areas. Certainly some functions are more important than others and may be more relevant for a particular situation or community. Combining functions in a single activity improves efficiency. For example, participatory functions dealing with needs assessment and with monitoring and communicating activities can be carried out together, as we discussed in the needs-assessment section. So too can the areas of community liaison, placement, and follow-up activities be coordinated, as the description of a counselor's day illustrated.

Fulfilling the role as described may require guidance personnel to make substantial behavior and attitude changes. With this fact in mind, the American Personnel and Guidance Association (Association for Counselor Education and Supervision, 1976, pp. 6 – 7) has indicated change implications, of which the following are most significant:

1. a change toward further emphasis on the counselor as a member of the career-education team and away from emphasis on the counselor as isolated professional;
2. a change toward greater counselor involvement in the business/labor/ industrial community, as well as in the home environment;
3. a change toward emphasizing career guidance in lifestyle terms and away from the narrow view of occupational guidance of the past;
4. a change toward treating the counselor as a major influencer of curriculum change and away from a view of the counselor as one who helps students adjust to the existing curriculum;
5. a change toward using the concept of work as a means of helping students acquire self-understanding and personal meaning.

COUNSELOR COMPETENCIES FOR CAREER DEVELOPMENT

With its primary emphasis on self- and values development, career education in its broadest sense is the vehicle for providing career-guidance programs to all persons. The American Personnel and Guidance Association and the Association for Counselor Education and Supervision have advocated that the counselor assume a major leadership role in the development and promotion of guidance-based career-education programs in the public schools $(K-12)$, in postsecondary educational institutions, and in community agencies (Association for Counselor Education and Supervision, 1976).

Competency areas

Mitchell (1975) suggests seven counselor competency areas consistent with a view of career that is broader than the work-identification and job-placement approach. *Career-counseling competency* includes assessment, group and individual career counseling, and value- and decision-training skills. *Program-planning competency* involves the counselor as a team member having knowledge of career-development theory, cognitive theory, personality theory, decision theory, vocational-choice theory, employment trends and training routes, and curriculum-development strategies (p. 701). *Implementation competency* includes career-exploration techniques and the skills necessary to design career-awareness, self-development, and job-placement programs. *Consultation competency* emphasizes collaborative problem identification and utilization of available resources, including individual materials. *Linkage competency* stresses communication among agencies, as well as placement and follow-up skills. *Staff-development competency* requires instructional skills for training of parents, teachers, and educational support personnel in the client system through workshops and case conferences. *Evaluation competency* stresses the research skills involved in analysis of program-outcome information.

Kilby (1980) underscores the counselor's responsibility to be knowledgeable about research and theory in career development and to convey the knowledge to teachers and administration. By implication, the counselor must also have consulting and monitoring competencies in order to determine the relevancy and integrity of the career-education program. Miller (1980) also cites consultation competencies and adds the important knowledge of "unique career development needs of special student groups (minority students, girls, handicapped students) and skills in using strategies to reduce discrimination in order to broaden opportunities for these students" (p. 90).

Competencies for agency counselors

To date the effort to specify counselor competencies for promoting career development has been concentrated primarily within public-education programs. Counselors in mental-health centers have not elaborated their involvement in the career-development process. We assume that counselors outside the schools and within community agencies will clarify their roles in this area.

It seems that work-assessment and counseling competencies are needed by agency counselors who deal with career-decision and adjustment problems. From a program-planning view, however, the consultation and education efforts of mental-health agencies require additional competencies. For example, knowledge of career-development theory, the use and organization of career information, and so forth, would come into play in consultation with business and industry. Employers in a community often need assistance in ensuring, for example, that safety efforts include attention to psychological factors that can endanger worker health. Both the physical and interpersonal environments in a plant or office often require understanding of the stressors that exist within them. While some large, profit-making companies can hire psychologists to examine such issues, many of the smaller employers may have to rely on aid from the community.

Agencies serving welfare clients, minorities, older workers, veterans, disadvantaged persons, and youth must have knowledge of federal legislation. Special federal and state funds may influence the development and implementation of career-guidance programs.

Rehabilitation agencies usually require counselors to be proficient in training clients for job-seeking skills, job placement, comprehensive work evaluation, Social Security disability determinations, and personal adjustment training (Brolin, 1975). Job placement in particular offers a special challenge for the rehabilitation counselor. The rehabilitation process will become fragmented if placement is not carefully integrated with career preparation and career enhancement (Dunn, 1974; Zadny & James, 1976). Rehabilitation counselors are being required to develop additional competencies in working with school-age handicapped persons in accordance with Public Law 94-142, which mandates mainstreaming of special-education students into regular classes. Many school counselors do not yet have the career knowledge and skills applicable to handicapped persons, and many rehabilitation counselors are not familiar with the characteristics of the younger members of this population. Competencies will need to be shared between these two groups of professionals to ensure effective service to the school-age handicapped.

Brolin (1975) suggests that agency personnel should provide education on how noneducational agencies can contribute to career education. Volunteers from the business community could be coordinated by agency personnel to provide career-guidance services for students and adults in the community. Agencies can assume a leadership role in identifying referral systems for career development and providing an extension of the school's effective career guidance to adults who are not part of a formal educational system.

Career issues precipitate many of the developmental crises of adulthood. Often they affect marriage and family adjustment. While school-based career guidance is expected to be preventive treatment for later career problems, counselors oriented toward developmental processes still attempt to monitor life changes stage by stage. The agency counselor may need to consult regularly with school personnel for assistance in developing adult programs. However, once adult programs are established, school counselors can benefit from the agency counselor-consultant in order to appreciate more fully the home or family factors affecting student career development. Thus, promoting community relations and cooperation of career-development specialists is also an important competency for the counselor working in mental health.

DEVELOPMENTAL GUIDANCE PROGRAMMING

Developmental career-guidance programs focus on the individual self-concept as a predominant theme. Typically, the period of development is viewed as either K−12 or K−productive work years. Developmental career-guidance programs are usually organized around life stages or phases of development consistent with Super's (1953, 1957) developmental stages. The process of making career choices is emphasized more than the choice itself. Many career and developmental specialists (Havighurst, 1953, 1964; Rhodes, 1970; Super, 1957; Tiedeman & O'Hara, 1963) have linked the concept of developmental stages with potential for career development. As certain developmental tasks are realized or developmental stages reached, the individual either has achieved or has the potential to achieve increased vocational maturity. Havighurst (1953, p. 2) defines a *developmental task* as "a task which arises at or about a certain period in the life of the individual, successful achievement of which leads to happiness and success with later tasks, while failure leads to unhappiness in the individual, disapproval by society, and difficulty with later tasks."

Developmental programs usually have behavioral objectives appropriate for various age and grade levels. They use curriculum materials and planned, sequenced guidance experiences that match the objectives. The team concept is another important characteristic. The counselor, teachers, and other resource personnel from school and community function in concert to provide broad and diverse experiences. The developmental career counselor designs activities and objectives around an organizing concept such as Havighurst's (1964, p. 216) proposed sequence of vocationally oriented developmental tasks. The four general stages are:

1. Identification with a worker—father, mother, or other significant persons (ages 5 – 10): the concept of working becomes an essential part of the ego-ideal.
2. Acquiring the basic habits of industry (ages 10 – 15): learning to organize one's time and energy to get a piece of work done (school, work, chores); learning to put work ahead of play in appropriate situations.
3. Acquiring identity as a worker in the occupational structure (ages 15 – 25): choosing and preparing for an occupation; getting work experience as a basis for occupational choice and for assurance of economic independence.
4. Becoming a productive person (ages 25 – 40): mastering the skills of one's occupation; moving up the ladder within one's occupation.

Stages and tasks, although general, can be translated into a series of learning activities to provide developmental competence at one level while creating readiness for the next level or stage.

Another conceptualization of the development of vocationally related behavior is provided by Herr and Cramer (1972, pp. 104 – 107). They present a comparative vocational-development chart that illustrates the relationships between developmental stages or periods, as represented by seven theorists: Tiedeman (1961), Gesell, Ilg, and Ames (1956), Ginzberg and others (1951), Buehler (1933), Havighurst (1964), Erikson (1963), and Super (1969). The theories differ on the nature of tasks and exact intervals between developmental stages. However, Herr and Cramer's (1972) chart does present development as sequential, with critical stages that must be successfully negotiated for optimal future development.

Further to elucidate the developmental guidance process, we have matched Havighurst's stages with Hansen's (1972, p. 243) career-guidance curriculum strategies and goals and related them to behavioral objectives or outcomes (see Table 11-1).

A comparable program could be constructed just as readily using another model, such as Super's stages. The important consideration is the interrelationship of each strategy level with the one before and the one that follows. In our example, Strategy I Step 1, Strategy II Step 1, and Strategy III Step 1 are logically sequenced and keyed to the child's developing cognitive ability to deal with abstraction as well as concreteness and to make "other" references as readily as "self" references.

With any system, counselors must be aware of the necessity to modify programs for specific populations. Special groups may have unique needs that need to be considered as part of a developmental approach. Beane and Zachmanoglou (1979), for example, present five psychosocial components important for career education of the handicapped. Career education assists individuals in:

1. becoming aware of the relationship between their maturity and their evolving aspirations, values, and potentialities;
2. developing a sense of worth, purpose, and direction in life;
3. becoming a part of, rather than apart from, society;
4. developing the security of legitimization in relation to the norms of achieving adult status;
5. becoming fully capacitated to perform all of life's roles more effectively.

Although specifying career education, these components provide direction for developing career-guidance-program goals and objectives.

Within the developmental approach, stages or levels of development are anticipated and the counselor's role is to determine readiness for required tasks. Counselors may identify developmentally appropriate materials and activities and advise curriculum teams on integrating career information and sequencing experiences. Teachers need to be supplied not only with career information but with an evaluation of the strengths and weaknesses of that information and the necessary understanding for utilization.

In selecting developmental-guidance strategies, counselors should consider four questions (Miller and Benjamin, 1975):

1. How appropriate is the strategy? No matter what the setting or population, strategies may have characteristics that cause them to be more effective with certain educational levels, abilities, sex and ethnic characteristics, and aspirational levels.
2. What is the expertise of available staff? Clearly, strategies requiring skills or resources that are unavailable or unobtainable should be avoided.

3. What program resources are available? Consider the cost and benefits of a strategy as well as existing resources.
4. What impact will the strategy have on the existing program? Strategies that require only minimal change or are compatible with existing programs are usually preferable.

CAREER COUNSELING IN THE 1980s

An example of a significant effort in conceptualizing and implementing comprehensive career-guidance programs was a series of projects sponsored by the Bureau of Occupational and Adult Education, a division of the U.S. Office of Education. In 1978, the Bureau funded a project entitled "Legislative Provisions for the Improvement of Guidance Programs and Personnel Development." This became a joint effort of the National Center for Research in Vocational Education, the American Personnel and Guidance Association (APGA), and the American Institute for Research. A follow-up project substituted the University of Missouri—Columbia for APGA as one of the subcontractors. This second project was entitled "Guidance Team Training Program."

One of the most significant parts of the first project was a listing of 200 critical competencies needed by guidance personnel to operate career programs for an entire community. This list was grouped into 31 competency areas. Under the direction of Harry N. Drier, The National Center for Research in Vocational Education developed training modules for each of the competency areas. This agency's address is 1960 Kenny Road, Columbus, Ohio 43210.

The next major phase of the "Legislative Provisions Project" was the organization of a series of regional and state workshops to train career-development specialists in accord with the conceptual framework (31 competency areas) for the project. In all states there are now individuals who have undergone training and may serve as consultants to local career-guidance programs.

The second project to be funded, the "Guidance Team Program," was to build on the first project. Some of the trained specialists were to assist in the development of a local career-guidance team in one community in each state and to help that team to execute a comprehensive career-guidance program. In addition, national consultants funded by the project were to assist. This second project would produce more than 50 comprehensive career-guidance programs "without walls" to serve all age groups in the community, including special and handicapped populations. Since the programs were viewed as demonstrations of principles and procedures with the potential for broad application, well-controlled research was to assess both the process and the outcomes of the effort.

In 1978 the Office of Career Education of the U.S. Office of Education provided funds for the APGA to conduct a one-year study of the role of the school

TABLE 11-1. Developmental guidance strategies

Strategy (Hansen)	Stage (Havighurst)	Goals	Behavioral objectives
I. Orientation and awareness (primary years)	Identification with a worker (ages 5 – 10)	1. Beginning to develop self-awareness and positive self-concept.	Using the activity "Family Crest," the student produces a coat of arms indicative of dominant personal and/or family characteristics.
		2. Building communications and interpersonal skills for everyday function.	Given a conflict or problem-solving situation on the playground, the student role-plays two possible resolutions with consequences.
		3. Ideas and information about the work world in a broad sense.	In an oral presentation, the student identifies at least six of the types of workers who are associated with the functioning of his or her school.
II. Prevocational self-exploration experiences (middle school)	Identification with a worker (ages 5 – 10) and acquiring the basic habits of industry (ages 10 – 15)	1. Recognition of personal strengths and emerging values and goals.	The student role-plays his or her interpretation of the values that workers might hold in four different occupations and identifies those values that are similar to his or her own.
		2. Awareness of individual potentials and ultimate need to choose those that need fuller development to achieve life goals.	The student verbally differentiates his or her self-characteristics (for example, interests, values, abilities, and personality traits) and expresses tentative occupational outlets for each.
		3. Exploration of the worlds of education, occupation, and work.	The student reviews a selection of tools or instruments on a table and selects those used in ten different occupations; or, in an oral exercise, the student states how different workers contribute to his or her well-being and the welfare of the community.
III. Career exploration module (8th or 9th grade)	Acquiring the basic habits of industry (ages 10 – 15)	1. Decision-making process: Values, alternatives, probabilities, possibilities, consequences, action plans.	From a dramatization portraying five different value-revealing ways of handling daily events, the student identifies and describes the value set with which he or she feels most comfortable.

Program	Developmental task	Activity	Student objective
		2. Simulation experiences: Motivational job problem solving; adult decision making in areas of family, education, occupation, and leisure.	The student identifies, in a gaming situation, future decisions he or she must make in order to reach various goals.
		3. Classifying the work world.	The student places 20 occupations about which he has read on a continuum from unskilled to skilled.
IV. Senior high career-information program (grades 9–12)	Acquiring the basic habits of industry (ages 10–15) and acquiring identity as a worker in the occupational structures (ages 15–25)	1. An elective course in the psychology of careers.	The student completes specified academic assignments or, as a general objective, completes the course with a grade of at least "B."
		2. Occupational information programs, focusing each month on broad occupational families in two-hour weekly sessions.	The student differentiates among the major occupations that make up a broad occupational area, or cluster, in terms of (1) amount and type of education needed for entry, (2) content, tools, setting, and products or services of the occupations, (3) value to society, (4) probability of providing the type of lifestyle the student desires, and (5) relationship to student's interests and values.
V. Exploratory occupational information interviews (grades 10–12)	Acquiring identity as a worker (ages 15–25)		The student provides data as a result of the interview, to answer questions developed prior to the interview.
VI. Career contacts with counselor (grades 11–12)	Acquiring identity as a worker (ages 15–25)	1. Become aware of the forces and events that influence their decisions.	The student verbalizes feelings of competence and adequacy in those tasks that relate to his or her vocational preference.
		2. Obtain specific information about postsecondary educational and work options.	The student develops a plan of access to his or her next step after high school, either educational or occupational, listing possible alternatives, whom to contact, capital investment necessary, and self-characteristics to be included on a résumé.

counselor in career education. APGA collected and analyzed career-related literature and information on exemplary career-guidance programs. Regional conferences and a national conference were held to discuss prepared issue papers and solicit input from counseling professionals as well as from related school and community personnel. The goal of the project was to draw distinctions between the school counselor's roles in career education, career guidance, and career development. One of the end products of this effort was the collection of position papers and bibliographic references entitled *The School Counselor's Involvement in Career Education,* published by the American Personnel and Guidance Association (Burtnett, 1980). This extensive and definitive collection is of major value to practitioners and students of career guidance. Again, it is clear that the federal government views comprehensive career guidance as an important national priority.

In the coming decade, and probably throughout much of the balance of this century, themes that have been established in the 1970s will continue to emerge. Change in the nature and availability of work in our society and what we hope will be greater research and sophistication in career development will be the key factors in the career-guidance movement of the 1980s.

The following listing is intended not to cover all possibilities but to stimulate thinking about future needs and directions. Counselors must anticipate trends and be proactive if they are to be instruments of change.

Research in career-development and assessment techniques will be an increasingly important theme. Vocational-development theory still does not adequately account for leisure time (Winters & Hansen, 1976) and the potential for development of minorities and the economically disadvantaged. Most vocational-development theories are still basically middle class oriented.

More sophisticated assessment techniques in areas of career choice, work characteristics (of both the job and the individual), and vocational maturity are essential. Counselors must collect local data for validation of the relevance of career-guidance material and assessment to their areas. Better definitions of developmental tasks and more information concerning the role of significant others in affecting career choice will be required if more effective programs of career guidance are to be developed.

The counselor must be, in addition to a change agent, an expert in the dynamics of change. Students of the 1980s and beyond will need to be educated for flexibility in job-related skills and for an increased capacity not only to tolerate change but to manage it smoothly and creatively from one occupation or lifestyle to another (Messing & Jacobs, 1976). The ability to move from occupation to occupation, change geographic areas, and accommodate new work-week formats will be essential to effective career development of the individual. Workers will be able to spend more time away from their places of employment, keeping in contact via phone and computer-terminal links. As more youth and older workers (with delayed retirement) having differing values populate the work force and more women and minorities continue to enter supervisory and management positions, the work force will become much more heterogeneous than it has ever been. Counselors must emphasize the processes of exploring and experiencing career as a primary guidance activity.

As we have already suggested, continued emphasis on career development for women, minorities, and special or exceptional populations will be required. We have done very little with the area of careers for physically and intellectually disabled. Should there be—as we have proposed—a common core of experiences for all individuals, with individualized options or tracks appropriate to unique characteristics and needs?

Career-guidance programs will need to promote the effective use of leisure time (Edwards & Bloland, 1980; McDaniels, 1977). The relationships among work, leisure, and craftsmanship, although not yet well investigated, hold great promise. A reemergence of the valuing of craftsmanship and folk art is currently visible. To the degree that work and the pleasure of creating are once again linked, the possibility exists to combine work and leisure. In another combination of work and leisure, companies are beginning to provide leisure opportunities during work, such as breaks for tennis, swimming, and jogging, and increased recreational facilities as worker benefits.

As opportunities for leisure increase, more attention must be given to career values. Counselors must effect a curriculum that helps individuals to learn to value themselves for reasons beyond their paid employment. Career-guidance themes of energy conservation and ecology will be important for shaping values and preparing the individual for maximum life-career effectiveness. Sutton (1976) points out that under our present values system we are prepared to do great violence to the earth and its energy stores in order to continue our technological progress. Schools can reinforce the concept of waste or conservation in their own utilization of energy and materials and through their curriculum.

Career-education resource centers and increased community participation will be themes of the 1980s. Resource centers can provide adult counseling services for mid-life career change or worker relocation. Hoffman and Rollin (1977) have suggested "situational groups" as preventive strategies for persons required to relocate for manpower reasons or who are recently unemployed. The center is also the source of current career information for students and new guidance techniques for staff.

The themes of the 1980s are varied but converge on the issues of career change and flexibility, outreach and community-based extension programs, values and lifestyle counseling. A true community theme can be realized as career guidance moves toward an integrated and coordinated effort among schools, agencies, parents, business, and industry. The emphasis is on collaboration. The challenge for the counselor is well defined.

SUMMARY

Career guidance must serve all clients, and counselors play a significant role in all career-development programs, whether they are in educational, agency, or industrial settings. The concepts of career education, career development, and career guidance have again been reviewed and four models of career education described. The importance of a comprehensive career-guidance program was discussed and the needs-assessment activity identified as a key process and tool in program development. A systematic approach for conducting needs assessments includes 13 phases or activities from the initial approval of activity to the final assessment and feedback activities.

Career-education counselors are involved in both leadership and participatory functions (Association for Counselor Education and Supervision, 1976), and the six areas of leadership and seven participatory activities have been described. Counselors in all settings may be required to effect significant behavior and attitude change in the process of developing the competencies needed to function in the essential career-education role. The counselor must be active across community institutions, including the schools, agencies, and industry. A collaborative effort is required, with the counselor in a coordinating position. Community resources must be maximally utilized and the concept of career development expanded to life-career development (Gysbers & Moore, 1975), including the effective use of leisure time and the emphasis on special populations.

RECOMMENDED READINGS

Beane, A., & Zachmanoglou, M. A. Career education for the handicapped: A psychosocial impact. *The Vocational Guidance Quarterly,* 1979, *28,* 44 – 47.

A brief introduction to career-development and guidance concepts for handicapped populations. This is a major area of challenge for the development of career-guidance programs and activities.

Brewer, J., Hanson, M., VanHorn, R., & Moseley, K. A new dimension in employee development: A system for career planning and guidance. *Personnel Journal,* 1975, *54,* 228 – 231.

The presentation of a comprehensive career-development and guidance program housed within an industrial setting. Employee motivation and job satisfaction are emphasized.

Brown, F. G., & Wedel, K. R. *Assessing training needs.* Washington, D. C.: National Training and Development Service Press, 1974.

This is a very useful basic reference for both program evaluation and the development of needs assessment. "System mapping," a most important concept for expediting change, is well described in this work.

Burtnett, F. E. *The school counselor's involvement in career education.* Falls Church, Va.: American Personnel and Guidance Association, 1980.

This reference represents the culmination of a nationwide project exploring the role of the school counselor in career education. It provides information on the distinction between guidance and career-education activities, as well as a review of relevant literature and exemplary career-guidance programs. A recommended reference for school counselors.

Hoyt, K. B., Evans, R., Mangum, G., Bowen, E., & Gale, D. *Career education in the high school.* Salt Lake City: Olympus, 1977.

The authors provide an extensive overview of career-education concepts and guidance applications for the secondary school. Specific activities and techniques are described, as well as strategies for program development.

Super, D. E. *The psychology of careers.* New York: Harper & Row, 1957.

A classic reference in career psychology; part 3, discussing dynamics and factors in career development, is a particularly extensive reference on that subject. More recent works of Super, as well as related material, should also be consulted in order to update this reference.

Terkel, S. *Working.* New York: Avon, 1975.

A very readable bestseller briefly describing individuals' career paths. This book illustrates the dynamics of job satisfaction and worker frustration, which are important areas of exploration for career-guidance programs.

LEARNING ACTIVITIES

1. Visit a school or agency (depending on your career goals) and obtain a description of the career-education and career-guidance programs.
   a. What populations are served?
   b. If the setting is a school, how does career guidance interface with career education?
   c. How is the program evaluated?
   It is helpful to interview the staff involved in the program to learn about the services they provide. If possible, visit a career-education class or career-guidance group.
2. Brainstorm with your group ways in which to get the community educated and involved in a career-education/career-guidance program. It may be helpful first to identify an actual career-development problem in the community through contact with the local employment service or director of school guidance programs.
3. In a small group or individually, identify a setting for assessing career-guidance needs. Using the outline for needs assessment from this chapter, obtain appropriate permissions, and then develop a needs-assessment instrument for use in that setting. Focus the instrument on only one popula-

tion, such as representative ninth-grade students, counseling staff, or employees. Pilot-test the instrument using a small sample of individuals from this group (5 to 15) and then conduct a follow-up interview during which the individuals surveyed can criticize your instrument. Explore questions such as:

a. Did they understand the questions?

b. Were the questions relevant to the situation?

c. What did they believe you were trying to accomplish? (Does this perception match your intent?)

d. Was the instrument too long? Did it leave out information?

e. Are the results usable—could you identify needed services or information based on this information?

4. Develop a brief outline of an in-service program to explore attitudes toward and describe career guidance for a group of persons representing the setting in which you hope to work.

5. Try to identify one of the four models of career education described in this chapter that is operating in your community. Visit this program and learn about the program philosophy, activities, and evaluation. Do you observe any impact on the community?

6. In a small group, role-play an agency or school staff meeting in which a counselor, teacher(s) or other agency personnel, and an administrator are present. The counselor is to describe his or her role in career education or the provision of career guidance. Evaluate the effectiveness of the presentation in a postgroup discussion. Exchange roles and have a new counselor role-play the presentation, incorporating the group's recommendations.

REFERENCES

A comparison of four experienced-based career education programs: What they offer. How they differ. ED 140 031. Arlington, Va.: ERIC Document Reproduction Service, 1976.

Adams, W. W. Knowledge about work: A career information model and system. In J. H. Magisos (Ed.), *Career education.* Washington, D.C.: American Vocational Association, 1973, 141–156.

Aiken, J., & Johnston, J. A. Promoting career information seeking behaviors in college students. *Journal of Vocational Behavior,* 1973, *3,* 81–87.

Alderfer, C. P., & McCord, C. G. Personal and situational factors in the recruitment interview. *Journal of Applied Psychology,* 1970, *54,* 377–385.

American Personnel and Guidance Association. *Career guidance: Role and functions of counseling and guidance practitioners in career education.* A position paper. Washington, D.C.: American Personnel and Guidance Association, March 1975.

American Personnel and Guidance Association. *Ethical standards of the American Personnel and Guidance Association.* Washington, D.C.: American Personnel and Guidance Association, 1974.

American Psychiatric Association. *Diagnostic and statistical manual of mental disorders* (2nd ed.). Washington, D.C.: American Psychiatric Association, 1968.

American Psychiatric Association. *Diagnostic and statistical manual of mental disorders* (3rd ed.). Washington, D.C.: American Psychiatric Association, 1979.

American Psychological Association. *Standards for educational and psychological tests and manuals.* Washington, D.C.: American Psychological Association, 1966.

American Psychological Association. *Ethical standards of psychologists.* Washington, D.C.: American Psychological Association, 1972.

American Psychological Association. *Ethical principles in the conduct of research with human participants.* Washington, D.C.: American Psychological Association, 1973.

Anderson, J. *Job seeking skills project.* Minneapolis: Minneapolis Rehabilitation Center, 1968.

Anderson, N. J., & Ramer, B. Career dress-up day: Who will I be today? *Elementary School Guidance and Counseling,* 1976, *10,* 288–289.

Anthony, W. A. Job interviewing skill program. Unpublished manuscript, Boston University, 1973.

Appalachia Educational Laboratory. *Career information system.* Bloomington, Ill.: McKnight Publishing, 1978.

Arensberg, C. M., & Niehoff, A. H. *Introducing social change: A manual for Americans overseas.* Chicago: Aldine-Atherton, 1964.

Association for Counselor Education and Supervision (ACES) Position Paper Commission on Counselor Preparation for Career Development/Career Education. Paper presented at the American Personnel and Guidance Association Convention, Chicago, Ill., April 1976.

281

Axelrod, V., Korfhage, M., & Whitson, K. *Career guidance, counseling, placement and follow-through program for rural schools, career guidance program process, planning and implementation: A coordinator's guide to career guidance program development.* Rural America Series. Research and Development Series No. 118D2. Arlington, Va.: ERIC DRS, 1977.

Azrin, N. H., & Besalel, V. B. *Job club counselor's manual: A behavioral approach to vocational counseling.* Baltimore: University Park Press, 1979.

Azrin, N. H., Flores, T., & Kaplan, S. J. Job-finding club: A group-assisted program for obtaining employment. *Behavior Research and Therapy,* 1975, *13,* 17–27.

Azrin, N. H., & Philip, R. A. The job club method for the job handicapped: A comparative outcome study. *Rehabilitation Counseling Bulletin,* 1979, *23,* 144–155.

Azrin, N. H., Philip, R. A., Thienes-Hontos, P., & Besalel, V. B. Comparative evaluation of the job club program with welfare recipients. *Journal of Vocational Behavior,* 1980, *16,* 133–145.

Bagby, J. M., & Kimmel, K. S. *Career guidance information needs for rural and small schools.* R & D Series No. 130, ED 149 133. Arlington, Va.: ERIC DRS, 1977.

Bailey, L. J., & Stadt, R. W. *Career education: New approaches to human development.* Bloomington, Ill.: McKnight Publishing Co., 1973.

Bank, I. M. Children explore careerland through vocational role models. *The Vocational Guidance Quarterly,* 1969, *17,* 284–289.

Barak, A., Carney, C. G., & Archibald, R. D. The relationship between vocational information seeking and educational and vocational decidedness. *Journal of Vocational Behavior,* 1975, *7,* 149–159.

Barlow, M. L. Community involvement in career education: A metropolitan area example. Washington, D.C.: U.S. Department of Health, Education and Welfare, Office of Education, Office of Career Education, 1978.

Barnett, J. Therapeutic intervention in the dysfunctional thought processes of the obsessional. *American Journal of Psychotherapy,* 1972, *26,* 338–351.

Barron, F. An ego-strength scale which predicts response to psychotherapy. *Journal of Consulting Psychology,* 1953, *17,* 327–333.

Barry, R., & Wolf, B. *Epitaph for vocational guidance.* New York: Columbia University Press, 1962.

Beane, A., & Zachmanoglou, M. A. Career education for the handicapped: A psychosocial impact. *The Vocational Guidance Quarterly,* 1979, *28,* 44–47.

Bender, R. C. Vocational development in the elementary school: A framework for implementation. *The School Counselor,* 1973, *21,* 116–120.

Berdie, R. Editorial. *Journal of Counseling Psychology,* 1973, *20,* i–ii.

Bergan, J. R. *Behavioral consultation.* Columbus, Ohio: Charles E. Merrill, 1977.

Bergin, A. E. Some implications of psychotherapy research for therapeutic practice. *Journal of Abnormal Psychology,* 1966, *71,* 235–246.

Berry, J. B. Counseling older women: A perspective. *Personnel and Guidance Journal,* 1976, *55,* 130–131.

Bettelheim, B. Psychiatric consultation in residential treatment: The director's view. *American Journal of Orthopsychiatry,* 1958, *28,* 256–265.

Binderman, A. J. The psychologist as a mental health consultant. *Journal of Psychiatric Nursing,* 1964, *2,* 367–380.

Binet, A., & Henri, V. The individual psychology. *Année Psychologie,* 1895, *2,* 411–463.

Blake, R. R., & Mouton, J. S. *Consultation.* Reading, Mass.: Addison-Wesley, 1976.

Blinder, M. *The treatment of depression.* New York: Psychotherapy Tape Library, 1977.

Blocher, D. H. Social change and the future of vocational guidance. In H. Borow (Ed.), *Career guidance for a new age.* Boston: Houghton Mifflin, 1973, 41–81.

Bloom, B. L., Asher, S. J., & White, S. W. Marital disruption as a stressor: A review and analysis. *Psychological Bulletin,* 1978, *85,* 867–894.

Bloom, B. S., Engelhart, M. D., Furst, E. J., Hill, W. H., & Krathwohl, D. R. *Taxonomy of educational goals: Handbook I: Cognitive domain.* New York: Longmans, Green, 1956.

Bodden, J., & James, L. Influence of occupational information giving on cognitive complexity. *Journal of Counseling Psychology,* 1976, *23,* 280–282.

Bolles, R. N. *What color is your parachute?* Berkeley, Calif.: Ten Speed Press, 1979.

Bordin, E. S. Effective consultation: Behind the questions. *Adult Leadership,* 1955, *3,* 25–26.

Bordin, E. S. *Psychological counseling* (2nd ed.). New York: Appleton-Century-Crofts, 1968.

Bordin, E. S., & Kopplin, D. A. Motivational conflict and vocational development. *Journal of Counseling Psychology,* 1973, *20,* 154–161.

Bordin, E. S., Nachmann, B., & Segal, S. J. An articulated framework for vocational development. *Journal of Counseling Psychology,* 1963, *10,* 107–116.

Borman, C. Effects of a reinforcement style of counseling on information-seeking behavior. *Journal of Vocational Behavior,* 1972, *2,* 255–259.

Bottoms, G., & Sharpe, D. Career education: A broadening educational perspective. *The School Counselor,* 1973, *21,* 121–128.

Boyd, V. S. Neutralizing sexist titles in Holland's Self-Directed Search: What differences does it make? *Journal of Vocational Behavior,* 1976, *9,* 191–199.

Brewer, J., Hanson, M., VanHorn, R., & Moseley, K. A new dimension in employee development: A system for career planning and guidance. *Personnel Journal,* 1975, *54,* 228–231.

Brodsky, C. M., & Byl, N. Treatment of work-related health problems in a work clinic. *Hospital and Community Psychiatry,* 1976, *27,* 116–120.

Brolin, D. E. Agency settings for career guidance. *Personnel and Guidance Journal,* 1975, *53,* 686–690.

Brolin, D. E., & Gysbers, N. C. Career education for persons with handicaps. *Personnel and Guidance Journal,* 1979, *58,* 258–262.

Brown, D., Wyne, M., Blackburn, J., & Powell, W. *Consultation: Strategy for improving education.* Boston: Allyn and Bacon, 1979.

Brown, D. G. *The mobile professors.* Washington, D.C.: American Council on Education, 1967.

Brown, F. G., & Wedel, K. R. *Assessing training needs.* Washington, D.C.: National Training and Development Service Press, 1974.

Browning, R. C. Validity of reference ratings from previous employers. *Personnel Psychology,* 1968, *21,* 389–393.

Bruch, M. A. Holland's typology applied to client-counselor interaction: Implications for counseling with men. *The Counseling Psychologist,* 1978, 7(4), 26; 32.

Buehler, C. *Der menschliche Lebanslau als psychologisches Problem.* Leipzig: Hizel, 1933.

Buffington, T., & Associates. *Profiles of career education projects.* Washington, D.C.: U.S. Government Printing Office, 1978.

Burke, R. J., & Weir, T. Marital helping relationships: The moderators between stress and well-being. *Journal of Psychology,* 1977, *95,* 121–130.

Buros, O. K. (Ed.). *The mental measurements yearbook.* Highland Park, N.J.: Gryphon Press, irregular years.

Burtnett, F. E. *The school counselor's involvement in career education.* Falls Church, Va.: American Personnel and Guidance Association, 1980.

Cahn, S. *The treatment of alcoholics: An evaluative study.* New York: Oxford University Press, 1970.

Calia, V. F. Vocational guidance: After the fall. *Personnel and Guidance Journal,* 1966, *45,* 320–327.

Campbell, D. P. Stability of interests within an occupation over thirty years. *Journal of Applied Psychology,* 1966, *50,* 51–56.

Campbell, D. P. *Manual for the SVIB-SCII* (2nd ed.). Stanford, Calif.: Stanford University Press, 1977.

Campbell, N. Techniques of behavior modification. *Journal of Rehabilitation,* 1971, *37,* 28–31.

Campbell, R. E. Special groups and career behavior: Implications for guidance. In J. S. Picou & R. E. Campbell (Eds.), *Career behavior of special groups: Theory, research and practice.* Columbus, Ohio: Charles E. Merrill, 1975, 424–444.

Caplan, G. *Concepts of mental health and consultation.* Washington, D.C.: U.S. Children's Bureau, 1959.

Caplan, G. *The theory and practice of mental health consultation.* New York: Basic Books, 1970.

Caplow, T. *The sociology of work.* Minneapolis: University of Minnesota Press, 1954.

Carkhuff, R. R. *Helping and human relations. Vol. I: Selection and training.* New York: Holt, Rinehart & Winston, 1969.

Carkhuff, R. R., Pierce, R. M., Friel, T. W., & Willis, D. G. *Get a job.* Amherst, Mass.: Human Resource Development Press, 1975.

Cattell, J. M. Mental tests and measurements. *Mind,* 1890, *15,* 373–381.

Cheek, J. G. A strategy for establishing a school-based job placement program. In H. J. Peters & J. C. Hansen (Eds.), *Vocational guidance and career development.* New York: Macmillan, 1977, 246–250.

Christiani, T. S., & Christiani, M. F. The application of counseling skills in the business and industrial setting. *Personnel and Guidance Journal,* 1979, *58*(3), 166–169.

Ciborowski, P. J. Guidelines for armed services recruiters. *The School Counselor,* 1978, *25,* 285–286.

Ciborowski, P. J. In-school military recruiting: A counseling perspective. *The School Counselor,* 1980, *28,* 22–25.

Clowers, M. R., & Fraser, R. T. Employment interview literature: A perspective for the counselor. *The Vocational Guidance Quarterly,* 1977, *26,* 13–26.

Coleman, J. S. *The adolescent society.* New York: Free Press, 1971.

Coleman, J. S. *The transition from youth to adult.* New York: The New York University Extension Quarterly, II, 1974.

Colligan, M. J., Smith, M. J., & Hurrell, J. J. Occupational incidence rates of mental health disorders. *Journal of Human Stress,* 1977, *3,* 34–39.

Conrad, T., Gulick, S., & Kincaid, M. B. In-school military recruiting: An appraisal. *Personnel and Guidance Journal,* 1977, *56,* 85–88.

Coombs, J., & Sklare-Lancaster, A. Career guidance every day of the week. *Elementary School Guidance and Counseling,* 1978, *12,* 295–298.

Cooper, C. L., & Marshall, J. Occupational sources of stress: A review of the literature relating to coronary heart disease and mental ill health. *Journal of Occupational Psychology,* 1976, *49,* 11–28.

Cooper, C. L., & Payne, R. (Eds.). *Stress at work.* Chichester, England: Wiley, 1978.

Coopersmith, L. *The antecedents of self-esteem.* San Francisco: W. H. Freeman, 1967.

Cormier, W. J., & Cormier, L. S. *Interviewing strategies for helpers: A guide to assessment, treatment, and evaluation.* Monterey, Calif.: Brooks/Cole, 1979.

Crites, J. O. Ego-strength in relation to vocational interest development. *Journal of Counseling Psychology,* 1960, *7,* 137–143.

Crites, J. O. A model for the measurement of vocational maturity. *Journal of Counseling Psychology,* 1961, *8,* 225–259.

Crites, J. O. *Vocational psychology: The study of vocational behavior and development.* New York: McGraw-Hill, 1969.

Crites, J. O. *Career maturity inventory: Administration and use manual.* Monterey, Calif.: CTB/McGraw-Hill, 1973.

Crites, J. O. Career counseling: A review of major approaches. *The Counseling Psychologist,* 1974, *4,* 3–23.

Crites, J. O. Career counseling: A comprehensive approach. *The Counseling Psychologist,* 1976a, *6,* 2−11.

Crites, J. O. A comprehensive model of career development in early adulthood. *Journal of Vocational Behavior,* 1976b, *9,* 105−118.

Crites, J. O. Career counseling: A review of major approaches. In J. M. Whiteley & A. Resnikoff (Eds.), *Career counseling.* Monterey, Calif.: Brooks/Cole, 1978, 18−56.

Cronbach, L. J. The Armed Services Vocational Aptitude Battery—A test battery in transition. *Personnel and Guidance Journal,* 1979, *57,* 232−237.

Crowther, B., & More, D. M. Occupational stereotyping on initial impressions. *Journal of Vocational Behavior,* 1972, *2,* 87−94.

Cunnick, W. R., & Smith, N. J. Occupational related emotional problems. *New York State Journal of Medicine,* 1977, *77,* 1737−1741.

Cusick, P. A. *Inside high schools: The student's world.* New York: Holt, Rinehart & Winston, 1973.

Dalton, G. W., Thompson, P. H., & Price, R. L. The four stages of professional careers: A new look at performance by professionals. *Organizational Dynamics,* 1977, *6*(1), 19−42.

Detre, T. P., & Jerecki, H. J. *Modern psychiatric treatment.* Philadelphia: Lippincott, 1971.

Dinkmeyer, D., & Carlson, J. *Consulting: Facilitating human potential and change processes.* Columbus, Ohio: Charles E. Merrill, 1973.

Dinkmeyer, D., & Carlson, J. Consulting: Training counselors to work with teachers, parents, and administrators. *Counselor Education and Supervision,* 1977, *16,* 172−177.

Dipboye, R. L., Wibach, K., & Fromkin, H. L. Relative importance of applicant sex, attractiveness, and scholastic standing in evaluation of job applicant resumes. *Journal of Applied Psychology,* 1975, *60,* 39−43.

Dipboye, R. L., & Wiley, J. W. Reactions of college recruiters to interviewee sex and self-presentation style. *Journal of Vocational Behavior,* 1977, *10,* 11−12.

Dipboye, R. L., & Wiley, J. W. Reactions of male raters to interviewee self-presentation style and sex: Extensions of previous research. *Journal of Vocational Behavior,* 1978, *13,* 192−203.

Dortch, R. N. What businessmen look for in a resume. *Personnel Journal,* October 1975, 516−522.

Drake, L. R., Kaplan, H. R., & Stone, R. A. How do employees value the interview? *Journal of College Placement,* 1972, *32,* 47−51.

Droege, R. C., & Hawk, J. Development of a U.S. Employment Service interest inventory. *Journal of Employment Counseling,* 1977, *14,* 65−71.

Droege, R. C., & Padgett, A. Development of an interest-oriented occupational classification system. *The Vocational Guidance Quarterly,* 1979, *27,* 302−310.

Dunn, D. *Placement services in the vocational rehabilitation program.* Menomonie, Wis.: University of Wisconsin—Stout, 1974.

Edington, E. D. Evaluation of methods of using resource people in helping kindergarten students become aware of the world of work. *Journal of Vocational Behavior,* 1976, *8,* 125−131.

Edwards, K. J., Nafziger, D. H., & Holland, J. L. Differentiation of occupational perceptions. *Journal of Vocational Behavior,* 1974, *4,* 311−318.

Edwards, P. B., & Bloland, P. A. Leisure counseling and consultation. *Personnel and Guidance Journal,* 1980, *58*(6), 435−440.

Egan, G. *The skilled helper: A model for systematic helping and interpersonal relating.* Monterey, Calif.: Brooks/Cole, 1975.

Eisenberg, S. Understanding and building self-esteem. In S. Eisenberg & L. Patterson (Eds.), *Helping clients with special concerns.* Chicago: Rand McNally, 1979, 9−34.

Ellis, A. *Reason and emotion in psychotherapy.* New York: Lyle Stuart, 1962.

Ellis, A. *Humanistic psychotherapy: The rational-emotive approach.* New York: Julian Press, 1973.

Elseroad, H., & Hensley, G. *Synthesizing work and schooling: The role of community and society.* Report No. 91. Denver, Colo.: Education Commission of the States, 1976.

Encyclopaedia Britannica. *Career kits for kids.* New York: Author, 1974.

Erikson, E. H. The problem of ego identity. *Journal of the American Psychoanalytic Association,* 1946, *4,* 56–121.

Erikson, E. H. *Young man Luther.* New York: Norton, 1956.

Erikson, E. H. *Childhood and society* (2nd ed.). New York: Norton, 1963.

Erikson, E. H. *Identity: Youth and crisis.* New York: Norton, 1968.

Farmer, H. Inquiry project: Computer-assisted counseling centers for adults. In N. K. Schlossberg & A. D. Entine (Eds.), *Counseling adults.* Monterey, Calif.: Brooks/Cole, 1977.

Farr, J. L. Response requirements and primacy-recency effects in a simulated selection interview. *Journal of Applied Psychology,* 1973, *57,* 228–232.

Faunce, W. A. *Problems in an industrialized society.* New York: McGraw-Hill, 1968.

Faure, L. S. *The conflict of generations.* New York: Basic Books, 1969.

Faust, V. *The counselor-consultant in the elementary school.* Boston: Houghton Mifflin, 1968.

Feild, H. S., & Holley, W. H. Resume preparation: An empirical study of personnel managers' perceptions. *The Vocational Guidance Quarterly,* 1976, *24,* 229–237.

Feinberg, A. M., Stabler, B., & Coley, S. B. Electrically induced relaxation in systematic desensitization: A case note. *Psychological Reports,* 1974, *35,* 75–78.

Ferkiss, V. C. *Technological man.* New York: Mentor Books, 1970.

Field, T. F., & Field, J. E. (Eds.). *The classification of jobs according to worker trait factors (An addendum to the 1977 edition of the Dictionary of Occupational Titles).* Athens, Ga.: McGregor Company, 1980.

Fielding, J., & Fielding, M. R. *Conducting job placement programs: Planning pre-employment programs, module 3.* Palo Alto, Calif.: American Institute for Research, 1976.

Flannagan, T. W. Placement: Beyond the obvious. *Rehabilitation Counseling Bulletin,* 1977, *21,* 116–120.

Forbes, R. F., & Jackson, P. R. Non-verbal behavior and the outcome of selection interviews. *Journal of Occupational Psychology,* 1980, *53,* 65–72.

Forer, B. R. *Manual for the Forer Vocational Survey.* Los Angeles: Western Psychological Services, 1957.

Form, W. H., & Miller, D. C. Occupational career pattern as a sociological instrument. *American Journal of Sociology,* 1949, *54,* 317–329.

Forsyth, L. B. The hat exhibit. *Elementary School Guidance and Counseling,* 1972, *7,* 52.

Friedman, M., & Rosenman, R. H. *Type A behavior and your heart.* Greenwich, Conn.: Fawcett Publications, 1974.

Friel, T., & Carkhuff, R. R. *The art of developing a career.* Amherst, Mass.: Human Resource Development Press, 1974.

Fröberg, J. Stress. In International Labour Office, *Encyclopedia of occupational health and safety.* New York: McGraw-Hill, 1972, 1359–1360.

Galinsky, M. D., & Fast, J. Vocational choice as a focus of the identity search. *Journal of Counseling Psychology,* 1966, *13,* 89–92.

Galton, F. *Inquiries into human faculty and its development.* London: Macmillan, 1883.

Gambrill, E. D. *Behavior modification: Handbook of assessment, intervention, and evaluation.* San Francisco: Jossey-Bass, 1977.

Garfield, S. L., & Kurtz, R. Clinical psychologists in the 1970s. *American Psychologist,* 1976, *31,* 1–9.

Garrison, C. B., McCurdy, W. J., Munson, P. J., Brolie, D., Saunders, J. D., Sims, K., & Telis, D. *Finding a job you feel good about.* Niles, Ill.: Argus Publishing, 1977.

Gelatt, H. B. Decision making: A conceptual frame of reference for counseling. *Journal of Counseling Psychology,* 1962, *9,* 240–245.

Gelso, C. J., Collins, A. M., Williams, R. O., & Sedlacek, W. E. The accuracy of self-administration and scoring on Holland's Self-Directed Search. *Journal of Vocational Behavior,* 1973, *3,* 375–382.

Gesell, A., Ilg, F. L., and Ames, L. *Youth: The years from ten to sixteen.* New York: Harper & Row, 1956.

Ginzberg, E. Toward a theory of occupational choice. *Personnel and Guidance Journal,* 1952, *30,* 491–494.

Ginzberg, E. *Career guidance.* New York: McGraw-Hill, 1972a.

Ginzberg, E. A critical look at career guidance. *American Vocational Journal,* 1972b, *47,* 51–54.

Ginzberg, E. Toward a theory of occupational choice: A restatement. *The Vocational Guidance Quarterly,* 1972c, *20,* 169–176.

Ginzberg, E. *Good jobs, bad jobs, no jobs.* Cambridge, Mass.: Harvard University Press, 1979.

Ginzberg, E., Ginsburg, S. W., Axelrad, S., & Herma, J. L. *Occupational choice: An approach to a general theory.* New York: Columbia University Press, 1951.

Giovacchini, P. L. *Treatment of primitive mental states.* New York: Aronson, 1979.

Goeke, J. D., & Salomone, P. R. Job placement and the school counselor. *The Vocational Guidance Quarterly,* 1979, *27,* 209–215.

Goldberg, H. *The hazards of being male: Surviving the myth of masculine privilege.* New York: The New American Library, 1976.

Goldhammer, K. *Extending career awareness beyond the school house walls.* Columbus, Ohio: Center for Vocational Education, 1974.

Goldhammer, K., Gardner, R., Heilman, C., Mokma, A., Libby, R., & Rietfors, G. *Experience based career education: A description of four pilot programs financed through the National Institute of Education.* Washington, D.C.: National Institute of Education, ED 118 833, 1975.

Goldhammer, K., & Taylor, R. E. (Eds.). *Career education: Perspective and promise.* Columbus, Ohio: Charles E. Merrill, 1972.

Goldman, L. A revolution in counseling research. *Journal of Counseling Psychology,* 1976, *23,* 543–552.

Goldstein, A. P. *Therapist-patient expectancies in psychotherapy.* New York: Pergamon Press, 1962.

Goldstein, A. P. *Psychotherapeutic attraction.* New York: Pergamon Press, 1971.

Granovetter, M. S. *Getting a job.* Cambridge, Mass.: Harvard University Press, 1974.

Granovetter, M. S. Placement as brokerage—Information problems in the labor market for rehabilitated workers. In D. Vandergoot and J. D. Worrell (Eds.), *Placement in rehabilitation: A career development perspective.* Baltimore: University Park Press, 1979, 83–101.

Green, T. *Work, leisure and the American schools.* New York: Random House, 1968.

Gregory, R. J. The application for employment. *The Vocational Guidance Quarterly,* 1966, *15,* 131–134.

Gribbons, W. D., & Lohnes, P. R. *Emerging careers.* New York: Columbia University, Teachers College Press, 1968.

Griffith, A. R. A survey of career development in corporations. *Personnel and Guidance Journal,* 1980, *58,* 537–543.

Guidance Associates (Producer). *First things.* Pleasantville, N.Y.: Guidance Associates, 1973. (Filmstrip)

Gysbers, N. C., Miller, W., & Moore, E. J. *Developing careers in the elementary school.* Columbus, Ohio: Charles E. Merrill, 1973.

Gysbers, N. C., & Moore, E. J. Beyond career development—life career development. *Personnel and Guidance Journal,* 1975, *53,* 647–752.

Haase, R. F., Reed, C. F., Winer, J. L., & Bodden, J. L. Effect of positive, negative, and mixed information on cognitive and affective complexity. *Journal of Vocational Behavior*, 1979, *15*, 294–302.

Hall, D. T., & Schneider, B. *Organizational climates and careers*. New York: Seminar Press, 1973.

Hamilton, J. S., & Krumboltz, J. D. Simulated work experience: How realistic should it be? *Personnel and Guidance Journal*, 1969, *48*, 39–44.

Hansen, L. S. A model for career development through curriculum. *Personnel and Guidance Journal*, 1972, *51*, 243–250.

Hansen, L. S. Commentary during the USOE National Conference on Guidance at Baltimore, April 1978.

Hansen, L. S., & Keierleber, D. L. Born free: A collaborative consultation model for career development and sex-role stereotyping. *Personnel and Guidance Journal*, 1978, *56*, 395–399.

Harris, E. F., & Fleishman, E. A. Human relations training and the stability of leadership patterns. *Journal of Applied Psychology*, 1955, *39*, 20–25.

Harris, S. Sex typing in girls' career choices: A challenge to counselors. *The Vocational Guidance Quarterly*, 1974, *23*, 128–133.

Harrison, L., & Entine, A. D. Existing programs & emerging strategies. In N. K. Schlossberg & A. D. Entine (Eds.), *Counseling adults*. Monterey, Calif.: Brooks/Cole, 1977, 108–121.

Hartz, J. D., & Kosmo, S. J. *Career guidance, counseling, placement, and follow-through program for rural schools. Career guidance and counseling for groups and individuals. An individualized approach to career counseling and career placement: Introduction, background and rationale*. Rural America Series, R&D Series No. 118 C3, ED 142 759. Arlington, Va.: ERIC DRS, 1977.

Havighurst, R. J. *Human development and education*. New York: Longmans, 1953.

Havighurst, R. J. Successful aging. In R. H. Williams, C. Tibbetts, & W. Donahue (Eds.), *Process of Aging*. Vol. 1. New York: Atherton, 1963, 299–320.

Havighurst, R. J. Youth in exploration and man emergent. In H. Borow (Ed.), *Man in a world at work*. Boston: Houghton Mifflin, 1964, 215–236.

Hayes, J. A. Automation: A real "H" bomb. In C. Markham (Ed.), *Jobs, men, and machines: Problems of automation*. New York: Praeger, 1964.

Hedgepeth, A. The popcorn factory: An artificial work experience. *Elementary School Guidance and Counseling*, 1972, *6*, 198–200.

Heller, K., & Goldstein, A. P. Client dependency and therapist expectancy as relationship maintaining variables in psychotherapy. *Journal of Consulting Psychology*, 1961, *25*, 371–375.

Helms, S. T. Practical applications of the Holland occupational classification in counseling. *Communique*, 1973, *2*, 69–76.

Herr, E. L. Trends in guidance: A national view. In *Leadership in guidance: Perspectives on content, process and directions*. Harrisburg, Pa.: Bureau of Instructional and Support Services, Pennsylvania Department of Education and The Pennsylvania State University, 1979, 8–56.

Herr, E. L., & Cramer, S. H. *Vocational guidance and career development in the schools: Toward a systems approach*. Boston: Houghton Mifflin, 1972.

Herr, E. L., & Cramer, S. H. *Career guidance through the life span: Systematic approaches*. Boston: Little, Brown, 1979.

Herr, E. L., & Whitson, K. S. Career guidance of urban adults: Some perspectives on needs and action. *The Vocational Guidance Quarterly*, 1979, *28*, 111–120.

Hershenson, D. G. Sense of identity, occupational fit, and enculturation in adolescence. *Journal of Counseling Psychology*, 1967, *14*, 319–324.

Herzberg, F. *Work and the nature of man*. Cleveland: The World Publishing Co., 1966.

Hewett, K. D., Warner, D. D., and Wolff, P. *Eleven career education programs*. Cambridge, Mass.: Abt Publications, 1975.

Hinsie, L. E., & Campbell, R. J. *Psychiatric dictionary* (4th ed.). New York: Oxford University Press, 1970.

Hoffman, S. D., & Rollin, S. A. Implications of future shock for vocational guidance. In H. J. Peters & J. C. Hansen (Eds.), *Vocational guidance and career development* (3rd ed.). New York: Macmillan, 1977, 33–40.

Holcomb, W. R., & Anderson, W. P. Vocational guidance research: A five year overview. *Journal of Vocational Behavior,* 1977, *10,* 341–346.

Holland, J. L. A theory of vocational choice. *Journal of Counseling Psychology,* 1959, *6,* 35–45.

Holland, J. L. *Manual for the Vocational Preference Inventory.* Palo Alto, Calif.: Consulting Psychologists Press, 1965.

Holland, J. L. *The psychology of vocational choice.* Waltham, Mass.: Blaisdell, 1966.

Holland, J. L. *Making vocational choices: A theory of careers.* Englewood Cliffs, N.J.: Prentice-Hall, 1973.

Holland, J. L. A new synthesis for an old method and a new analysis of some old phenomena. *The Counseling Psychologist,* 1976, *6,* 12–15.

Hollis, J. W., & Hollis, L. U. *Personalizing information processes.* New York: Macmillan, 1969.

Homans, G. C. *The human group.* New York: Harcourt Brace Jovanovich, 1950.

Hoppock, R. *Occupational information* (4th ed.). New York: McGraw-Hill, 1976.

Hornstein, H., Bunker, B., Burke, W., Gindes, M., & Lewicki, R. *Social intervention: A behavioral science approach.* New York: Free Press, 1971.

Horowitz, M. J. *Stress response syndromes.* New York: Aronson, 1976.

Hoyt, K. B. Career education: Challenges for counselors. *The Vocational Guidance Quarterly,* 1975, *23,* 303–310.

Hoyt, K. B. *Career education and the business, labor, industry community.* Monographs on career education. Washington, D.C.: U.S. DHEW, OE, OCE, 1976.

Hoyt, K. B. *Career education: Contributions to an evolving concept.* Salt Lake City: Olympus Publishing Company, 1977a.

Hoyt, K. B. *A primer for career education.* Monographs on career education. Washington, D.C.: U.S. DHEW, OE, OCE, 1977b.

Hoyt, K. B. Contrasts between the guidance and the career education movements. In F. E. Burtnett, *The school counselor's involvement in career education.* Falls Church, Va.: American Personnel and Guidance Association, 1980, 1–11.

Hoyt, K. B., Evans, R. N., Mackin, E. F., & Mangum, G. L. *Career education: What it is and how to do it* (2nd ed.). Salt Lake City: Olympus, 1974.

Hoyt, K. B., Evans, R., Mangum, G., Bowen, E., & Gale, D. *Career education in the high school.* Salt Lake City: Olympus, 1977.

Hoyt, K. B., Pinson, N. M., Laramore, D., & Mangum, G. L. *Career education and the elementary school teacher.* Salt Lake City: Olympus Publishing Company, 1973.

Huggins, O. Job hunting: The resume is the foot in the door. *Canadian Business,* July 1977, 35–39.

Human Resources Center. *Modular placement training program: Module 10, self-placement skills I (Leader's guide).* Albertson, N.Y.: Author, 1977.

Ironside, D. J., & Jacobs, D. E. Trends in counseling and information services for the adult learner. Occasional Paper 17. Toronto, Canada: Ontario Institute for Studies in Education, 1977.

Isaacson, L. E. *Career information in counseling and teaching* (3rd ed.). Boston: Allyn & Bacon, 1977.

Jackson, I. The elementary school employment service. *Elementary School Guidance and Counseling,* 1972, *6,* 285–286.

Jacobson, M. D. Adult Career Advocates Training Program. Unpublished interim report, Northwestern University, Evanston, Ill., January 1979.

Jarvik, L. F. Thoughts on the psychobiology of aging. *American Psychologist,* 1975, *30,* 576–583.

Jenkins, C. D. Psychologic and social precursors of coronary disease. *New England Journal of Medicine,* 1971, *284,* 307–317.

Jenks, C. L. *The theoretical basis of experience-based career education.* San Francisco: Far West Laboratory of Education Research and Development, 1976.

Jewish Vocational Service. *Job placement and job development.* Chicago: Jewish Vocational Service, 1976.

Job Experience Kit. Chicago, Ill.: Science Research Associates, Inc., 1970.

Johnson, R. G. Job simulations to promote vocational interests. *The Vocational Guidance Quarterly,* 1971, *20,* 25–30.

Johnson, R. H. Individual styles of decision making: A theoretical model for counseling. *Personnel and Guidance Journal,* 1978, *50*(9), 530–536.

Johnson, W. F., Korn, T. A., & Dunn, D. J. Comparing three methods of presenting occupational information. *The Vocational Guidance Quarterly,* 1975, *24,* 62–66.

Jones, K. K. Holland's typology and the new Guide for Occupational Exploration: Bridging the gap. *The Vocational Guidance Quarterly,* 1980, *29,* 70–76.

Jones, R. L., & Azrin, N. H. An experimental application of a social reinforcement approach to the problem of job-finding. *Journal of Applied Behavior Analysis,* 1973, *6,* 345–353.

Kaback, G. R. Occupational information in elementary education. *The Vocational Guidance Quarterly,* 1960, *9,* 55–59.

Kaback, G. R. Occupational information for groups of elementary school children. *The Vocational Guidance Quarterly,* 1966, *14,* 163–168.

Kaniuga, N., Scott, T., & Gade, E. Working women portrayed on evening television programs. *The Vocational Guidance Quarterly,* 1974, *23,* 134–137.

Karoly, P. Operant methods. In F. H. Kanfer & A. P. Goldstein (Eds.), *Helping people change.* New York: Pergamon Press, 1975.

Kasl, S. V. Epidemiological contributions to the study of work stress. In C. L. Cooper & R. Payne (Eds.), *Stress at work.* Chichester, England: Wiley, 1978, 3–48.

Katz, M. *Decisions and values: A rationale for secondary school guidance.* New York: College Entrance Examination Board, 1963.

Keil, E. C., & Barbee, J. R. Behavior modification and training the disadvantaged job interviewee. *The Vocational Guidance Quarterly,* 1973, *22,* 50–55.

Keith, R. D., Engelkes, J. R., & Winborn, B. B. Employment-seeking preparation and activity: An experimental job-placement training model for rehabilitation clients. *Rehabilitation Counseling Bulletin,* 1977, *21,* 159–165.

Kemp, B. J., & Vash, C. L. A comparison between two placement programs for hardcore unemployed persons. *Journal of Employment Counseling,* September 1971, 109–115.

Kernberg, O. *Object-relations theory and clinical psychoanalysis.* New York: Aronson, 1976.

Kilby, J. School counselor collaboration with teachers and other education personnel in the delivery of career education. In F. E. Burtnett, *The school counselor's involvement in career education.* Falls Church, Va.: American Personnel and Guidance Association, 1980, 111–122.

Klein, S. M. *Workers under stress.* Lexington, Ky.: University Press of Kentucky, 1971.

Korman, A. K. Hypothesis of work behavior revisited and an extension. *Management Review,* 1976, *1,* 50–65.

Kornhauser, A. *Mental health of the industrial worker: A Detroit study.* New York: Wiley, 1965.

Krathwohl, D. R., Bloom, B. S., & Masia, B. B. *Taxonomy of educational objectives. Handbook II: The affective domain.* New York: David McKay, 1964.

Krumboltz, J. D. *Vocational problem solving experiences for simulating career exploration and interest.* Final report. Stanford, Calif.: Stanford University Press, 1967.

Krumboltz, J. D. A social learning theory of career selection. *The Counseling Psychologist,* 1976, *6*(1), 71–81.

Krumboltz, J. D., & Baker, R. D. Behavioral counseling for vocational decisions. In H. Borow (Ed.), *Career guidance for a new age*. Boston: Houghton Mifflin, 1973, 235–284.

Krumboltz, J. D., Mitchell, A. M., & Jones, G. B. A social learning theory of career selection. In J. M. Whiteley & A. Resnikoff, *Career counseling*. Monterey, Calif.: Brooks/Cole, 1978, 100–127.

Krumboltz, J. D., & Schroeder, W. W. Promoting career planning through reinforcement. *Personnel and Guidance Journal*, 1965, *44*, 19–26.

Krumboltz, J. D., & Thoresen, C. E. The effect of behavioral counseling in group and individual settings on information seeking behavior. *Journal of Counseling Psychology*, 1964, *11*, 324–333.

Krumboltz, J. D., & Thoresen, C. E. *Behavioral counseling: Cases and techniques*. New York: Holt, Rinehart & Winston, 1969.

Krumboltz, J. D., & Thoresen, C. E. *Counseling methods*. New York: Holt, Rinehart & Winston, 1976.

Kurpius, D. J. Consulting theory and process: An integrated model. *Personnel and Guidance Journal*, 1978, *56*, 335–338.

Kurpius, D. J., & Brubaker, J. C. *Psychoeducational consultation: Definition—functions—preparation*. Bloomington, Ind.: Indiana University, 1976.

Lambert, N. M. A school-based consultant model. *Professional Psychology*, 1974, *5*, 267–276.

Landy, F. J., & Bates, F. Another look at contrast effects in the employment interview. *Journal of Applied Psychology*, 1973, *58*, 141–144.

Lange, A., & Jakubowski, P. *Responsible assertive behavior: Cognitive/behavioral procedures for trainers*. Champaign, Ill.: Research Press, 1976.

Laramore, D., & Thompson, J. Career experiences appropriate to elementary school grades. *The School Counselor*, 1970, *17*, 262–264.

Lasson, K. *The workers: Portraits of nine American jobholders*. New York: Bantam Books, 1972.

Leonard, G. E. *The developmental career guidance project: An interim report*. Detroit, Mich.: Wayne State University, 1968a. (ERIC DRS No. ED 35 31)

Leonard, G. E. *Developmental career guidance project: Career guidance manual for teachers*. Detroit: Detroit Public Schools, 1968b.

Leonard, G. E. Career guidance in the elementary school. *Elementary School Counseling and Guidance*, 1971, *6*, 124–126.

Leonard, G. E. *The developmental career guidance project: 1965–1970*. Detroit: Wayne State University, 1972a.

Leonard, G. E. Living in a medieval town. *Elementary School Guidance and Counseling*, 1972b, *6*, 283–284.

Leonard, G. E., Jeffries, D., & Spedding, S. Career guidance in the elementary school. *Elementary School Guidance and Counseling*, 1974, *9*, 48–51.

Leonard, G. E., & Vriend, T. J. Update: The developmental career guidance project. *Personnel and Guidance Journal*, 1975, *53*, 668–671.

Levine, E. L., & Rudolph, S. M. *Reference checking for personnel selection: The state-of-the-art*. Berea, Ohio: American Society for Personnel Administration, 1977.

Levinson, D. The mid-life: A period of adult psychosocial development. *Psychiatry*, 1977, *40*, 99–112.

Levinson, D., Darrow, C., Klein, E., Levinson, M., & McKee, B. *The seasons of a man's life*. New York: Knopf, 1978.

Lippett, G. L. A study of the consultation process. *Journal of Social Issues*, 1959, *15*, 43–50.

Lippitt, G., & Lippitt, R. *The consultation process in action*. La Jolla, Calif.: University Associates, Inc., 1978.

LoCascio, R. Delayed and impaired vocational development: A neglected aspect of vocational development theory. *Personnel and Guidance Journal*, 1964, *42*, 885–887.

Lofquist, L. H., & Dawis, R. V. *Adjustment to work.* New York: Appleton-Century-Crofts, 1969.

Lumsden, H. H., & Sharf, J. C. Behavioral dimensions of the job interview. *Journal of College Placement,* 1974, *34,* 63–66.

Magisos, J. H. (Ed.). *Career education.* Washington, D.C.: American Vocational Association, 1973.

Mahler, W. R., & Monroe, W. H. *How industry determines the need for and effectiveness of training.* Personnel Research Section Report 929. Washington, D.C.: Department of the Army, 1952.

Mahoney, M. J., & Thoresen, C. E. *Self-control: Power to the person.* Monterey, Calif.: Brooks/Cole, 1974.

Mangum, G. L., Becker, J. W., Coombs, G., & Marshall, P. *Career education in the academic classroom.* Salt Lake City: Olympus, 1975.

Mann, F. C. Studying and creating change: A means to understanding social organization. In H. A. Hornstein et al. (Eds.), *Social intervention: A behavioral science approach.* New York: Free Press, 1971.

Marland, S. P., Jr. Marland on career education. *American Education,* 1971, *7,* 25–28.

Marland, S. P., Jr. Career education now. *The Vocational Guidance Quarterly,* 1972a, *20,* 188–192.

Marland, S. P., Jr. Career education now. In K. Goldhammer & R. E. Taylor (Eds.), *Career education: Perspective and promise.* Columbus, Ohio: Charles E. Merrill, 1972b.

Marland, S. P. *Career education: A proposal for reform.* New York: McGraw-Hill, 1974.

Marshall, A. *How to get a better job.* New York: Hawthorn, 1976.

Maslow, A. H. *Motivation and personality.* New York: Harper & Row, 1954.

Mayfield, E. C. The selection interview. A reevaluation of published research. *Personnel Psychology,* 1964, *17,* 239–260.

Maynard, J. *Growing up old in the sixties.* Garden City, N.Y.: Doubleday, 1973.

McBeath, M. Consulting with teachers in two areas—Grief and mourning: Relaxation techniques. *Personnel and Guidance Journal,* 1980, *58,* 473–476.

McClure, D. Placement through improvement of clients' job seeking skills. *Journal of Applied Rehabilitation Counseling,* 1972, *3,* 188–196.

McClure, L., & Buan, C. (Eds.). *Essays on career education.* Portland, Ore.: Northwest Regional Educational Laboratory, 1973.

McDaniels, C. Leisure and career development in mid-life: A rationale. *The Vocational Guidance Quarterly,* 1977, *25,* 344–350.

McGovern, T. V., & Tinsley, H. E. Interviewer evaluations of interviewee nonverbal behavior. *Journal of Vocational Behavior,* 1978, *13,* 163–171.

McKinnon, B. E., & Jones, G. B. Field testing a comprehensive career guidance program, K-12. *Personnel and Guidance Journal,* 1975, *53,* 663–667.

McLean, A. (Ed.). *Occupational stress.* Springfield, Ill.: Charles C Thomas, 1974.

McQuade, W., & Aikman, A. *Stress.* New York: Bantam Books, 1974.

Meichenbaum, D. H. *Cognitive behavior modification.* New York: Plenum, 1977.

Meichenbaum, D., Turk, D., & Burstein, S. The nature of coping with stress. In S. G. Sarason & C. D. Spielberger (Eds.), *Stress and anxiety* (Vol. 2). New York: Wiley, 1975.

Messing, J. K. *Job accessibility beliefs of minority junior high school students.* Unpublished manuscript, Syracuse University, 1964.

Messing, J. K., & Jacobs, E. E. Students and change: Challenge for the school counselor. In D. P. Garner (Ed.), *The career educator* (Vol. 2). Charleston, Ill.: Eastern Illinois University, 1976, 69–75.

Messing, J. K., & Jones, L. *Career awareness: A community based approach.* Unpublished manuscript, West Virginia University, 1980.

Miller, C. D., & Form, W. H. *Industrial sociology.* New York: Harper & Row, 1951.

Miller, C. H. *Foundations of guidance* (2nd ed.). New York: Harper & Row, 1971.

Miller, J. V. The role of the counselor in elementary school career education. In F. E. Burtnett, *The school counselor's involvement in career education.* Falls Church, Va.: American Personnel and Guidance Association, 1980, 73–92.

Miller, J. V., & Benjamin, L. New career development strategies: Methods and resources. *Personnel and Guidance Journal,* 1975, *53,* 694–699.

Milt, H. *Basic handbook on alcoholism.* Maplewood, N.J.: Scientific Aids Publications, 1969.

Mitchell, A. Emerging career guidance competencies. *Personnel and Guidance Journal,* 1975, *53,* 700–703.

Molinaro, D. A placement system develops and settles: The Michigan model. *Rehabilitation Counseling Bulletin,* 1977, *21,* 121–129.

Moore, R. K., & Sanner, K. Helping teachers analyze and remedy problems. In J. D. Krumboltz & C. E. Thoresen (Eds.), *Behavioral counseling: Cases and techniques.* New York: Holt, Rinehart & Winston, 1969, 250–259.

Moreland, J. R. Some implications of life-span development for counseling psychology. *Personnel and Guidance Journal,* 1979, *57,* 299–304.

Morrison, R. F. Career adaptivity: The effective adaptation of managers to changing role demands. *Journal of Applied Psychology,* 1977, *62,* 549–558.

Mosel, J. N., & Goheen, H. W. Agreement among replies to an employment recommendation questionnaire. *American Psychologist,* 1952, *1,* 365–366.

Mosel, J. N., & Goheen, H. W. The employment recommendation questionnaire: III. Validity of different types of references. *Personnel Psychology,* 1959, *12,* 469–477.

Muchinsky, P. M. The use of reference reports in personnel selection: A review and evaluation. *Journal of Occupational Psychology,* 1979, *52,* 287–297.

MultiResource Center. *Minnesota job seeking skills program.* Minneapolis: Author, 1971.

Munley, P. H. Erikson's theory of psychosocial development and career development. *Journal of Vocational Behavior,* 1977, *10,* 261–269.

Munson, H. L. Career education reconsidered: A life-experience model. *Personnel and Guidance Journal,* 1978, *57,* 136.

Munsterberg, H. *Psychology and life.* Boston: Houghton Mifflin, 1889.

Munsterberg, H. *Psychology and industrial efficiency.* Boston: Houghton Mifflin, 1913.

Musselman, D. L. Career exposition: Big-time version of an old guidance technique. *The Vocational Guidance Quarterly,* 1969, *18,* 49–53.

Nachman, B. Childhood experience and vocational choice in law, dentistry, and social work. *Journal of Counseling Psychology,* 1960, *7,* 243–250.

National Manpower Institute. Consortium activities. *The Work-Education Exchange,* 1978, *2,* 4–5.

National Training Laboratory in Group Development. Consultation as a training function. *Explorations in human relations training.* Washington, D.C.: National Education Association, 1953.

National Vocational Guidance Association. *NVGA bibliography of current career information.* Washington, D.C.: Author, 1979 (updated biennially).

National Vocational Guidance Association. Guidelines for the preparation and evaluation of career information literature. *The Vocational Guidance Quarterly,* 1980, *28,* 291–296.

Newman, R. G. *Psychological consultation in the schools.* New York: Basic Books, 1967.

Nida, R., & Messing, J. *Staff training needs assessment.* Dunbar, W.V.: West Virginia Research and Training Center, 1979.

Norris, W. *Occupational information in the elementary school.* Chicago: Science Research Associates, 1969.

Norris, W., Hatch, R. N., Engelkes, J. R., & Winborn, B. B. *The career information service* (4th ed.). Chicago: Rand McNally, 1979.

Northwest Regional Education Laboratory. *Final evaluation report of NWREL experience based career education program.* Portland, Ore.: Northwest Regional Educational Laboratory, 1974.

Oetting, E., & Miller, C. D. Work and the disadvantaged: The work adjustment hierarchy. *Personnel and Guidance Journal,* 1977, *56,* 29–35.

Osipow, S. H. *Theories of career development* (2nd ed.). Englewood Cliffs, N.J.: Prentice-Hall, 1973.

Pacific Consultants. *Profiles of career education projects.* Washington, D.C.: U.S. Government Printing Office, 1976.

Parkinson, T., Bradley, R., & Lawson, G. Career counseling revisited. *The Vocational Guidance Quarterly,* 1979, *28,* 121–128.

Parsons, F. *Choosing a vocation.* Boston: Houghton Mifflin, 1909.

Patterson, C. H. Counseling: Self-clarification and the helping relationship. In H. Borow (Ed.), *Man in a world of work.* Boston: Houghton Mifflin, 1964, 434–459.

Patterson, C. H. A current view of client-centered or relationship therapy. *The Counseling Psychologist,* 1969, *1,* 2–24.

Peres, S. H., & Garcia, J. R. Validity and dimensions of descriptive adjectives used in reference letters for engineering applicants. *Personnel Psychology,* 1962, *15,* 279–286.

Peters, H. J., & Hansen, J. C. (Eds.). *Vocational guidance and career development: Selected readings* (3rd ed.). New York: Macmillan, 1977.

Piaget, J. *Structuralism.* New York: Basic Books, 1970.

Poor, C., & Delaney, J. Houston job fair for the handicapped. *Journal of Rehabilitation,* 1974, *40,* 26–30.

Prazak, J. A. Learning job-seeking interview skills. In J. D. Krumboltz & C. E. Thoresen (Eds.), *Behavioral counseling: Cases and techniques.* New York: Holt, Rinehart & Winston, 1969, 414–428.

Quinn, I. T. *Consulting in the area of career guidance.* National Consortium on Competency Based Staff Development in Career Guidance. Palo Alto, Calif.: American Institute for Research, 1978.

Radin, S. S. Job phobia: School phobia revisited. *Comprehensive Psychiatry,* 1972, *13,* 251–257.

Rappoport, L. Adult development: "Faster horses . . . and more money." *Personnel and Guidance Journal,* 1976, *55,* 106–108.

Reardon, R. C., & Burck, H. D. Training of the career development specialist within counselor education. *Counselor Education and Supervision,* 1980, *19,* 210–215.

Remenyi, A. G., & Fraser, B. J. Effects of occupational information on occupational perceptions. *Journal of Vocational Behavior,* 1977, *10,* 53–68.

Rhoads, J. M. Overwork. *Journal of the American Medical Association,* 1977, *237,* 2615–2618.

Rhodes, J. A. *Vocational education and guidance: A system for the seventies.* Columbus, Ohio: Charles E. Merrill, 1970.

Richards, L. S. *Vocophy.* Marlboro, Mass.: Pratt Brothers, 1881.

Riggs, R. T., & Kugel, L. F. Transition from urban to rural mental health practice. *Social Casework,* 1976, *57,* 562–567.

Robbin, A. Who is building the bridges? *Personnel and Guidance Journal,* 1971, *49,* 693–697.

Roe, A. *The psychology of occupations.* New York: Wiley, 1956.

Roe, A. Reactions to Krumboltz and Crites. *The Counseling Psychologist,* 1976, *6,* 16–17.

Roe, A., & Siegelman, M. The origin of interests. *APGA Inquiry Studies,* No. 1, 1964.

Roethlisberger, F. J., & Dickson, W. J. *Management and the works.* Cambridge, Mass.: Harvard University Press, 1964.

Rogers, C. R. *Counseling and psychotherapy.* Boston: Houghton Mifflin, 1942.

Rogers, C. R. *Client centered therapy.* Boston: Houghton Mifflin, 1951.

Rogers, C. R. The necessary and sufficient conditions of therapeutic personality change. *Journal of Consulting and Clinical Psychology,* 1957, *21,* 95–103.

Rosenman, R. H., Friedman, M., & Jenkins, C. D. Clinically unrecognized myocardial infarction in the Western Collaborative Group Study. *American Journal of Cardiology,* 1967, *19,* 776–782.

Rosenman, R. H., Friedman, M., & Strauss, R. A predictive study of coronary heart disease. *Journal of the American Medical Association,* 1964, *189,* 15–22.

Rosenman, R. H., Friedman, M., & Strauss, R. Coronary heart disease in the Western Collaborative Group Study. *Journal of the American Medical Association,* 1966, *195,* 86–92.

Rost, P. The career pyramid. *Elementary School Guidance and Counseling,* 1973, *8,* 52–53.

Rungeling, B., Smith, L. H., & Scott, L. C. Job search in rural labor markets. *Industrial Relations Research Association Series, Proceedings of the twenty-eighth winter meeting,* 1976, *120*–128.

Russell, M. L. Behavioral consultation: Theory and process. *Personnel and Guidance Journal,* 1978, *56,* 346–350.

Rust, H. L. *Job search: The complete manual for job searchers.* New York: Amacon, 1979.

Ryan, T. A. A systems approach to career education. *The Vocational Guidance Quarterly,* 1974, *22,* 172–179.

Sankowsky, R. Audiovisuals: A valuable tool. *Journal of Rehabilitation,* 1973, *39,* 14–15.

Sarason, S. B. Toward a psychology of change and innovation. *American Psychologist,* 1967, *22,* 227–233.

Sarason, S. B., Sarason, E. K., & Cowden, P. Aging and the nature of work. *American Psychologist,* 1975, *30,* 584–592.

Schein, E. H. *Process consultation.* Reading, Mass.: Addison-Wesley, 1969.

Schein, E. H. The role of the consultant: Content expert or process facilitator? *Personnel and Guidance Journal,* 1978, *56,* 339–343.

Schiller, B. R. Winning the job search. *Manpower,* 1975, *7,* 17–19.

Schlossberg, N. K., & Goodman, J. A. A woman's place: Children's sex stereotyping of occupations. *The Vocational Guidance Quarterly,* 1972, *20,* 266–270.

Schmidt, J. A. Career guidance in the elementary school. *Elementary School Guidance and Counseling,* 1976, *11,* 149–153.

Schofield, W. *Psychotherapy: The purchase of friendship.* Englewood Cliffs, N.J.: Prentice-Hall, 1964.

Schroeder, C. S., & Miller, F. T. Entry patterns and strategies in consultation. *Professional Psychology,* 1975, *7,* 182–186.

Schwab, J. J. *Handbook of psychiatric consultation.* New York: Appleton-Century-Crofts, 1968.

Selye, H. *Stress without distress.* New York: New American Library, 1974.

Selye, H. *The stress of life* (Rev. ed.). New York: McGraw-Hill, 1976.

Sexton, R. F. *Experimental education and community involvement practices at the post secondary level: Implications for career education.* Washington, D.C.: National Advisory Council for Career Education, 1977.

Shartle, C. L. *Occupational information: Its development and application* (3rd ed.). Englewood Cliffs, N.J.: Prentice-Hall, 1959.

Sheppard, H. C., & Herrick, N. Q. *Where have all the robots gone? Worker dissatisfaction in the 70s.* New York: Free Press, 1972.

Sheppard, H. L. The emerging pattern of second careers. In H. J. Peters & J. C. Hansen, *Vocational guidance and career development* (3rd ed.). New York: Macmillan, 1977, 335–342.

Sheppard, H. L., & Belitsky, A. H. *The job hunt: Job-seeking behaviors of unemployed workers in a local economy.* Baltimore: Johns Hopkins Press, 1966.

Sherfey, M. N. Psychopathology and character structure in chronic alcoholism. In O. Diethelm (Ed.), *Etiology of chronic alcoholism.* Springfield, Ill.: Charles C Thomas, 1965.

Shertzer, B. *Career exploration and planning* (2nd ed.). Boston: Houghton Mifflin, 1976.

Siegel, A. 1921 to 1971: 50 years of the P&G. *Personnel and Guidance Journal,* 1972, *50,* 513–521.

Sinick, D. Counseling the dying and their survivors. *Personnel and Guidance Journal,* 1976, *55,* 122–123.

Slakter, M. J., & Cramer, S. H. Risk taking and vocational or curriculum choice. *The Vocational Guidance Quarterly,* 1969, *18,* 127–132.

Sleight, R. B., & Bell, G. D. Desirable content of letters of recommendation. *Personnel Journal,* 1954, *32,* 421–422.

Snyder, J. I. Epilogue: The implications of automation. In C. Markham (Ed.), *Jobs, men, and machines: Problems of automation.* New York: Praeger, 1964, 152–154

Souther, J. W. A three phase experiment in minority placement. *Journal of College Placement,* 1972, *33,* 59–61.

Spriegel, N. R., & James, V. A. Trends in recruitment and selection practices. *Personnel,* 1958, *35,* 42–48.

Springbett, B. M. Factors affecting the final decision in the employment interview. *Canadian Journal of Psychology,* 1958, *43,* 395–401.

Srivastava, A. K. Anxieties pertaining to job-life: A universal psychological problem of the modern age. *Indian Journal of Social Work,* 1977, *38,* 149–155.

State University of New York. The State Education Department, Bureau of Guidance. *Needs assessment; A step in program planning.* Albany, N.Y.: Author, 1976.

Stefflre, B. Run, mama, run: Women workers in elementary readers. *The Vocational Guidance Quarterly,* 1969, *18,* 99–102.

Stellman, J. M., & Daum, S. M. *Work is dangerous to your health.* New York: Pantheon, 1973.

Stephens, D. B., Watt, J. T., & Hobbs, W. S. Getting through the résumé preparation maze: Some empirically based guidelines for résumé format. *The Vocational Guidance Quarterly,* 1979, *28,* 25–34.

Strassberg, D. S., Anchor, K. N., Cuningham, J., & Elkins, D. Successful outcome and number of sessions: When do counselors think enough is enough? *Journal of Counseling Psychology,* 1977, *24,* 477–480.

Super, D. E. Vocational adjustment: Implementing a self-concept. *Occupations,* 1951, *30,* 88–92.

Super, D. E. A theory of vocational development. *American Psychologist,* 1953, *8,* 185–190.

Super, D. E. *Career patterns as a basis for vocational counseling. Journal of Counseling Psychology,* 1954, *1,* 12–20.

Super, D. E. Transition: From vocational guidance to counseling psychology. *Journal of Counseling Psychology,* 1955, *2,* 3–9.

Super, D. E. *The psychology of careers.* New York: Harper & Row, 1957.

Super, D. E. Vocational development theory: Persons, positions, and processes. *The Counseling Psychologist,* 1969, *1,* 2–9.

Super, D. E. (Ed.). *Measuring vocational maturity for counseling and evaluation.* A monograph of the National Vocational Guidance Association. Washington, D.C.: American Personnel and Guidance Association, 1974.

Super, D. E. *Career education and the meaning of work.* Monographs on career education. Washington, D.C.: U.S. DHEW, OE, OCE, 1976.

Super, D. E., & Bohn, M. J. *Occupational psychology.* Belmont, Calif.: Wadsworth, 1970.

Super, D. E., Bohn, M. J., Jr., Forrest, D. I., Jordaan, J. P., Lindeman, R. H., & Thompson, A. S. *Career development inventory.* New York: Columbia University Press, 1971.

Super, D. E., Crites, J. O., Humme, R. C., Moser, H. P., Overstreet, P. L., & Warnath, C. F. *Vocational development: A framework for research.* New York: Teachers College, 1957.

Super, D. E., & Hall, D. T. Career development: Exploration and planning. In *The Annual Review of Psychology,* Vol. 29. Palo Alto, Calif.: Annual Reviews, Inc., 1978, 290–372.

Super, D. E., & Overstreet, P. L. *The vocational maturity of ninth-grade boys.* New York: Teachers College, 1960.

Super, D. E., & Thompson, A. S. A six-factor measure of adolescent career or vocational maturity. *The Vocational Guidance Quarterly,* 1979, *28,* 6–15.

Sutton, K. Career education in the next century. In D. P. Garner (Ed.), *The career educator* (Vol. 2). Charleston, Ill.: Eastern Illinois University, 1976, 165–175.

Svetlik, R. L. Job interviewing: State specific subject area, then listen. *Administrative Management,* 1973, *34,* 63–64.

Terkel, S. *Working.* New York: Avon Books, 1975.

The community is the teacher. Descriptive brochure. Washington, D.C.: National Institute of Education, 1974.

Thomas, L. E. Causes of mid-life change from high status careers. *The Vocational Guidance Quarterly,* 1979, *27,* 202–208.

Thoresen, C. E., & Mahoney, M. J. *Behavioral self-control.* New York: Holt, Rinehart & Winston, 1974.

Tiedeman, D. V. Decision and vocational development: A paradigm and its implications. *Personnel and Guidance Journal,* 1961, *40,* 15–20.

Tiedeman, D. V., & O'Hara, R. P. *Career development: Choice and adjustment.* New York: College Entrance Examination Board, 1963.

Tiedeman, D. V., Schreiber, M., & Wessell, T. R. *Key resources in career education: An annotated guide.* De Kalb, Ill.: ERIC Clearinghouse in Career Education, 1976.

Tolbert, E. L. *Counseling for career development.* Boston: Houghton Mifflin, 1974.

Trice, H. M., & Roman, P. M. Alcoholism and the worker. In P. G. Bourne & R. Fox (Eds.), *Alcoholism: Progress in research and treatment.* New York: Academic Press, 1973, 359–384.

Turner, C. Systematic decision-making by career counselors. *The Vocational Guidance Quarterly,* 1979, *27,* 341–349.

Tyler, L. E. *The work of the counselor* (3rd ed.). New York: Appleton-Century-Crofts, 1969.

Ugland, R. P. Job seeker's aids: A systematic approach for organizing employer contacts. *Rehabilitation Counseling Bulletin,* 1977, *21,* 107–115.

Ulrich, L., & Trumbo, D. The selection interview since 1949. *Psychological Bulletin,* 1965, *63,* 100–116.

U.S. Department of Health, Education and Welfare. *Work in America.* Cambridge, Mass.: MIT Press, 1973.

U.S. Department of Labor. *Dictionary of occupational titles* (2nd ed.). Washington, D.C.: U.S. Government Printing Office, 1939.

U.S. Department of Labor. *Dictionary of occupational titles* (3rd ed.), Vol. I & II. Washington, D.C.: U.S. Government Printing Office, 1965.

U.S. Department of Labor. *A supplement to the dictionary of occupational titles: Selected characteristics of occupations (Physical demands, working conditions, training time).* Washington, D.C.: U.S. Government Printing Office, 1966.

U.S. Department of Labor. *Supplement to the dictionary of occupational titles: Selected characteristics of occupations by worker traits and physical strength.* Washington, D.C.: U.S. Government Printing Office, 1968.

U.S. Department of Labor. *Handbook for analyzing jobs.* Washington, D.C.: U.S. Government Printing Office, 1972.

U.S. Department of Labor, Bureau of Labor Statistics. *Job-seeking methods used by American workers.* Bulletin 1886. Washington, D.C.: U.S. Government Printing Office, 1975a.

U.S. Department of Labor. *Manpower report of the President.* Washington, D.C.: U.S. Government Printing Office, 1975b.

U.S. Department of Labor. *Recruitment, job search, and the United States Employment Service.* Washington, D.C.: U.S. Government Printing Office, 1976.

U.S. Department of Labor. *Dictionary of occupational titles* (4th ed.). Washington, D.C.: U.S. Government Printing Office, 1977.

U.S. Department of Labor. *Occupational outlook handbook* (1978–79 ed.). Washington, D.C.: U.S. Government Printing Office, 1978 (revised biennially).

U.S. Department of Labor. *Guide for occupational exploration.* Washington, D.C.: U.S. Government Printing Office, 1979a.

U.S. Department of Labor. *Occupational outlook for college graduates.* Washington, D.C.: U.S. Government Printing Office, 1979b (revised biennially).

U.S. Department of Labor. *Occupational outlook quarterly.* Washington, D.C.: U.S. Government Printing Office, 1980 (published quarterly).

U.S. Executive Office of the President. *Standard industrial classification manual.* Washington, D.C.: U.S. Government Printing Office, 1972.

Vandergoot, D., & Engelkes, J. R. An application of the theory of work adjustment to vocational counseling. *The Vocational Guidance Quarterly,* 1977, *26,* 45–53.

Vandergoot, D., & Worrell, J. D. (Eds.). *Placement in rehabilitation: A career development perspective.* Baltimore: University Park Press, 1979.

Vetter, L. The majority minority: American women and careers. In J. S. Picou & R. E. Campbell (Eds.), *Career behavior of special groups.* Columbus, Ohio: Charles E. Merrill, 1975.

Vincenzi, H. Minimizing occupational stereotypes. *The Vocational Guidance Quarterly,* 1977, *25,* 265–268.

Vogler, R. W., Weissbach, T. A., Compton, J. V., & Martin, G. T. Integrated behavior change techniques for problem drinkers in the community. *Journal of Consulting and Clinical Psychology,* 1977, *45,* 267–269.

Wagner, R. The employment interview: A critical summary. *Personnel Psychology,* 1949, *2,* 17–46.

Walz, G., & Benjamin, L. A change agent strategy for counselors functioning as consultants. *Personnel and Guidance Journal,* 1978, *56,* 331–334.

Wangler, L. A. The employee reference request: A road to misdemeanor? *Personnel Administrator,* 1973, *18,* 45–47.

Warnath, C. F. Vocational theories: Direction to nowhere. *Personnel and Guidance Journal,* 1975, *53,* 422–428.

Warren, S. L. Problems in the placement and follow-up of the mentally retarded. *American Journal of Mental Deficiency,* 1955, *59,* 406–412.

Webster, E. C. *Decision making in the employment interview.* Montreal: Industrial Relations Centre, McGill University, 1964.

Weinrach, S. G. *How career choices are made.* New York: MSS Information Center, 1975.

Weinrach, S. G. *Career counseling: Theoretical and practical perspectives.* New York: McGraw-Hill, 1979.

Westbrook, B. W. *Cognitive vocational maturity test.* Raleigh, N.C.: North Carolina State University, 1970.

Westbrook, B. W. Content analysis of six career development tests. *Measurement and Evaluation in Guidance,* 1974, *7,* 172–180.

Whiteley, J. M., & Resnikoff, A. *Career counseling.* Monterey, Calif.: Brooks/Cole, 1978.

Wiener, Y., & Schneiderman, M. L. Use of job information as a criterion in employment decisions of interviewers. *Journal of Applied Psychology,* 1974, *59,* 699–704.

Williamson, E. G. *How to counsel students: A manual of techniques for clinical counselors.* New York: McGraw-Hill, 1939.

Williamson, E. G. *Counseling adolescents.* New York: McGraw-Hill, 1950.

Williamson, E. G. An historical perspective of the vocational guidance movement. *Personnel and Guidance Journal,* 1964, *42,* 854–859.

Williamson, E. G. *Vocational counseling: Some historical, philosophical, and theoretical perspectives.* New York: McGraw-Hill, 1965.

Williamson, E. G., & Darley, F. C. *Student personnel work: An out-line of clinical procedures.* New York: McGraw-Hill, 1937.

Wilstach, I. M. Career guidance center sponsored by office of Los Angeles County Superintendent of Schools. *The Vocational Guidance Quarterly,* 1962, *10,* 245–247.

Winefordner, D. W. *Worker trait group guide.* Bloomington, Ill.: McKnight Publishing, 1978.

Winters, R. A., & Hansen, J. C. Toward an understanding of work-leisure relationships. *The Vocational Guidance Quarterly,* 1976, *24,* 238–243.

Wolberg, L. R. *The technique of psychotherapy* (3rd ed.). New York: Grune & Stratton, 1977.

Wool, H. What's wrong with work in America? A review essay. *The Vocational Guidance Quarterly,* 1975, *24,* 155–164.

Wright, O. R., Jr. Summary of research on the selection interview since 1964. *Personnel Psychology,* 1969, *22,* 341–413.

Wubbolding, R., & Osborne, L. B. Career guidance in the elementary school. *Elementary School Guidance and Counseling,* 1976, *10,* 214–217.

Wurtz, R. E. Test review. *The School Counselor,* 1977, *25,* 58–60.

Yeomans, W. N. *Jobs, 80–81: Where they are. How to get them.* New York: Paragon, 1979.

Yerkes, R. M. (Ed.). Psychological examining in the U.S. Army. *Memoirs of the National Academy of Sciences,* 1921, Whole No. 15.

Young, D. M., & Beier, E. G. The role of applicant non-verbal communication in the employment interview. *Journal of Employment Counseling,* 1977, *14,* 154–165.

Zadny, J., & James, L. *Another view on placement: State of the art, 1976. Portland State University studies on placement and job development for the handicapped.* Studies in Placement. Monograph No. 1. Portland, Ore.: Regional Rehabilitation Research Institute, Portland State University, 1976.

Ziller, R. C. Vocational choice and utility for risk. *Journal of Counseling Psychology,* 1957, *4,* 61–64.

Zuger, R. R. To place the unplaceable. *Journal of Rehabilitation,* 1971, *37,* 122–123.

Zytowski, D. G. Psychological influences on vocational development. In S. C. Stone & B. Shertzer (Eds.), *Guidance Monograph Series, IV: Career information and development.* Boston: Houghton Mifflin, 1970.

Zytowski, D. G. Four hundred years before Parsons. *Personnel and Guidance Journal,* 1972, *30,* 443–450.

AUTHOR INDEX

301

SUBJECT INDEX